THE CROOKED MIRROR

THE CROOKED MIRROR

Plays from a Modernist Russian Cabaret

Edited and translated from the Russian
by Laurence Senelick

NORTHWESTERN UNIVERSITY PRESS
EVANSTON, ILLINOIS

Northwestern University Press
www.nupress.northwestern.edu

10 9 8 7 6 5 4 3 2 1

Library of Congress Cataloging-in-Publication Data

Names: Senelick, Laurence, editor, translator.
Title: The Crooked Mirror : plays from a modernist Russian cabaret / edited and translated from the Russian by Laurence Senelick.
Description: Evanston, Illinois : Northwestern University Press, 2023. | Includes bibliographical references.
Identifiers: LCCN 2023005929 | ISBN 9780810146136 (paperback) | ISBN 9780810146143 (cloth) | ISBN 9780810146150 (ebook)
Subjects: LCSH: Krivoe zerkalo—History. | Satirical plays, Russian—Translations into English. | Russian drama (Comedy)—Translations into English. | Music–halls (Variety–theaters, cabarets, etc.)—Russia—History—20th century.
Classification: LCC PG3245 .C76 2023 | DDC 891.72308—dc23
LC record available at https://lccn.loc.gov/2023005929

For Dassia

who carries on the tradition

CONTENTS

ACKNOWLEDGMENTS

My interest in the Crooked Mirror grew out of a fascination with Nikolay Evreinov that dates back to my undergraduate days. So my first expressions of appreciation go to Spencer Golub of Brown University and Sharon Carnicke of the University of Southern California, who published the earliest monographs about him in English. We have been close colleagues and regular conference companions ever since.

Many Russian scholars and artists have cleared the paths of research for me in Moscow and Leningrad/Petersburg from the last days of Brezhnev's stagnation to the glimmers of glasnost to the turbulent changes that followed the demise of the Soviet Union. I learned much from Aleksey Bartoshevich, Aleksandr Chepurov, Slava Ivanov, Vitas Saliunas, Valery Semenovsky, Mikhail Shvidkoy, Inna Solovyova, Lidiya Tikhvinskaya, and especially my good friend Tolya Smeliansky. In Europe and America, I owe a great deal to fellow experts in Russian theater and culture: they include Claudine Amiard-Chevreul, Stefan Aquilina, J. Douglas Clayton, Donald Fanger, Christine Hamon-Siréjols, Irena Makaryk, Fausto Malcovati, John Malmstad, Sergei and Arkady Ostrovsky, Béatrice Picon-Villon, Dassia Posner, Nicholas Rzhevsky, Maria Shevtsova, and Stuart Young. Those whose demise has been a great loss to scholarship and to me personally include Jean Benedetti, Victor Borovsky, Dan Gerould, Yuly Kagarlitsky, Adrian Kiernander, Alma Law, Sasha Popov, Jurij Striedter, and Andrzej Wirth.

Of those who share my love of cabaret and helped me understand how it works, often as participants and/or spectators, let me single out Will Baynes, Charles Cermele, Barbara Wallace Grossman, Peter Jelavich, Veronica Kelly, Roy Kift, Helen Palmer, Joshua Rifkin, Lisa Peschel, and Lynn Torgove. A special thanks goes to the members of the satirical improvisational revue the Proposition, which I directed in Cambridge,

Massachusetts, in the late 1960s, among them Jane Curtin, John Forster, Fred Grandy, Judy Kahan, Ken Tigar, and Alaina Warren. Thanks are also due to the ingenious teaching assistants in my cabaret course at Tufts University—Megan Hammer, Pat King, Helen Lewis, and Reza Mirsajadi—and the many undergraduates who took part in those classes. Irina Yakubovskaya and Hesam Sharifian have aided me in solving problems linguistic and technological.

Ultimately, I ought to acknowledge my grandparents Lyov and Roza Sinel'nikov, who, by leaving the tsar's empire for Chicago in 1905 and reinventing themselves as Leslie and Rose Senelick, set the example for conveying things Russian into English.

EDITOR'S INTRODUCTION

By the end of the nineteenth century, although ornate academic paint-ing, grand opera, and the three-decker novel persisted, a high-spirited revolt against grandiosity was being fomented in the arts: painters re-belled against the vast canvases of the annual expositions; many com-posers turned to chamber music; poets explored the villanelle and free verse; prose writers worked on the *novella* and the *conte*. In the theater, an analogous development was the growing popularity of the one-act play.

Originally dismissed as a curtain raiser or an after-piece, the one-act's new prominence emerged from the naturalistic school promoted by Émile Zola. The playwrights featured at André Antoine's Théâtre Libre in Paris in the 1880s claimed to be presenting "slices of life," best exposed in short, striking format. These *comédies rosses* (slang for "nasty or raw-boned plays") or *quarts d'heure* (though they ran well beyond fifteen minutes) were aimed to hit the spectators in the gut and leave them reeling. A short jab was more effective than a prolonged bout. No wonder the naturalist school's most enduring offshoot was the Grand Guignol, which could pack a sensation drama of acid burns, gouged eyes, and lunacy into a hysterical forty-five minutes, the brevity contributing to the stomach-churning effect.

The growing taste for short plays was promoted with differing agendas by both the young would-be naturalist August Strindberg and a standard-bearer of symbolism, Maurice Maeterlinck; but it was also catered to by the emergent *cabarets artistiques*. These had begun as haunts for poets and humorists reading their latest efforts to one another; success and public-ity brought a wider popularity, and by the 1890s a more diverse public was flocking to such nightspots as the Chat Noir and the Mirliton in Montmartre. Cabarets offered attractions common to lowbrow entertain-ments: varied, rapidly alternating acts, and eating, drinking, smoking, and good fellowship, along with the more rarefied lure of rubbing elbows with artists, if only in their housebroken guise. To amuse this mixed crowd of bohemians, bourgeois pleasure-seekers, and tourists, poetry recitals and songs accompanied by a piano needed to be enhanced by more elaborate diversions. Puppet shows and shadow plays helped fill the bill. The sketch, already familiar from the variety stage, showed signs of evolving into a comic one-act.

In Paris, the cabaret's founding geniuses were men of letters who wrought the *chanson* into a terse and sardonic art form. In Berlin and Munich, the promulgators often included actors and directors, so that the offerings tended to run more to one- or even two-act comedies, exploiting the in-crowd's awareness of the latest trend in staging or playwriting. The one-act thus became a vehicle for attacks on both innovation and convention in the arts and occasionally in social life (censorship prevented the fin de siècle cabaret from being political in any overt way, although its sympathies were libertarian, proletarian, and antinomian, not to say anarchic). The terse cabaret one-act needed to develop innovative features to convey its satiric message with as much impact as possible in a short time span.

Cabaret in Russia followed the German, rather than the French, model by originating in a theatrical milieu, but from its inception, the word "cabaret" (*kabaré*) was seldom used. To Russian ears, it bore a connotation of un-Russian sexually tinged frivolity, more blackguard than avant-garde. After the Revolution, the constructivist director Nikolay Foregger would condemn cabaret as "a filthy, petty art, the imperial-capitalist, decadent and bourgeois product of a fading Europe, shoddy hackwork which sins against Faith, Hope, Charity and their common mother Wisdom."[1] Shorn of its Bolshevik rhetoric, this denunciation might characterize the tsarist Russian intelligentsia's view as well. The Germans had a neutral term for lesser, unorthodox types of performance—*Kleinkunst*. As defined by one of its proponents, Ernst von Wolzogen, *Kleinkunst* was refined art made accessible to the general public in an *Überbrettl*, or "Super-gaff," the intimate and relaxed atmosphere taking the curse off the preciosity of the material. The Russian equivalents were *teatr miniatyur* (theater of miniatures) and *teatr malykh form* (theater of small formats). They evoke the legitimate stage rather than the beer hall and suggest a succession of carefully burnished gems.[2]

In Russia the century had begun with a millennial feeling of hope. Maksim Gorky and his circle of popular writers still invested expectation for the future in the peasantry and working class, but the old "civic" goals of public enlightenment and political reform were being eclipsed by more transcendental notions of salvation and redemption. The artist began to be interpreted as a moribund humanity's savior who held the passkey to a new life. The Russian symbolists preached a coming age of *sobornost'* (ecumenism), when artists and the masses would merge in a quasi-religious communion. All this optimism foundered on the Russo-Japanese War, the failed Revolution of 1905, and the disheartening dissolution of one Duma after another.

Idealistic dreams of communal love and the power of the Beautiful evaporated with these rude awakenings. The loyal opposition Kadet Party was calling for rigorous self-scrutiny of the traditional values of the Russian intelligentsia. According to the historian Bernard Pares, "a mood of general egoism"[3] signaled a retreat from social reforms to private and personal matters. In the arts, individuality, cynicism, and frivolity replaced the quest for communion, redemption, and salvation.

The Russian theater's long-proclaimed mission to improve and uplift society was obscured by theatricality for theatricality's sake. Playwrights turned from models of Greek ritual and medieval mysteries to the *commedia dell'arte* and premodern *kabotinstvo* or histrionics. The playgoing public was no longer interested in messianic messages or political exhortations. It wanted to lose itself in entertaining illusion at its most blatant and disingenuous. The period between 1909 and 1914 saw the proliferation of operetta and farce theaters, music halls and cheap cinemas, "gypsy" choirs and circus attractions. Experimental studio theaters, artists' cabarets, and clubs sprung up like the proverbial mushrooms, and Russians are old hands at serving mushrooms. This trend was deplored by nationalists, who thought all this fluff was Europe-inspired and inimical to the Russian character, especially as the Russian tendency to excess exacerbated the abuse. One commentator wryly noted that once "our nation sets out to copy foreign vulgarity, it will out-spit the whole universe from the get-go."[4]

THE CROOKED MIRROR

"Don't blame the mirror if your mug is crooked," reads the epigraph to Nikolai Gogol's comic masterpiece *The Inspector General*. Aptly enough,

"The Crooked Mirror" (Krivoe Zerkalo, which may also be translated "Distorting Mirror" or "Funhouse Mirror") was the name given to a satirical "theater of miniatures" that opened in Saint Petersburg in December 1908 in the Yusupov Palace Club, a luxurious gambling casino that had been taken over by the Union of Dramatic and Musical Authors.[5] Originally, the Crooked Mirror was the midnight show that followed Vsevolod Meyerhold's experimental workshop The Strand. The late hour (it ran until 2 a.m.) had the advantage of enlisting actors who had finished their work at other theaters. Meyerhold's enterprise proved to be too Hoffmannesque and pretentious for the knowing Petersburg public and folded after one performance. The Crooked Mirror, on the other hand, soon became one of the permanent features of Petersburg nightlife.

The Crooked Mirror had been founded, nominally, by Zinaida Khol'mskaya, a buxom comedienne of the Maly Theater who lent it much of its farcical exuberance.[6] However, the aesthetic policymaker was her husband, Aleksandr R. Kugel', editor of *Theater and Art*, the most influential performing-arts journal in Russia (see the introduction to plays by Kugel'). His editorials and reviews were unsparing in their attack on what he considered artistic sham, hackwork, irresponsible experimentation, or obscurantism. Observing the German *Überbrettl*, he declared it a step in a new and necessary direction. Its intimacy, refinement, and surprise element, unsuitable for and distasteful to a mass public, guaranteed its distinction. "Cabaret doesn't require an ensemble, all it needs is artistic individuality,"[7] he insisted. Freed from traditional structures and subject matter, the highbrow cabaret offered a brilliant opportunity for unfettered talent.

Like many thinkers of the time, Kugel' believed that the theater had reached an impasse: "The evolutionary process demands a certain decadence, a disintegration, so that a social phenomenon, weighed down by an overly regular development, can go on evolving. The complication, mechanization and proliferation of the theater have reached such a pitch that they impede its growth and condemn it to routine." New forms had to be found to impel progress, "to fracture the theater into its primary elements, to compress and condense it."[8]

Rival cabarets, such as the Bat in Moscow, relied on a witty master of ceremonies, solo recitations, song, and dance, along with satirical skits and decorative tableaux. The Mirror differed from its counterparts by special-

izing exclusively in the one-act play. Kugel', aware of his European pre-
cursors, was taken more with their ideals than with their practice. Eager
to transfer the format to Russian soil, he scrapped any appeal to a general
public, as well as the standard cabaret convention of the *compère* (host).
Instead, he encouraged a new literary genre, the parody of art forms, ex-
quisitely staged and performed for an audience of sophisticated intellec-
tuals alert to the *dernier cri* in modern culture. Inspired by the pioneers in
Montmartre, he envisaged the Mirror less as a theater than as an experimental studio where an author would perform his own creations. "Such a
cabaret needs first of all its own authors who will write, compose, versify
and produce their own poems, sketches, comic skits, songs, and ditties."[9]
He also stressed the "aesthetic significance of laughter," usually undervalued as an element in "legitimate" theater. The Crooked Mirror was to
be a "theater of smiles."[10]

Although his connections enabled Kugel' to draw on outstanding
humorists, journalists, and playwrights, the earliest contributions, as
Khol'mskaya recalled, were "written in an old, stereotyped form of familiar vaudevilles, farces, and revues, whereas I envisaged a theater of new
forms."[11] The Mirror's first authors were literary celebrities, the likes of
Leonid Andreev, Fyodor Sologub, and Natalya Teffi, who contributed
one-acts similar to offerings at other such theaters. The initial Mirror program opened with Teffi's sketch "Love throughout the Ages," mocking
"the sexual problem," the current literary dabbling in pornographic decadence. In *Salome's Funeral*, the drag artist and dancer Ikar parodied "barefoot Isadora Duncan" to the music of Richard Strauss.[12] Its first real play,
Days of Our Life by "We" (Zinaida Bukharova and Kugel' himself), was
a lampoon of Andreev's hit drama of student life. Someone in Gray, the
mysterious Fate figure from Andreev's *Life of Man*, was interpolated in a
nightcap, dressing gown, and slippers to comment on the complaints of
the student Kol'-Kol'. Other references to Andreev's synthetic symbolism
were inserted, but, far from being alienated, he jovially submitted his own
efforts (see the introduction to Andreev's plays).

Satire was the bread and butter of Russian cabaret,[13] but it was the
Crooked Mirror that emphasized parody of theatrical practice and situations seen from multiple points of view. Kugel' later boasted that the
Crooked Mirror had invented a new dramatic form, a theatrical "theory
of relativity," expanding and exploiting the one-act's potential by playing

variations on a single theme. It was the Mirror's unique and influential contribution to the theater of its time, and both Khol'mskaya and Kugel' attributed it and most of its innovations to Boris Geyer and Viktor Érenberg,[14] while Nikolay Evreinov took the credit to himself. (See the introductions to plays by Volkonsky, Geyer, and Evreinov.)

The main currents of Silver Age literature flowed across the stage of the Crooked Mirror. The first decade of the twentieth century in Russia bred a controversy known as "the crisis in the theater." Debate raged on the lack of relevance of traditional theatrical forms to modern life and thought. Various alternatives were offered by the symbolists and the proto-expressionists; realists and naturalists came up with modified approaches to their pet modes. Extremists on both sides called for the abolition of the theater entirely.

Out of these turbulent arguments, the director emerged like Athena from the head of Zeus. The ideas and practices of Antoine, Lugné-Poë, Gordon Craig, Georg Fuchs, and Max Reinhardt were already reforming the European stage. In Russia, Konstantin Stanislavsky and Vladimir Nemirovich-Danchenko in Moscow and Meyerhold and Fyodor Kommissarzhevsky in Saint Petersburg enjoyed similar prestige. Kugel' was strongly opposed to directorial preeminence; in the pages of *Theater and Art* he attacked what he considered the excesses of overproduction when it perverted or distorted the author's meaning.

The first season had been somewhat unfocussed, shooting its satiric darts in all directions. Parodies of this early period attacked melodrama, classical ballet, undisciplined acting troupes, and the symbolist verse of Aleksandr Blok, Valery Bryusov, and Fyodor Sologub, which did not prevent the last from allowing the Mirror to stage his own comedy *The Same Old Tricks* (1911). This back-and-forth between writers who were both the creators and the subjects of the satire lent a certain cliquish atmosphere to the program. All this was to change with *Vampuka*.

Prince Mikhail Volkonsky had pseudonymously published his parody of grand opera, *The Princess of Africa*, in the conservative journal *New Times* in 1900 as an oblique comment on the Boer War (see the introduction to Volkonsky's plays). But, as with Andreev's *The Lovely Sabine Women*, the topical aspect was eclipsed by the cultural when staged by Baron Rudol'f Ungern, one of the Crooked Mirror's more ingenious directors. With music by Viktor Érenberg, *Vampuka, the Bride of Africa*, an "opera ideal in every respect," opened on January 18, 1909, and went far beyond satire of the clichés of the musical stage. It became the hit of the season, the trademark and flagship of the theater. The word *Vampuka* entered the language as a byword for hackwork of every kind. As Nikolay Evreinov was later to write, "I know of no other example in the history of theater of a parody, at first glance insignificant, which exercised such an irresistible influence and which finally modified the style of scenic interpretations."[15]

The Crooked Mirror toured to actor's clubs in Moscow and the provinces, bringing it steady recognition and scattering seeds of its irreverence toward establishment art. What began as diversion for "our crowd," mocking outworn routines and conventions, became a constitutive element in the theatrical sphere. This was made clear in fall 1910 when the Mirror stopped performing in the late-night Teaklub and settled into the 750-seat Catherine Theater on 90, Ekaterinsky Canal. Playing to seats upholstered in sky-blue velvet, it could compete with legitimate theaters during standard performance hours on a nightly basis.

Reviewing the theater's tour to Odessa in 1909, the leftist humorist Vatslav Vorovsky noted that the theater's repertory clearly bespoke a "shrinking from, a 'non-acceptance' of the hustle and bustle of everyday life [which] suggests it is in danger of degenerating into an in-joke society for the literati and theater people."[16] Attacking the "apoliticism" of the Crooked Mirror became something of a party line after the Revolution,[17] but the Soviet historians who dutifully trotted out Vorovsky's remark failed to cite his further observation that the Russian general public was not mature enough for subtle satire (many provincial spectators took *Vampuka* to be a genuine grand opera). He feared that for the sake of the box office the Crooked Mirror would have to follow the trend of European cabarets and turn into a mere music hall. That was, in fact, the case with some of the Mirror's competitors: the Liteyny Theater, which had begun as Grand-Guignol, switched to operetta and recitations by 1910, and two years later the Troitsky Theater, best-known for its ingenious scenery, was showing silent films between the acts.

That the Crooked Mirror, after two successful seasons, avoided these fates is due to three factors. The first was Kugel's artistic puritanism; he refused to cater to the lowest common denominator. The second was the Mirror's special audience in the capitals. From the 1870s on, a new theater public had developed, which was educated, well read, politically progressive, economically comfortable, and interested in artistic developments. Private stage and amateur dramatic societies had proliferated in the wake of the 1882 cancelation of the imperial monopoly on theaters in Moscow and Petersburg. The limited size and intimacy of the cabaret had snob appeal not just for the in-crowd cited by Vorovsky but also for those who wanted to be "insiders" in the glamorous yet alien world of actors and journalists and who prided themselves on being *au courant* regarding the latest backstage gossip and cultural book chat. It was the same left-leaning, right-thinking audience of students and professionals that attended, in Moscow, the Art Theater, its competitor Nezlobin's, and its offshoot, the Independent, and, in Saint Petersburg, Vera Kommissarzhevskaya's theater on Office Street, the Theater in the Passage, and the Liberated Theater, all of them respectably "advanced" in their programs. This relatively homogeneous community, whose members shared tastes and backgrounds, could be expected to catch hints and allusions to the latest thing in the art world. It was also demanding, with a voracious appetite for novelty.

ENTER EVREINOV

The third factor in the Mirror's survival was the annexation in October 1910 of thirty-one-year-old Nikolay Evreinov as artistic director and member of its literary council, a move that answered Vorovsky in an unexpected manner (see the introduction to Evreinov's plays). With an idiosyncratic aesthetic agenda of his own, Evreinov kept the Mirror's comic dragnet spread over all forms of theatrical extremism and vulgarity, as before, but his opinions about the "intimization of theater" and its interrelationship with life promoted the repertoire's wider application to human behavior and social institutions. He had always taken the ludic element of theater, its appeal to children and illiterates, to be testimony to the theatrical faculty in human nature. During the controversy over "rejecting the theater," he concurred with Kugel' that companies like the Moscow Art Theater, those overly dependent on literature and social purpose, should be discarded but that the principle that lies at the base of all human behavior, *theatricality*, should be cherished. "Theater without theatricality is a rabbit stew minus the rabbit . . . Burn, Theater, burn, reduce to ashes! I kiss thy very ashes, because from them, like the Phoenix, thou shalt be reborn, each time more and more beautiful!"[18]

Evreinov's philosophic outlook informed his leadership. A talented designer, musician, and director, he turned the Mirror from a sophisticated nightspot to a distinctively experimental theater, thus enabling its authors, especially Boris Geyer, to venture more boldly into "new forms."[19] He brought in the impressionist painter Mikhail Yakovlev, who also worked for the Bolshoy Theater, as chief designer, and the talented composer Il'ya Sats, an associate of the Moscow Art Theater, as musical director. In Evreinov's words, he intended to make the Crooked Mirror "flexible, buoyant, audacious, giving free rein to individuality and absolutely independent of anything routine in its satirical criticism of social life."[20]

From this point on, the Crooked Mirror stopped being reactive and derivative, battening on satire of preexisting work. It adopted fresh perspectives and ventured into territory that had independent artistic significance. The company was also renovated. The actors who took part after performing in other theater troupes were replaced by a regular ensemble, many drawn from Evreinov's Merry Theater for Grownup Children.[21] The press was quick to notice these developments.

> The directors of the theater have attempted to broaden the bounds of its former programs and to deepen its subject matter . . . There is a sense of a firm directorial hand at work. Staging, scenery, costumes and makeup are superb. Those who wish to see the Crooked Mirror as a "cabaret" will be disappointed, but those wishing to descry a reflection of true art with its indispensable element of talent even in trifles will have no doubt discerned in the debut of the reformed Crooked Mirror the precursor of a new, original phenomenon in the realm of stage art.[22]

A BERGSONIAN PERSPECTIVE

Evreinov was later to claim that the goal of the Crooked Mirror was "to use *negative* treatments of a theme to create a *positive* work of art."[23] If Geyer's cynicism was unrelenting, the prerevolutionary Evreinov could still be classified as an ironic optimist, accentuating the positive even when his characters face death. What the two playwrights shared, perhaps unwittingly, was the impress of the French philosopher Henri Bergson that colored so much psychological and aesthetic thought from 1900 to the outbreak of the Great War. In those decades Bergson's fundamental ideas were the common currency of every educated European, much as Sigmund Freud's would be after the war. Russia was no exception.

Henri Bergson (1859–1941) was probably the most influential thinker in the Western world at the fin de siècle. His prime significance for the literary world was his distinction between the continual flow of time (durée) and time as it is usually measured in ordinary life. This concept had a significant impact on Maurice Maeterlinck, the Decadents, Anton Chekhov, Marcel Proust, and, later, the Russian Formalists and Samuel Beckett.[24] Bergson goes unmentioned among the names dropped in Evreinov's "Introduction to Monodrama," but they clearly saw eye to eye concerning the meaning of laughter. Like Freud, Bergson believed that the artistic consciousness when creating comedy becomes fragmented in its attitude toward reality.

> There is something aesthetic about the comic, because it comes into being just when society and the individual, freed from care of self-preservation, begins to regard himself as a work of art . . . It is only . . . in light comedy and farce that the comic is in striking contrast to reality . . . Art has no other object than to brush aside . . . everything that veils reality from us, in order to bring us face to face with reality itself . . . Art is only a more direct vision of reality.[25]

Bergson's notion that fictional characters seem lifelike because they are "a multiplication or division" of the author "plumbing the depths of his own nature" would also appeal to the Crooked Mirror's fondness for fragmenting experience by comic distortion.

The concept of l'expérience vécue, the flow of immediate subjective experience ungraspable by thought, was anti-abstract, an attempt to break the bonds of scientific determinism and religious predestination that fettered human freedom. Such an idea would obviously appeal to radical Russian thinkers; the literary critic Boris Eikhenbaum wrote of his publications in 1916 and 1917 that he was striving for "an epistemologically based aesthetics" to deal with the nature of time and space.[26] It would also chime in with the innate skepticism of the Crooked Mirror's leaders, who opposed both the positivism of the Moscow Art Theater and the mysticism of the symbolist school. Bergson insisted on the mutability and subjectivity of perception, not only among individuals but also within the individual consciousness. Constantly moving within time,

> the same reasons may dictate to different persons, or to the same person at different moment, acts profoundly different, although equally reasonable. The truth is that they are not quite the same reasons, since they are not those of the same person, nor of the same moment. That is why we cannot deal with them in the abstract, from outside, as in geometry, nor solve for another the problems by which he is faced in life.[27]

Any artist who hoped to re-create *l'expérience vécue* had to discover how to represent directly its dynamism, velocity, and fluidity. This last quality particularly required an illusion of spontaneity. As William James clarified Bergson, "What really exists is not things made but things in the making." "The dramatic flux of personal life," wrote James, is composed of "the unstructured, but introspectable confusion of thoughts, sensations, and images."[28] He called the flux "dramatic," but traditional dramatic techniques could not capture it.

In rejecting the notion that one could section a "slice" out of life for stage consumption, the Bergsonian idea breaks ground for a new theatrical method. Two generations later, Bertolt Brecht would make similar demands. Brecht's insistence that dramatic action be presented not as foregone conclusions to be passively accepted by the audience but as rational options chosen for a number of evident causes sanctions such action's fragmentation and contingency. His Epic Theater, with its disjunct tableaux, was one way of doing it, which has provided a model for less politically minded dramatists. In some respects, the mono- and polydramatic experiments at Kugel's cabaret were bold steps toward solving the problem of putting Bergson's notion of *l'expérience vécue* onstage.

Pre-Brechtian innovators who sought to dramatize *l'expérience vécue* had perforce to reject standard act and scene structures without a precedent. Evreinov's *Backstage at the Soul* purports to bring us inside a human psyche, the dramatic conflict playing out among its various constituents and their warring visions of reality. Geyer's *Memories* refracts an event through the consciousness of five different individuals, embodying Bergson's idea that "all sensation is already memory." Geyer's *Water of Life* alters an environment as the characters become progressively inebriated. Their collaboration *Aeolian Harps* demonstrates how the reception of a play varies according to the fixations of the spectator. The relativistic, fractional method they employed bore some resemblance to the impressionist painters' disintegration of volume into atoms of light and color and the expressionist painters' shattering of objective reality into idiosyncratic, distorted nightmares.

The analogy between painting and the dramaturgy of the Crooked Mirror did not go unremarked at the time. Valerian Chudovsky, a member of the World of Art circle, writing in its journal *Apollon* in 1912, specifically associated the Mirror with contemporary aesthetic trends. After Romanticism, after naturalism, after symbolism, wrote Chudovsky, the art world is dominated by the "school of no schools" (*shkola bezshkol'nosti*), the movement of individualism and anarchic subjectivity. If, in the graphic arts, each individual is permitted a personal vision, then in the theater the concept of monodrama comes to the same thing, the subjectivity of apprehension. Taken separately, the Crooked Mirror's sketches may seem trivial, but in aggregate they appear as significant inquiries in that direction. Their farcical nature is appropriate, since, in Chudovsky's view, "all extreme subjectivity is comic" and farce is one of the few wholly admissible ways of structuring life.[29]

Chudovsky warned against exaggerating this significance; he carefully relegated the work of the Crooked Mirror to the category of *Kleinkunst*. In our time, however, the hierarchies of art no longer apply, so that we do not have to apologize for admiring so-called minor forms. The cabaret play, as practiced at the Crooked Mirror, may be ranked with the most interesting experiments of the modernist stage, their brevity not a drawback but a handicap overcome. Its best works, in their unpretentious way, focus the converging rays of popular philosophies—Bergson's theory of life's flux, Eduard von Hartmann's pessimistic view of human aspiration and dream sublimation, the Nancy school of psychology's concept of the multifaceted personality—and rediffuse them as derisive comedy. One critic characterized this compression and saturation as a theatrical "theory of relativity."[30] The Crooked Mirror refracted modern concerns about subjectivity and the subliminal self, then shattered them into a myriad of shards, each one reflecting a separate reality.[31]

WHAT NEXT?

The theater did not renounce parody. A companion piece to *Vampuka* by the same authors was *The Guest Artist*, a hilarious depiction of a provincial theater. Other targets were a puppet "tragicomedy," a detective play, a French melodrama about Russian life, a Ukrainian musical comedy, a bedroom farce, and a frantic film comedy. Kugel's conservatism surfaced in the attacks on artistic innovation; the Mirror's contrarianism was indiscriminate, merrily assailing symbolists, futurists, and nihilists, poking fun at both Stanislavsky's naturalism and Meyerhold's stylization. While the theater claimed to be protecting sacred tradition, Evreinov, Geyer, and their colleagues were in fact advancing their own experiments in playwriting, directing, and acting. Geyer continued to explore the discrepancy between illusion and reality. Evreinov's version of Gogol's *Inspector General* offered a kaleidoscope of directorial styles. *The Dream of Major Kovalyov* presented Gogol's *Nose* as a lampoon of symbolist drama, but the staging and lighting were themselves symbolist. They prefigured the postrevolutionary provocations of the Factory of the Eccentric Actor and the Proletkul't.

Another novelty was the "tribute ceremony," using the bombastic format to direct polemic at some contemporary folly. What begins as a panegyric turns into a roast. Its patron saint was Koz'ma Prutkov, a figment of the imagination of Aleksey Tolstoy and his cousin Aleksei Zhemchuzhnikov, conjured up in the 1850s. Prutkov was alleged to be an employee in the Assay Office who had pretensions to literature. His fatuous, philistine, tin-ear poems, aphorisms, and plays are precocious exercises in nonsense and absurdism.[32] Prutkov became something of a mascot for Evreinov, who had produced his effusions at the Theater for Grownup Children and later promoted him in his Parisian exile. "The Tribute Ceremony, in Honor of the Memory of K. Prutkov" mocked jubilee blather: an old general related his memories of "Kirill Prutkov," and his works were sung and performed, while a mock lecture, "Prutkov and the Antichrist," skewered the god-seeker Mezherepius—merging the writing couple Dmitry Merezhkovsky and Zinaida Gippius, apostles of "mystical anarchism."

A CLOUDED MIRROR

By 1913 there were 250 miniature theaters throughout Russia, but it was the Great War that caused the real boom in cabaret. The worse the news from the front, the longer the queues to get into these shows. A temporary prohibition of alcohol in catering establishments led restaurateurs and liquor dealers to go into the entertainment business. Cabarets became mass entertainment, and while the Crooked Mirror persisted in its elitism, its sophisticated audience evaporated, its creativity began to run dry, and many of its exponents left, among them Evreinov. To boost the catastrophically ailing box office, the theater offered fashionable "full-length" novelties, chiefly translations of foreign drama. These included George Bernard Shaw's *The Doctor's Dilemma*, Arthur Schnitzler's *La Ronde*, and J. M. Barrie's *The Admirable Crichton*, all directed by the hack Sergey Nadezhdin, who later made a career abroad in film. A satire once banned by the tsarist censor, *The Prince of Lutonia*, failed to attract the dwindling public. As the Revolution and Civil War made artistic endeavors seem futile, Kugel' shut the theater down in 1918.

When Lenin proclaimed the New Economic Policy, allowing a limited form of capitalism, Kugel' and Khol'mskaya collected a few remaining colleagues for a revival. The Crooked Mirror reopened on December 30, 1922, in the uncomfortable Murmansk Culture Department Theater with a "Tribute Ceremony in Honor of the Renovation of the Crooked Mirror." The next season it moved to the Slav Bazaar Hotel in Moscow and continued touring the provinces, with some success in its old repertoire. However, Bolshevik agitprop theater and more aggressive forms of ridicule proliferated as competition: Teresvat, the Free Comedy, the People's Comedy, Mastfor, and eventually the Moscow and Leningrad Theaters of Satire. Since the main targets at the Mirror had been art and literature, its sidelining of everyday life and politics made it seem irrelevant and out of date. The first programs offered familiar fare made up-to-date: *Love of a Russian Cossack* became *Love of a Russian Bolshevik*; a fifth episode was added to *The Evolution of the Theater* to mock constructivism. A half-hearted attempt was made to address contemporary issues. *Among the Red*

Muscovites was postrevolutionary Russia as seen through the eyes of a naive Frenchman; *Modern Times (The Party Card)* partly preempted the theme of Nikolay Érdman's later comedy *Credentials.* These efforts went unappreciated. "Untalented, tactless, narrow-minded, counterrevolutionary," ranted one reviewer.[33] "All this reeks of the malignant stench of the White Guard," *Pravda* railed.[34]

The repertory's perceived triviality was not the only problem. Unprotected by any government agency, the theater had to find a new space every season. In 1923, Érenberg died and several of the veteran actors transferred to the Moscow Theater of Satire. Evreinov returned to join a tour to Warsaw, which proved to be a disaster. The Russian émigré press denounced the Crooked Mirror as Soviet propaganda; it urged the troupe to defect and the public to boycott the shows. Back in Russia, Kugel' put all the blame on Evreinov, who left for New York and eventually settled in Paris. Kugel' then brought in young Georgy Kryzhitsky. A former member of FÉKS (the Petrograd Factory of the Eccentric Actor) who had helped draft its "Manifesto of Eccentric Theater," he formed a new troupe and found new venues, eventually moving the Mirror into a shared space with the Technical School of Stage Art. The bills now featured an emphasis on the travails of the Soviet citizen: sketches dealing with housing shortages and governmental decrees; peasant encounters with modern ideas; and a satire of ZAGS, the state wedding bureau. Theatrical parody did not vanish entirely, for Meyerhold's innovations continued to be teased, along with the pseudohistorical plays of Aleksey Tolstoy, "the Red Count" and the hit heroic drama of the Civil War, *Lyubov' Yarovaya.*

Under constant bombardment from the authorities and the press, the Mirror cautiously sought to straighten out its crookedness. It set itself the difficult task of seeming to be an unobjectionable theater of miniatures, while preserving its originality. Kryzhitsky advertised it as being in line with Soviet policy by "battling philistinism in life, routine and tastelessness in art, standing up for realism in the tough skirmishes with pseudo-innovators, decadents, naturalists and futurists."[35]

Events were, however, condensing inexorably into an atmosphere unpropitious for satire. The first Five-Year Plan was initiated in 1927, demanding single-minded participation in the industrialization of the nation. The following year Trotsky was expelled, and the collectivization of agriculture, with the attendant destruction of "kulaks," was under way. The death of Kugel' in 1928 may be seen as the symbolic end of the Crooked Mirror theater, even though in March 1929 it moved to a new performance space, the basement of the Splendid Palace cinema, and a new director-in-chief—Isaak Kroll, a student of Meyerhold—took over. One of its last successes was *The Rails Are Whistling* by the popular humorist Mikhail Levitin, a takeoff on Vladimir Kirshon's revolutionary drama *The Rails Are Humming*. But parody, particularly of patriotic works, was out of step with the times. "The Year of the Great Turning Point," 1930, initiated a new form of public spectacle: show trials. The declaration of socialist realism as the unique mode of expression put a full stop to individuality in the arts. The Mirror's last premiere, on November 15, 1930, offered a play about market prices and the new industrial plan called *Come Back, All Is Forgiven . . .*

Nothing was forgiven, however, and in January 1931 the papers reported the theater's liquidation. Everything it had stood for was now anathema. It is no surprise that when Mikhail Bulgakov's satire *The Crimson Island* opened at the Kamerny Theater around the time of Kugel's death, one of the first of many hostile reviews declared, "Basically this is a rehash of the Crooked Mirror's classic parody productions."[36] It was not meant as a compliment.

NOTES

1. Nikolay Foregger, "Avangardnoe iskusstvo i music-xoll," *Ėrmitazh* 6 (1922): 6. Foregger had directed some early Crooked Mirror plays, and after his studio Mastfor was closed by the Soviets, he choreographed a Crooked Mirror revival. All translations, unless otherwise indicated, are the editor's.
2. On Russian terminology, see Béatrice Picon-Vallin, "L'atelier de Foregger et le courant comique dans le théâtre soviétique," in *Du Cirque au théâtre*, ed. Claudine Amiard-Chevrel (Lausanne: L'Âge d'Homme, 1983), 135. For a comprehensive account of prerevolutionary Russian cabaret, see Yury Dmitriev, "Teatry miniatyur," in *Russkaya khudozhestvennaya kul'tura kontsa XIX–nachala XX veka (1908–1917): Kniga tret'ya. Zrelishchnie iskusstvo, muzyka* (Moscow: Nauka, 1977), 191–207; and Lidiya Tikhvinskaya, *Kabaré i teatry miniatyury v Rossii 1908–1917* (Moscow: RIK-Kultyura, 1995).
3. Bernard Pares, *A History of Russia* (New York: Alfred A. Knopf, 1928), 443.
4. Aleksandr Amfiteatrov, "O kinematografi," *Artistichesky Mir* 5 (1912): 5.
5. Zinaida Khol'mskaya later claimed the name derived from the mirror in Hans Christian Andersen's fairy tale *The Snow Queen*, but the homonymous collection of verse parodies by A. A. Izmaylov, published by Kugel' in 1908, is a more likely origin.

6. Firsthand accounts of the Crooked Mirror are Kugel's *List'ya s dereva: Vospominaniya* (Leningrad: Vremya, 1926); Nikolay Evreinov, *V shkole ostroumiya*, ed. Aleksandra Deich and Anna Kashina-Evreinova (Moscow: Iskusstvo, 1998); Khol'mskaya's "Krivoe Zerkalo," *Rabochy i Teatr* 9 (September 1937): 52–56; A. Deych, "Vospominaniya minuvshee," *Zvezda* 5 (1966): 173–83; and Georgy Kryzhitsky, "Vospominaniya: Laboratoriya smekha," *Teatr* 8 (August 1967): 110–20. Later scholarship includes Tikhvinskaya, *Kabaré i teatr miniatyury*, 205–84; and Yury Alyansky, *Uveselitel'nye zavedeniya starogo Petersburga* (Saint Petersburg: Avrora/Stroyizdat SPb, 2013), 170–75. In English, see C. Moody, "The Crooked Mirror," *Melbourne Slavonic Studies* 7 (1972): 25–37; and Spencer Golub, *Evreinov: The Theatre of Paradox and Transformation* (Ann Arbor, MI: UMI Research Press, 1984), 145–90.

7. A. R. Kugel', "Iz zagrannichnykh skitanii. III," *Teatr i iskusstvo* 34 (August 1905): 455–56.

8. Kugel', *List'ya s dereva*, 196.

9. Kugel', "Iz zagrannichnykh skitanii. III," 455–56; N. Negorev [Kugel'], "Artisticheskie kabachki," *Teatr i iskusstvo* 33 (August 13, 1906): 504.

10. Kugel', "Teatral'nye zametki," *Teatr i iskusstvo* 10 (March 7, 1910): 220.

11. Khol'mskaya, "Neskol'ko slov o moem 'detishche,'" program for *Teatr Krivoe Zerkalo* (1928), 13.

12. Ikar (i.e., Icarus; Nikolay Fyodorovich Barabanov), a humble employee of the Ministry of Land Management, became so famous for his cross-dressed dance parodies that he was invited to London in 1910 and between 1922 and 1947 lived and worked in Rome and Paris. He died in 1975 at the age of ninety-five in a Leningrad home for theatrical veterans.

13. Evreinov identified sixteen distinct literary and theatrical genres parodied at the Crooked Mirror. Evreinov, *V shkole ostroumiya*, 40–41.

14. "Almost everything at the Crooked Mirror that was new in the sense of creative ideas came from Geyer and Érenberg." Kugel', *List'ya s dereva*, 200. Kugel' wrote this after he had broken with Evreinov, but it is clear from Kugel's earlier writings that his admiration for those two creators was sincere. Evreinov, on the other hand, constantly downplayed the significance of others' contributions in his writing about the Crooked Mirror.

15. Nikolay Evreinov, *Histoire du théâtre russe* (Paris: Éditions du Chêne, 1947), 398.

16. "P. Orlovsky," "Neskol'ko slov o 'Krivom Zerkale,'" in V. V. Vorovsky, *Sochineniya* (Leningrad: Gos. Sotsekgiz, 1931), 2:373–75.

17. See, e.g., A. G. Alekseev, *Ser'yoznoe i smeshnoe: Polveka v teatre i na éstrade* (Moscow: Iskusstvo, 1972), 21–22.

18. Nikolay Evreinov, "Ob otritsanii teatra: Polemika serdtsa," *Strelets* 11 (1914): 36–51.

19. Boris Zaytsev, *Moskva* (Paris: Russkie Zapiski, 1939), 136–37.

20. Evreinov, *V shkole ostroumiya*, 40–41.

21. A list of the premieres at the Crooked Mirror under Evreinov's directorship, 1910–17, appears as appendix C in Golub, *Evreinov*, 229–35.

22. M. Veykone, *Rech'* (October 1910), quoted from M. K. Yarotskaya, "Letopis' teatra 'Krivoe Zerkalo,'" in Golub, *Evreinov*, 156.

23. Evreinov, *V shkole ostroumie*, 40–41.

24. See Hilary L. Fink, *Bergson and Russian Modernism, 1900–1930* (Evanston, IL: Northwestern University Press, 2012); Igor Evlampiev and Inga Matveeva, "The Philosophy of Time of Henri Bergson and Russian Culture of the Nineteenth–Early Twentieth Centuries," *Studies*

in East European Thought 74, no. 3 (2021): 401–17; James H. Curtis, "Bergson and Russian Formalism," *Comparative Literature* 28, no. 2 (Spring 1976): 109–21; and Daria A. Kirjanov, *Chekhov and the Poetics of Memory* (New York: Peter Lang, 2000).

25. Henri Bergson, *Laughter: An Essay on the Meaning of the Comic*, trans. Cloudesley Brereton and Fred Rothwell (New York: Macmillan, 1911). Translation revised by Laurence Senelick.

26. Boris Eikhenbaum, *Shvoz' liteaturu* (1924; reprint, The Hague: Brill, 1962), 3.

27. Henri Bergson, *Creative Evolution* (1907), trans. A. Mitchell (New York: Macmillan, 1911), 7.

28. William James, *A Pluralistic Universe* (New York: Longmans, Green, 1909), esp. 233–74. An unexpected echo sounds in the title of Fyodor Sologub's 1908 novel *Trovimaya legenda*: not, as English translations have it, *The Created Legend*, but *A Legend in the Making*.

29. Valerian Chudovsky, "'Krivoe Zerkalo' i monodrama," *Russkaya khudozhestvennaya letopis'* (supplement to *Apollon*) 5 (March 1912): 75–76.

30. A. G. [Avvakumov?], "O teatr 'Krivoe Zerkalo,' in the Mirror's program" (1928): 3–8.

31. In this respect, these innovations prefigure some of the devices of the American satirical revue of the 1960s, such as Second City or the Proposition, with their improvised scenarios in a given style suggested by the audience.

32. Simon Karlinsky, "The Alogical and Absurdist Aspects of Russian Realist Drama," *Comparative Drama* 3, no. 3 (Fall 1969): 147–55.

33. ESGE, "Nichego udivitel'nogo," *Novy Zritel'* 10 (1924): 13.

34. *Pravda*, May 12, 1924.

35. Quoted in Golub, *Evreinov*, 185.

36. *Krasnaya gazeta, vecherny vypusk* 342 (December 12, 1928).

THE CROOKED MIRROR

ANCHAR MANTSENILOV
(PRINCE MIKHAIL VOLKONSKY)
AND VLADIMIR ÉRENBERG

INTRODUCTION

Prince Mikhail Nikolaevich Volkonsky (1860–1917) was a prolific writer who penned more than twenty historical novels, their plots often dealing with clandestine intrigue. His plays were successfully produced at the leading theaters in Moscow and Petersburg. He even translated Rabindranath Tagore. For all his reputation as a gregarious habitué of green rooms, however, Volkonsky was an unlikely participant in Kugel's enterprise, for he was reactionary in his politics, a contributor to the monarchist newspaper *New Times* and a conscientious member of the Union of Russian People, a far-right faction that supported the antisemitic armed bands the Black Hundreds. Yet both *Vampuka* and *The Guest Star*, which he published under the pseudonym Anchar Mantsenilov (from the names of two poisonous trees), were for years the signature comedies of the Crooked Mirror.

The standard origin story of *Vampuka* derives from the memoirs of the playwright and all-round theater man Pyotr Gnedich: "More than once we were outraged by the 'conventions' of the stage. Aspiring to eliminate affectation and mugging onstage, we kept constantly on the alert for the mannerisms that flourished fully even on exemplary stages and especially in opera. Volkonsky often said to me, 'We have to make a note of such gobbledygook so as to destroy this foolery once and for all.' He wrote *Vampuka* in one go, but it had been gestating for many years."[1] The name came about when a relation of Gnedich's wife told Volkonsky how

3

schoolgirls at the Smolny Institute presented flowers to the philanthropist Alexander Duke of Oldenburg as they sang a famous air from Meyerbeer's *Robert le diable*, "Vam puk, vam puk, vam puk tsvetov podnosim" (T'you a bunch, t'you a bunch, t'you a bunch of flowers we bring). The baffled Duke inquired, "What kind of a name is Tyuabunch [*Vampuk*]?" Volkonsky exclaimed, "Eureka! I've found the name for my heroine: it will be Vampuka," and so *The Princess of Africa* duly appeared in the pages of *New Times* on September 8, 1900.

There it might have stayed, given that the text was as much a mild attack on British colonialism and the Boer War as it was a spoof of operatic clichés, had it not been for a young lawyer, Vladimir Georgievich Érenberg (1875–1923). Although devoid of formal musical training, he dabbled in composing mournful ballads. When he came to Kugel' and proposed writing an opera parody, the director pulled out the old issue of *New Times* with Volkonsky's piece.[2] The text seemed chiefly to mock Meyerbeer's *L'Africaine* and Verdi's *Aïda*, so Érenberg's score incorporated motifs from these and other works by the same composers.

The music and Érenberg's grace notes added to the libretto inspired the performers and the director Ungern to improvise their own bits of dialogue and business that turned a topical squib into an hilarious takeoff on all that was hackneyed in the performing arts. Merinos's water aria was packed with vocal embellishments as he circled the stage, his arms raised to heaven. After their lengthy duet, exhorting one another to make haste, the lovers exited slowly, smiling and waving goodbye to the audience. The soldiers were played by four extras who went out one side and came in another like a road show of the triumphal march in *Aïda*. In imitation of Chaliapin, Strafokamil would lean on the flimsy backdrop and wipe his nose with a handkerchief taken from his half-naked body. He kept preventing the axe from falling on his neck by raising his hand and carrying on singing. Once more in drag, Ikar made a mockery of prima ballerinas. Kugel' himself showed up in the crowd of priests in a red wig, while Érenberg, also disguised in wig and beard, conducted.

Now titled *Vampuka, the Bride of Africa*, it opened on January 17/30, 1909, and immediately became the hit of the season and eventually the enduring emblem of the theater. One critic wrote that *Vampuka* showed "how one must not compose an opera, must not stage an opera, and must not sing an opera." Stripped of its political allusions, the parody actually gained in currency by enlarging its scope. *Vampuka* entered the language as a metonym for every kind of stereotype, fakery, and outworn convention in the arts. A verb, *vampuchit'* (to vampuke it up), was coined. The parody enjoyed its hundredth performance on December 17, 1909, and on December 11, 1911, its three hundredth. It was included in most of the theater's tours, spreading its infectious derision throughout the Russian empire. (In 1914, Crimean secondary school students were banned from attending the Crooked Mirror, on the grounds that *Vampuka* "can evoke a critical attitude toward art.") With various changes in cast, it reached its thousandth performance by spring 1927.

Once *Vampuka* turned out to be a runaway success, Volkonsky proclaimed far and wide that he was its "onlie begettor." One of his collaborators, the actress M. M. Karmina-Chitau, claimed in print that much had come from anecdotes told by actors whom Volkonsky frequented, and much was contributed by the Crooked Mirror performers. A court case declared in Volkonsky's favor, but the facts remain murky. Relations between the author and the theater became embroiled and led to a quarrel. Eager to showcase *Vampuka* under other auspices, Volkonsky sought someone else to write music for his libretto. Learning of this, on November 6, 1909, the composer V. Shpis-Éshebruk, known as Shaé, addressed Volkonsky thus: "I have written music and have some suggestions for its performance onstage. Please, do not think that I am a member of the Theater Club" (i.e., Crooked Mirror). This led to the publication of "*Vampuka*, parody opera in 2 acts, written to the music of V. Shaé," but no productions of this variant ensued.

Like the genre that bred it, *Vampuka* vanished for most of the Soviet period, but the liberalism of the 1990s led to its rediscovery. On February 9, 1995, the Saint Petersburg Theater Museum held a scholarly conference devoted to the stage history of *Vampuka*. In April of the following year the studio theater O'Key staged it as a televised adaptation, along with *The Guest Star*. In 2005 the Galina Vishnevskaya Opera Center presented it, followed by Moscow's provocative Helicon (Gelikon) Opera, which in 2010 staged an hour-and-a-half revival that is still in its repertory. The following year Vampuka, a "synthetic music-theater," opened in Saint Petersburg to present outlandish spectacles with puppets and Spike Jones–style instrumentation. *Vampuka* bids fair to become immortal.

According to Khol'mskaya, the Crooked Mirror took the initiative in bringing Volkonsky and Érenberg together again for another assault on operatic worst practices. *The Guest Star* (*Gastrol' Rychalova*)[3] is an outrageous spoof of both inept provincial theater companies and the pretensions of moth-eaten touring stars. Its second act, which shows the results of the previous awful rehearsals, is one of the funniest versions of a dramatic device that goes back at least as far as Shakespeare's *Midsummer Night's Dream*, the Duke of Buckingham's *The Rehearsal*, and Richard Sheridan's *The Critic*. There are Russian forebears in the comedies of Aleksandr Shakhovskoy and the vaudevilles of Dmitry Lensky. Looking forward, it predicts the Marx Brothers' *A Night at the Opera* and Michael Frayn's farce *Noises Off*.

To mollify the touchy Volkonsky, the director Evreinov invited the author to sit in so that they could "benefit from his advice." He didn't. Despite or because of that absence, the opening proved to be an enormous success, and the play stayed in the repertoire for years. Even in the early Soviet period it proved to be a surefire attraction. Of a 1925 revival at the Free Theater, one Communist reviewer wrote in a magazine meant for workers, "'The Guest Star' has still not lost its relative value as a minor satiric buffonade, cleverly and pungently mocking the hackwork of guest stars from the big cities in the provinces. A very musical play, abounding in a series of winning stage situations, gives the full possibility for the performers to show off, and one must give them credit, they did everything in their power: the whole play proceeds to the unabating laughter of the auditorium."[4] Bad theatrical habits die hard.

Neither author nor composer had long to enjoy his success. Volkonsky died in Petrograd a week before the October Revolution; although he had abandoned far-right political activity long before, it was just as well he did not survive the Bolshevik takeover. With the advent of Evreinov and his replacement as musical director by Il'ya Sats, Érenberg's influence at the Crooked Mirror waned. He gravitated to the Petrograd literary cabarets, the Stray Dog and Comedians' Rest. His most famous work for the Crooked Mirror after his Volkonsky collaborations was a satiric symphonic cantata, "May Our Mirror Never Dim," and "Musical Illustrations to the Work of Koz'ma Prutkov." He also set Chekhov's one-act comedy *The Wedding* as an opera and wrote serious ballads based on the poems of Aleksey Tolstoy. During the Civil War, he and his German wife, who had played piano at the Crooked Mirror, headed south to avoid the conflict. He passed away in Khark'ov in 1923.

NOTES

1. P. P. Gnedich, *Kniga zhiz'ni* (Leningrad: Priboy, 1929), 245.
2. A. R. Kugel', *List'ya s dereva* (Leningrad: Vremya, 1926), 201.
3. Literally, *Rychalov on Tour.* The name Rychalov might be translated as "Bellow."
4. *Rabochy i teatr* 43 (1925): 18.

VAMPUKA, OR THE BRIDE OF AFRICA
(*Vampuka, ili Nevesta afrikanskaya*)

An opera libretto ideal in all respects*

by Anchar Mantsenilov (Prince Mikhail Volkonsky)

Music by Viktor Érenberg

1909

Dedicated to Roberts and Chamberlain†

CHARACTERS‡

Strofokamil IV, king of Ethiopia

Vampuka, princess of Africa

Merinos, a disinterested admirer of Vampuka

Lodyray, a young man with feathers wherever necessary

A Page

The High Priest

Velim, executioner for southeastern Ethiopia

Ethiops, standard-bearers, priests, common people,
warriors and soldiers, doges, fishermen, senators, minnesingers,
major-domos, pages, and other courtiers of both sexes

---

* "The present libretto observes all the so-called stage-worthy conventions, which makes it in the highest degree suitable for both dramatic presentation and potential adaptation by some 'high-ranking' amateur or brand-new talent as a short story, novel, etc."—AUTHOR'S NOTE. "In all respects" is a nod to how Gogol describes the "affable" ladies in his novel *Dead Souls*.—EDITOR'S NOTE.

† A thrust at British imperialism: General Frederick "Bobs" Roberts (1832–1914) and Prime Minister Joseph Chamberlain (1836–1914) were major players in the Boer War in South Africa. Russian volunteers fought on the Boer side; the British action was excoriated by most European nations.

‡ *Strofokamil* is an obsolete Russian word for "ostrich." *Merinos* is Russian for "merino sheep." *Velim* means "We're in charge." *Lodyray* means a loafer or good-for-nothing; the character is supposed to be disguised as a naked South Sea islander barely covered in feathers.

9

Act 1

The set depicts a sandy desert in full bloom with an unbounded horizon.

CHORUS OF ETHIOPS:

Of Eth . . . of Eth . . . of Ethiops, we're the best,

And Eur . . . and Eur . . . and Europe we detest . . .

Our orders are to go and seize

Vampuka, fairest in the land—

Our ruler wants, upon his knees,

To offer her his regal hand! . . .

Afri . . . Afri . . . Africa's where we dwell,

Vampu . . . Vampu . . . Vampuka we'll compel!

[*They withdraw.*]

[*Enter* VAMPUKA *and* MERINOS.]

MERINOS:

Oh fair Vampuka! Here

Are buried the remains of your unhappy

Father. He fell in battle 'gainst the Ethiops.

VAMPUKA [*weeping*]:

For he who's buried in the sand

I stand and weep sublimely.

I can't help weeping for a man

Who was cut off untimely.

MERINOS:

O weep, Vampuka, o'er his tomb!—

For destiny has sealed your doom!

VAMPUKA:

Unceasing flow my bitter tears,

They veil my eyes so thick,

I've felt no rosebuds these last years,

But just their thorny prick.

MERINOS:

O weep, Vampuka, o'er his tomb!—

For destiny has sealed your doom!

VAMPUKA:

My weeping offers no relief,

Nor surcease from my plaint.

My strength's exhausted by my grief,

I fall into a faint!

[*She falls unconscious.*]

MERINOS:

She has fainted! Oh free-wheeling whirlwind!

In a blanket of storm clouds, in a plague of tempests,

Hasten to veil the sky above us

From one end of the earth to the other

—Let the downpour pour down,

A second deluge menacing dry land,

Let the snow and ice on the

Inaccessible, primeval heights thaw

And melt into deafening torrents;

Let the seas, the rivers,

And the ocean itself overflow

Their banks, and hurry toward us on the plain,

To bring one drop of liquid to Vampuka!

[*Pause.*]

The whirlwind makes no reply. A solemn stillness

Hugs the snowy mountain summits,

And as before the ocean lazily

Laps the shore with its drowsy waves.

I have it—five minutes' walk from here

There is a spring. Its icy water

I shall bring. On the wings of hurricane

I'll speed to her, swifter than a wild, fleet-footed

Fallow deer—the speediest runners

Shall I outdistance in this fast-paced race.

Oh, how I'll run! Achilles himself

Will lag behind me like a tortoise,

And faster than lightning shall I rush,

And lightning, envious of me, will stand stock still!

[*He goes on singing for a long time yet about how he will run quickly,
then looks at* VAMPUKA, *shakes his head, and exits slowly.*]

LODYRAY [*running in*]:

What's this?—Alone and on the ground,

Vampuka is defenseless.

But my behavior's honor bound—

She's coming to her senses.

[*Kisses her.*]

VAMPUKA [*jumping up*]:

Is't thou, Lodyray?

LODYRAY:

'Tis I, Lodyray!

VAMPUKA:

Ah, all my strength was fled,

I suffered in my love . . .

LODYRAY:

A kiss revived the dead,

That's you, my turtle dove . . .

[*The moon begins to shine down on them.*]

TOGETHER:

How comforting to be in love

In one another's arms.

The moon shines on us from above,—

How full it is of charms!

LODYRAY:

Hark! Vampuka, lend an ear,

The sound of footsteps I do hear . . .

VAMPUKA:

The Ethiops are on my trail—

They soon will be here without fail.

[*They hurriedly sit on a boulder and start to sing.*]

TOGETHER:

They come in hot pursuit

Let's fly, let's flee this place,

In hot pursuit they come,

How dreadful is the chase.

Let's make our swift escape,

Or else we shall be caught.

They come in hot pursuit,

Let's fly, make no delay,

Make no delay, let's fly,

In hot pursuit they come . . .

Ma-ake no de-lay!

Let's flee! . . .

[*They withdraw.*]

ETHIOPS [*running in, rushing down to the footlights, and starting to stamp in place*]:

Behold, they run from us!

Speed after them in haste,

Ah, they run at such a pace! . . .

Increase the speed of the pursuit,

The speed of the pursuit increase,

The pursuit's speed you must increase . . .

Time is flying, waste not a minute,

We haste to overtake them!

Act 2

The same desert setting. Two thrones have been set up in the desert.

ETHIOPS:

Strofokamil is our king

And he's just the nicest thing.

As his servants we must sweat.

Even so we've no regret.

Long live Strofokamil!

[STROFOKAMIL *enters, leading* VAMPUKA *by the hand.
They walk around the* ETHIOPS. *Bows.*]

VAMPUKA:

Ah, once my love was Lodyray,

When I chose without trammel,

But now I must this love betray

For hated Strofokamil.

Him I loathe, him I detest

For he is my tormentor.

He my fatherland oppressed

And enslaved me instanter!

STROFOKAMIL:

I've loved her from afar—

She's my sunshine, my star—

O Vampuka so bright,

Deign my love to requite! . . .

[*Everyone exits. A* PAGE *enters.*]

PAGE [*singing, accompanying himself on the flute*]:

Ah, tell her the tale,*

You flowers, without fail,

Tell her, I besee-ech,

Of my love, give it spe-ech . . .

She pays not the least heed

To how my heart doth bleed.

My loving heart so sore

She chooses to ignore,

As if she did not know,

. That I do love her so-oo.

[*Hurriedly withdraws.*]

[STROFOKAMIL, VAMPUKA, *their retinue, and* ETHIOPS *enter.*]

STROFOKAMIL:

So let the games proceed. Summon dancers, singers.
Let them sing and dance.

[*He and* VAMPUKA *sit on the thrones.*]

[*Dancers enter. A folk dance.*]

CHORUS:

Look at them dancing

Till they're quite out of breath.

Three cheers for our king,

May he ne'er encounter death! . . .

---

* Parody of Siébel's aria in Gounod's *Faust*: "Faites-lui mes aveux, / Portez mes voeux, / Fleurs écloses près d'elle" (Make my confession to her, / Bring her my vows, / Blossoming flowers beside her).

[*The* DANCERS, *once the dance is over, run off. Enter the* ETHIOPIAN MINNESINGERS, *among them* LODYRAY *in disguise with a gusli.*]

LODYRAY [*sitting on a tree stump planted in the ground, which has been brought for him from offstage*]:

From dreamland I come,

A lovelorn balladeer,

As my lyre I do strum,

I crave love with a tear . . . ,

Ah, love is holy in my eyes . . .

Oh, my love casts a spell,

My love is a true paradise

But also bloody hell!

STROFOKAMIL:

I have recognized thee. Thou art my sworn enemy Lodyray!

[*Rises.*]

VAMPUKA AND LODYRAY [*standing on either side of the prompter's box,* STROFOKAMIL *between them. They sing*]:

O horrors! We're found out,

Lodyray is unmasked

Within the foe's redoubt.

Friendless, we stand aghast!

STROFOKAMIL:

What are they saying,

What are they whispering?

VAMPUKA, LODYRAY:

No matter that we'll soon be dead,

Victims of the headsman's blade—

By the headsman we'll be wed,

And die together with his aid.

STROFOKAMIL:

What are they saying,

What are they whispering?

VAMPUKA, LODYRAY:

O gods! In agonized dismay

I see the axe fall on our nucha,

O Vampuka, o Lodyray,

O Lodyray, Vampuka!

STROFOKAMIL:

What are they saying,

What are they whispering?

HIGH PRIEST [*crossing down from far upstage*]:

I overheard them. Order the traitor to be executed forthwith!

STROFOKAMIL:

Velim!

THE EXECUTIONER VELIM:

I am here, o sovereign! . . .

STROFOKAMIL:

Right on cue. Execute Lodyray for me at once.

VELIM [*merrily*]:

Hey, the axe!

[*Pages bring in the axe.*]

VAMPUKA:

Lodyray, for this poor maid

You die, so young a varlet.

The headsman will with his keen blade

Stain your shirt collar scarlet.

LODYRAY:

The headsman may with his keen blade

Stain my shirt collar scarlet.

I'm glad to die for you, fair maid,

Though still so young a varlet! . . .

MERINOS [*suddenly appearing*]:

Why is there talk of death in this place?

Believe I speak the truth,

Death has no truck with youth,

Naught but joy

Should be the lot of every girl and boy!

STROFOKAMIL:

Who art thou, come in costume like a Papuan,

To dare with your bass voice our quietude to ruin?

[MERINOS *throws off his costume of nudity and appears in European dress.*]

ETHIOPS:

A European!

MERINOS:

Yes, I am a European and I have conquered you!

ETHIOPS:

He has conquered us! . . .

STROFOKAMIL:

Many thanks—this is quite unexpected! . . .*

[MERINOS *orders* STROFOKAMIL's *execution and marries* LODYRAY *to* VAMPUKA.]

---

* A line from one of V. A. Sologub's impromptus of the 1860s, familiar from its citation in P. A. Vyazemsky's comic verse.

THE GUEST STAR
(Gastrol' Rychalova)

by A. Mantsenilov (Prince Volkonsky)
Music by V. G. Érenberg
1911

Act 1

[*Behind the Scenes*]

CHARACTERS[*]

V. P. Rychalov, an actor in Moscow and other big city theaters

Marina Isidorskaya, a prima donna

A. A. Lapsheev, a *jeune premier*

Borzoy-Nevzorov, an actor

S. S. Krutikov, an operetta comedian

Impresario

Psoy Maksimovich Korovkin, assistant stage manager [*His cheek is bound up in a kerchief. He is suffering a toothache and often lays his hand on his cheek.*]

1st
2nd
3rd
4th
} Soldiers from the local garrison

Tailor

Tailor's Wife

---

[*] Once again, the names are evocative. *Rychalov* suggests Bellow; *Lapsheev*, Noodles; *Borzoy-Nevzorov*, Whippet-Dimsight (provincial tragedians often took hyphenated stage names); *Krutikov*, Twirling; and *Korovkin*, Lady-bird.

SOLDIERS *dressed not as Chouans* but in their ordinary uniforms, stand onstage, at attention.*

PSOY MAKSIMOVICH: You know your parts. Have you gone over the chorus with the bandmaster?

SOLDIERS: Righto.

PSOY MAKSIMOVICH: Then you should be standing like so . . . [*Shows them.*] You know what Chouans are?

SOLDIERS: Righto . . . We know . . .

PSOY MAKSIMOVICH: You know. Then what are Chouans?

SOLDIERS: How're we s'posed to know?

PSOY MAKSIMOVICH: You just said you know . . .

SOLDIERS: Righto, we know . . .

PSOY MAKSIMOVICH: So I'm asking you, what are Chouans?

SOLDIERS: How're we s'posed to know . . .

PSOY MAKSIMOVICH [*impatiently*]: Chouans are French pissants, understand, French pissants . . . Well, long story short, you do know what French pissants are . . .

BORZOY-NEVZOROV [*in a shabby costume, which is supposed to represent the sumptuous apparel of an aristocrat of the time of Louis XVI, is at a table drinking from a bottle and eating sausage*]: Not pissants, but *paysans.*†

PSOY MAKSIMOVICH: What's that, sir?

BORZOY-NEVZOROV: *Paysans* . . . I said, pay . . . pay . . . and not pis, pissants . . .

PSOY MAKSIMOVICH: Pay . . . pay . . . All you do is drink . . . Is that vodka you've got? . . . [*Comes closer.*]

BORZOY-NEVZOROV: Vodka, sir . . . Only not for you . . . [*Slips the bottle into his pocket.*]

---

* Chouans were counterrevolutionaries in Normandy during the French Revolution of 1789.
† *Paysans* is French for "peasants," "farmers."

PSOY MAKSIMOVICH: You better behave yourself at least today for Mr. Rychalov's guest appearance, Mr. Borzoy-Nevzorov.

BORZOY-NEVZOROV: I'll behave . . . [*Yawns.*] A lot I care about your Rychalov. You think *he* doesn't drink . . . Sure he does . . . We used to drink in Moscow . . .

PSOY MAKSIMOVICH: You and Rychalov . . .

BORZOY-NEVZOROV: What do you think . . . with the prompter Institutov or like you under the stage? . . . No sir, my good sir, Moscow trembled when we drank . . . A torch was lit on the Sukharev Tower . . .*

PSOY MAKSIMOVICH: So he drinks . . .

BORZOY-NEVZOROV: Who . . . Rychalov? . . . Russian talent cannot fail to drink . . . [*Takes out the bottle and drinks.*]

PSOY MAKSIMOVICH [*waving his hand in dismissal and turning back to the soldiers*]: Now then, you Chouans: . . . You enter with farm implements . . . you know what farm implements are? . . .

SOLDIERS: No way . . .

PSOY MAKSIMOVICH: How can you not know? Never mind . . . They'll give you something to hold . . . [*Shouts offstage.*] Hey, props!

VOICE [*offstage*]: Here . . .

PSOY MAKSIMOVICH: Before the farmers' entrance, give the soldiers farm implements.

VOICE: What kind of farm implements . . .

PSOY MAKSIMOVICH: Well, different kinds of farm implements, whatever you've got . . . Don't *you* know? [*To the soldiers*] Now then, you make your entrance and sing:

> Now work is done,
> Now work is done,
> We stretch, we stretch
> Our weary limbs one by one . . .

---

* The Sukharev Tower, a Moscow landmark erected by Peter the Great to celebrate a victory, was torn down on Stalin's orders in 1934, allegedly because it blocked traffic but actually to make way for his preferred form of architecture.

That's when you stretch out, you stretch your weary arms, like after work . . . Got it?

SOLDIERS: Righto, got it . . .

PSOY MAKSIMOVICH: Then the Marquis Parbleu de Cassagnac appears and sings an appeal to you: "O, you loyal Chouans," meaning, Chouans—that's you, pissants, sort of French for farmers, got it . . . Borzoy-Nevzorov, what exactly are Chouans?

BORZOY-NEVZOROV [*yawning*]: French aristocrats . . .

PSOY MAKSIMOVICH: Aristocrats . . .

BORZOY-NEVZOROV [*yawning*]: Sure . . . Princes, counts . . . barons . . .

PSOY MAKSIMOVICH: What kind of nonsense are you spinning . . . After all, they come in from farm work in pissant costumes, and you're on about aristocrats . . .

BORZOY-NEVZOROV: Don't believe me—I could care less . . .

PSOY MAKSIMOVICH: For pity's sake, every moment is precious and you and your clowning around . . . [*The* IMPRESARIO *bustles in, his arms raised.*] Vasil Yakich, what in the world are Chouans? . . .

IMPRESARIO: Chouans are . . . hmm . . . [*Confidently.*] There was a queen in Spain . . .

PSOY MAKSIMOVICH: A queen . . .

IMPRESARIO: Donna Juana the Mad . . . Gorelova played her once . . . it went over swell . . .

BORZOY-NEZVOROV: Donna Juana the Mad is one thing, but Chouans are quite another . . . You gotta know your history . . .

IMPRESARIO: That's enough out of you, actually, you and your history . . . My head's spinning without that, and there's you and your Chouans . . . [*To* PSOY MAKSIMOVICH] What's going on here?

PSOY MAKSIMOVICH: I hired these singing soldiers here. They say they've learned their parts . . . They're supposed to represent Chouans, but they can't get it right. I've killed a good hour on them.

IMPRESARIO: Didn't they learn it at rehearsal?

PSOY MAKSIMOVICH: They've got a sergeant-major who set up shifts. They send some to the rehearsals, and others to the performance . . . These ones here don't know a thing . . . I was trying to drill them . . .

IMPRESARIO: As if we've got the time for drill . . . A-hunting we shall go, so first feed the hounds . . .

PSOY MAKSIMOVICH: So what's to be done, Vasil Yakich?

IMPRESARIO [*imitating him*]: "What's to be done" . . . [*To the* SOLDIERS] When you come onstage, lads, look over there in the wings . . . Psoy Maksimych will be standing there, and whatever he does, you do . . . Like wave your arms or whatever . . . Got me?

SOLDIERS: Righto, gotcha . . .

IMPRESARIO [*to* PSOY MAKSIMOVICH]: So you stand in the wings and show them . . . It'll be all right . . . [*To the* SOLDIERS] Go on . . .

[SOLDIERS *exit.*]

Put them in costume . . . Get 'em dressed fast.

PSOY MAKSIMOVICH: Vasil Yakich, I'm afraid there'll be a misunderstanding . . .

IMPRESARIO: What kind of misunderstanding . . .

PSOY MAKSIMOVICH: Between Rychalov and the soldiers. After all, he sings an appeal to them . . . He'll see them gesticulate and get angry . . . They say he's got quite a temper . . .

IMPRESARIO: Eh, sweetheart . . . whenever a tenor sings onstage, he turns to the audience. Naturally, he'll have his back to them and his face to the audience and 'll even walk down to the footlights . . . so whatever the soldiers do behind his back, he won't notice . . . Has Rychalov come?

PSOY MAKSIMOVICH: They told me he arrived on the five o'clock train. They arranged to bring him to the hotel . . .

IMPRESARIO: Yes, I drove him there myself. I was asking whether he's in the theater now?

PSOY MAKSIMOVICH: No, we're still waiting . . .

IMPRESARIO [*looking at his watch*]: Ay, ay, ay . . . the audience is already gathering. We've got a more-than-full house . . . even standing room is sold out . . . We can't postpone it . . . Is Isidorskaya here? . . .

PSOY MAKSIMOVICH: She came here straight from home in her costume.

IMPRESARIO: What about the rest, all present and accounted for?

PSOY MAKSIMOVICH: Oof, I don't know, honestly . . . After all, we've got no one to sing Selina.

IMPRESARIO: What do you mean, no one? I arranged for them to cast our ingénue from the farce, she's got a nice little voice, and the role of Selina isn't big . . . Why doesn't she know it?

PSOY MAKSIMOVICH: Didn't I tell you, Vasil Yakich, that our ingénue is pregnant for the seventh time?

IMPRESARIO: A mere detail, sweetheart . . .

PSOY MAKSIMOVICH: She's giving birth today . . .

IMPRESARIO: Giving birth . . . So we'll cut her role, that's all . . . After all, she doesn't have a scene with Rychalov.

PSOY MAKSIMOVICH: But it'll make no sense . . .

IMPRESARIO: Eh, sweetheart, who's looking for sense in an opera . . . You can't figure out a word of it . . . So long as there's music and a guest star, no sense is called for . . . "Tra-ta-ta, tra-ta-ta," and what "tra-ta-ta" means, nobody knows. What's wrong with you, toothache? . . .

PSOY MAKSIMOVICH: Ugh, yes . . . [*Touches his cheek.*]

IMPRESARIO: You should see a dentist, dear boy.

PSOY MAKSIMOVICH: I'd like to . . . I thought if I rinsed it with vodka . . .

IMPRESARIO [*alarmed*]: No vodka, no vodka, sweetheart . . . Psoy Maksimych, I'll telling you seriously that if you get drunk today . . .

PSOY MAKSIMOVICH: No matter what, you shouldn't engage in personal remarks . . .

BORZOY-NEVZOROV [*looks at the stage*]: Vasil Yakich, Rychalov's here.

RYCHALOV [*entering rapidly, in an overcoat. His throat is enswathed above the overcoat in a big muffler*]: What's going on . . . What's going on, I ask you . . .

IMPRESARIO: What's the matter, my dearest boy, sweetheart . . .

RYCHALOV: Excuse me . . . There was no one to meet me . . . After all, I'm used to such things . . . Where are the reporters, the interviewers?

IMPRESARIO: Sweetheart . . . they . . . they . . . will be here any minute. Mark my words, they'll be here . . .

RYCHALOV: I'm used to being a mentor to the younger generation. Where is your younger generation, may I ask?

IMPRESARIO: Sweetheart, our younger generation has aged . . . Forgive us, our climate . . . our climate is so brutal . . . but here's the thing, darling . . . it's late . . . the audience is gathering, and you still haven't got into costume . . . postponing things is not a good idea, my dear boy . . .

RYCHALOV [*with imposing and deliberate emphasis*]: You may tell your audience that in the big cities VIPs wait for me, let alone the likes of them. [*To* PSOY MAKSIMOVICH] Are your dressing rooms heated?

PSOY MAKSIMOVICH: For heaven's sake, overheated, you might say . . . We've got Homeric stoves . . .

IMPRESARIO: Hermetic.

PSOY MAKSIMOVICH: For heaven's sake, isn't that what I said, emetic . . .

RYCHALOV [*to* PSOY MAKSIMOVICH]: And have you got Clos de Vougeot?

PSOY MAKSIMOVICH: What's that, sir?

RYCHALOV: Clos de Vougeot.

PSOY MAKSIMOVICH: Tha-at . . . I mean . . . ye-yess . . . the last door on the right in the corridor.

RYCHALOV: Clos de Vougeot . . . it's a wine, a red wine . . . Don't you know that Caruso and I always drink red wine in the course of an act? Whenever I feel the need, I go and drink . . . Especially before my big aria . . . When the interviewers come,—let me know . . . [*Exits.*]

PSOY MAKSIMOVICH: Yes . . . a man of character . . . they weren't mistaken . . .

BORZOY-NEVZOROV: A Russian talent . . . The amount of drink we've downed together . . .

PSOY MAKSIMOVICH: He didn't even recognize you . . .

BORZOY-NEVZOROV: Of course he didn't . . . How could he . . . after all we used to drink ourselves senseless . . . Get me, totally unconscious . . . But how could you understand?

IMPRESARIO: My dear boy, you're an educated man, so just make an effort, darling, today . . .

BORZOY-NEVZOROV: How could you, Vasil Yakich . . . Haven't I sung such roles as . . . Susanin, Mephistopheles, Marcel . . .* that's what Borzoy-Nevzorov is all about . . . [*Yawns.*]

RYCHALOV: Oh, by the way, you wrote me that you held ensemble rehearsals . . .

IMPRESARIO: Incredibly ensemble . . . I mean, like one man . . . there's no need for them to rehearse with you.

RYCHALOV: As if I came all this way for a rehearsal . . . I do have the time, though . . . Is the first chorus before my entrance ready to go?

IMPRESARIO: No . . . we don't have our own chorus, so for you we got wonderful singers from the local regiment.

RYCHALOV: That's clever . . . And have them put another carpet in my dressing room . . . [*Exits.*]

IMPRESARIO [*to* PSOY MAKSIMOVICH]: Go, sweetheart, and arrange for them to take the rug out of the manager's box for him . . .

---

* Susanin is the lead in the opera *A Life for the Tsar* by Mikhail Glinka (1836), Mephistopheles appears in Gounod's *Faust* (1859), and Marcel is the hero of Meyerbeer's *Les huguenots* (1836). Susanin and Mephisto are bass roles; Marcel is a tenor!

PSOY MAKSIMOVICH: We have to get *clozhevo* too . . .

IMPRESARIO: Ah, that wine . . . Send to the refreshment stand and have them get some Crimean red . . . and don't get it wrong.

TAILOR [*running in*]: Mr. Rychalov orders the candles on the mirror an inch higher . . .

IMPRESARIO: Higher . . . Won't they burn the same way?

TAILOR: The gent's language is getting pretty salty . . . he no sooner looks at you than he picks a fight . . . Please, candles, an inch higher . . .

IMPRESARIO: And why does he need candles, when there's electric light in the dressing room?

TAILOR: I don't know, he says, for eff-ekt . . .

IMPRESARIO: Well, take the candles out of the emergency lamps by the fire exits . . . I suppose the lamps can get along without candles . . .

[TAILOR *exits*.]

KRUTIKOV [*entering*]: Listen here, Vasil Yakich . . . I'm a born operetta comic, and they're making me sing a funeral part.

IMPRESARIO: A tragic part, dear boy . . .

KRUTIKOV: So I came to say that if it's not too late I can't sing.

IMPRESARIO: What do you mean, "if it's not too late". . . The curtain's just about to go up . . . Where could I get another innkeeper right now instead of you? And even if your role is a tragic one, in the big cities, sweetheart, all the best comic actors invariably want to be tragedians . . . And you refuse . . .

KRUTIKOV: Well, if you insist . . . I'll sit astride a chair . . . That's the best I can do . . . The audience is bound to laugh the minute I come onstage. [*Exits*.]

IMPRESARIO: I don't care if you sit astride three chairs . . .

PSOY MAKSIMOVICH [*entering*]: Ugh, I can't cope . . . My teeth . . . Borzoy-Nevzorov . . . Favor me with a sip of what you've got . . . Just to rinse my tooth . . .

[*Offstage* ISIDORSKAYA's *squealing is heard.*]

Ugh, Isidorskaya's here . . . She should only drop dead . . .

ISIDORSKAYA [*entering in a very low-cut ball gown, followed by the* IMPRE-SARIO]: This is intolerable, it's impossible. I won't sing like this, I won't sing . . . Where's your guest star—where's your famous Rychalov? . . . Introduce him to me . . .

TAILOR [*running in to the* IMPRESARIO]: There ain't no candles in the 'mergency lamps . . .

IMPRESARIO: In what emergency lamps? . . . What candles?

TAILOR: An inch higher, for Mr. Rychalov. I ran round to all the 'mergency lamps . . . there ain't no candles . . .

ISIDORSKAYA: Candles for Mister Rychalov . . . Why does he get candles? . . .

IMPRESARIO: I don't know why. For effect, he says . . . Psoy Maksimych . . .

PSOY MAKSIMOVICH: What, sir?

IMPRESARIO: Where are the candles?

PSOY MAKSIMOVICH: What candles?

IMPRESARIO: In the lamps in case of fire.

PSOY MAKSIMOVICH: They were pilfered long ago . . . With these people anything's possible . . . The other day they swiped the white linen underpants from the ladies' dressing room.

TAILOR: What should I tell Mister Rychalov?

IMPRESARIO [*looking around and picking up a wooden board*]: Here, take this. Lay it on the table and put the candles on it . . . They'll be an inch higher . . .

ISIDORSKAYA: Where's your Rychalov, though? Tell him that Isidorskaya wants to make his acquaintance.

TAILOR [*returning*]: Mister Rychalov asks if the reporter is here . . .

IMPRESARIO: Tell him he'll be here right away. [*To* ISIDORSKAYA] Well, you're already dolled up in your outfit, sweetheart . . . That's splendid, darling . . .

ISIDORSKAYA: Do you really like it? [*Turns around.*]

PSOY MAKSIMOVICH [*glumly*]: Vasil Yakich, that gown won't do for the stage . . .

ISIDORSKAYA: What do you mean, it won't do?

PSOY MAKSIMOVICH: Well, the whole act takes place in a pissant village . . . A farmyard . . . a tavern . . . and all of a sudden a low-cut gown . . .

ISIDORSKAYA: You can install a green rococo box-set . . . It'll be beautiful . . .

IMPRESARIO: Darling . . . Perhaps Psoy Maksimych is right. Please, a low neckline here, sweetheart, doesn't quite fit . . .

ISIDORSKAYA: You're against me too . . . I know that your Psoy Maksimych hates me . . . I sing a countess, but according to you I have to come on as a housemaid . . . Well, allow me to know better than you how to dress . . . This is all a conspiracy by that Psoy Maksimych of yours. I know he hates me. And don't object. All because I didn't invite him to the supper after the benefit. And the moon didn't shine while I was singing, there was no moon . . . [*To* PSOY MAKSIMOVICH] Where was the moon? . . . Where was the moon? . . . Oh, shut up . . .

[PSOY MAKSIMOVICH, *holding his cheek, waves his hand in dismissal.*]

IMPRESARIO: Sweetheart, sweetheart . . .

ISIDORSKAYA: So I'm telling you now . . . [*Screams.*] If the next time I sing there's no moon, I'll leave the stage . . . So now you know, I'll walk out, I'll walk out . . . [*Leaves.*]

PSOY MAKSIMOVICH [*desperately shouting upward*]: Hey, you up in the flies, whenever there's Isidorskaya, there's a moon . . . If there's a moon, then there's Isidorskaya . . . She can go to blue blazes . . .

IMPRESARIO: Psoy Maksimych . . .

PSOY MAKSIMOVICH: What, sir?

IMPRESARIO: You're playing the ghost.

PSOY MAKSIMOVICH: What else can we do, Vasil Yakich? There's no-body left . . .

IMPRESARIO: The trapdoor is in good working order?

PSOY MAKSIMOVICH: I can't manage that, Vasil Yakich . . . My legs are too weak for the trap . . . And what with my teeth . . .

IMPRESARIO: Then how are you going to disappear?

PSOY MAKSIMOVICH: Very simple: I'll pop behind a bush, and I'll sit back there, as if I'd vanished . . .

TAILOR'S WIFE [running in]: Miss Isidorskaya is asking for candles . . .

IMPRESARIO: What does she need candles for?

TAILOR'S WIFE: So things'll be like for Mr. Rychalov.

IMPRESARIO: I don't have any candles . . . Tell her, tomorrow I'll buy her a whole pound, but not today . . . [To PSOY MAKSIMOVICH] Oof, if the performance were only over . . . Have you settled matters with Lapshev?

PSOY MAKSIMOVICH: The bandmaster whistled the part over with him . . . They worked on it for two days . . .

IMPRESARIO: Well, what do you think? Can he sing the young Chouan?

PSOY MAKSIMOVICH: He'll sing it as a singer. But he doesn't know a word of it. The bandmaster whistled it to him without words . . .

IMPRESARIO: You think it'll work?

PSOY MAKSIMOVICH: Well, he'll pick up something from the prompter, and otherwise he can go, "Tra-la-la, tra-la-la" . . . He wasn't born yesterday, he'll figure something out . . . You can count on Lapshev . . .

LAPSHEV [entering]: Speak of the devil and his tail appears . . . You say "Lapshev" and here I am . . .

IMPRESARIO: What is this, my sunshine? . . . They tell me you don't know a word of it?

LAPSHEV: What are words? Life is but a melody . . . All you need are sounds . . .

IMPRESARIO: Can you hear the prompter all right? After all, you have to sing. This is an opera, not an improvised play . . .

LAPSHEV: Do you think the main thing in an opera is the singing?

IMPRESARIO: And what is the main thing, according to you?

LAPSHEV: Legs, of course.

IMPRESARIO: Legs are legs, but bone up on the words, sweetheart . . .

LAPSHEV: When I come onstage—the theater will go crazy . . . That's been my experience . . . Women will sob . . .

TAILOR [entering]: Mister Rychalov demands to see the shurnalist . . . the gent sez as how he won't sing and bangs on the table . . .

IMPRESARIO: Where am I supposed to get a journalist?

TAILOR'S WIFE [running in]: Miss Isidorskaya demands candles this very minute . . . The same as Mister Rychalov . . .

IMPRESARIO: Oh, you . . . [To LAPSHEV] Sweetheart, dear boy, you'll play the journalist . . . the interviewer . . . Come to my aid, darling . . .

LAPSHEV: You ask me as a gentleman?

IMPRESARIO: Darling, like your own father . . . Come to my aid . . .

LAPSHEV: For a bottle of bubbly . . .

TAILOR'S WIFE: What should I tell Miss Isidorskaya about the candles?

IMPRESARIO: I'll go to her myself . . .

[Banging offstage.]

TAILOR [running in]: Mister Rychalov is angry, he's banging . . .

IMPRESARIO [*to* LAPSHEV]: All right . . . a bottle of bubbly . . . [*To the* TAILOR] Go and tell him the newspaperman is waiting for him here . . . [*To* LAPSHEV] Got a pencil?

LAPSHEV: A pencil? . . . What kind of pencil?

IMPRESARIO: Here's one . . . There . . . Got a notebook? . . .

LAPSHEV: What notebook? I'll write on my cuff . . . just like the reviewers in the big cities . . .

[RYCHALOV *enters. The* IMPRESARIO *exits.*]

RYCHALOV [*to* LAPSHEV]: You're the interviewer?

LAPSHEV: The copy editor.

RYCHALOV: Ask your questions, I am listening.

LAPSHEV: Please, where have you just come from?

RYCHALOV: Rio de Janeiro.

LAPSHEV: How many performances?

RYCHALOV: . . . teen . . .

LAPSHEV: And how was the box office?

RYCHALOV: . . . dred trillion . . .

LAPSHEV: Tell me, what's your opinion of smallholder farming?

RYCHALOV: There should be water pipes on all farms. Chicken coops are very prone to fires . . .

LAPSHEV: And tell me . . . How many battleships do you consider necessary to defend Russia's shoreline?

RYCHALOV: Fifty-seven. [*Walks over to* LAPSHEV *and speaks directly to him.*] The laughter of genuine humor is the pitiful cry of the doleful grief for the interior of our motherland . . . [*Turns around to leave, but, having seen* BORZOY-NEVZOROV's *extended hand, gives him money instead of a handshake, and says:*] Send for some rose water. [*Exits.*]

LAPSHEV: I enjoy talking with an intelligent man. [*Exits.*]

BORZOY-NEVZOROV [*after a pause*]: Yes, I was quite forgetting . . . I should be wearing a beard. Psoy Maksimych, Psoy Maksimych . . . A beard for me.

PSOY MAKSIMOVICH [*who has run in when called*]: Sorry, it's too late. Where can I get you a beard? Go to the hairdresser yourself . . . [*Runs out.*]

[IMPRESARIO *enters along with* PSOY MAKSIMOVICH.]

PSOY MAKSIMOVICH: Ugh, Vasil Yakich, aren't we giving ourselves grief with all this? . . . I told you there's no way to put on a real opera with an operetta company. They'll up and start asking for their money back . . .

IMPRESARIO: Wha-a-at? . . . Money? . . . What money? . . . Didn't I make them a promise? A guest appearance by Rychalov? And here's the honest-to-God Rychalov, and that's all I promised the public. They're familiar with what we're capable of . . . Good lord, I almost forgot . . . [*To the orchestra, to the bandmaster*] Maestro, please, dear boy, see to it that if things get too badly mixed up—have the bass drum cover it up with a "boom," cover it up with a "boom". . . It should work . . .

RYCHALOV [*entering*]: How's it going, is everything ready?

IMPRESARIO: We're waiting, dear boy, we're waiting . . .

RYCHALOV: And who here is singing the Papal Nuncio?

IMPRESARIO [*interrupting*]: Ayvazovsky is singing it . . . an experienced, veteran performer . . .

RYCHALOV: That's good . . . Now remind Countess Margarita not to forget to bring her dagger either, that's happened to me once before.

IMPRESARIO: For heaven's sake . . . do you think we'd allow such a thing?

RYCHALOV: And do you have the appropriate stage pieces? You should place some sort of armchair and table for me . . .

PSOY MAKSIMOVICH: We have a superb ancient Roman throne . . .

RYCHALOV: What?

IMPRESARIO: A throne . . . a Roman one . . .

RYCHALOV: No, that's not period . . .

PSOY MAKSIMOVICH: It's a period but somewhat later . . . Louis Quatorze the Sixteenth, for instance . . .

RYCHALOV: Yes, yes, that'll do . . . [*Tries out his voice, pacing the stage.* PSOY MAKSIMYCH *and the* IMPRESARIO *follow him, hustling to get started. Angrily:*] Will you get away from me or not? Maybe I won't sing. My voice doesn't sound right . . .

IMPRESARIO: What do you mean "I won't," sweetheart! What's "I won't" mean?

RYCHALOV [*holding a note and saying resolutely*]: You may begin. [*Exits quickly.*]

Act 2

[*On the Stage*]

CHARACTERS

Marquis Parbleu de Cassagnac, secretly a
Knight of the Order of Malta . . . . V. P. Rychalov

Countess Margarita (Margot) . . . . Marina Isidorskaya

*Pibrac the Black,** a cousin of the Marquis . . . . Borzoy-Nevzorov

Innkeeper, Margot's grandfather . . . . S. S. Krutikov

Young Chouan . . . . A. A. Lapshev

Ghost . . . . V. P. Samoylov

Papal Nuncio . . . . Ayvazovsky

Chouans, troops, guests, servants, etc.

With the participation of the entire company

---

* Daniel Germain du Fair de Pibrac (1750–1826), known as the Black Musketeer, was a major landowner in the area that swore allegiance to the Chouans.

CHORUS OF CHOUANS:

[*The soldiers sing*]

Now work is done, now work is done

We stretch, we stretch,

We stretch, we stretch

We stretch our limbs one by one,

Our weary limbs

We stretch, we stretch.

Honest toil and rest,

Leisure time's the best

And quiet, and quiet

And quiet, and quiet,

Quiet, quiet

Songs and honest toil . . .

[*The* SINGING SOLDIERS *come onstage. They are dressed as Chouans: in Indian file, in cadence, they mark out the steps; holding sheet music, rakes, shackles, a broom over their shoulders, they form up in a line and stare into the second wing.*]

[*The* MARQUIS PARBLEU *enters, walks to the forestage, and stops with his back to the Chouans. The Chouans during the* MARQUIS's *address to them perform an awkward mime, slavishly copying whatever* PSOY MAKSIMO-VICH *does as he stands in the wings; he clutches his cheek, waves his arms, etc.*]

MARQUIS [*singing*]:

Oh, Chouans, brave and true,

I've come to inform you

That Robespierre wants to

By scheming us undo . . .

I have come of this to inform you . . .

CHORUS:

Then inform us, speak out, do . . .

ARIOSO WITH CHORUS:

O, Chouans brave and true, I have come to inform you,

That Robespierre wants to by scheming us undo.

CHORUS:

Yes, Robespierre wants to

By scheming us undo . . .

MARQUIS:

As friends let us close ranks tightly,

And boldly to the fray let us hie . . .

And if any need there chance to be . . .

Then let us die, let us die, let us die . . .

CHORUS:

Yes, if any need there be, we shall die, we shall die, we shall die.

[*They exit.*]

MARQUIS [*alone*]:

But where can my queen of beauty be,

O tell, ye heavens, where is she, where is she, where is she?

If only an apparition might appear

From the other world that I might hear . . .

GHOST [*entering*]:

Before thee stands a man expired

'Tis thy most unhappy sire . . .

MARQUIS:

Horrors, horrors, my blood runs cold,

What new tale has he to unfold?

GHOST [*merrily, but with peals of thunder*]:

In sunlight or in moonlight's ray,

On distant shores, in distant bay,

In suit of armor, in swordplay,

When your dashing steed doth neigh,

Remember, remember what I say . . .

And now? Alas, I must away . . . alas, I must away, alas, I must away . . .

MARQUIS:

Do not disappear—I pray . . .

[*The* GHOST *disappears behind a bush; the bush falls and the* GHOST *is seen squatting humbly, back to the audience, unaware that the bush has fallen.*]

MARQUIS [*singing to the audience, unaware of what has happened*]:

That wondrous vision now has fled . . .

Be at peace, oh ghostly rover . . .

Thy torments I shall put to bed

And shall avenge thee two times over . . .

Thy torments I shall put to bed

And shall avenge . . .

I shall avenge thee, thee shall I avenge,

I shall avenge thee two times over . . .

[PSOY MAKSIMOVICH, *dressed as the* GHOST, *turns around, sees that the bush has fallen, and scuttles offstage. The* MARQUIS, *having finished singing, goes to the left wing and drinks wine, which is handed to him on a tray from the wings. Then the singing continues.*]

MARQUIS:

But, heavens above, he did not tell,

Where my beauty fair doth dwell . . .

Who will hasten to my aid,

Who will to my pain put paid . . .

Where is he, the modern Brutus?

Where is he, the modern Brutus?

Where is he, the modern Brutus?

[*Confusion in the orchestra. The bass drum gives out a "boom," then a pause. The orchestra stops playing. Offstage we hear the patter of running feet and, like a bomb, the belated* BORZOY-NEVZOROV, *who plays* PIBRAC THE BLACK, *flies onstage with a beard he hasn't had time to glue on, and holding a chewed sausage.*]

BLACK [*singing*]:

Whose groans so tenderly uproot us?

MARQUIS:

Whom do I see? . . . 'Tis Pibrac the Black . . .

BLACK:

Yes, I'm back, I'm back, I'm back . . .

I am Pibrac the Black, I am Pibrac the Black . . .

Yes, I'm back, I'm back, I'm back . . .

I am Pibrac the Black, I am Pibrac the Black . . .

MARQUIS:

And I am Parbleu de Cassagnac . . .

BLACK:

I don't recognize you, alack . . .

MARQUIS:

Greetings, greetings, I'm quite moved . . .

You're my cousin, twice removed,

You're my cousin, twice removed.

BLACK:

What a happy state I'm in, he's my cousin, he's my
kin . . .

He's my cousin, he's my kin, what a happy state I'm
in . . .

TOGETHER:

To glad reunion, mine and thine,

Let us drink a glass of wine . . .

Hey, landlord, waiter, what's to do?

Here's a tavern, right on cue . . .

Here's a tavern, right on cue, right on cue . . .

[*They exit into the tavern.*]

COUNTESS MARGARITA [*entering. The moon suddenly shines on her.*]:

Grandfather dear, you seem depressed,

You seem depressed, my dearest one . . .

INNKEEPER [*entering simultaneously with*
COUNTESS MARGOT, *sitting astride a chair*]:

Granddaughter dear, I am depressed,

The grief I suffer weighs a ton . . .

COUNTESS MARGARITA:

Granddad dear, please tell me why

The grief you suffer weighs a ton . . .

Come, I'll sing a song to you,

Lend an ear once I've begun . . .

[*She sings a coloratura trill and dances.*]

INNKEEPER:

Granddaughter, thank you for your song,

My grief as if by magic's gone . . .

Stay here a while, but not too long,

While I step in my tavern yon . . .

[*Exits.*]

COUNTESS MARGARITA [*singing, telling her fortune by plucking a daisy*]:

Was he a simple peasant sort

Or someone noble from the court,

Who rescued me all by himself

As with the bears he singly fought . . .

Yea, nay, yea, nay, yea, nay, yea, yea

Yea, nay, yea, nay, yea, yea, yea.

Yea, yea, yea, yea, nay, nay, yea, yea . . .

[*Footsteps heard offstage.*]

Hark! Someone's coming . . .

Who has dared intrude on my solitude? . . .

Who comes here, who comes here?

Ah, 'tis you . . .

LAPSHEV [*entering, in his cups, giving the prompter a dirty look, and then, having made up his mind, singing*]:

Alas, alas, alas, alas . . .

COUNTESS MARGARITA:

Time and again I have you told

That talk of love from you

I will not listen to . . .

LAPSHEV:

Alas, alas, I forgot all the words,

All that's left is dreams, dreams, alas . . .

COUNTESS MARGARITA [*losing her temper*]:

What are you on about?

LAPSHEV [*remembering the tune, but not
knowing the words, very lyrically*]:

I don't know, I don't know . . .

Whatever the prompter sends me,

Whatever the prompter sends . . .

[*then suddenly very martially*]

I don't know, I do not know . . .

Whatever the prompter sends me,

I don't know, I do not know,

Yes, whatever the prompter sends me,

Yes, whatever the prompter sends me . . .

[*That's all he knows. The orchestra stops.* LAPSHEV *looks at the prompter and finally sings pathetically:* "Alas . . ." *The music goes* "Boom". . .]

COUNTESS MARGARITA [*resolutely stepping forward and,
leading the scene to its end, singing*]:

Your aria's conclusion

You cut short as a fluke,

Consign yourself to oblivion,

You flunky, you're no duke . . .

[*Exits proudly.*]

[LAPSHEV, *somewhat lost, looks around, bends down to the prompter, stares at the orchestra. From offstage is heard the* IMPRESARIO'S *whisper: "Sweetheart, beat it . . ."* LAPSHEV *shudders and takes himself off the stage. Enter* PIBRAC THE BLACK, *the* INNKEEPER, *the* MARQUIS, *and the* CHOUANS.]

PIBRAC:

Tell us how it was,

So we can while away the time . . .

INNKEEPER:

Tell us how it was

So we can while away the time.

MARQUIS [*recitative*]:

My friends, pray lend an ear

To a tale of love's white heat . . .

Upon the road quite near

A maiden I did meet:

At once a clan of bears

Came growling from their cave . . .

The maid burst into tears.

She prayed me her to save;

Then I devised a plan

To disembowel the bruins . . .

So for an axe I ran,

Then honed it, then cut down

A branch of aspen wood,

Which sharpened to a stake,

Which sharpened to a stake,

I rammed into their throats . . .

A minute did it take,

For me to do the deed . . .

The maiden senseless fell

And my Pauline I beheld . . .

COUNTESS MARGARITA [*appearing*]:

'Twas I . . .

MARQUIS:

'Tis she . . . my lost Pauline . . .

COUNTESS MARGARITA:

No, I am Margarita . . .

But, Marquis, were my name Ortrud,

What matters it to you . . .

You lot withdraw, do not intrude,

And leave alone us two . . .

[*Everyone exits.*]

MARQUIS [*aside*]:

Now I shall make my declaration . . .

[*To her, very tenderly*]

My heart's a fervid beater

For you, o Margarita . . .

COUNTESS MARGARITA:

I'm swooning helplessly,

So raise me up, Marquis . . .

MARQUIS:

My heart's a fervid beater

For you, o Margarita . . .

COUNTESS MARGARITA:

I'm swooning helplessly,

So raise me up, Marquis.

TOGETHER:

O . . .

[*Coming together again and she in his arms*]

O happiness, o joy.

In an embrace we lie . . .

Being young will not cloy,

Why should we have to die . . .

MARQUIS:

O, Margarita, as a knight of Malta,

I made a vow to remain celibate . . .

COUNTESS MARGARITA:

O horrors, can it be? . . . My God, what have you said? . . .

Then let us die together, here is my dagger's blade . . .

[*Spoken, to him*]

I forgot the dagger.

MARQUIS [*losing his temper*]:

I knew it . . .

[MARGARITA *gives an order into the wings to bring her a dagger, then returns and again stands beside the* MARQUIS.]

MARQUIS [*indicating to the orchestra to begin again, singing.
· During the singing painfully squeezing* MARGARITA'S *hand.*]:

My heart's a fervid beater

For thee, o Margarita . . .

COUNTESS MARGARITA [*speaking*]:

If you go on pinching me, I'll tell my husband . . .

[*Singing*]

I'm swooning helplessly,

So raise me up, Marquis . . .

MARQUIS [*speaking*]:

I don't care two hoots about your husband . . . Stop leaning on me, you're keeping me from singing . . .

My heart's a fervid beater

For you, o Margarita . . .

COUNTESS MARGARITA:

Ignoramus . . .

I'm swooning helplessly,

So lift me up, Marquis . . .

MARQUIS:

Idiot . . .

COUNTESS MARGARITA:

Wise-ass . . .

TOGETHER [*running to their places*]:

O . . .

[*coming together*]

O happiness, o joy.

In an embrace we lie . . .

Being young will not cloy,

Why should we have to die . . .

MARQUIS:

O, Margarita, as a Knight of Malta

I made a vow of celibacy . . .

COUNTESS MARGARITA:

O horrors, can it be? . . . My God, what have you
said? . . .

Then let us die together, here is my dagger's
blade . . .

Then we shall die together, we'll die, here, here,
here . . .

[*Grabs the dagger handed to her from offstage.*]

Here is my dagger's blade, dagger's blade, my
dagger's blade . . .

PIBRAC [*entering*]:

Don't die too soon if that's your plan,

To cancel the vow of celibacy,

Here comes the emissary of the Vatica-a-an.

[*Before the* NUNCIO *appears, after a trumpet blast—general entrance.* PSOY
MAKSIMYCH *enters in the costume of a Catholic monk. He has put on a gray*

*wig but has forgotten to remove from his cheek the black kerchief, which has
literally grown to his skull.*]

PSOY MAKSIMYCH:

I am the pupal nancio . . . [*"Boom" from the music*]

I am the nupal pancio . . . [*"Boom"*]

I am the nansal pupcio . . . [*"Boom"*]

I am the panc . . . [*"Boom"*]

RYCHALOV [*beginning to stamp and shout*]:

I can't take any more of this, I can't take it . . . Curtain,
curtain . . . The lot of you . . . I can't . . . [*Runs off.*]

[*The* NUNCIO *goes on bellowing. The curtain comes down. The* NUNCIO *bellows behind the curtain. The orchestra plays the final finale.*]

LEONID ANDREEV

INTRODUCTION

Leonid Nikolaevich Andreev (1873–1919) is one of those authors who enjoys controversial and noisy celebrity during his lifetime but then is forgotten by all except specialists and revisionists. Even at the height of his fame he was not wholly accepted; opinions of his works ranged from ecstatic praise to the most savage vituperation. At his best, in many of his stories he can create a powerful and lingering if morbid effect; at his worst, he becomes shrill and willfully obscure.

He was born in Oryol, the son of a land surveyor whose early death left the family impoverished. Like so many men of letters of this period, he attended the law faculty of the Saint Petersburg University and obtained a degree, but his poverty led him to multiple suicide attempts (on one occasion, he lay down on the railway tracks), a nervous breakdown, and paranoia. He lived off portrait painting and law reporting.

In 1898 he was encouraged by Maksim Gorky, who published his early stories in his journal *Znanie* (*The Banner*). Andreev at first copied Gorky's style and subject matter, but, as a fan of Edgar Allan Poe, he colored social issues with a sensational tinge of sex and violence. In 1902 he contracted a happy marriage with Shura Veligorskaya, and until 1908 every one of his stories was a literary event. He became immensely popular and wealthy, with a flamboyant wardrobe and a villa in Finland.

The failed Revolution of 1905 affected Andreev as it did so many of his contemporaries, and the death of his wife the following year brought on an emotional crisis. He began to find Gorky's belief in social revolution naive; his whole outlook became pessimistic, nihilistic, his philosophy a "scientific agnosticism." Human freedom was a mere illusion. His work became shrouded in a kind of shallow and derivative symbolism.

At this time, Andreev began to write for the stage, producing nearly thirty plays by 1916. Despite critical disdain, he was the preeminent dramatist of the post-Chekhov era, and directors vied to stage his dramas. They appeared on the leading stages, dominating critical debate and salon conversation. Although a few of his plays have a veneer of everyday life, he nevertheless rejected "the realistic theater" as being "a gabby old trollop" (*salopnitsa*).[1] Four of his dramas were produced by the Moscow Art Theater, including the most oppressively "symbolist" examples, *The Life of Man* (1906) and *Anathema* (1909). The former is a doleful account of the futility of human life, couched in a monotonous chant intoned by allegorical characters. The latter is a Faustian parable of a Satanic figure endowing David Leizer, a poor Jewish peddler, with four million rubles. Leizer gives the fortune away to the poor, and when he has nothing left to give, they stone him. Both plays were ripe for parody and consequently showed up in spoofs at the Crooked Mirror.[2]

The strident sensationalism and overheated eroticism of the period suffuse *Ekaterina Ivanovna* (1912), in which a wife, unjustly accused of adultery by her hysterical husband, decides to confirm his worst fears by giving in to her seducer and eventually takes any number of lovers. This too became grist for the satire mill.

Andreev exploited blatant sensation to jump-start dramatic conflicts, in hopes of reaching a wider audience. In a letter from 1914 he wrote that a play should be something over which "Schopenhauer and his cook can cry together": "The hero, the masses, the heroic in the masses and the individual, broad brushstrokes and extreme stylization, the loudest words and unbridled poses, a stentorian voice, hymns, wonders and bluntness, Sinai and Sabaoth—that is the truth and the future in this good decade."[3]

Like Gorky, he was fascinated by the advent of cinema. Andreev was willing to relinquish to this "artistic apache of modernity" the life of external action and everything that might interest the "crowd." The movies were better than the theater at depicting duels, passionate embraces, and rapid shifts of locale. In recompense, Andreev argued for the "theater of panpsychism": modern drama was to concentrate on "the depths of the soul—the quiet and internal immobility of mental experiences."[4] Similar ideas had been floated by the influential Belgian playwright Maurice

Maeterlinck in his *Trésor des humbles* (1896), but Andreev propounded Chekhov's plays as the best models for the intellectual "internal" drama in which "all subjects of the world visible and invisible enter only as part of one great soul."

Andreev's most successful attempt to embody panpsychism in a play is *Professor Storitsyn* (1912), in which a world-famous scientist is suffocated and beaten down by the circumambient vulgarity, represented by his depraved son, his dissolute wife, and her paramour, a conniving high school teacher. A Lear of the mind, Storitsyn wanders into a dark and stormy night and dies at the home of an old friend and colleague. The panpsychic element is present in Andreev's tuning all the external factors to the inner drama of the protagonist. The landscape, the weather, and the Professor's illness are all images of Storitsyn's frame of mind. It is obvious how these devices chime in with the concept of monodrama circulated by Evreinov (see the introduction to Evreinov's plays).

Prince Dmitry Mirsky opined that Andreev's sense of humor was "heavy, joyless, and stilted,"[5] but Evreinov chose to differ. Quoting Andreev's frequent remark "Fools, fools, the world is full of fools," Evreinov explained that Andreev's comedy cannot be dismissed as "gallows humor," ridiculing a tragic situation. Rather, it is paradoxical in demonstrating how the dismal or horrible can evoke not tears or disgust but laughter, even gales of laughter. Certainly, Andreev was not offended by the mockery directed at his plays in the early seasons of the Crooked Mirror and not averse to making his own contributions. Unfamiliar with the form of the cabaret sketch, he tended to overwrite and ignore exigencies of cast size. But he admired Evreinov's production of his one-act *Love Thy Neighbor* (1909) and was willing to make cuts in his other plays if Evreinov agreed to direct them.

Another problem Evreinov detected in Andreev's playlet was lack of action, but he believed that the actors could make up for it with lively playing. *Love Thy Neighbor* is a sardonic comment on the exploitation of both the best and worst impulses of human beings. A man is seemingly stuck on a ledge over a precipice, with no means of rescue. A crowd of onlookers and sightseers turn this into a carnival atmosphere, until it appears that a local hotelier has staged the crisis as a catchpenny attraction. He is then almost lynched for having exploited the public's love of its neighbor. Andreev provides a colorful panorama of responses, with particular jabs at

yellow journalism and old-time religion. The play is a remarkable forecast
of Billy Wilder's film *Ace in the Hole* (1951), in which Kirk Douglas as a
shrewd newscaster similarly bloats a local accident into a national tragedy.

The Lovely Sabine Women (*Prekrasnie sabinyanki*), directed by Evreinov, opened at the Crooked Mirror on November 30, 1911. It began as
a political statement. Andreev would explain to anyone who asked, "You
must understand, the Sabines are the Kadets—Ka-dets. They talk about
constitution and law, but it's only lip service, face-making!" The Kadets,
or Constitutional Democrats, had been founded by Professor Pavel Mil-
yukov, an energetic tactician, by uniting many of the Liberals from the
rural councils with moderate professional men. In the first Duma of 1906,
they prevailed and tried to make it into an English Parliament rather
than a Reichstag. Led by Vladimir Dmitrievich Nabokov, father of the
novelist, it passed a broad reform bill but was told by the prime minister
that such a thing was "inadmissible." The Kadets then passed a unanimous
bill of censure, and the tsar dissolved the Duma. The Kadets' presence in
the short-lived second Duma of 1907 was ineffectual. They set themselves
up as a regular parliamentary opposition, but when the Third Duma took
shape they had to surrender leadership of the debates to the Octobrists.

For those not conversant with the intricacies of tsarist politics, the
American fellow traveler H. W. L. Dana explained:

> The Sabines are those "constitutional democrats" ("Kadets")
> whose wives are none other than freedoms which the Sabines
> think they discovered in 1905. These freedoms are abducted by
> the Roman soldiers who represent the Tsarist government (in
> Russia). Andreev ruthlessly mocks the constitutional democrats,
> that is, the Sabines, who, trying to fight for their wives, i.e., their
> freedoms, think that using physical force does not correspond
> to their dignity and have recourse (as their sole weapon) to a
> document proving the legality of their marriages. Their motto—
> "two steps forward" (to demonstrate firmness—their will) and
> "one step back" (to demonstrate their opportunism).[6]

The Crooked Mirror audiences, generally liberal and supporters of decisive action against Nicholas II, caught the allusions, which made the play
both an artistic and a political success.

When *The Pretty Sabine Women* was published in Andreev's complete works, it contained a footnote about the production's music: "The Petersburg theater 'The Crooked Mirror' very successfully made use of the "Marseillaise"; in the first two acts, resounding triumphantly and boldly, it transitions to something doleful—like a painful belch."[7] Evreinov concocted a refinement to that, and the composer Érenberg made it work: as the Sabines shouldered their heavy code of laws like a spear, they took two steps forward to "Allons enfants de la patrie" and one step back to the first two bars of "God Save the Tsar." Evreinov convinced Kugel' that the police wouldn't recognize the tune without the words and wouldn't suspect subversion from a well-regarded theater like the Crooked Mirror.

The rape of the Sabines had long been a topic of satire: John Leech and Honoré Daumier had drawn derisive caricatures of it, and later the Broadway stage would convert it into the musical comedy *Seven Brides for Seven Brothers*. Aside from the topical aspect, Andreev's version works on a protofeminist level. Irrespective of whether the wives are allegories of constitutional liberties, they are clearly more sensible and more effective than the men on either side. The intentional anachronisms give the comedy a tinge of urbanity, and many of the male/female interchanges have a Shavian flavor. Discussions of whether might makes right have not lost their potency.

Andreev's last contribution to the Mirror was *Monument* (1916), a genre piece set in a provincial town, where the city fathers decide to put up a statue to Alexander Pushkin. The Gogolian types debate the direction it should face; prospective sculptors propose a classical Pushkin with bare legs or a futurist Pushkin blowing his nose.

The war years and the rise of the Bolsheviks bore out Andreev's pessimism. By this time he had fallen out of fashion and was living an indigent life in Finland with his second wife. He died of a heart attack, possibly brought on by both personal and political stress. Although his play *He Who Gets Slapped* (*Tot, kto poluchaet poshchechiny*), a melodrama set in a circus, was often revived in the West (a silent-film version starred Lon Chaney), the Soviet literary establishment definitively sidelined him. With the fall of communism, a renewal of interest in the Silver Age led some Russian theaters, such as the Moderne in Moscow, to revive his plays. Still, despite his academic standing as a representative literary figure, production of his dramatic work is honored more in the breach than in the observance.

NOTES

1. Quoted in Homo Novus (A. R. Kugel'), "Zametki," *Teatr i iskusstvo* 2 (1914): 41.

2. The American Slavicist Leo Wiener believed that Andreev copied whichever play had been produced ahead of his at the Moscow Art Theater or Vera Kommissarzhevskaya's theater in Saint Petersburg. Leo Wiener, *The Contemporary Drama of Russia* (Boston: Little, Brown, 1924), 147–48.

3. Quoted in B. A. Bialik, *Literaturnoe-esteticheskie kontseptsii v Rossii kontsa XIX–nachala XX veka* (Moscow: Nauka, 1975), 274.

4. *Literaturno-khudozhestvennye almanalkh izd. "Shipovnik,"* 12 (1914): 252; reprinted as *Pis'ma o teatre* (Letchworth, UK: Prideaux Press, 1974). A translation appears in Laurence Senelick, ed. and trans., *Russian Dramatic Theory from Pushkin to the Symbolists* (Austin: University of Texas Press, 1981), 223–72.

5. Prince D. S. Mirsky, *Contemporary Russian Literature, 1881–1925* (London: George Routledge & Sons, 1926), 138.

6. Henry Wadsworth Longfellow Dana, *A History of Modern Drama*, chap. 7, 433; manuscript in the Harvard Theatre Collection.

7. Free supplement to *Niva* 7 (1913): 35.

LOVE THY NEIGHBOR
(*Lyubov' k blizhnemu*)

by Leonid Andreev

1909

A wild locale in the mountains.

On a rock that is almost perfectly perpendicular to the ground, on a small, barely noticeable ledge, stands a man in a pose of despair. How he got there is not easy to explain, but there is no way to reach him either from above or below; short ladders, ropes, and poles reveal that some attempts to rescue him have been made, but to no avail.

Evidently, the wretched fellow has been in this desperate situation for a long while, for there has been time for a variegated crowd of considerable size to assemble. Here are vendors of cold drinks and even a well-stocked little bar around which a breathless attendant, all in a sweat, is rushing around—he is on his own and has no time to fill all the orders. Peddlers are walking up and down, with postcards, coral beads, souvenirs, and all sorts of rubbish; one individual is trying insistently to dispose of a tortoiseshell comb, which is not actually tortoiseshell. And from all sides tourists keep flooding in, attracted by rumors of a catastrophe about to take place: English, German, Russian, French, Italian, etc., with all their national peculiarities of character, manners, and dress. Almost all of them have alpenstocks, binoculars, and cameras. The talk is polyglot, but for the reader's convenience we translate it into our language.

At the foot of the rock, where the stranger must fall, two police sergeants are shooing away children and are fencing off the area with a slender rope attached to stakes.

It is noisy and rollicking.

FIRST POLICEMAN: Get out of here, you scamp! If he falls on your head, what will your mother and father say?

BOY: Is this where he'll fall?

FIRST POLICEMAN: Right here.

BOY: What if it's farther off?

SECOND POLICEMAN: The kid's right. In his desperation he might jump, fall beyond the rope, and injure the spectators. He must weigh at least two hundred pounds.

FIRST POLICEMAN: Beat it! Where are you getting to, little girl? This your daughter, madam? Please take her away. The young man might fall any minute now.

LADY: Any minute now! Ah, my goodness! My husband's not here!

LITTLE GIRL: He's at the bar, mama.

LADY [*distressed*]: Of course, he's always at the bar! Call him, Nelly, tell him: he's going to fall any minute. Hurry! Hurry!

VOICES: Kellner!

Garçon!

Waiter!

Beer!

There's no beer.

What? What'd you say? Call this a bar . . .

They're bringing some right away.

Hurry it up!

Kellner!

Kellner!

Garçon!

FIRST POLICEMAN: Here again, you little brat!

BOY: I wanted to take that stone away.

POLICEMAN: What for?

BOY: So he won't get so badly hurt when he falls.

SECOND POLICEMAN: The kid's right: we should remove the stones, we've got to clear the whole area. Is there any sand or sawdust around here?

[*Two* ENGLISH TOURISTS *approach. They stare at the stranger through binoculars and exchange remarks.*]

FIRST ENGLISH TOURIST: Young.

SECOND ENGLISH TOURIST: How young?

FIRST ENGLISH TOURIST: Twenty-eight.

SECOND ENGLISH TOURIST: Twenty-six. Fear makes him seem older.

FIRST ENGLISH TOURIST: Bet.

SECOND ENGLISH TOURIST: Ten to one. Make a note.

FIRST ENGLISH TOURIST [*writing a note, to the* POLICEMAN]: Can you please tell us how he got there? Why haven't they removed him?

POLICEMAN: They tried, but couldn't manage it. The ladders are too short.

SECOND ENGLISH TOURIST: Has he been there long?

POLICEMAN: Two whole days.

FIRST ENGLISH TOURIST: Oho! He'll fall tonight.

SECOND ENGLISH TOURIST: Two hours from now. Hundred to one.

FIRST ENGLISH TOURIST: Make a note! [*Shouts to the* STRANGER] How do you feel? What? I can't hear.

STRANGER [*barely audible*]: Lousy!

LADY: Ah, good heavens! And my husband not here!

LITTLE GIRL [*running up*]: Papa said he'll hurry, he's playing chess with some gentleman.

LADY: Ah, good heavens! Tell him, Nelly, that I insist. And yet . . . Will he be falling soon, officer? No, Nelly, you'd better go, while I hold a place for Papa.

[*A tall, thin lady, with an unusually self-possessed and aggressive look, is arguing with some tourist about her place. The* TOURIST *is puny, frail, and bad at
defending his rights. The lady takes a decisive step forward.*]

TOURIST: But this is my place, madam, I've been standing here for the
last two hours.

AGGRESSIVE LADY: What do I care how long you've been standing here?
I want to stand here, do you understand? I'll have a better view from
here, understand?

TOURIST [*meekly*]: But I have a better view from here.

AGGRESSIVE LADY: Is that so? And what do you know about it?

TOURIST: What's there to know? The man's going to drop, and that's that.

AGGRESSIVE LADY [*imitating*]: The man's going to drop, and that's that!
Is that so! Have you ever seen a man drop? Well? No? Well, I've seen
a good three: two acrobats, one tightrope walker, and three aviators.

TOURIST: That makes six.

AGGRESSIVE LADY [*imitating*]: That makes six! You've got a brilliant
aptitude for mathematics, I must say! Have you ever seen before your
very eyes a tiger in a menagerie tear a woman to pieces? Eh? What's
that? I thought not! Well, I have! Step aside! Step aside!

[*With a shrug the humiliated* TOURIST *steps aside, and the thin lady triumphantly plants herself, sitting down on the stone she has conquered. She
arranges around her a reticule, handkerchiefs, peppermint drops, a small flask
of some kind of elixir; removes her gloves; and wipes the lenses of her binoculars,
affably glancing at the bystanders. She turns to the* LADY *who is waiting for
her husband to come from the bar.*]

AGGRESSIVE LADY [*condescendingly*]: You're still on your feet, dearie. You
should sit down.

LADY: Ah, don't mention it! I can't feel my legs anymore.

AGGRESSIVE LADY: Men nowadays are so rude, they never give their
places to ladies. Have you brought any peppermint drops?

LADY [*panicked*]: No. Are they necessary?

AGGRESSIVE LADY: When you have to look up a long time, you're bound to feel sick to your stomach. And do you have any smelling salts on you? No? Goodness me, how thoughtless of you! How will they bring you round when he drops? No ether either? Of course not! If that's the state you're in . . . Isn't there anyone to look after you?

LADY [*panicked*]: I'll tell my husband. He's at the bar.

AGGRESSIVE LADY: Your husband is a brute!

POLICEMAN: Whose jacket is that? Who threw that rag down here?

BOY: I did. I threw down the jacket so he won't get so hurt when he falls.

POLICEMAN: Take it away.

[*A couple of tourists, armed with Kodaks,* argue over the most advantageous position.*]

FIRST PHOTOGRAPHER: I wanted to stand here.

SECOND PHOTOGRAPHER: You wanted, but I'm already standing here.

FIRST PHOTOGRAPHER: You just got here, but I've been standing here for two whole days.

SECOND PHOTOGRAPHER: Then why did you go away without leaving even your shadow?

FIRST PHOTOGRAPHER: Am I supposed to starve to death, damn it?

PEDDLER WITH A COMB [*mysteriously*]: Tortoiseshell.

TOURIST [*fiercely*]: So what?

PEDDLER WITH A COMB: Genuine tortoiseshell.

TOURIST: Go to hell!

THIRD PHOTOGRAPHER TOURIST: For heaven's sake, madam, you're sitting on my camera.

LITTLE LADY: Ah, where is it?

---

* George Eastman's Kodak Brownie camera, encased in a cheap cardboard box, was introduced in 1900 and quickly gained an international market. Its slogan, "You press the button, we do the rest," was heard wherever vacationers gathered.

TOURIST: Underneath you, underneath!

LITTLE LADY: But I was so tired! Foo, what a nasty camera you've got! Now I see—something was lying there and I was wondering, can it be a stone—why is it so black? And now it turns out to be your camera.

TOURIST [*in agony*]: Madam, for heaven's sake!

LITTLE LADY: Why is it so big? Cameras are little things, and this one's so big! Honestly, I never suspected that it was a camera. Could you take my picture? I'd like the mountains as a background, that kind of setting.

TOURIST: How can I take your picture when you're sitting on the camera!

LITTLE LADY [*jumps up in fright*]: Really? Why didn't you say so? Is it taking a picture now?

VOICES: Kellner, beer!

Why don't you serve wine?

I put in my order a long time ago.

What would you like?

Right away!

This minute!

Kellner!

Kellner!

A toothpick!

[*A* FAT TOURIST, *breathing hard, enters quickly, surrounded by a numerous brood.*]

FAT TOURIST [*shouting*]: Masha! Sasha! Petya! Where's Masha! Ah, for heaven's sake, where is Masha?

HIGH SCHOOL BOY [*dully*]: She's here, Daddy.

FAT TOURIST: Well, where is she? Masha!

YOUNG LADY: I'm here, Papa dear.

FAT TOURIST: Well, where are you? [*Turns around.*] Ah, there you are! Who stands behind a person's back? Look, look! Where are you looking, for heaven's sake!

YOUNG LADY [*dully*]: I don't know, Papa dear.

FAT TOURIST: No, this is impossible! Can you imagine, never once has she seen lightning: she makes goo-goo eyes as big as buttons, but as soon as it flashes—she shuts them. So she's never seen it a single time! Masha, you're yawning again! There he is, take a look!

FIRST HIGH SCHOOL BOY: She sees him, Daddy.

FAT TOURIST: Look after her. [*Suddenly shifting to a tone of the deepest pity*] Ah, poor young fellow! No, can you imagine how he's going to fall? Look, children, how pale he is. You see how dangerous climbing can be!

FIRST HIGH SCHOOL BOY [*dully*]: He won't fall today, Daddy.

FAT TOURIST: Nonsense! Who said so?

SECOND YOUNG LADY: Papa, Masha's closed her eyes again.

FIRST HIGH SCHOOL BOY: May I sit down, Daddy. After all, he won't fall today . . . The doorman at the hotel told me. I can't take any more of this! You've been dragging us through all those art galleries from morning to night . . .

FAT TOURIST: So what? For whose benefit am I doing it? Huh? You think I enjoy being with you, you blockhead . . .

SECOND YOUNG LADY: Papa, Masha's blinking again.

SECOND HIGH SCHOOL BOY: I can't take it either. I keep having horrible dreams. All last night I dreamed of waiters.

FAT TOURIST: Petka!

FIRST HIGH SCHOOL BOY: And I've lost so much weight I'm nothing but skin and bones. I can't keep this up, Daddy. Train me to be a shepherd, a pig farmer . . .

FAT TOURIST: Sashka!

FIRST HIGH SCHOOL BOY: As if he were really going to fall—everybody lies to you and you believe them. Baedeker too. Your Baedeker's a liar!*

MASHA [*dully*]: Papa dear, children, he's starting to fall.

[*On high the* STRANGER *shouts something. General movement. Voices: "Look, he's falling"; binoculars are raised, the few* PHOTOGRAPHERS *excitedly snap their Kodaks; the* POLICEMEN *energetically clear the area for the fall.*]

FIRST PHOTOGRAPHER: Confound it! How in the world did I . . . When you're in a blasted hurry!

SECOND PHOTOGRAPHER: Partner, your lens cap is still on.

FIRST PHOTOGRAPHER: Damn and blast!

VOICES: Ssh! He's getting ready to fall.

No, he's saying something.

No, he's falling!

Ssh!

STRANGER [*faintly*]: Help!

FAT TOURIST: Ah, the poor young fellow! Masha! Petya! This is what is called a tragedy: a clear sky, lovely weather, but any minute he is bound to fall and be injured to death. Sasha, isn't this awful!

HIGH SCHOOL BOY [*dully*]: I get it.

FAT TOURIST: Masha, do you get it? Just think, out here there's the sky, out here people are eating, everything's so pleasant, and he has to drop. What a tragedy! Petya, do you remember Hamlet?

SECOND YOUNG LADY [*prompting him*]: Hamlet, Prince of Denmark, Olsinore.

---

* The German publishing house Baedeker (1827–1948) put out a series of popular guidebooks in several languages in familiar red covers.

PETKA [*gloomily*]: Helsingfors, I know. Why do you keep at me, Daddy?

MASHA [*dully*]: All night long he was dreaming about garçons.

SASHKA: Better order some sandwiches.

PEDDLER WITH THE COMB [*mysteriously*]: Tortoiseshell. Genuine.

FAT TOURIST [*gullible*]: Is it stolen goods?

PEDDLER WITH THE COMB: How dare you, sir!

FAT TOURIST [*angrily*]: If it's not stolen goods, how can it be genuine?

AGGRESSIVE LADY [*condescendingly*]: Are all these your children?

FAT TOURIST: Yes, madam. A father's responsibilities . . . But, as you see, they protest: the age-old conflict between father and child, madam. Such a dreadful tragedy is taking place here, it's heart-rending . . . Are you starting to blink again, Masha?

AGGRESSIVE LADY: You're absolutely right: children must be inured to it. But why do you call this a dreadful tragedy? Any roofer can fall from a great height. And how far is it here—a hundred, two hundred feet? And I've seen a man fall right out of the sky.

FAT TOURIST [*delighted*]: You don't say so! Sasha, children, listen up. Right out of the sky.

AGGRESSIVE LADY: Quite so. An aviator. He flew out of the clouds and *bang!* on to an iron roof.

FAT TOURIST: What a horror!

AGGRESSIVE LADY: That's what I call a tragedy! They had to pour water from a pump on me for two whole hours before I came to. Nearly drowned me, the scoundrels! Ever since then I carry smelling salts.

[*A troupe of itinerant Italian singers and musicians appears. The short, stout tenor with a reddish beard and big, watery, stupidly dreamy eyes; he sings unusually sweetly. A skinny hunchback in a jockey cap sings in a shrill baritone; the bass, who looks like a highway robber, also plays the mandolin; a gaunt girl with a fiddle rolls her eyes so that only the whites are visible. They strike a pose and sing:*]

ITALIANS [*singing*]:

> Sul mare luccica l'astro d'argento
> Placida è l'onda, prospero è il vento.
> Venite all'agile barchetta mia
> Santa Lucia, Santa Lucia.*

MASHA [*dully*]: Papa, children, look: he's starting to wave his arms around.

FAT TOURIST: Could it be the effect of the music?

AGGRESSIVE LADY: Highly likely. Generally speaking all these things are done to music. Only it may make him fall before he should. Hey, you, musicians, go away—go away!

[*A* TALL TOURIST, *with a turned-up mustache, gesticulating heatedly, steps up, accompanied by a few sympathetic sightseers.*]

TALL TOURIST: It's outrageous! . . . Why don't they take him down? Gentlemen, didn't you all hear him shout "Save me"?

SIGHTSEERS [*in unison*]: We all heard, all of us.

TALL TOURIST: There you are! And I heard it perfectly plainly: "Save me. Why don't they save me?" It's outrageous! Officers, officers! Why don't you rescue him? What are you doing here?

POLICEMAN: We're clearing a space for the fall.

TALL TOURIST: Ah! That makes sense. But why don't you rescue him? You ought to be rescuing him. That's your duty in loving your fellow man. When a man asks to be rescued, he has to be rescued. Isn't that so, gentlemen?

SIGHTSEERS [*in unison*]: Right, absolutely right! He has to be rescued.

TALL TOURIST [*heatedly*]: We're not heathens, we're Christians, we have to love our neighbor. Once he asks to be rescued, all measures that lie at the disposal of the authorities must be taken to rescue him. Officers, are you taking all measures?

---

* "The silver star shines on the sea / The wave is placid, the wind is propitious. / Come to my nimble little boat / Santa Lucia, Santa Lucia." [I have corrected Andreev's Italian.—TRANS.]

POLICEMAN: All of 'em.

TALL TOURIST: Every single one? Gentlemen, all measures are being taken. Young man, listen—all measures are being taken to rescue you. Do you hear me?

STRANGER [*barely audible*]: Save me! . . .

TALL TOURIST [*agitated*]: Gentlemen, you heard him: again he shouted, "Save me." Officers, did you hear him?

ONE OF THE SIGHTSEERS [*meekly*]: In my opinion he ought to be saved.

TALL TOURIST: That's just the point! That's what I've been saying for the last two hours. Officers, did you hear? This is outrageous!

THE SAME SIGHTSEER [*a bit more boldly*]: In my opinion, we ought to apply to the highest authorities.

THE REST [*in unison*]: Yes, yes, we must complain. This is outrageous! The authorities should not abandon its citizens in danger. We all pay our taxes. He has got to be rescued.

TALL TOURIST: And isn't that what I've been saying? Of course we must go and register a complaint . . . Young man, do you hear, did you pay your taxes? I can't hear you.

FAT TOURIST: Petya, Katya, listen, what a tragedy!—Ah, the poor young fellow! He's about to fall at any minute, and they're asking for his residential rent receipt.

KATYA [*a girl in eyeglasses, pedantically*]: But, Papa, can this be called a residence? The meaning of residence . . .

PETKA [*pinches her*]: Suck-up!

MASHA [*dully*]: Look, Papa—he's about to fall.

[*In the crowd, more excitement, with the same shouting and bustling among the photographers.*]

TALL TOURIST: We'd better hurry. Gentlemen, we must rescue him at all costs! Who's with me?

SIGHTSEERS [*in unison*]: All of us, all of us!

TALL TOURIST: Officers, did you hear that? Let's go, gentlemen.

[*They leave, gesticulating heatedly. From the bar, increased liveliness; we hear the clink of beer mugs and the start of loud German singing. The* WAITER, *finally and totally swamped, runs to one side, looks up in despair at the sky, and mops his sweaty brow with a napkin. Frenzied orders: "Kellner! Kellner!"*]

STRANGER [*rather loudly*]: Kellner, can't you bring me some soda water?

[*The* WAITER *shudders, looks in horror up at the sky, till he spies the* STRANGER; *he leaves, pretending he has heard nothing. Enraged voice: "Kellner, beer!"*]

WAITER: Right away, this minute! Right away.

[*Two* DRUNKS *come out of the bar.*]

LADY: Ah, there's my husband! Over here, come over here at once!

AGGRESSIVE LADY: What a brute!

FIRST DRUNK [*waving his hand*]: Hey, you up there—feeling rotten? Huh?

STRANGER [*rather loudly*]: Rotten. Sick and tired of it.

FIRST DRUNK: And no way to get a drink.

STRANGER: Not likely!

SECOND DRUNK: Why are you talking to him about a drink? The man's about to die, and you're getting him excited with all these temptations. Listen, we're spending our time drinking to your health. That can't do you any harm, can it?

FIRST DRUNK: What are you on about, how could that harm him? It could only buck him up. Listen! We feel sorry for you, honest to God, but don't mind us: we're going back to the bar now.

SECOND DRUNK: Just look at how many people there are!

FIRST DRUNK: Let's go. Otherwise, if he falls, they'll close the bar.

[*A new bunch of tourists appear, led by an extremely elegant gentleman— the correspondent of leading European newspapers. They surround him with whispers of respectful admiration and disinterested excitement; many people leave the bar to have a look at him, and even the waiter makes a slight detour, takes a quick look, smiles blissfully, and hurries along, spilling a gravy boat.*]

VOICES: The journalist, look!

LADY: Ah, goodness me—and my husband's not here again!

FAT TOURIST: Petya, Masha, Sasha, Katya, Vasya, look—that's a famous journalist . . . the most famous. Whatever he writes, that's how it'll be.

KATYA: Mashechka, you're not looking in the right place again.

SASHKA: Let's order some sandwiches instead! I've had it, Papa! A fellow has to eat . . .

FAT TOURIST [*thrilled*]: What a tragedy! Katechka, sweetie, do you realize how awful this is: such fine weather—and a famous journalist! Take out your notebook, Petya, take out your notebook.

PETKA: I lost it, Papa.

JOURNALIST: Where is he?

VOICES [*obliging*]: There he is, up there!

A little higher, even higher!

A bit lower!

No, higher!

JOURNALIST: Please, please, gentlemen. I'll find him myself. Aha, there he is! Mm-yes, his situation . . .

TOURIST: Wouldn't you like a campstool?

JOURNALIST: Thank you. [*Sits.*] Mm-yes, his situation! Very, very interesting. [*Takes out his notebook; to the photographers, graciously.*] Have you already snapped him, gentlemen?

FIRST PHOTOGRAPHER: Yes, of course, of course! We've covered the general nature of the locale . . .

SECOND PHOTOGRAPHER: The tragic situation of the young man . . .

JOURNALIST: Re-ally? Very, very interesting.

FAT TOURIST: You hear, Sashka; a clever fellow, a famous journalist, and he says: how interesting it is. And you want sandwiches! . . . Blockhead!

SASHKA: Maybe he's already eaten . . .

JOURNALIST: Gentlemen, I pray you to observe silence.

AN OBLIGING VOICE: Quiet, you there in the bar!

JOURNALIST [*shouting upward*]: Allow me to introduce myself: chief correspondent of the European press, sent here on special assignment by the editors. I should like to ask you some questions concerning your situation. What is your name? Your name, social standing, age?

[*The* STRANGER *mumbles something.*]

JOURNALIST [*not quite making it out*]: I can't hear a thing. Is he like that all the time?

VOICES: Yes, you can't make out a word.

JOURNALIST [*jotting something down*]: Splendid! Are you unmarried?

[*The* STRANGER *mumbles something.*]

JOURNALIST: I can't hear you! Married, yes! Please repeat it.

FIRST TOURIST: He said he's a bachelor.

SECOND TOURIST: No he didn't! Of course he's married . . .

JOURNALIST [*casually*]: You think so? Let's put down: married. How many children? What? I can't hear you. I think he said three? Hmm . . . let's put down five to be sure.

FAT TOURIST: Ah, what a tragedy! Five children! Can you imagine!

AGGRESSIVE LADY: He's lying.

JOURNALIST [*shouting*]: How did you get into this situation? What? I can't hear you, louder! Repeat what you just said. [*Not making it out, to the public.*] What is he saying? He's got a confoundedly faint voice.

FIRST TOURIST: I thought he shouted he just got lost.

SECOND TOURIST: No, he doesn't know himself how he wound up there.

VOICES: He was hunting!

He was rock climbing.

No, no, he's simply a madman.

JOURNALIST: Please, please, gentlemen—whatever the case, he didn't drop down from the sky. However . . . [*Makes a quick note.*] The unfortunate young man . . . has from childhood suffered fits of insanity . . . The bright radiance of a full moon . . . rugged rocks . . . a drowsy doorman . . . failed to notice . . .

FIRST TOURIST [*to the* SECOND, *quietly*]: But it's only a new moon now.

SECOND TOURIST: Ah, you think the public knows anything about astronomy?

FAT TOURIST [*in ecstasy*]: Masha! Pay attention—here before you is a shining example of the influence of the moon on living organisms. But what a terrible tragedy: to go for a stroll on a moonlight night— and climb up and suddenly find you can't be rescued!

JOURNALIST [*shouting*]: How do you feel? I can't hear you. Louder! Ah, that's it! Mm-yes, the situation.

PUBLIC [*engrossed*]: Listen, listen to how he feels. Isn't it awful!

JOURNALIST [*making notes, uttering detached remarks aloud*]: A mortal terror shackles his limbs . . . Icy fear runs coldly down his spine . . . No hope at all . . . In his mind's eye pictures arise of his domestic bliss: his wife making bread-and-butter, his five children babbling tender feelings in their angelic innocent voices . . . Grandmother in an armchair, smoking a pipe . . . I mean, grandfather smoking a pipe, while grandmother . . . Deeply moved by the sympathy of the public . . . He expressed a pre-death wish that his last gasp should be printed in our paper . . .

AGGRESSIVE LADY [*indignantly*]: The liar!

MASHA [*dully*]: Papa, children, look—he's starting to fall again.

FAT TOURIST [*angrily*]: Don't interrupt! A tragedy like this is taking place, and you . . . Why are you blinking?

JOURNALIST [*shouting*]: Hold fast! That's it, that's it! One last question: What would you like to convey to your fellow citizens as you depart for a better world?

STRANGER [*faintly*]: They can all go to hell!

JOURNALIST: What? Ah yes! [*Makes a quick note.*] "Ardent love . . . A final farewell . . . A firm opponent of the law granting equal rights to Negroes . . . Last wish was that never should those black-faced . . . "

PASTOR [*out of breath, making his way through the crowd*]: Where is he? Ah, there he is! Unhappy young man! Gentlemen, has no one of my spiritual vocation been here yet? No? Thank you. Am I the first?

JOURNALIST [*making a note*]: A highly emotional moment . . . A clergy-man has arrived . . . Everyone is frozen in suspense, some are weeping! . . .

PASTOR: If I may! If I may, gentlemen. An erring soul wishes to be rec-onciled with heaven at the end. [*Shouts.*] Don't you wish, my son, to be reconciled with heaven? Reveal to me your sins, and I will swiftly grant you absolution. What? I can't hear you.

JOURNALIST [*making a note*]: Sobs rend the air. In heart-rending terms the minister of the gospel exhorts the criminal, I mean the wretched man . . . With tears in his eyes, in a faint voice, the unhappy youth gives thanks . . .

STRANGER [*faintly*]: If you . . . don't clear out, I'll land on your head. I weigh three hundred pounds.

[*They all jump aside in fear and try to hide behind each other.*]

VOICES: He's falling, he's falling!

FAT TOURIST [*excitedly*]: Masha, Sasha, Petya!

POLICEMEN [*energetically*]: Stand back, please stand back.

LADY: Nelly, quick, run for Papa, tell him he's falling.

PHOTOGRAPHER [*in desperation*]: Good grief, I'm out of film. [*Rushes around, looking at the* STRANGER *plaintively.*] Just one little minute, I won't be long. I've got some in my overcoat. [*He moves back a step, keeping his eyes on the* STRANGER, *and returns.*] No, I can't, what if . . . Ah, good grief! It's there in my coat! I'll be right back, this minute. What a mess!

PASTOR: Make haste, my friend, gather your strength if only for the most important sins. We shall defer the lesser ones.

FAT TOURIST: What a tragedy!

JOURNALIST [*making notes*]: The criminal, I mean the unfortunate man, expresses general contrition . . . terrible mysteries come to light . . . The villain, having robbed a banker . . .

FAT TOURIST [*gullible*]: What a scoundrel!

PASTOR [*shouting*]: Firstly, have you killed anyone? Secondly, have you stolen anything? Thirdly, have you committed adultery? . . .

FAT TOURIST: Masha, Petya, Katya, Sasha, Vasya, cover your ears!

JOURNALIST [*writing*]: The indignant crowd . . . cries of outrage . . .

PASTOR [*hurriedly*]: Fourthly, have you taken the Lord's name in vain? Fifthly, have you coveted your neighbor's ass? His ox, his bondwoman, his wife? Sixthly . . .

PHOTOGRAPHER [*startled*]: What's that about an ass?

SECOND PHOTOGRAPHER: Where, where is there an ass? I don't see it.

FIRST PHOTOGRAPHER [*calming down*]: I thought I heard one.

PASTOR: I congratulate you, my son, you have made your peace with heaven. Now you may rest easy . . . Ah, good Lord, what do I see? The Salvation Army? Officers, chase them away!

[*A few members of the Salvation Army, men and women, in parade uniforms, with musical instruments, come near the place of action. There are only three instruments: a bass drum, a fiddle, and an unusually squeaky trumpet.*]

FIRST SALVATIONIST [*drumming furiously, drawls loudly and nasally*]: Brethren and sistren . . .

PASTOR [*trying to drown him out, shouting even more loudly and more nasally*]: He's already repented, brothers. Gentlemen, you are my witnesses! He's already repented and made his peace with heaven.

SECOND SALVATIONIST, A LADY [*climbing on to a rock, wailing*]: Like that sinner, I too dwelt in darkness and evilly abused alcohol, when the light of truth . . .

VOICE: She's drunk as skunk right now.

PASTOR: Officers, you heard how he repented and made his peace with heaven?

[*The* FIRST SALVATIONIST *drums furiously; the rest strike up a song. Shouts, roars of laughter, whistles. They're singing in the bar as well and calling for the waiter in every language. The frantic* POLICEMEN *are seeking to break away from the* PASTOR, *who is trying to pull them somewhere; the photographers are spinning around as if possessed. An English lady tourist appears on a donkey, which, sprawling its forelegs, refuses to go any farther and lends its voice to the others. The noise gradually subsides. The Salvation Army withdraws solemnly. The* PASTOR, *waving his arms, follows it.*]

FIRST ENGLISH TOURIST [*to another*]: How uncouth. This mob has no idea how to behave.

SECOND ENGLISH TOURIST: Let's get out of here.

FIRST ENGLISH TOURIST: Just a minute. [*Shouts.*] See here, my good man, can't you speed up this falling business?

SECOND ENGLISH TOURIST: What are you saying, Sir William?

FIRST ENGLISH TOURIST [*shouting*]: Can't you see that's what they're all waiting for? And, as a gentleman, it behooves you to give them satisfaction, and avoid disgracing yourself by suffering in public before this mob.

SECOND ENGLISH TOURIST: Sir William!

FAT TOURIST [*excitedly*]: That's it, that's the truth! Sasha, Petya, listen: they're telling the truth. What a tragedy!

SOME OTHER TOURIST [*stepping up to the* FIRST ENGLISH TOURIST]: How dare you!

FIRST ENGLISH TOURIST [*pushing him away*]: Come down from there at once, do you hear? If you haven't the nerve, I shall help you with a well-aimed shot. Do you agree or not?

VOICES: That red-headed devil is out of his mind!

POLICEMAN [*grabbing the* FIRST ENGLISH TOURIST *by the arm*]: You have no right to do that. I arrest you.

SOME OTHER TOURIST: A nation of barbarians!

[*The* STRANGER *shouts something. Excitement below. A Voice:* "*Listen, listen!*"]

STRANGER [*loudly*]: Send that jackass to the devil, he's going to shoot me. And tell the boss I've had it up to here.

VOICES: What's that?

What boss?

He's gone out of his mind, poor fellow!

FAT TOURIST: Sasha, Masha, the picture of insanity. Petya, quick, remember Hamlet!

STRANGER [*angrily*]: Tell 'im, the small of my back is killing me.

MASHA [*dully*]: Papa, children, look, he's starting to jerk his legs.

KATYA: Is that what's called convulsions, papa?

FAT TOURIST [*thrilled*]: I don't know. I think so. What a tragedy!

SASHKA [*gloomily*]: Katya, you goose! She reads books but she doesn't know what death throes look like. And yet she wears glasses! I can't take any more of this, daddy.

FAT TOURIST: Just think, children. Any minute now a man will be dashed to his death, and what is he thinking about? The small of his back!

[*A noise is heard. A few infuriated tourists almost drag in a rather terrified gentleman in a white waistcoat. He is smiling, he bows in all directions, splays his hands as if to say, "I can't help it." At times, pushed, he quickly runs forward; at times tries to slip into the crowd but is caught and dragged again.*]

VOICES: A brazen hoax!

It's outrageous!

Police, police!

He's got to be taught a lesson!

OTHER VOICES:

What's the matter?

What hoax?

What's going on?

Gentlemen, they've caught a thief.

GENTLEMAN [*bowing and smiling*]: It's a joke, ladies and gentlemen. Simply a joke! The public gets bored, and I wanted to amuse them a bit.

STRANGER [*furiously*]: Boss!

GENTLEMAN: Right away, right away!

STRANGER: What, am I supposed to stay here until Doomsday?! We contracted for twelve o'clock, and how late is it now?

TALL TOURIST WITH THE TWIRLED MUSTACHE [*beside himself with indignation*]: You hear that, gentlemen? It turns out that this scoundrel, this gentleman in a white waistcoat hired some another scoundrel and easy as you please tied him to that rock.

VOICES: He's tied on?

TALL TOURIST WITH THE TWIRLED MUSTACHE: Yes indeed, he's tied on and cannot fall. And here we are getting all excited, getting all upset, and he cannot fall! . . .

STRANGER: Even if I wanted to! You suppose I'm going to break my neck for twenty-five rubles! Boss, I can't stand it anymore. Some ass wanted to take a shot at me. A pastor preached at me for two hours straight—that's not in the contract!

SASHKA: I told you, Papa dear, that Baedeker is a liar, but you always believe everybody, drag us all over the place, without a bite to eat.

HOTELKEEPER: The public gets bored . . . My only wish was to entertain the respected public . . .

AGGRESSIVE LADY: What's all this? I don't understand? Why won't he fall? Then who is going to fall?

FAT TOURIST: I don't understand either. Of course he has to fall.

PETKA: You never understand anything, Papa dear. They're telling you he's tied on.

SASHKA: Just try and convince him! He loves any old Baedeker more than his own children.

PETKA: Call him a father!

FAT TOURIST: Silence!

AGGRESSIVE LADY: What is this? He has to fall!

TALL TOURIST WITH THE TWIRLED MUSTACHE: No, the very idea, what a swindle! You've better explain yourself, my dear sir.

HOTELKEEPER: The public gets bored. Forgive me, gentlemen. But in my wish to please . . . A few hours of pleasant thrills . . . nervous stimulation . . . inspiring altruistic feelings . . .

ENGLISHMAN: The bar is yours?

HOTELKEEPER: It's mine.

ENGLISHMAN: And the hotel down there is yours?

HOTELKEEPER: It's mine. The public gets bored . . .

JOURNALIST [*making a note*]: A brazen hoax . . . A hotelkeeper, eager to increase his profits from alcoholic beverages, is exploiting the finest of human feelings . . . The indignation of the public . . .

STRANGER [*furiously*]: Are you going to take me down soon, boss, or not?

HOTELKEEPER: What's got into you? What have you got to complain about? Don't we take you down at night?

STRANGER: You'd better, that's all I need, to be left here all night long.

HOTELKEEPER: Well, you can hold on a few more minutes. The public gets bored . . .

TALL TOURIST WITH THE TWIRLED MUSTACHE: No, do you have any idea what you've done, you scoundrel! For the sake of your sordid profits you are godlessly exploiting the love of one's neighbor. You made us undergo fear, compassion, poisoned our hearts with pity—and what's the result? The result is that this scoundrel, your wretched accomplice, is tied to the rock and not only won't fall the way we all expect, but can't fall.

AGGRESSIVE LADY: What do you mean? He's got to fall!

FAT TOURIST: Police, police!

[*The* PASTOR *reappears, out of breath.*]

PASTOR: What, still alive? Aha, there he is. What charlatans, that Salvation Army!

VOICE: You haven't heard yet: he's attached.

PASTOR: What? Attached to what? To life? Oh, we are all attached to life, until death releases us. But whether he is attached or not, I have reconciled him with heaven and *basta*! While those charlatans . . .

TALL TOURIST WITH THE TWIRLED MUSTACHE: Police! Police, you have to draw up an official report!

AGGRESSIVE LADY [*stepping up to the* HOTELKEEPER]: I cannot allow anyone to cheat me. I have seen an aviator drop out of the clouds and *ba-ang* onto a roof, I have seen a tiger tear a woman to pieces . . .

PHOTOGRAPHER: I've spoiled three rolls of film shooting that scoundrel. You'll answer for that, my good sir!

FAT TOURIST: An official report, an official report! What effrontery! Masha, Petya, Vasya, call the police.

HOTELKEEPER [*falling back in despair*]: But I can't force him to fall if he doesn't want to. I've done all I can. Gentlemen, gentlemen! . . .

AGGRESSIVE LADY: I won't let you get away with it!

HOTELKEEPER: Please, gentlemen. Word of honor, he'll fall the next time, but he doesn't want to now!

STRANGER: What next time?

HOTELKEEPER: Shut up, you there!

STRANGER: For twenty-five rubles?

PASTOR: Well, I never, what an insolent fellow! Only now at the risk of my own life I reconciled him with heaven—you heard how he threatened to fall on my head? And he's still dissatisfied. Adulterer! Thief! Murderer! Coveter of your neighbor's ass!

PHOTOGRAPHER: Gentlemen, an ass!

SECOND PHOTOGRAPHER: Where's the ass? I don't see it.

FIRST PHOTOGRAPHER [*calming down*]: I heard something . . .

THIRD PHOTOGRAPHER: You're the ass. You're making me cross-eyed.

MASHA [*dully*]: Papa, children, look, the police are coming.

[*Excitement, noise. On one side the* POLICEMAN *is mobbed, on the other the* HOTELKEEPER, *and they are both shouting: "If I may, if I may!"*]

FAT TOURIST: Officer, constable! Here he is, that con man, swindler . . .

PASTOR: Officer! There he is, the adulterer, thief, murderer, coveter of his neighbor's ass . . .

POLICEMAN: If I may, if I may, gentlemen, we'll teach him what's what and make him sorry for what he's done.

HOTELKEEPER: But I can't force him to fall if he doesn't want to!

POLICEMAN: Hey, you up there, youngster, can you fall or not, tell the truth!

STRANGER [*surly*]: I don't want to fall.

VOICES: Aha, he admits it! What a scoundrel!

TALL TOURIST WITH THE TWIRLED MUSTACHE: Write this down, Officer. Wishing . . . for the sake of profit . . . to exploit the feeling of love for one's neighbor . . . a sacred feeling . . . ex . . . ex . . . ex . . .

FAT TOURIST: Children, listen, an official report is being drawn up. How descriptive!

TALL TOURIST WITH THE TWIRLED MUSTACHE: Sacred feeling, which . . .

POLICEMAN [*writing painstakingly, his tongue in the corner of his mouth*]: Love for one's neighbor . . . sacred feeling, which . . .

MASHA [*dully*]: Papa, children, look: here comes an advertisement.

[*A few musicians with trumpets and bass drums appear. They are headed by an individual carrying a long pole with an enormous poster depicting a desperately long-haired man with the caption "I used to be bald."*]

STRANGER: You're too late! Pals, they're drawing up the report right now! You'd better scram.

INDIVIDUAL [*stopping and speaking in a high voice*]: I used to be bald from the day of my birth and a long time thereafter. That sparse growth which covered my skull by my tenth year resembled fleece rather than hair. When I entered into matrimony, my skull was as bare as a pillow, and my young bride . . .

FAT TOURIST: What a tragedy! Newly wed, and such a head—you understand, children, how horrible that must be!

[*Everyone listens with interest and even the* POLICEMAN *freezes, pen in hand.*]

INDIVIDUAL [*inspired*]: And the moment came when conjugal bliss literally depended on a hair. All methods of growing hair recommended by quacks . . .

FAT TOURIST: Pull out your notebook, Petya.

AGGRESSIVE LADY: But when is he going to fall?

HOTELKEEPER [*obligingly*]: Next time, madam, next time! I won't tie him on so tightly . . . you know what I mean . . .

Curtain.

THE LOVELY SABINE WOMEN
(*Prekrasnye Sabinyanki*)

A bit of Roman history in three acts

by Leonid Andreev

1911

Act 1

A wild, rugged terrain. Daybreak. Armed Romans appear over the hills, dragging along the lovely, half-naked SABINE WOMEN, *who resist, screaming and scratching, except for one, who lies perfectly quiet, seemingly asleep, in the arms of her Roman. Each time they are scratched, the Roman captors yelp with pain. They quickly dump the women in a heap, then hastily leap away and try to recover. They pant in exhaustion. The screams abate. The women also recover, warily watching the abductors' movements, whispering and prattling in subdued tones.*

FIRST ROMAN: By Hercules! I'm dripping sweat like a water rat. I'll bet my woman weighs a ton.

SECOND ROMAN: Who told you to go for the biggest one in the place? I took a little thing all skin and bones, so—

FIRST ROMAN: You did, did you? How about your face? You mean to tell me that skinny little thing did that?

SECOND ROMAN: Alas! She scratches like a cat.

FIRST ROMAN: They all scratch like cats. I've fought in a hundred battles. I've been hacked with swords, thumped with clubs, battered with stones, walls, and gates, but this takes the cake. My Roman nose is out of joint for good.

THIRD ROMAN: If I weren't clean-shaven, like all ancient Romans, I wouldn't have a hair on my face. You know what dainty slender fingers and exceptionally sharp nails they've got. Cats, you say! Bah! Cats can't compete. Mine managed to scratch the hair off my arms and was so caught up in her work all the way here she even forgot to scream.

A TALL, FAT ROMAN [*in a bass voice*]: Mine managed to get under my armor and kept tickling my armpits the whole way. I nearly died laughing.

[*Low, malicious laughter from the* SABINE WOMEN.]

FIRST ROMAN: Ssh, they can hear us.

SECOND ROMAN: Take it easy, gentlemen, and stop whining. Smarten yourselves up. You don't want them to lose respect for us the very first day. Look at Æmilius Paulus. There's a man who knows how to behave with dignity.

THIRD ROMAN: He shines resplendent as Aurora!

FOURTH ROMAN: By Hercules! Not a single scratch on him. How did you manage it, Paulus?

PAULUS [*with false modesty*]: Oh, I don't know. Nothing to it. Right from the start she clung to me as if I were her husband. The minute I lifted her up, she spontaneously threw her arms around my neck. My only fear was she might choke me in her tight embrace. Her arms are slender but very strong.

FIRST ROMAN: Lucky dog.

PAULUS: Easy as pie, I tell you. Her innocent, trusting heart whispered for me to love her dearly and respect her. Believe it or not, it's true. She slept like a baby half the way here.

FAT ROMAN: Now, Roman sirs, how are we going to tell whose is which? We abducted them in the dark like chickens from a coop.

[*Indignant outcry from the heap of* SABINE WOMEN: "What a revolting comparison!"]

FIRST ROMAN: Ssh! They can hear us!

FAT ROMAN [*lowering his voice an octave*]: Well, how can we tell them apart? Mine was an awfully jolly girl, and I won't give her up to anyone. Nobody can put one over on me.

SECOND ROMAN: Don't be a jerk!

THIRD ROMAN: I'll recognize mine by her voice. I'll never forget her screams till the birth of Christ.

FOURTH ROMAN: I'll recognize mine by her nails.

SCIPIO: And I'll know mine by the wonderful fragrance of her hair.

PAULUS: And I, mine, by the modest beauty of her soul. O Romans! We now stand on the threshold of a new life. All the torments of the single state, farewell! Farewell, sleepless nights with their confounded nightingales! Let the nightingale sing whatever it damn well pleases, or any other bird, for that matter—I can stand it.

FAT ROMAN: Yes, it's time we entered the state of matrimony.

[*Sarcastic exclamations from the* SABINE WOMEN: "Yes, go ahead!" "Just you try it!" "Let's see you do it!"]

FIRST ROMAN: Ssh! They can hear us.

SECOND ROMAN: It's about time, you hear me, about time.

THIRD ROMAN: Roman sirs, who'll go first?

[*Silence. All stand motionless. Low, malicious laughter from the women.*]

FAT ROMAN: For my part, I've had all the tickling I can stand. Let someone else get tickled. I won't let anybody put one over on me. Hey, Paulus, you go forth.

PAULUS: Don't push me! Can't you see my little darling is still asleep? There—you see that little dark lump under that rock? That's her. Oh, innocent heart!

SCIPIO: Romans, I can see by your hesitation and justifiable confusion that none of you has the courage to approach those relentless creatures by himself. My plan, therefore, O gentlemen of ancient Rome, is this—

FAT ROMAN: That Scipio's got his head screwed on right.

SCIPIO: My plan is this . . . Let's all advance upon them in a body, casually, each hiding behind the other. After all, since we weren't afraid of their husbands—

FAT ROMAN: Oh, their husbands, that was a cinch.

[*Loud groans among the women and outbursts of weeping.*]

FIRST ROMAN: Ssh! They can hear us.

SCIPIO: There you go again, Marcus Antonius, with your leather lungs! Anyway, we must try to avoid that unfortunate word "husband." You see the dreadful effect it has on the poor women. Now then, gentlemen, do you agree to my plan?

ROMANS: We do, we do.

SCIPIO: Well then, gentlemen!

[*The* ROMANS *prepare for attack, the* WOMEN *for defense. In place of charming features, only sharp nails are seen ready to plunge into face and hair. A low snakelike hissing. The* ROMANS *advance according to plan, that is, hiding behind each another; this leads to their all falling back and disappearing offstage. Laughter among the* WOMEN. *The* ROMANS *reenter, in disarray.*]

FIRST ROMAN: There seems to be a flaw in your plan, Scipio. We advanced in retreat, as Socrates might have said.

FAT ROMAN: It's got me stumped.

PAULUS: Courage, Roman sirs! What matter a scratch or two? It's in the cause of everlasting bliss! Forward, gentlemen of Rome! Prepare to board them!

[*The* ROMANS, *all except* PAULUS, *his eyes raised dreamily to heaven, advance on the* WOMEN *as a disorderly mob but, after a moment's silent struggle, quickly retreat, all rubbing their noses.*]

SCIPIO [*through his nose*]: Did you notice, gentlemen, they didn't even scream? That's a sinister omen. I prefer women who scream.

FIRST ROMAN: What's to be done?

SECOND ROMAN: I want married life!

THIRD ROMAN: I want a hearth and home. What's life without a hearth and home? We have been founding Rome long enough, damn it! It's time we had some rest and recreation.

FAT ROMAN: Unfortunately, ancient Romans, there isn't one man among us well acquainted with female psychology. Constantly at war and founding Rome, we've grown coarse, lost all refinement, and forgot what a woman is.

PAULUS [*modestly*]: Not all of us.

SCIPIO: But didn't these women already have husbands, the fellows we beat yesterday? This leads me to conclude that there must be some way, some special mysterious way of approaching a woman which we do not know. How can we find it out?

FAT ROMAN: We must ask the women themselves.

SECOND ROMAN: They won't tell.

[*Malicious laughter from the* WOMEN.]

FIRST ROMAN: Ssh! they can hear us.

SCIPIO: Listen, I have a plan.

FAT ROMAN: That Scipio's got his head screwed on right.

SCIPIO: Our charming captors—for don't you think, gentlemen, that, far from capturing them, they have captivated us?—our charming captors, I say, preoccupied in scratching our faces, pulling the hair from our skins, and tickling our armpits, could not possibly have heard us. And unable to hear us, how could they be open to persuasion? And if we were unable to persuade them, how could they be persuaded? QED!

ROMANS [*repeating*]: QED!

[*They sink into an attitude of despondency. The* WOMEN *eavesdrop.*]

SCIPIO: This, then, is my plan. Let us, in accord with the rules of war, select an envoy from among us, and propose to our captivating foes that they do the same. I trust that the representatives of both warring camps, enjoying complete security under the protection of a white flag [*He feels his nose.*] will be able to arrive at a definite *modus vivendi*, as we say in Latin. And then—

[*The* ROMANS *interrupt his brilliant speech with loud shouts of "Hurrah!" They unanimously elect him envoy. He raises a white flag.*]

SCIPIO [*cautiously approaching the* WOMEN, *speaking over his shoulder*]: Now don't go too far away, boys. [*Ingratiating.*] Fair Sabines, please, please stay where you are. You see, I am under the protection of the white flag. The white flag is sacred, and my person, too, is inviolable—that's a fact, word of honor! Fair Sabines, only yesterday we had the pleasure of abducting you, and today dissension, squabbles, and strange misunderstandings have already arisen between us!

CLEOPATRA: What impudence! Don't think because you put that white rag on a stick you can utter all sorts of obscenities.

SCIPIO [*conciliating*]: Goodness me—what obscenities? On the contrary, I am delighted—I mean, to tell the truth, we are all perfectly miserable, and—[*with desperate resolution*] we are consumed with love. By Hercules, we are all aflame! Lady, I see you sympathize, and so I make bold to ask a slight favor, to select, as we have done, an env—

CLEOPATRA: We know; we heard all about it. You needn't repeat.

SCIPIO: Why, we talked under our breaths.

FIRST SABINE WOMAN: But we heard you all the same.

CLEOPATRA: Go back with your rag now and wait where you belong. We'll talk it over. No, no, not here—farther off, please. No listening in. And who is that mama's boy standing there with his mouth wide open? [*She points to the dreaming* PAULUS.] Take him away, please.

ROMANS [*tiptoeing off, whispering*]: Now we're getting somewhere. [*Some conscientiously plug their ears.*]

FIRST SABINE WOMAN: What gall! How insulting! How heavy-handed! Oh, our poor husbands!

SECOND SABINE WOMAN: I swear I'd rather scratch out a thousand eyes than cheat on my unhappy husband the least little bit. Sleep in peace, beloved. I shall guard your honor well.

THIRD SABINE WOMAN: I swear too.

FOURTH SABINE WOMAN: So do I.

CLEOPATRA: Ah, my dear friends, we all can swear, but what's the point of our swearing? These people are so uneducated and uncouth they can't appreciate it. Take my man. Even though I chewed on his nose—

FIRST SABINE WOMAN: How can you tell them apart?

CLEOPATRA [*spitefully*]: I shall never forget him to my dying day. He smelled so badly of armor and swords and all that pertains to a common soldier and he squeezed me without the slightest consideration. My poor, dear husband!

FIRST SABINE WOMAN: They all have that soldier smell.

SECOND SABINE WOMAN: And they all squeeze like grizzly bears! Maybe it's a custom among them.

THIRD SABINE WOMAN: When I was a little girl, a soldier boy came to our house and said he was from a far-off land where—

CLEOPATRA: Ladies, this is no time for reminiscing.

THIRD SABINE WOMAN: But this soldier boy—

CLEOPATRA: My dear little Juno, I swear by Venus, we are not in the least interested in your soldier when each of us is saddled with a soldier of her own. What shall we do now, my dears? Here's what I suggest—

VERONICA [*a skinny Sabine of advanced years, just awakened, approaches, sleepily squinting*]: Where are they? Why are they so far away? I want them to come closer. I feel at a loss when they are so far away. I was in a trance this whole time, and now I can't find the youth who carried me here. He smelled like a soldier.

CLEOPATRA: He's standing over there with his mouth wide open.

VERONICA: I'll go to him. I'm at such a loss.

CLEOPATRA: Hold her back! Now, Veronica, how can you have forgotten your unhappy husband?

VERONICA: I swear I shall love him forever. But why don't we go over there? Is there something in the way? What is it? Personally, I'm ready for anything. Let them come over here. Once you let a man know you're not angry with him, the next minute he starts to take all sorts of uncalled-for liberties.

CLEOPATRA: Now then, my dear friends, my first suggestion is that we swear never to betray our dear unhappy husbands. Whatever these men choose to do with us, we shall remain as steadfast as the Tarpeian rock. When I think of how my husband must be missing me now, and how he is crying in vain to his empty couch: "Cleopatra! Oh, where art thou, Cleopatra!" When I think of how much he loved me—

[*The* WOMEN *weep.*]

CLEOPATRA: Let us swear, then, dear friends, for these men are waiting.

SABINE WOMEN: We swear, we swear! Whatever these men do to us, we'll remain true to our husbands.

CLEOPATRA: Now my mind is at ease about our husbands. Sleep in peace, dear husband! The next thing to do is to select an envoy to meet their request, and let her—

FIRST SABINE WOMAN: Scratch out his eyes.

CLEOPATRA: No, let her give the scoundrel a piece of her mind. That bunch think all we can do is scratch. We'll show them how we can talk.

VERONICA [*shrugging her skinny shoulders*]: Ah, what's the point of talking when they have might on their side?

CLEOPATRA: Hold her back! Veronica, might is not right, whatever Roman law may say. Let *me* go, and I'll show them they have no right to keep us here, that they are duty bound to let us go, that by the laws of God and man *et alia*, as they say in Rome—they acted like perfect swine.

SABINE WOMEN: Go, go, Cleopatra!

FIRST SABINE WOMAN: Hold Veronica back!

CLEOPATRA: Hey, you envoy there with the white rag, come over here—I want to talk to you.

SCIPIO: Shall I unbuckle my sword?

CLEOPATRA: No. What for? Do you think we're afraid of your swords? Come on. Please don't be afraid. I won't bite. Last night when you broke into our peaceful homes and roughly tore me out of my poor husband's arms you weren't so timid. Why are you so timid now? Come over here!

[SCIPIO *approaches cautiously. The* ROMANS *and* SABINE WOMEN *arrange themselves in two symmetrical groups, stage right and left, and listen attentively.*]

SCIPIO: I am delighted, lady—

CLEOPATRA: Delighted, are you? Then let me tell you: you're a scoundrel, a madman, a thief, a robber, a murderer, a monster! Your behavior is blasphemous, contemptible, disgusting, repulsive, unheard-of, unprecedented!

SCIPIO: Lady!

CLEOPATRA: I despise you; you turn my stomach; I can't bear the sight of you; you smell of soldier. If your nose weren't so scratched, I'd—

SCIPIO: Excuse me, you were the one who scratched it.

CLEOPATRA: Did I? Then you were the one who—[*She eyes him contemptuously.*] Pardon me, I didn't recognize you.

SCIPIO [*gleefully*]: I recognized you at once. Doesn't your hair smell of verbena?

CLEOPATRA: What do you care what it smells of? Verbena is as good as any other perfume.

SCIPIO: Why, I didn't mean—

CLEOPATRA: I don't care what you meant. I didn't say what you smell of. Anyway, what's all this weird talk about smells? All I ask of you, my good sir, is to tell me plain and simple, as a man of honor, what do you want of us?

[SCIPIO *looks down, embarrassed, but, unable to restrain himself, snickers behind his hand. All the* ROMANS *snicker. The* WOMEN *take offense.*]

CLEOPATRA [*blushing*]: Snickering is not an answer. It's nasty. I ask you, what do you want of us? I hope you know that we are all married women.

SCIPIO: How shall I put it, lady? For our part we are prepared to offer you our hands and hearts.

CLEOPATRA: Aha! So you're serious? Are you in your right mind?

SCIPIO: Lady, look at us. We are not just anybody. We are not some street-corner Romeo. We have just founded Rome and are eager to eternalize it. Put yourself in our sandals, lady, and take pity on us! Wouldn't you, for example, feel sorry for your husbands if they woke up one fine day and found they'd been left entirely womanless? We are lonely, lady.

FAT ROMAN: Ever so lonely.

VERONICA [*wiping her eyes*]: I feel sorry for them.

SCIPIO: In the midst of war's alarums, preoccupied with the founding of Rome, we allowed the moment to slip by, so to speak, when—lady, we pity your husbands from the bottom of our hearts.

CLEOPATRA [*with dignity*]: I am very glad to hear it.

SCIPIO: But why the devil did they let you go?

ROMANS [*egging him on*]: That's right, that's right, Scipio.

SABINE WOMEN [*resentfully*]: Disgraceful! They're insulting our husbands. What a snide insinuation!

CLEOPATRA [*dryly*]: If you wish to continue the negotiations, I must ask you to speak of our husbands with respect.

SCIPIO: With pleasure! But, lady, much as we may respect them, we cannot help stating the fact that they are unworthy of you. While you are here breaking our hearts with your inhuman suffering; while your hot tears, wrung from you by your bereavement, flow like a mountain torrent in the spring; when even the rocks, quaking with pity, murmur and repine; when your charming noses, swollen with piteous tears, lose their exquisite form—

CLEOPATRA: That's not true.

SCIPIO: When all nature and so forth—at such a time as this, where are your husbands? Nowhere to be seen. They are not present. They are absent. They have abandoned you. At the risk of provoking your anger, I will say it—they have basely abandoned you!

[*The* ROMANS *strike an arrogant pose, with their hands on their hips. Distress and tears among the* WOMEN.]

PROSERPINA [*gently*]: Really, why *don't* they come for us? It's about time.

CLEOPATRA: That sounds very high and mighty, my good sir, and I cannot deny a certain element of grace in your posture. But what would you have done if men broke in on you at night to abduct us?

SCIPIO: We would have kept watch all through the night.

CLEOPATRA: And in the daytime?

SCIPIO: Oh, you wouldn't be willing to go away in the daytime.

VERONICA [*languorously*]: Why are they so far away? I'm at a loss when they're so far away. I want them to be closer.

SABINE WOMEN [*whispering*]: Hold her back!

CLEOPATRA: How conceited! Still, I'm sorry for you, sir. True, I do feel some respect and consideration for your suffering. But your youth has led you astray. I shall now set forth an argument that will instantly destroy your pipe dreams, and I hope will make you blush. How about the children, sir?

SCIPIO: What children?

CLEOPATRA: The children we left behind.

SCIPIO: I admit, lady, that's a serious problem. Permit me to withdraw an instant to confer with my colleagues.

[CLEOPATRA *goes back to her group,* SCIPIO *to his. They confer in whispers.*]

SCIPIO: Lady!

CLEOPATRA: I'm listening.

SCIPIO: After lengthy deliberation, my colleagues, the Ancient Romans, have instructed me to inform you that you will have new children.

CLEOPATRA [*startled*]: Aha! You think so!

SCIPIO: We swear it. Gentlemen, swear.

[*The* ROMANS *swear in a discordant chorus.*]

CLEOPATRA: But this place of yours is highly unattractive.

SCIPIO [*offended*]: Of ours?

CLEOPATRA: Yes, it's a horrid location—all hills, gullies, quite unattractive. What's this rock lying here for? Please remove it.

[SCIPIO *removes the rock with great effort.*]

CLEOPATRA: What do you call this sort of tree? God only knows what it is. I can hardly breathe. Do tell me what sort of silly tree that is? Does this embarrass you, dear sir? Then permit me to withdraw. I suppose you have to have an answer, don't you?

SCIPIO: An answer to what?

CLEOPATRA: You asked me a question, didn't you?

SCIPIO: I did? Excuse me, lady. I seem to losing my wits. What did I ask you about?

CLEOPATRA: There you are! Now you're insulting me!

SCIPIO: I am?

CLEOPATRA: You certainly are. You say you're losing your wits.

SCIPIO: I do?

CLEOPATRA: Yes, of course. It isn't me. You're forgetting yourself, sir.

SCIPIO: I am?

CLEOPATRA: Well, I shall withdraw. And smarten yourself up a bit, sir, if you expect us to proceed with our negotiations. You look a sight. Don't you have a handkerchief? Wipe your face. It's dripping with sweat, as if you had been hauling rocks all day. [*She starts to go.*]

SCIPIO: No, lady, excuse me. I believe I really did pick up a rock, but you made me do it—

CLEOPATRA: Did I? I never had the faintest notion of such a thing.

SCIPIO: Pardon me, lady. What's this all about?

CLEOPATRA: How do I know? It's nothing to do with me.

SCIPIO: I think you're pulling my leg.

CLEOPATRA: So you've noticed?

SCIPIO: I won't allow you to pull my leg.

CLEOPATRA: What are you going to do about it?

SCIPIO: I'm not a husband yet, thank the gods!

CLEOPATRA: Aha! Now you say "Thank the gods." Not bad, sir. We'd be in a fine fix if we believed your oaths. [*To the* WOMEN] Do you hear? Now they're already glad we're not their wives.

SCIPIO: Good grief, this is insufferable! Either you stop this—

CLEOPATRA: Or else?

SCIPIO: Or else go home! Yes, yes, go home, ladies. Enough is enough! By Hercules! We didn't found Rome just to get bogged down in your ridiculous negotiations like flies in jam.

CLEOPATRA: Ridiculous?

SCIPIO: Yes, yes, idiotic!

CLEOPATRA [*weeping*]: You're insulting me.

SCIPIO: O Jupiter, now she's crying. Lady, what do you want? Why are you sticking to me like glue? Ancient Roman I may be, but by Olympus this woman is driving me crazy. Do, please, stop crying. I can't figure out what you're blubbing about.

CLEOPATRA [*crying*]: So you'll let us go?

SCIPIO: Yes, yes. [*Turning toward the* ROMANS] Friends, Romans, and countrymen, do you agree? I've reached the end of my tether.

FAT ROMAN: Let them go. We'll abduct the wives of the Etruscans.

SCIPIO: These creatures are not women, but—

CLEOPATRA [*crying*]: Word of honor?

SCIPIO: Word of honor what?

CLEOPATRA: Word of honor, you're going to let us go? Maybe you're just saying so, and the moment we start you'll snatch us back.

SCIPIO: No—not at all, go. Sticks like glue!

CLEOPATRA [*weeping*]: And will you carry us back home?

SCIPIO: What!

CLEOPATRA: Well, you must realize you brought us here, so you should carry us back. It's a very long way.

[*Malicious laughter from the* WOMEN. SCIPIO, *gasping with anger, glares at them fiercely and is about to say something, but merely stamps his foot and goes back to the* ROMANS. *All the* ROMANS *demonstratively turn their backs on the* WOMEN *and sit like that during what follows. The* WOMEN *calmly confer together.*]

CLEOPATRA: Did you hear, dear friends? They'll let us go back.

VERONICA: Isn't it awful!

SECOND SABINE WOMAN: No, what you mean is, they're kicking us out. It's outrageous! To abduct perfectly innocent women for no reason at all, break into their homes in the middle of the night, turn their furniture upside down, wake the children—and now, if you please, they don't want us!

FIRST SABINE WOMAN: What about our poor husbands! Consider what they have had to suffer.

SECOND SABINE WOMAN: Can you imagine! At night, when everybody's asleep.

THIRD SABINE WOMAN: Say, do you know the way back home?

FOURTH SABINE WOMAN: Do you suppose I was memorizing the route while I was carried here? Of course I don't. All I know is it's awfully far.

THIRD SABINE WOMAN: Well, it's pretty clear they won't carry us back.

[*Quiet laughter from the* ROMANS.]

VERONICA [*moaning*]: Look, they have made my poor boy sit down with his back to us, too. I'll go to him.

FIRST SABINE WOMAN: Hold on, Veronica, your boy won't run away. We've got to talk this over.

PROSERPINA: Here's what I think—what difference does it make what husbands we have, these here, or those there? These are all right and those are all right and others are all right, too. I'll bet the first thing mine'll ask me to do is to cook him a hot meal. I rather like the idea of having a new husband. My present husband is already sick and tired of my menu, and that numbskull there will be delighted.

CLEOPATRA: Proserpina, don't be cynical. History will judge us.

PROSERPINA: Ah, a lot history knows about what we women get up to. It's not so bad here, either.

CLEOPATRA: You're awful, Proserpina. What if they heard us? Here's what I suggest, dear friends. Naturally, we'll head for home and our dear peace-loving husbands right now. But the way is long and we're so tired—

FIRST SABINE WOMAN: My nerves are in tatters.

SECOND SABINE WOMAN: Nobody's got the stamina to stand this sort of thing—all of a sudden having your house turned upside down in the middle of the night.

CLEOPATRA: Let's stay here for a couple of days. That won't commit us to anything, will it? And they'll be so pleased. And when they see how cheerful and meek we are, they won't find it so hard to part with us. I'll admit I feel a little sorry for mine. His nose is in a terrible state.

THIRD SABINE WOMAN: But only for two days.

FOURTH SABINE WOMAN: I think one's enough. We'll just rest up a bit and have some fun. Quick, Cleopatra. I think they've fallen asleep already.

CLEOPATRA: Sir.

SCIPIO [not turning around]: What can I do for you?

CLEOPATRA: Come here a minute.

SCIPIO: At your service.

CLEOPATRA: We have decided to accept your generous offer and go away at once. You're not angry?

SCIPIO: No.

CLEOPATRA: But first we should like to rest up a little. Will you allow us to stay here a day or two, until we recover? This place of yours is quite a beauty spot.

[Simultaneously the ROMANS turn around and spring to their feet.]

SCIPIO [in raptures]: Dear lady, what does the place matter! What matters—O Jupiter! Lady, I swear by Hercules! I swear by Venus! I swear by Bacchus! Lady, I'll be thrice accursèd, if—By Aphrodite! Gentlemen of ancient Rome, prepare for boarding!

CLEOPATRA: We'll take a little stroll, shall we?

SCIPIO: Lady!—Ancient Romans, quick march! Dress front. Left, right—column of twos. [He takes CLEOPATRA's arm and leads her toward the hills. Each of the ROMANS, at his command, seizes a Sabine woman and proudly marches in file behind him.]

SCIPIO: Left, right! Left, right! One, two! One, two!

ÆMILIUS PAULUS [*left behind, spinning around, crying piteously*]: Where is she? Gentlemen, Ancient Romans, wait. I've lost her. Where is she?

[VERONICA *stands, her eyes modestly downcast, like a bride.* PAULUS *accidentally bumps into her.*]

PAULUS: Sorry. Have you seen her, lady?

VERONICA: You fool!

PAULUS: You talking to me?

VERONICA: Yes, you. You're a fool.

PAULUS: Why are you insulting me?

VERONICA: Oh, you fool! Don't you see? My darling boy, I have waited for you thirty years. Here, here for the taking—

PAULUS: Taking what?

VERONICA: Me. It is I—she. Oh, you fool.

PAULUS: You? No, not you.

VERONICA: Yes, I'm the one.

PAULUS: No, you're not. [*He sits on the ground, weeping.*]

VERONICA: Listen—they've left us all alone here. I'm at a loss. Let's go.

PAULUS: You're not the one. It's not you.

VERONICA: I tell you—I am. Drat! Of all things! My husband never stopped saying for thirty years "You're not the one" and this mama's boy here says the same thing. Give me your hand.

PAULUS [*rising in terror*]: You're not the one. Oh, oh, oh! Help! She's abducting me!

Act 2

An extremely gloomy scene depicting the woeful situation of the despoiled husbands. It may be raining. The wind is howling; black clouds overcast the sky.

But it may be that it only seems this way. Horrors! The very landscape should suggest how overwhelmed the SABINE HUSBANDS *are with grief.*

As the curtain rises the characters are arranged in two symmetrical groups, one on either side, some Sabines engaged in gymnastic exercises and zealously muttering in rhythm with their arm movements: "Fifteen minutes' exercise and you'll be strong and twice the size."

Center stage on a long bench sit a row of the husbands who have children, each with a baby in his arms. Their heads droop despondently to one side, their whole attitude expressing stylized despair. Horrors! For a long time all that is heard is the ominous, barely audible mutter "Fifteen minutes' exercise, and you'll—"

Enter ANCUS MARTIUS, *waving a letter.*

ANCUS MARTIUS: The address! Sabine sirs, we have our wives' address. The address!

SABINES [*in hushed voices*]: Listen up, listen up! The address! We've got the address.

[ANCUS MARTIUS *whips a dinner bell out of his pocket and rings it.*]

SABINES: Sh! Sh!

ANCUS MARTIUS: Sabine sirs, history can reproach us neither for procrastination nor for hesitation. Neither procrastination nor hesitation is an attribute of the Sabines, whose fierce impetuosity can scarcely be restrained by the barricades of prudence and experience. Do you remember, o plundered Sabine husbands, whither you raced headlong that memorable morning that followed that memorable night when those pirates basely abducted our hapless wives? Do you remember, Sabines, whither our fleet feet, obliterating distance, overcoming all obstacles, and filling the land with clamor, carried us? Well? Try to remember, gentlemen!

[*The* SABINES *maintain a meek silence.*]

A TIMID VOICE: O Proserpina, Prossy pussy, where art thou? Ow!

[*The* SABINES *maintain a rapt silence and stare in suspense at the speaker's mouth.*]

ANCUS MARTIUS [*not waiting for an answer, exclaiming emotionally*]: To the Information Office, that's where! Remember our grief, gentlemen, when we found that the Information Office, that obsolescent institution, knew nothing as yet and gave us the former address, and for a whole week continued to provide us with that cruelly ironic address, until finally it imparted this bitter bit of information. [*Reads*] "Moved. Destination unknown." Well, what did we do, Sabines? Did we settle for that? Try to remember.

[*The* SABINES *are silent.*]

ANCUS MARTIUS: No, we did not settle for that. Here is a bald but eloquent summary of our actions during the brief period of a year and a half. We placed advertisements in the better newspapers offering a reward to anyone who would discover the address. We summoned all the celebrated astrologers and got them to read the stars every night in order to divine the address of our unhappy wives.

TIMID VOICE: Prossy pussy! Ow!

ANCUS MARTIUS: We sacrificed thousands of chickens, ducks, and geese, and disemboweled all the cats, in an attempt to elicit the fateful address. But, alas, it was the will of the gods that our superhuman efforts did not meet with success. Remember, Sabine sirs—well, don't bother. I'll put it this way—neither experiential science nor nonexperiential science came up with an answer. The very constellations to whom our stargazers turned with mournful questions did deign to reply, but offered no more than the Information Office: "Moved, moved, moved" . . . but where to?

[*The* SABINES *weep quietly.*]

TIMID VOICE: Prossy pussy! Ow!

ANCUS MARTIUS: Yes, a strange answer to receive from the constellations, if you consider that they can see everything from up there. Well! I will proudly continue the recital of our deeds. Remember, gentlemen, what our learned jurists were busy with while the astrologers were interpreting the stars—well, well?

[*The* SABINES *are silent.*]

ANCUS MARTIUS: Please, gentlemen, try to remember. It's tough talking to you. You stand there like statues, for heaven's sake! I'm sure you remember. Only you're too embarrassed to speak. Now then, gentlemen—well? well? Remember. What were our jurists doing while—

TIMID VOICE: Prossy pussy! Ow!

ANCUS MARTIUS: Stop that! Stop interrupting with your "Prossy pussy." Well, I'll give you a hint, gentlemen. Remember why you have been doing gymnastics. Well?

TIMID VOICE [*from the back row*]: To develop our muscles.

ANCUS MARTIUS: Absolutely right. Top marks! But what do we want our muscles developed for? Well? Gentlemen, you'd try the patience of a demigod. Remember what we Sabines use muscles for.

HESITANT VOICE: To fight.

ANCUS MARTIUS [*raising his arms in despair*]: Ye gods in heaven! To fight! And these are the words of a Sabine, the friend of law and order, the bulwark of peace, the only genuine, twenty-four-carat model of conscience in the world. To fight! I'm ashamed of this lapse into hooliganism, worthy of the piratical Romans, the base abductors of our lawful wives.

TIMID VOICE: Prossy pussy! Ow!

ANCUS MARTIUS: Shut up! You and your "Prossy pussy"! This is a matter of principle. And he keeps on with his "Prossy pussies"! I see, gentlemen, that your loss has somewhat beclouded your ordinarily brilliant memories, so I repeat in brief: the reason we need muscles is that when we march upon the Romans—now that we've found the address—you understand?—we shall be carrying the heavy code of laws the whole way, as well as a collection of the decisions of the appeals court, and also—do you now understand?—those four hundred volumes of research which our legal scholars compiled to confirm the legality of our marriages—do you understand?—and the illegality of abduction. Our weapons, Sabine sirs, are our rights and our clear conscience. We shall prove to the vile abductors that they are indeed abductors; to our wives we shall prove that they have indeed been abducted. And the heavens will tremble, for now that we have the address it's in the bag. Here! [*He waves the letter. The* SABINES *stand on tiptoe to see it.*] A registered letter with the signature "A Repentant Abductor!" In it an unknown friend expresses regret for the thoughtless crime he committed, assures us that never again will he abduct, and pleads with the fates to deal mercifully with him. The name is undecipherable, a big blot, apparently caused by his tears. There, gentlemen! That's what I call conscience. By the way, he says that our wives' hearts are broken.

TIMID VOICE: Proserpina—

ANCUS MARTIUS: Once and for all, you and your "Proserpina" don't let me get a word in edgewise. Please understand that yours is a private matter. When all of us are so enthusiastically debating a general question and working up a plan—I'll tell you about it in a minute—and preparing for victory or death, you are whining about your Prossy pussy! In the name of the assembly I call you to order. Now then, gentlemen, prepare to march. Wait for the command! Fall in line. On the double, gentlemen. This is too much—you still can't tell right from left. Where are you going? Halt! [*He takes hold of a* SABINE *who has fallen out of line and instructs him.*] To learn which is right, stand still— look at me!—stand with your face to the north—or no, with your face to the south, and your back to the east—well, where is your face? That's not your face; that's your back. Here—this is your face. Do you understand? It's maddening! I can't spend any more time on you. Look at your neighbor and see what he's doing and where your right is. Now, gentlemen, any of you carrying penknives? Turn your pockets out. Fine. Anybody carrying toothpicks? Leave them here. We don't want the least hint of violence, gentlemen. Nothing that cuts or pricks. Our weapons are our rights and our clear conscience. Now each one pick up a volume of the laws and decisions—that's right—I should have had them bound, but we'll do that later—here's where the muscles come in. You see? Fine, fine. Trumpeters to the fore. Do you remember the march of the plundered husbands? Forwa—Oh, right, you do remember how to march?

[*The* SABINES *are silent.*]

ANCUS MARTIUS: No? I'll remind you. Two steps forward, one step back; two steps forward, one step back. The first two steps, Sabines, express the inextinguishable fire of our ardent hearts, the firm will, the indomitable spirit and determination to advance. The step backward stands for the step of prudence, the step of experience and the mature mind. In taking it we reflect on what comes next; in taking it we cling to the great link with tradition, with our ancestors, our great past. History does not leap before it looks; and we, Sabines, are at this momentous moment in history. Trumpeters, trumpet.

[*The trumpets blow a dismal note, lurch forward convulsively, then draw back smoothly, the host of plundered husbands in their wake. Making two steps forward and one step back, the company slowly crosses the stage.* The curtain falls, the trumpets blow dismally, and the second act passes into the third.*]

Act 3

The same wild terrain as in the first act, although there are now some rudiments of improvement. Near one of the huts stands a ROMAN *in an indolent attitude, blissfully picking his nose. From offstage left the army of* SABINE HUSBANDS *is seen marching diligently in the same tempo as before: two steps forward, one step back. The* ROMAN, *at first sight of them, shows signs of life, and, leaving off his nasal excavations, watches them with good-natured curiosity. However, the slowness of their movements apparently makes him drowsy. He resumes his indolent pose, yawns, stretches languidly, and casually glides onto a stone. At a signal from* ANCUS MARTIUS, *the trumpets fall back.*

ANCUS MARTIUS [*shouting desperately*]: Sabine sirs, halt! Halt, for pity's sake! Please halt! O ye gods? What power can stay a falling avalanche? Will nothing—

[*The* SABINES *halt abruptly and stand as if rooted to the spot.*]

ANCUS MARTIUS: Thank the gods, they've halted! Attention! Trumpeters, to the rear! Professors, to the fore! The rest, stand at attention!

---

* "The Crooked Mirror Theatre in Saint Petersburg successfully adapted the "Marseillaise," opening with two bold notes of triumph held, and then emitting a doleful note of retreat, like a painful belch" (Andreev's note).

[*The* TRUMPETERS *retreat, the* PROFESSORS *advance. The rest stand motionless.*]

ANCUS MARTIUS: Professors, make ready!

[*The* PROFESSORS *quickly squat down, unfold small tables, put thick tomes on them, and throw the covers of the books open with a bang. This gives the impression of a field artillery firing. The Roman*—SCIPIO—*rousing himself, apparently takes an interest.*]

SCIPIO [*friendly*]: What's up, gentlemen? What can I do to help? If this is a circus, I might as well tell you the Coliseum isn't ready yet.

ANCUS MARTIUS [*casually*]: Silence, you base abductor. [*To the* SABINES] So now, Sabine sirs, we have arrived at our longed-for goal. Behind us stretches a long path of privation, starvation, isolation, and canned food; before us a historical conflict such as has never been known before. Screw your courage to the sticking place, Sabine sirs, but keep your feelings in check. Stay calm. Cherish the sense that you have been wronged, and quietly await the unfolding of the fateful drama. Remember, Sabines, why we have come here.

[*The* SABINES *are silent.*]

ANCUS MARTIUS: Ransack your memories, gentlemen. We didn't lug these thick tomes all the way here for a book club. Now remember, gentlemen—why did we come here?

SCIPIO: Come now, gentlemen, try to remember.

ANCUS MARTIUS [*to* SCIPIO]: Can you imagine?—that's how it's been the whole time.

SCIPIO: Is that right?

ANCUS MARTIUS: Honestly, all they do is stand there like graven images. I ask you, why can't a man deliver a top-notch speech without having to resort to the exhortation "Remember"?

SCIPIO [*amiably shaking his head*]: I don't know. A funny sort of speech that would be!?

ANCUS MARTIUS: You see, even you understand. And these gentlemen here—

A TREMULOUS VOICE FROM AMONG THE SABINES: Prossy pussy, where art thou? Ow!

SCIPIO [*hesitantly*]: *He* seems to remember something.

ANCUS MARTIUS [*contemptuously*]: Bah, he always remembers *that*. [*To the* SABINES] Attention! We are about to demand our wives back. Woe betide the abductors, if their consciences have not yet awakened! We will force them to obey the law. Hey, you base abductor, summon your vile colleagues and prepare for the terrible reckoning.

SCIPIO: I'll go call my wife this minute. [*He walks into the hut, calling*] Cleopatra! Patsy, dear! There are people here to see you.

ÆMILIUS PAULUS [*peeking from around the corner, he recognizes the* SABINES *and shouts with joy*]: The husbands have come! The husbands have come! Gentlemen of ancient Rome, awake, the husbands are here!

[*He rushes out and flings himself around* ANCUS MARTIUS*'s neck with tears in his eyes.* ANCUS MARTIUS *is dumbfounded.* PAULUS *runs around, still joyously shouting, "The husbands are here!" The drowsy Romans come out of their huts and fill the right side of the stage.* ANCUS MARTIUS, *with his hands on his hips, military fashion, haughtily waits until they are all assembled.*]

FAT ROMAN: By Bacchus! I was sleeping as sweetly as the day we founded Rome. Who are these scarecrows?

FIRST ROMAN: Ssh! It's the husbands.

FAT ROMAN: Oh. I'm thirsty. Prossy pussy, please bring me a glass of beer, sweetheart!

FAINT VOICE FROM AMONG THE SABINES: Prossy pussy! Ow-w-w!

FAT ROMAN: What does that fellow want? He's calling my wife too.

FIRST ROMAN: Ssh! That's her husband.

FAT ROMAN: Oh. I forgot. By the gods, I'm so thirsty. After that hot meal and that sound sleep I could drink the whole Tiber! My, Proserpina is a fine cook! Really, gentlemen of ancient Rome, it's a gift from the gods.

FIRST ROMAN: Ssh!

FAT ROMAN: Oh, I forgot. I just had a very peculiar dream. I dreamed I was asleep and suddenly I saw Rome beginning to decline, decline, decline, and then fall.

FIRST ROMAN: What's the matter with our wives? These fellows here come calling on them and they don't show themselves. It's rather awkward.

SECOND ROMAN: I suppose they're dressing.

FIRST ROMAN: Woman, thy name is vanity! Why bother primping when these men are only their ex-husbands? But no, they have to live up to the eternal feminine. I'll never figure out female psychology!

FAT ROMAN: By Olympus, I'm so thirsty. Are these mummies going to stand there forever? They might at least play us a tune. They've got a brass section. Look, look, they're moving!

ANCUS MARTIUS: Gentlemen of Rome, now we stand face to face, I hope you will no longer seek to dissemble and will give us a straight-forward, honest answer. Remember, Romans, what took place on the night of the twentieth to twenty-first of April?

[*The* ROMANS *glance at each other in bewilderment and remain silent.*]

ANCUS MARTIUS: Please remember! Can't you understand? Try to remember, gentlemen. I won't budge from this spot until you do.

FAT ROMAN [*scared, whispering to another*]: Maybe you can remember, Agrippa. It must be something really important, huh?

AGRIPPA: No, I can't.

FAT ROMAN: Ever since my nap my memory's like a sieve.

AGRIPPA: I think I'd better go. You can tell me about it later.

FAT ROMAN: All right. But what does he want?

ANCUS MARTIUS [*in a loud voice*]: Then I will remind you, Romans. On the night of the twentieth to the twenty-first of April there was committed the greatest villainy that history has ever known. On that night, which I shall have cause to refer to later, our wives, the fair Sabine women, were outrageously abducted.

THE ROMANS [*recollecting, they nod gleefully and nudge each other*]: "Yes, yes, yes!" "So that's what it's all about?" "True enough, true enough." "It really was the twentieth of April."

FAT ROMAN [*deeply impressed*]: These Sabines have got their heads screwed on right!

ANCUS MARTIUS: And the ravishers who carried out this abduction are you Romans. Oh, I know you'll try to rationalize, deny the facts, basely pervert the course of justice, using that disgusting sophistic reasoning which is the invariable resort of all who break the law. But we are prepared. Professors, begin.

PROFESSOR AT THE END OF LINE [*beginning in a singsong voice that seems to emanate from beyond the bounds of time and space*]: Concerning crimes against property, volume 1, book 1, section 1, chapter 1, page 1, paragraph 1, line 1. Concerning theft in general. In the most ancient times, even more ancient than the present time, when the birds and insects and beetles fluttered about freely in the sunshine and the idea of crime against property never entered anyone's consciousness, for consciousness itself was nonexistent—in those far-off times—

ANCUS MARTIUS: Listen up, Romans, listen up!

SCIPIO: Can't you cut it short?

ANCUS MARTIUS: Out of the question!

SCIPIO: But you're putting them to sleep.

ANCUS MARTIUS: Do you think so?

SCIPIO: Look, they're already dozing off, and if they doze they can't hear. Can't your man begin at the bottom line? Do us a favor and tell us straight out what you want.

ANCUS MARTIUS: Verily, this is a strange dispute! Be it so, then. I shall indulge your friends' frailty and tell you straight out—we have come to prove that you were wrong in snatching our wives away and are abductors—you Romans, that is—and that no cunning sophistry can justify your abominable behavior. And the heavens will tremble!

SCIPIO: As a matter of fact, my good sir, we don't dispute it.

ANCUS MARTIUS: No? Then what have we come here for?

SCIPIO: Maybe you wanted a walk in the country.

ANCUS MARTIUS: No, the reason we came here is to prove it to you. Most peculiar! So you admit you are abductors?

SCIPIO: Absolutely. I think that's definitely the right word—"abductors."

ANCUS MARTIUS: But perhaps you are not fully convinced. If so, the professor is ready and willing—aren't you, professor?—ready and willing to—

SCIPIO: Never mind, never mind.—We are perfectly convinced! Gentlemen of Rome, back me up, or else he'll begin again.

ROMANS: We admit it—we admit it.

ANCUS MARTIUS: Then what's the point?

SCIPIO: I don't know.

ANCUS MARTIUS: There's an odd misunderstanding here! Sabine sirs, celebrate your victory. The culprits admit their guilt. The mere sight of our awe-inspiring preparations awakened the voice of conscience and legality; and the heavens trembled. All that's left is to return, aware that we have done our duty, and—

A TREMULOUS VOICE: And how about Prossy pussy?

ANCUS MARTIUS: Ah, yes! Badly expressed your words may be, but the thought is perfectly correct. Gentlemen of Rome, here is a detailed and accurate inventory of our wives. Be kind enough to return the goods. For any loss, injury and—what's it called, Professor?

PROFESSOR: Spoilage, shrinkage—

ANCUS MARTIUS: No, no—damages, that's it. Yes, you are responsible for all damages. Read the law on this point, Professor.

[*Enter the* WIVES.]

ANCUS MARTIUS: Ah, but here are our wives. Attention, Sabine sirs. Keep yourselves in check, I entreat you. Moderate your passion, until the legal question is settled—two steps forward, one step back. 'Tenshun! Greetings, Sabine women! Good morning, Cleopatra!

[*The* WOMEN *take center stage, their eyes downcast, their bearing modest, dignified, and submissive.*]

CLEOPATRA [*without looking up*]: If you have come to rebuke us, Ancus Martius, I must tell you we don't deserve your scolding. We put up a long, hard fight, and if we did yield, it was to force alone. I swear to you, Martius, beloved, I haven't stopped crying over you a minute. [*She weeps. All the women follow suit.*]

ANCUS MARTIUS: Calm yourself, Cleopatra. They have already confessed they are abductors. Come, let us return to our household gods.

CLEOPATRA [*without looking up*]: I'm afraid you'll scold us, but we have already grown accustomed to this place. Don't you like these hills, Martius?

ANCUS MARTIUS: I don't understand you, Cleopatra. What have the hills to do with it?

CLEOPATRA: I'm afraid you'll get angry. But it really isn't our fault. I have already wept over you properly, Martius. I can't begin to understand—what more do you want? More tears, is that it? As many as you please. Dear friends, they think we haven't cried enough for them. Let us prove them wrong. Weep, weep, dear friends! Martius, I did love you so!

[*The* WOMEN *cry rivers of tears.*]

SCIPIO: Patsy dear, calm down. Excitement is bad for you in your present condition. My dear sir, did you hear? Now turn around and retrace your steps. [*To* CLEOPATRA] Come, Patsy, darling, lie down and rest. I'll see to the soup myself.

ANCUS MARTIUS: Excuse me. What's soup got to do with it? Do calm down, Cleopatra. There's been some misunderstanding. You obviously don't realize that you have been abducted.

CLEOPATRA [*weeping*]: There, I said you were going to scold us. Scippy darling, have you got my hanky?

SCIPIO: Here it is, sweetheart.

ANCUS MARTIUS: I beg your pardon, what's a hanky got to do with it?

CLEOPATRA [*weeping*]: Making such a fuss over a hanky! How am I supposed to do without a hanky when I'm crying? And it's all your fault I'm crying. This is cruel. You're a monster, Ancus Martius!

[*By this time everyone is weeping, the* SABINE WOMEN *and the* SABINE MEN, *and even some of the* ROMANS.]

A TREMULOUS VOICE: Prossy pussy! Ow-w-w!

ANCUS MARTIUS [*very loudly*]: Calm yourselves, Sabine sirs; get a grip! Don't stir from this spot. I'll settle things in a jiffy. There is obviously a misunderstanding here of a legal nature. The wretched woman thinks we are accusing her of abducting a handkerchief. She doesn't realize that she herself has been the victim of an abduction. I'll prove it to her at once. Professors, step up.

[*The* PROFESSORS *prepare. The* ROMANS *are panic-stricken.*]

SCIPIO [*seizing* CLEOPATRA's *hand*]: Confess, Cleopatra! Quick! Oh, by the gods! He's about to begin!

CLEOPATRA [*crying*]: I have nothing to confess. It's slander.

ANCUS MARTIUS: Professor, we are waiting.

SCIPIO: Quick. Confess! Oh, Jupiter, he's opening his mouth. It's open! Sabine sirs, hold on! She has confessed. Shut your mouth, professor— she has confessed.

CLEOPATRA: All right. I confess. [*To the women*] Dear friends, do you confess too?

SCIPIO [*hastily*]: Yes, yes, they all confess. The matter is settled.

ANCUS MARTIUS [*puzzled*]: I beg your pardon. Cleopatra, you confess that you and the other Sabine women were abducted on the night of the twentieth to the twenty-first of April? You do, do you?

CLEOPATRA [*dripping with sarcasm*]: No, we ran away on our own.

ANCUS MARTIUS: There, you see, she doesn't understand. Prof—

CLEOPATRA: This is mean, Martius! We were abducted in our sleep. You didn't stand up for us, you surrendered us, forgot us, abandoned us, and now you charge us with running away. We were abducted, Martius, outrageously abducted. You can read about it in any history textbook, not to speak of [*weeps*] encyclopedias.

SCIPIO [*shouting*]: Shut your mouth, professor.

[*But the* PROFESSOR's *mouth remains open. The* ROMANS *are in a panic; some of them running offstage.*]

ANCUS MARTIUS: Roman sirs, Sabine sirs, come to order! I shall soon resolve the whole matter. There is a misunderstanding here of a technical nature. May I examine you, Professor? Ah, yes—of course—I knew it. The hinge is out of order and he can't shut his mouth. Never mind. We'll fix it when we get home. For now it's enough that I've heard it with my own ears. They have confessed that they were abducted. We have won our case, our aim has been achieved, and the heavens have trembled. Come along, Cleopatra, let's go back to our household gods.

CLEOPATRA: I don't want to go back to our household gods.

SABINE WOMEN: We don't want to go back to our household gods! Down with the household gods! We're going to stay here. They are insulting us! They are going to abduct us! Save us! Help! Help!

[*The* ROMANS, *rattling their weaponry, place themselves between the* WOMEN *and the* SABINES, *gradually moving the women upstage. They throw angry glances at the* SABINES, *and voices are heard calling*: "Romans, to arms! Defend your wives! To arms, Romans!"]

ANCUS MARTIUS [*ringing his bell*]: What's going on? Is there going to be a fight! My head is spinning. Sabine sirs, my head is spinning!

THE LOVELY SABINE WOMEN ❧ 111

PROSERPINA [*coming forward and speaking in a slow, matter-of-fact voice*]: Don't get excited, Romans. I'll speak to Martius.

A TREMULOUS VOICE [*from the Sabine ranks, a doleful declaration of love*]: Prossy pussy! Sweetie-pie—ow-w-w.

PROSERPINA [*matter-of-factly*]: Ow-w-w! My dear friend, are you feeling all right?—Come over here, Ancus Martius. Don't be afraid—your army won't run away. Don't you realize that none of us, not your wife, Cleopatra, nor I, nor any of us women wants to go back? Don't you understand?

ANCUS MARTIUS: My head is spinning. What shall I do without Cleopatra? I can't live without Cleopatra. She is my lawfully wedded wife. Is there any way of persuading her to go?

PROSERPINA: None whatsoever.

ANCUS MARTIUS: Then, what am I to do? I love her. How can I live without her? [*He weeps.*]

PROSERPINA: Calm down, Martius. [*Whispering*] I'm sorry for you. So I'll tell you a secret—there is still one way, but only one—abduct her.

ANCUS MARTIUS: And will she come?

PROSERPINA [*shrugging*]: How can she help it if you abduct her?

ANCUS MARTIUS: Why, that's outrageous! Are you suggesting I should commit an act of violence? How will I square it with my righteous conscience? Or do you women believe that might makes right? Oh, women, women!

PROSERPINA: We have heard that before—"Oh, women, women!" Ah, Martius, it was a sorry day when the gods created you. You are unutterably stupid. Yes, if I am to stay faithful to my husband, I want him to be a strong man, the very strongest. You think it's a picnic for us to be abducted, carried off, asked back, returned, lost and found—

A TREMULOUS VOICE: Prossy pussy! Sweetheart! Ow-w-w!

PROSERPINA: O-w-w, my dear, are you feeling all right?—to be treated like a parcel of goods. No sooner do I get used to one man than another comes along and carries me off—no sooner do I get used to him, the old one shows up and insists on having me back. Ah, Martius, if, as you insist so arrogantly, you want your wife to belong to you, to be your possession, just be the strongest, don't give her up her to anybody; fight for her, tooth and nail, and, if need be, die in her defense. Believe me, Martius, there is no greater joy for a woman than to die on the grave of a husband who fell defending her. And you may be sure, Martius, a woman proves false only when her husband proves false.

ANCUS MARTIUS: They have swords, and we are unarmed.

PROSERPINA: Arm yourselves.

ANCUS MARTIUS: They have mighty muscles, and we haven't.

PROSERPINA: Develop muscles! Honestly, Martius, you're an utter fool.

ANCUS MARTIUS [*recoiling*]: And you are a silly, trivial woman. All hail the law! Let brute force rob me of my wife; let it destroy my home; let it dowse the fire in my hearth. I shall never prove false to the law! Let the whole world laugh at the wretched Sabines, they shall not prove false to the law. The righteous man is honored even clad in rags. Sabines, retreat! And weep, Sabines, weep bitter tears; utter sobs; beat your breasts, and be not ashamed that you shed tears. Let them stone us; let them mock us. Weep, Sabines, for you are weeping for the scorned, downtrodden law. Forward, Sabines! Let them sling mud at us—'Ten-shun! Trumpeters, trumpet! Two steps forward, one step back! Two steps forward, one step back!

[*The* WOMEN *begin to weep.*]

CLEOPATRA: Martius, wait!

ANCUS MARTIUS: Hence, woman! I know thee not. Forward, march!

[*The trumpets blow a dismal note. The women, wailing and in tears, try to run to their ex-husbands. The* ROMANS *hold them back them by force. Laughter from the victors. Paying no heed to either the tears or the laughter, bending beneath the weight of the law, the* SABINES *slowly march off, two steps forward, one step back.*]

ALEKSANDR KUGEL'

INTRODUCTION

Aleksandr Rafailovich Kugel' (1843–1928) was originally named Abram when he was born in the Minsk province. His status as a Jew from the provincial Pale of Settlement makes his eventual influence and activity in the Petersburg art world all the more phenomenal. Like so many of his contemporaries in literature and theater, he graduated from the law school of Saint Petersburg University (1886); as a student he had been attracted to the fashionable nihilism of Dmitry Pisarev (as was Fyodor Dostoevsky) and the pessimism of Eduard von Hartmann (as was August Strindberg). From 1892 he began to moonlight as a journalist, contributing ephemeral columns and short articles on various themes to newspapers in the capital and Moscow. For financial reasons, in spring 1885 he wrote a review of a ballet at the Livadia Gardens, although he had never been to a ballet before; the next day he covered a French operetta at the Arcadia Gardens. This was the start of Kugel' the theater critic, an ardent playgoer and "chevalier of the stage." He was one of the founding members of the Theater Society and the Literary-Artistic Circle. The latter was to become Saint Petersburg's prominent Literary-Artistic Theater, under the management of the self-made millionaire, press magnate, and fervent antisemite Aleksey Suvorin.

In 1897, with the help of his wife, the prominent actress Zinaida Khol'mskaya, Kugel' founded the weekly journal *Theater and Art* (*Teatr i iskusstvo*) and served as editor for twenty years. As lead writer and frequent contributor, as well as occasional reviewer, under the pseudonyms Homo Novus, Negorev, and others, he made the magazine a tribune from which to expound his opinions and theories. "A critic devoid of passion is boring," he proclaimed, although he tried to be catholic in his outlook. His attitudes ranged from the sober, analytical, and closely observed to the temperamental and fulminous. "Art should rejoice people, this is its only meaning, assignment, goal and necessity,"[1] he asserted. In an argument with the symbolist poet Fyodor Sologub, Kugel' spoke of the necessity of "endowing life with ideas, and not forsaking life for the sake of ideas."

For Kugel' the prime mover in the theater was always the actor: "The laws of the theater are the laws of the actor." Consequently, he was a firm opponent of the nascent "director's theater," whether naturalistically inflected, as with Stanislavsky, or stylized, as with Meyerhold. He extended this belief in the performer's primacy to the world of popular entertainment and song; in his book *Theatrical Portraits*, he devoted chapters to the operetta diva Anna Judic as well as the folk singer Vera Panina. In their creativity he saw an art of primitives who bring "complicated reflexes, intricate shadows of spiritual suffering and outbursts to their . . . realistic archetypes."[2] The music hall was a performance art like any other, and he deplored society's valuation of actors according to the genres in which they appeared. "The complicated classification by external signs or the intended importance of the work usually accompanies periods and locales of stagnation."[3] He was particularly annoyed by contemporary associations of the actor's world with decadence and neurasthenia.

In his annual trips abroad Kugel' attentively studied the cabaret stages in Germany and France along with the "major" playhouses, seeing in them the quintessence of theater. He propagandized for them in the pages of *Theater and Art*. "Whatever is too intimate, subtle, individualistic in its creativity . . . and therefore boring for the petty-bourgeois public—all this aspires to cabaret."[4] In opposition to the aesthete Dmitry Filosofov, who saw in the artistic cabaret the rebirth of reaction, Kugel' stressed the significance of laughter. He considered disdain for laughter a sign of uncouthness. "Our severe climate, gloomy sky . . . our lack of culture, constraint, tension in people who came to culture very recently . . . they are afraid to be coarse, to show themselves unenlightened, vulgar"—hence the prejudice against laughter.[5]

On December 6, 1908, he and Khol'mskaya opened the Crooked Mirror, at first as a cabaret with little tables in the Theatrical Club of the Union of Dramatic and Musical Writers and then, from 1910, in a theater building on the Ekaterinsky Canal. "This is a first attempt at a theater 'of miniatures' which I consider the ultimate and therefore the inevitable phase in the development of theatrical affairs." Taking account of the peculiarities of Russian life and manners, Kugel' avoided the term "cabaret," which "gets associated with some kind of 'Apollo' with dolled-up girls."[6] He preferred 'theater of miniatures," with the stage miniature as a new scenic form, demanding a "specific tone" as "a special means of concentrating material, a special sketchiness and at the same tine a special precision of word and economy of means . . . either the essence is immediately grasped . . . or it eludes your understanding." He saw the Crooked Mirror's task as the search for new forms, a combination of comic and lyric, with significant attention to irony. Irony underlies *parody*, directed at the base of a phenomenon, at the "destruction of the ideology of what is coming unscrewed."[7]

Despite his distrust of directors, Kugel' felt the need for a firm directorial hand. Attracted by Nikolay Evreinov's ideas on monodrama and the widening sphere of theatricality, he invited him to be director in chief. Two years later he would write, "Cabaret with us now has scope, and is not the sort of operetta or farce theater, whose poster might read, 'And we also have a cabaret.' Strictly speaking, we have no cabaret . . . Let us avoid needless and noxious modesty. In Russian art there is much that is crude, gray, at times inchoate, but no art is more fresh and original than ours."[8]

Like two alpha dogs in the same yard, Kugel' and Evreinov were frequently at loggerheads. Evreinov not only kept moving in the direction of radical experimentation but was also exceptionally jealous of his reputation and chary of sharing the limelight. Meanwhile, as one of the founders of the Union of Dramatic Writers and Composers, an organization concerned with authors' rights, Kugel' had to look after Evreinov's royalties.

Kugel' seldom directed but would sit in the middle of the auditorium and observe. He would often jump up to shout, "Not like that! Not that way!," run onstage, and demonstrate what he had in mind. If Nikolay Urvantsov disagreed, Kugel' would take his hat and slam the door on his way out. Ten minutes later one would hear, "Lyovushka, it should be dead serious at this point," as if nothing had happened. He also carried a walking stick, half sawn through, so he could break it dramatically to make his point.

Kugel's own dramatic contributions to the Crooked Mirror were few. "A Little Night Music" was a piece he had seen in Vienna and adapted to a Russian setting. Although Evreinov considered it vulgar and said it embarrassed him, it had its premiere on October 1, 1910, during his first season as director. It is a neatly constructed anecdote with an O. Henry ending and might easily serve as a curtain-raiser to a more dramatic piece.

Kugel's other efforts included *Living Statues* (*Ozhivlennye statui*, 1911), in collaboration with Evreinov: it was based on a vaudeville routine of human automata epidemic in theaters of miniatures (actors portraying porcelain figurines, wooden soldiers, dolls, antique clocks, store dummies). In this Hoffmannesque piece, a self-styled poet evokes living statues whose Dionysian dance drives him to his death. With B. Bentovin, Kugel' wrote *Posthumous Letters* (*Posmertnye pis'ma*, October 30, 1911), about a love rivalry that outlives the love itself. The hero, an erstwhile philanderer, now Professor Dranitsyn, lives a quiet life, chatting with his old friend Professor Kolosov about gastronomic matters. They discover that the love letters of a famous actress have been published. Those letters contain romantic sentiments addressed to Dranitsyn. Suddenly he's assailed by journalists and glorified in headlines. But the actress had addressed similar letters to Kolosov. The friends quarrel; offense and jealousy revive in these decrepit old men. The play combines the pathos of Romanticism and the poetics of sentimentality.

Aloof from politics, Kugel' accepted the October Revolution with only the slightest degree of distrust. Nevertheless, it stripped him of his status and prestige. *Teatr i iskusstvo* shut down in 1918, the Crooked Mirror began to have problems, and his former authority evaporated. Younger movers and shakers eclipsed him. In the 1920s Kugel' concentrated on writing memoirs, collaborating on historical dramas that went unpublished, and occasionally directing his plays and those of others. Shortly before his death, he wrote *Marlborough Prepared His Campaign* (*Marl'bruk v pokhod sobralsya*, 1928) which attempted to show the rise of fascism and its dangers.

He had lost none of his sense of outrage. One observer who saw this short, stoop-shouldered figure with the "Assyrian" beard on a Leningrad platform of a dramatic society described him as a "geyser." "His eyes shot sparks, his hands formed exclamation marks in the air. His words seemed to summon the wind . . . His polemic fervor and passion turned into murderous irony . . . But when he spoke of great performers, naming their names, an exceptional tenderness crept into his voice."[9]

Against all odds, not least the competition of more Bolshevik-oriented satire theaters, Kugel' reopened the Crooked Mirror in December 1922. When an opportunity was offered to abandon Russia during the Polish tour of 1925, he chose not to take it. (Evreinov, however, remained abroad.) As sole and nominal artistic director, he began to turn into the kind of despotic stage manager he had deplored years earlier. In April 1928, as the troupe was preparing for tours to Siberia and the Far East, he let it travel without him, writing it a "Valedictory":

> Business, even last year, has retreated. Most of all I blame myself, because I was devoid of a free spirit and weary of the struggle with an alien element that penetrated even myself "somehow or other." The Crooked Mirror is a theater that does not allow the slightest (a) coarseness, (b) vulgarity, (c) negligence . . . Do not deviate a hair from the first performances. The most repulsive handwriting is that of a clerk, because it's all over "curlicues" which were concocted out of boredom.[10]

Kugel' was fortunate that he died while the company was away, for when it returned, it was in what Khol'mskaya called "the most banal form, with no individual profile whatsoever."[11] In 1931 she left in protest, and in a few months it had been reformed out of existence.

NOTES

1. Homo novus [A. R. Kugel'], "Zametki," *Teatr i iskusstvo* 1 (1911): 17.
2. *Teatral'nie portréty* (Moscow: "Petrograd," 1923), 165.
3. Homo novus [A. R. Kugel'], "Zametki," *Teatr i iskusstvo* 5 (1908): 100.
4. N. Negorev [A. R. Kugel'], "Teatr miniator," *Teatr i iskusstvo* 48 (1908): 845.
5. A. Kugel', "Teatral'nya zametki," *Teatr i iskusstvo* 50 (1908): 892.
6. Kugel', "Teatral'nya zametki," 893.
7. Homo novus [A. R. Kugel'], "Zametki," *Teatr i iskusstvo* 3 (1913): 68.
8. A. Kugel', "Teatral'nya zametki," *Teatr i iskusstvo* 10 (1910): 219.
9. Vladimir Polyakov, *Tovarishch Smekh* (Moscow: Iskusstvo, 1976), 43.
10. Given in its entirety in Polyakov, *Tovarishch Smekh*, 46.
11. Z. V. Khol'mskaya, *Memoirs*, quoted in *Kabaretnye p'esy serebryannogo veka*, ed. Nora Buks and Igor' Loshchilov (Moscow: OGI, 2018).

A LITTLE NIGHT MUSIC
(*Nemnozhko muzyki*)

A grotesque in one act: A borrowed subject

by Homo Novus

1910

CHARACTERS

The Musician

A Stranger

A Young Man

Two Attendants

The stage represents a tastefully furnished room. Many objets d'art. A grand piano. On the piano a violin case. The MUSICIAN *is seated at the piano, playing. The doorbell. A gesture of impatience. Doorbell again.*

MUSICIAN: Who is it? Christina . . . [*Tries to play the piano again. Doorbell.*] Hey . . . Christina . . . That's right, Christina's gone out . . . [*Gets up and goes to open the door. Returns after letting in a gentleman unknown to him.*]

STRANGER [*dressed in an immaculate black frock coat, sporting a lush, fashionable beard streaked with gray, and a high brow; his hat in his hand; smiles politely*]: Forgive me for making such an unexpected and unwarranted intrusion on your solitude. Count Maurice de Gragnac. Your neighbor . . .

MUSICIAN: Please, don't mention it . . . I'm delighted.

STRANGER: I took the liberty of resorting to this somewhat unusual means of striking up an acquaintance. I must tell you that I am here on no particular business of a personal nature. I am a dilettante, madly in love with music, paying a visit to an artist! Rather eccentric, perhaps, from a conventional bourgeois standpoint. But there are moments when the soul goes beyond the bounds to welcome music. And I said to myself quite simply: I shall drop in on this artist, who has given me so much pleasure so often, and offer my respects to him, and then simply take my leave.

MUSICIAN: For goodness' sake. This is such an honor, please, have a seat. [*They sit down: the* STRANGER *farther upstage, the* MUSICIAN *close to the forestage.*]

STRANGER [*rapidly glancing round the room and then transferring his gaze to the* MUSICIAN]: This is exactly how I imagined your artistic interior to be. [*Begins to smoke a cigar and offers one to the* MUSICIAN.] May I? Yes, music . . . You were playing Mendelssohn?

MUSICIAN: Oh, no, this is a composition of my own.

STRANGER: Your own? How enchanting . . . really, nothing in Mendelssohn has that ebullience, so to speak, that ebullience of the modern spirit . . .

MUSICIAN: Mendelssohn is a genius.

STRANGER: Oh, yes, of course. But even so, you must agree, modern boldness speaks more eloquently to us contemporary moderns . . . Quite so . . . yes.

MUSICIAN: You cannot imagine how pleasant it is for us artists to encounter such keen perception. Who are we usually surrounded by? Philistine souls . . .

STRANGER: To live with music, to die with music. You do live completely alone?

MUSICIAN: Oh yes, completely, unless you count the maid, but it's her day off. Though let's not talk about domestics, but about the philistine enviro . . .

STRANGER: Yes, alone . . . With your dreams. Surrounded by works of art. Ah, there was a time when I too played, dreamed about music . . . [*Notices the violin.*] So you play the violin, it would appear?

MUSICIAN: Yes, a bit, but of course my main instrument is the piano . . . This violin of mine is a very fine one. A genuine Amati . . . It cost seventy thousand francs.

STRANGER [*examining the violin and then carefully putting it in its case*]: Yes, so I see, it's a remarkable instrument . . . I believe you also have very interesting paintings. [*He examines the paintings on the back wall.*]

MUSICIAN: Yes, you might say so . . . That's a Gouché.

STRANGER: Gouché?

MUSICIAN: Yes, a copy. The original's in the Louvre.

STRANGER: A copy? . . . And yet, actually, now I remember, I did see it in the Louvre.

MUSICIAN: But that one is an original . . . A genuine little Meisonnier. It's a small picture, as you see—it cost forty thousand francs.

STRANGER [*looking it over*]: Yes, that is a Meisonnier. What wonderful coloring . . . [*Turning around to the* MUSICIAN] You are a happy man! Your artistic soul dwells among such treasures of art . . .

MUSICIAN: Oh, you're too kind . . . But some things that I have are not at all bad. Here, for instance, an antique bronze, if you'll be so kind as to look. This is Lalique. Here's a box carved with a coat of arms.

STRANGER [*examining it*]: Yes, your coat of arms . . .

MUSICIAN: This clock is Sèvres porcelain. It cost thirty thousand francs.

STRANGER: Enchanting, enchanting. This little museum has, of course, been acquired over generations. I have always held the view that true aristocracy is the fruit of continuity. We inherit a legacy of artworks and aristocratic tastes and talents . . . However, I dare not abuse your time. [*Takes his hat and heads for the door.*]

MUSICIAN [*seeing him out*]: Thank you . . . Goodbye, may I hope . . . [*Holds out his hand.*]

STRANGER: And yet, permit me to trouble you with a slight request. It may seem importunate, perhaps strange, but the glowing impressions left by art are so rare . . . Play that splendid piece again.

MUSICIAN: For heaven's sake, if you like it so much . . . [*Sits at the piano and begins to play.*]

[*The* STRANGER *stands by the piano and listens; a few minutes pass. Suddenly he covers his face with his hands and convulsively hunches his shoulders.*]

MUSICIAN [*stopping playing, walking over to him*]: What's wrong? . . . For heaven's sake, what's the matter?

STRANGER: Forgive me, it will pass presently . . .

MUSICIAN: Calm yourself, count . . .

STRANGER: Yes, my nerves have got the better of me. It's the divine music, it awoke in me memories of long ago. The past rose before me. Please forgive me. I shouldn't let myself go like this. It arrived unbidden, it upset you . . . Allow me to withdraw . . .

MUSICIAN: Oh no, no . . . I urge you to keep calm . . .

STRANGER: Music is capable of distressing even a calm, well-conducted heart. But mine is wounded to the core.

MUSICIAN: You've been unhappy?

STRANGER: I have been happy, yes, my artist! I am unhappy now . . . I don't know why, but I read in your artist's eyes . . . What am I trying to say? . . . yes . . . You can understand souls . . . You will understand me . . .

MUSICIAN: If I can make things easier for you somehow . . .

STRANGER: I am Count Maurice de Gragnac. Our race is long famous in Picardy. We have an estate there. We are bound by ancient friendships to the local families. We lived as neighbors to the Estrugon clan. Two splendid girls, Clotilda and Susanna, adorned the ancient

Château d'Estrugon. When still a babe I played with them both. And of course you will guess the rest?

MUSICIAN: You fell in love?

STRANGER: Yes, I fell in love with all the carelessness of a youthful heart. My chosen one was Clotilda. She was just as pretty as Susanna, but there was something angelic, modest, infinitely tender in her eyes and in her whole being. Clotilda loved me back. There was no objection to our marriage on the part of our parents. We were wed. [*Wipes his eyes.*] And we were happy. I was happy, my noble friend . . . Nothing, it seemed, could tarnish our immaculate happiness. But I had forgotten one thing . . . [*Stares fixedly at the* MUSICIAN.]

MUSICIAN: What . . . what had you forgotten?

STRANGER: I had forgotten that Susanna loved me with all the force of her proud nature, but she kept silent, concealing and suppressing her feelings. Still, the moment came when she no longer had the strength for self-control. She began to shower me with passionate avowals. She began to hate her sister, my little Clo. You understand?

[*The* MUSICIAN *nods his head.*]

STRANGER: She began to hate her . . . She persecuted Clo, gave her no peace. She tormented her in the most varied, most inventive ways. She turned my domestic life into a hell, dear artist. But I was patient, kept silent and trembled, trembled for my Clo. And then one fine day Susanna poisoned my wife! [*He sinks into an armchair.*]

MUSICIAN: What . . . what are you saying?

STRANGER: She dosed her with arsenic . . . a white powder for mice . . . Clo died . . . she died, died . . .

MUSICIAN: She . . . she died?

STRANGER: Yes, she died. [*Wipes away tears.*] But that's not all. Our family doctor, a young man, like you, yes, I don't believe he was any older than you . . . he had secretly loved Clo. When she died, he came into my room, left the door ajar, and said, "My dear sir, I am a physician, there are no secrets from me. Your wife died of poison. You poisoned her." "You're out of your mind," I said. "I poisoned my Clo, my dear little Clo? . . . I? I who loved her so . . ." "That's enough," he interrupted me, "you poisoned her in order to marry Susanna." You understand what he was saying?!

MUSICIAN: Oh, he . . . he said that to you?

STRANGER: There was no point in trying to disprove his accusation. He kept insisting over and over: "I shall have the law on you." And the only favor he did me was to lay a revolver on the table. "All right," I said, "if I have to pay with my life for someone else's crime, I shall do so, but I need to arrange my affairs, put them in order, meet with my lawyer."—"You'll run away," he replied. "If you have to go to town, you will go with me." So we set out. It was night. I got on to the back platform of the train, to breathe fresh air for the last time. And he, he, my jailer, my executioner, he followed me. He wouldn't leave me even there. Then I suddenly understood what I had to do . . . I grabbed him and with a powerful jolt tossed him underneath the train, as the wheels rattled and the rails gleamed . . . Ha, ha . . . He fell head first . . . And the wheels pounded . . . and the wind whistled, the train raced along into the distance, to freedom . . . I was alone. No one, no one knew my secret . . . Free . . . You understand . . . Play something to celebrate my freedom . . .

MUSICIAN: I . . . I . . . I . . .

STRANGER: Ah, you understand . . . a hymn to freedom . . . Because nobody knows, nobody can denounce me . . . [*Stares fixedly at the* MUSICIAN.] Not one man knows? No, there is one man who knows the tragedy . . . [*With sudden awareness*] You!

MUSICIAN: My God! . . . but you yourself . . .

STRANGER: Ah-ah-ah-ah . . . Damn this music . . . it made me blurt out my secret . . . I should have bitten off my tongue or smashed your piano [*Bangs his fist on the piano.*] . . . but it's too late now . . . You know . . . There is one man who knows, and I have to, yes, I have to kill him, annihilate him . . . Out there, down below, in the darkness of night. [*Pounds with his fists.*]

MUSICIAN: Help! My God . . . [*Moves backward to the door.*] What's going on? Leave me alone . . .

STRANGER: No, I won't . . . Ah, ah, ah. You think you can take advantage of music and use sounds to dig out secrets hidden in the depths of the soul . . . [*Shouts*] I'll kill you!

MUSICIAN: Help! Help! Save me!

STRANGER [*moving toward him*]: I'll kill you . . .

[*A* YOUNG MAN *in an overcoat enters with two attendants who seize the* STRANGER.]

YOUNG MAN: Here you are. [*To the* MUSICIAN] He escaped from us.

MUSICIAN: For heaven's sake, save me. He was about to kill me . . .

YOUNG MAN: He's a madman. We'll subdue him . . .

STRANGER [*roaring*]: Let me at him . . . I'll kill him . . .

YOUNG MAN: Of course, he told you about how they poisoned his wife . . .

MUSICIAN: Yes, yes . . . Help me, for heaven's sake!

[*The* STRANGER *roars.*]

YOUNG MAN: It's his obsession. But don't worry. Please, go into that room, we have got to pacify him completely.

MUSICIAN: Please, lock me in . . . Here's the key . . .

YOUNG MAN: With pleasure.

[*The* MUSICIAN *exits. The* YOUNG MAN *locks the door on him. Then all four immediately remove their outer garments and set about carrying off valuable items, stuffing them in their pockets and tying them up in knotted bundles.*]

STRANGER: I'll kill him . . . Where is he? [*Lays hands on the violin, the bronze, a vase.*] Ah, ah, I've got to kill him. [*To the* YOUNG MAN, *who is taking a painting off the wall*] Don't bother—it's a copy. There's an original. Ah, ah, ah . . . Where is he? A Meisonnier . . . Let me at him . . . I'll kill him . . . There's a coat of arms with a monogram. But by all means be careful. Ah, ah, ah . . . Leave the room quietly. I'll look and see if there's anything else. [*Knocks over the table and fumbles in drawers.*] Ah, ah . . . The villain . . . I won't let him . . . I won't let him . . . [*The others leave, he listens.*]

MUSICIAN [*knocking from behind the door*]: Open up . . . open up . . .

STRANGER: Well, you'll still have to wait a bit . . . sit quiet . . . sit quiet . . .

[*He puts on hat, overcoat, attentively looks round the room, exits in a gentlemanly fashion, with an elegant half-bow. The* MUSICIAN *knocks desperately on the locked door.*]

PYOTR POTYOMKIN

INTRODUCTION

In English, most parodists deal in prose; with a few exceptions such as Lewis Carroll, they are not known for their verse. Pyotr Petrovich Potyomkin (1885–1926) has the distinction of being both an accomplished poet of the Silver Age and a parodist of talent.

He was born in Oryol into the family of a top bureaucrat in the tax office, so grew up amid official circles. He took a degree in history and philosophy at Saint Petersburg University, and, when still a student, published his verses in the journal *Signal* (1905). His fables and fairy tales began to appear in all the current satirical magazines. In 1906 he was won over to symbolism, attending Fyodor Sologub's literary "Sundays," where he became acquainted with the leaders in the movement: Vyacheslav Ivanov, Georgy Chulkov, and Nikolay Gumilyov. He contributed to such symbolist publications as *The Golden Fleece* (*Zolotoe runo*) and *The Island* (*Ostrov*).

By 1908, his first collection of poems, *Comical Love* (*Smeshnaya lyubov'*, 1908), showed how far he had drifted from adherence to symbolist doctrine. He had developed his own light, urbane style, deemed "but for a day" by Valery Bryusov, who noted that Potyomkin had become a "petit maître."[1] Proficient in a variety of prosody, his poems subtly parodied Sologub, Aleksandr Blok, and Mikhail Kuzmin. He became celebrated for suffusing the banality of everyday life in the sublime pathos of the symbolists. In Potyomkin's interpretation, Blok's Beautiful Lady became a hairdresser's dummy. Poems regularly printed in the satirical journal *Satyricon* (*Satirikon*) reappeared in his second collection, *The Geranium* (*Geran'*, 1912). They ranged from Romantic parodies and lyrical satires to earthy humor with a psychological subtext.

His earliest dramatic miniature, the puppet play "Petrushka," had been performed in 1908 at Meyerhold's calamitous Strand, where the critic Lyubov Gurevich found it "pointless and puke-making [*toshnotvorno*]."[2] Evidently, his skill at the genre improved, for his later works were produced at all the literary cabarets: Meyerhold's House of Interludes (1910), the Stray Dog (1911–13), and Moscow's Bat ("Katen'ka," "Chinese Blocks," "Pavlov's Cossacks in Paris"). However, his most fruitful partnership was with the Crooked Mirror, where his wife, the beautiful actress E. A. Khovanskaya, played a prominent role.

Although poetry recitations were popular on the Russian platform, especially when performed to music (melodeclamation), Kugel' considered them too undramatic to feature at the Crooked Mirror. Consequently, many of Potyomkin's one-acts are "slices of life," anecdotal glimpses of ordinary people. One of these, *Shall We Let Down the Curtain?* (*A ne opustit' li nam zanavesku?*), was first played there on October 20, 1911. Its slightly racy nature gives it the flavor of a blackout sketch in a European revue. It enjoyed one hundred performances at the Crooked Mirror. (His longer one-act *The House in the Lane* [*Dom v pereulke*, 1912] expanded his sardonic view of working-class life to a whole neighborhood, not unlike Elmer Rice's *Street Scene*, but was performed at the Liteyny Theater, not the Mirror.)

Regrettably, Potyomkin's greatest success at the Mirror both defies translation and offends modern sensibilities. *Blék énd Uayt, a Negro Tragedy* is written in pidgin English, transcribed into Cyrillic characters, and then translated into Russian by an assistant director (played by K. É. von Gibshman, who wrote the Russian dialogue). It is a farce of miscegenation performed by an allegedly American troupe. Potyomkin was fluent in German but barely knew French and English, so the transcription mangles both grammar and pronunciation.

The alleged "American" language resembles phrases from a conversational primer, well in advance of Ionesco's *Bald Soprano*. "Yankee Doodle" is sung as the national anthem, and the standard greeting is "Westinghouse." In love with "Ayrish Molli" (who, despite her name, is black), the white man Dzhon asks to be made black (by means of makeup) so he may woo her. When Molli rejects him, he weeps, and his burnt cork dissolves. The outraged "Negroes" lynch him by hanging, and then they all dance to the destruction of the white race until the barman shouts, "Polisman énd konstebl'!" Removed from the noose, Dzhon comes back to life, Molli joins him, and the black characters fall down.

This was the 1910 version that was played on October 25. The revision, which opened on January 28, 1912, and remained in the repertoire till 1915, was played to music by Shaé, alias Vasily Avgustovich Shpis von Éshenbruk, the same interloper who had offered to score *Vampuka*. In this version Molli is not a "full-blooded Negro" but a cousin of an African king whose other cousin was mixed race. We are told by the assistant director that "the black-skinned race hates the white-skinned." Though the dialogue differs, the action is the same. This time the word "lynch" occurs, and the mob is dispersed not by police but by cries of "Sherlok Khol'ms, Nik Karter, Nat Pinkerton."

Potyomkin obviously favored this minstrel mode, for his next work was *Black Wedding* (*Chernaya svad'ba*), a ballet-pantomime to music for the Liteyny Theater in 1913, revived at the Stray Dog two years later. African American themes were very popular in Russian cabaret before and after the Great War. Evreinov included an American variant in his *Laughter Kitchen*, and Sergei Eisenstein featured "Negroes" in his adaptation of Jack London's *The Mexican* as his first work for the Proletkul't in 1920.

That was the year Potyomkin emigrated to Prague. His third book of verse, published in Berlin in 1923, was steeped in pessimism and despair, grief and longing. In 1924, he moved to Paris, where he continued to write sardonic sketches for émigré cabaret and helped create the theater *Jewish Mirror* (1925). At the Bat, now known as Le Chauve-Souris, he organized a "wake" for the Stray Dog. "Potyomkin's mourning on that evening was not elegiac, but bitter, tragic. The merest traces were left of his former merriment, he looked pinched and gloomy."[3] In his last years he took part in the filming of *Casanova* in Venice.[4] Back to Paris, as the émigré journalist and poet Don-Aminado recalled, "Pyotr Petrovich laid out portraits of his nearest and dearest, his engravings of Petersburg, old ribbons with theatrical wreaths . . . and died."[78] The Turgenev Society raised the funds to bury him in the Père Lachaise cemetery.

NOTES

1. Valery Bryusov, "Debiutanty (Sbornik stikhov H. Gulimeva, Potemkina, V. Khodasevicha, G. Novitskago, L. Zarianskago, Alexander," *Vesy* 3 (March 1908): 78.

2. The text was first published in I. Lezhava, "'Petrushka' Petra Potemkina," *Slavic Almanac* 16, no. 2 (2010): 149–60.

3. Nikolay A. Otsup, *Sovremenniki* (Paris: n.p., 1961), 115.

4. *Casanova* (1927), starring Ivan Mozzhukin, was one of a number of important French silent films directed, designed, and staffed by Russian émigrés.

5. Don-Aminado [Aminodar Peysakhovich Shpolyansky], "Pamyati P. P. Potyomkina," *Poslednye novosti* 2040 (October 3, 1926).

SHALL WE LET DOWN THE CURTAIN?
(*A ne opustit' li nam zanavesku?*)

Scene in one window

by Pyotr Potyomkin

1911

CHARACTERS

Manya } girlfriends and seamstresses

Nadya

Blond Young Man with a Little Mustache, an intellectual

A House Painter

The outer wall of a large building. All we can see is a single window on the third or fourth floor. Beside it is a drainpipe. Repairs are being made on the building: the walls are being whitewashed, as are the pipes. The window is open. We can see a tailor's dummy, a few chairs, a bed, and a table. The room is empty. On the wall, obviously directly opposite the window, a ray of light is dancing. MANYA *enters the room. The light hits her in the face. She squints, bangs on the wall, and calls to someone neither angrily nor happily.*

MANYA: Nadya, come and look at the Romeos! They're flashing lights again.

NADYA'S VOICE [*from offstage*]: No time, I got to sew on this ruffle.

MANYA: Drop it, you can speed it up later.

NADYA: Not now, I'm just about done.

MANYA: Do tell, what a hard worker. Acts like everything revolves around you. All day yesterday you spent looking out the window.

NADYA: I was looking at the monkey.

MANYA: Liar. Then why didn't you give me the binoculars?

NADYA: Take them, please.

MANYA: I don't need them now. I needed them yesterday.

NADYA: And I gave them to you yesterday.

MANYA: And who told me my eyesight's bad, I wouldn't see anything anyway.

NADYA: That was in fun.

MANYA: In fun, my eye. You're always like that. Showing off your superiority and your education.

NADYA: I don't think so.

MANYA: Well, don't you dare come into my room.

NADYA: We don't need to.

MANYA: Don't you want to have a look at my cute little dark-haired guy?

NADYA: Dark-haired guys mean nothing to me.

MANYA: Well, heaven only knows what does.

[*In a bad temper, she walks to the window. There is the sound of a harp in the courtyard and the voice of a female singer with the words "Ah, how sweet was all last night! Her breast was not sore, her heart did not grieve. He loved her, loved her passionately, and she looked on him so coldly."* MANYA *watches the female harpist, a flash of light dances on* MANYA, *she snorts, hides behind her hands, but keeps looking, fixes her hair, primps, laughs, and pretends that she's very interested in the harpist.* NADYA *enters the room.*]

NADYA: Mashenka, have you got a number fifty black?

MANYA: Well, good day to you too! Dark-haired guys mean nothing to me.

NADYA: I came for a spool of thread.

MANYA: Ah, thread! There's the thread. Take it out of that little box.

NADYA: *Merci* to you. [*Goes over, rummages.* MANYA *goes on looking as if nothing had happened. A flash of light falls on* NADYA.] They're flashing again. I can't stand it.

MANYA: Then why did you come in?

NADYA: I came in for thread.

MANYA: For thread? Come over here then. Look, there's your dark one making with the sunbeams.

[NADYA *walks over, and they both look out the window. Pause.*]

MANYA: The janitor chased away the music girl.

NADYA: There's no point in looking at him. You'll fall in love. He's not worth it.

MANYA: Who? The janitor?

NADYA: No, your blond guy.

MANYA: He's a civil servant. He's wonderful. He plays the guitar so nicely.

NADYA: I didn't see him.

MANYA: He does. I saw him myself yesterday. It was quiet last night. Hot. I was sitting there, looked out, after you'd left, he was playing so nicely.

NADYA: You want me to introduce him to you?

MANYA: Nadya! Darling! Only how could you do it?

NADYA: I'll set it up. Only I'm not crazy about doing it. Year before last I was living at a dressmaker's, at General Turina's wife's place. There too a neighbor was staring at us through binoculars. Really embarrassing. Whenever young ladies were in the fitting room or I would go to bed. And there he'd be, pulling out the binoculars. So I dressed up a dummy in a housecoat and put it in the window. There were no curtains. The general's lady said that a dressmaker shouldn't have curtains, and it was fine without.

MANYA: But you're looking through binoculars yourself.

NADYA: That's because he gave them to me.

MANYA: Which means, you've met.

NADYA: We've met. I went to meet him three months ago.

MANYA: And then what?

NADYA: And then . . . I poisoned myself.

MANYA: They pumped your stomach.

NADYA: They pumped my stomach.

MANYA: Well, I don't get it. When Kolenka dumped me, I cried like crazy. I ate a box of quinine pills. And nothing happened. Only Madam called me a little fool one extra time . . . For some reason these alterations are taking forever. Look, soon it'll be October.

NADYA: Yes.

MANYA: And I like the neighbor. His mustache has little points, it's white, just like my Kolenka's. Look—I think he's saying something.

NADYA: Can't understand it. I suppose he's saying good morning. [*Nods to him.*] Good morning, good morning, how are you?

MANYA: He's not listening.

NADYA: Good morning, I said. This girlfriend of mine here is very interested in you.

MANYA: Nadka! Shut up! [*Presses a hand over her mouth.*]

NADYA: What? I can't hear. Write it down.

MANYA: On a piece of paper! [*Shows her hand as if writing . . . Suddenly gets embarrassed.*] Ah, this is shameful, Nadka.

NADYA: What's up with you? If you want to meet him, you've got to be bold. Otherwise you look and look and waste your time.

MANYA: So what's going to happen? He'll come over here, I suppose.

NADYA: That's right.

MANYA: That's terrifying.

NADYA: Look there, he's written something. And there's another guy looking through the binoculars.

MANYA: I can't make it out. "What . . . what . . ." Can you see it?

NADYA: I'll get the binoculars right away. [*She goes out, returns with the binoculars.*] Now we'll read it. [*Reads*] "What's your name?"

MANYA: Is that all. Foo, how uninteresting.

NADYA: What'd you expect, he'd write "I love you" right off the bat?

MANYA: No, but all the same.

NADYA: Gotta answer back. Give me a scrap of paper.

MANYA: There isn't any.

NADYA: Give me one of the patterns.

MANYA: Here.

NADYA: Well, write.

MANYA [*writing on a scrap "I'm Manya and she's Nadya" and displaying it*]: Honest to God, they're laughing. And the other guy's writing.

NADYA: It'll be all right. Read what they wrote.

MANYA [*taking the binoculars and reading*]: "We like you a lot." Ay, what a thing to say!

NADYA [*writing*]: "And we like you a lot."

MANYA: Why did you write that?

NADYA: It's the truth, isn't it?

MANYA: One of them likes me, but not both.

NADYA: Read, read what's their answer.

MANYA [*reading*]: "May I come over?" There, you see what you've done.

NADYA [*writing*]: "Come over." Well done. Now I'll see how brave you are. [*Shows her the scrap.*]

MANYA: I don't dare, I don't dare. [*Tries to rip it up.*]

NADYA: It's too late. Look: he's nodding!

MANYA: He's gone out! Honest to God, he's gone out!

NADYA: And mine's laughing. What are you laughing at? At yourself! [*Sticks out her tongue at him.*]

MANYA: You started talking to him to get me in trouble. You're a pig.

NADYA [*teasing*]: Don't lose your temper. A guest will be arriving any minute.

MANYA: I won't let him in. I'll lock the door and won't let him in.

NADYA: You will.

MANYA: Oh my God! Oh my God! What am I going to do now! Get out of here, Nadka. You're a filthy slut!

NADYA: I'm going, I'm going. He's coming and I'm going. He's crossing the courtyard now. It won't be long to wait.

MANYA: Good grief, what a mess it is here. All these things strewn around. I'll have to straighten it up.

NADYA: But if you're not going to let him in.

MANYA: Idiot! Get out of here! Get out of here! You're a filthy slut.

NADYA: Give me the binoculars. Filthy slut yourself.

MANYA: Here, here, here are your binoculars. Shameless hussy.

NADYA: Listen, you're not so simon-pure yourself. Quinine guzzler!

MANYA: Yes, and you're a filthy slut, an alley cat, that's what you are!

NADYA: Just you wait.

[*A knock at the door. They both go quiet. A fair-haired fellow with a little mustache enters.*]

BLOND: Good morning. What are you arguing about?

MANYA: Us? . . .

NADYA: Nothing special, going about our business.

BLOND: It's naughty, Nadenka, to insult little girls. Naughty. What was she insulting you for? Poor creature! Give me your hand, let me have a look. That's right. Now don't be angry, don't be angry, I only wanted to comfort you. May I smoke?

NADYA: You may. Please do.

BLOND: Thanks. [*Sits down.*] Well, are you enjoying yourselves?

[NADYA *and* MANYA *look at one another and snort.*]

NADYA: How are we supposed to enjoy ourselves when our fingers keep swelling up?

BLOND: Ay, ay, how come?

NADYA: How come? From the needles.

BLOND: Poor things.

MANYA: It's true. Madam is strict with us.

BLOND: And where is she?

MANYA: She left with her whole family to their estate. She left us alone with the housekeeper. And she goes out every day.

BLOND [*to* NADYA]: I've got a message for you. My friend asked me to bring it. Whether you might drop in on him. He has something that needs sewing. And then you can sit down and take some tea.

NADYA: Why . . . I . . . really don't know.

BLOND: Go on, go on, he's a nice kid.

NADYA: After all, just for a minute.

BLOND: He says he's known you for a long time, he was immediately captivated by your beauty. I can't live without her, he says.

NADYA: Then I won't go.

BLOND: What's wrong, I was just joking, go ahead.

NADYA: Who can tell whether you're joking or not.

MANYA: Don't go, Nadya.

NADYA: What's it to you? If I want to, I'll go. Calls me bad names herself, bad names, and now decides to look out for me. So I'm going. Goodbye. Best wishes. [*Exits.*]

BLOND: Your girlfriend's a bit of shrew! How can you put up with such behavior?

MANYA: Honestly, what behavior! Only she's smart, she knows everything. She even poisoned herself once. And I'm like that too.

BLOND: But you don't want to be like that?

MANYA: Meaning, like what?

BLOND: Let me show you, tell you. Let me read your fortune in your palm.

MANYA: Excuse me, I've got hangnails. You know, we're always getting hangnails from the needles.

BLOND: Never mind, I'll figure it out. There, you see, you'll be rich, you'll find yourself a good fiancé.

MANYA: What'll he look like? Blond or brunet?

BLOND: Blond with a little mustache.

MANYA: Ay, you!

BLOND: Only you have to do what I say. Will you?

MANYA: That depends. If you tell me you won't go down the aisle with me, I won't do what you say.

BLOND: Well, suppose you and I were to go to the amusement park right now? You've been to the amusement park?

MANYA: I've been to the zoo. It was nice there. I like the parrots. They were lots of fun, but not the monkeys. They're disgusting.

BLOND: Do you find me disgusting?

MANYA: Are you a monkey?

BLOND: Thank you for that. Give me your hand. That's right. [*Kisses her hand and pulls* MANYA *to him.*]

MANYA: What are you doing? Leave off.

BLOND: What for? Nadya spoke the truth. You're a prude. Come and see how she's kissing my friend.

MANYA: It's true! The shameless hussy!

BLOND: Why shameless! He loves her and she loves him. And I love you. Here's how much I love you . . . [*Kisses her.*] That's how much I love you, my darling Manechka!

MANYA: Leave off. What's wrong with you. You mustn't, my dear. So you truly love me?

BLOND: Truly.

MANYA: Word of honor you love me?

BLOND: Word of honor I love you.

MANYA: And I love you. It's awful how I love you. I've been watching you through the window this whole time. Only . . .

BLOND: Only what?

MANYA: I don't know . . . what's your name.

BLOND: Call me whatever you like. Vanya or whatever.

MANYA: No, I don't like Vanya.

BLOND: Then Kolya.

MANYA: No, I'll call you Ferdinand. I like that name a lot, I read it in a book.

BLOND: Well, Manechka, kiss your Ferdinand.

MANYA: Ay, that's tickles, and I'm scared to death of tickling.

BLOND: Well, then, I won't. You know what . . . shall we let down the curtain?

MANYA: Isn't that risky?

BLOND: Not risky at all.

MANYA: Well . . . let it down.

[*The* BLOND *lets down the curtain. A long pause. We hear the creak of a block and tackle. The* HOUSE PAINTER *rises on a sling, paints the drainpipe, and sings:*]

> Dearest lady, my heart's queen,
> Can you forgive poor me
> I went and fell in love with you
> So disgracefully?
> Love me, love me, Vanyushka,
> Why would I angry be?
> But if you should betray our love
> I'll go drown in the sea.

[*A bare arm nervously makes an appearance and adjusts the curtain. The* HOUSE PAINTER *has noticed it.*]

HOUSE PAINTER: Looky there now, an arm! [*Draws near to the window, tries to look through a slit in the curtain.*] And what're they getting' up to in there! [*While the* HOUSE PAINTER *is pulled up higher, he shouts.*] Hold on, Vanka! Damn, don't yank it! Lemme have a look! [*They keep pulling him higher anyway. Then he waves his hand in despair and strikes up the song again.*] Dearest lady . . .

BORIS GEYER

INTRODUCTION

Scion of a poor family of Russified Germans, Boris Fyodorovich Geyer (1879–1916) was given a commercial education in Petersburg and became a bookkeeper with an insurance company. The success of his first story, printed in the magazine *Niva*, decided his fate. In the revolutionary year of 1905 he was active in creating two satirical journals and edited his own magazine, titled, rather unimaginatively, *Zhurnal* (*Journal*), mainly as an outlet for his own stories. In 1906 one of them earned its author a conviction of a year and a half solitary confinement in Petropavlovsk fortress for insulting the army. While there he wrote his first play, *Before Daybreak*, proclaiming that "only the nearsighted fail to notice the harbingers of dawn." This drama of a new generation that despises material wealth and struggles for social equality was, not surprisingly, banned for performance by the government censor. (Under the new title *In the Gloaming of the Dawning* [*V sumerkahkh rassveta*] it managed to get a hearing.)

Idealistic politics was not Geyer's strong suit; satire was. His *Nero*, in collaboration with the composer I. I. Chekrygin (1907), was a takeoff on Rubinstein's opera of the same name. (The censor granted it one performance.) So it can be seen as an obscure forerunner of *Vampuka*, which was bruited about salons but was not to be publicly performed for two years. Geyer found a haven in the humor journal *Satyricon* (*Satirikon*) with symbolist fairy tales and satirical playlets, among them a lampoon of spiritualism, *Chertoved* (*The Devilist*, 1908); Andreev and the Moscow Art Theater's misguided stabs at staging symbolist drama also came in for ridicule.

These began to appear on various Saint Petersburg stages, including the Crooked Mirror, whose literary council he joined in 1908 and for which he wrote original parodies, comic sketches, and miniature mono-dramas. As Kugel' testified, Geyer was apt for this theater "by the cut of his subtly humorous, intelligent and insuperable opposition to theatrical cliché and attraction to new forms of theatrical creativity."[1] He proved to be a major factor in the Mirror's success and moved Russian writing for cabaret in a new direction. A photograph in the Moscow Bakhrushin Theater Museum shows a short, bald, mustachioed man in pince-nez with a pretty wife, enjoying himself at a champagne luncheon. It is a graphic depiction of his happy-go-lucky, bohemian way of life and what Kugel' called his "Mozartian" insouciance.

In Geyer's writing, however, his insouciant flippancy often conceals a profound pessimism. In the Russian tradition, he sees rank, station, and ambition, rather than heredity, sex, war, or biological urges, as the impulses for action; at the bottom of every seemingly generous or unselfish deed is inevitably an egoistic motive. Geyer's parodies always strip human aspiration down to its basest, most despicable mainsprings. Kugel' attributed this to the profound depression that washed over the Russian intelligentsia following the abortive revolution and reforms of 1905–8.[2] Yet Geyer's cynicism seems deeper-dyed than that of his colleagues, a grittier version of the disillusionment in Aleksandr Blok's *The Little Show-booth* (*Balaganchik*, 1906) and *Incognita* (*Neznakomka*, 1906–7).

Geyer's Crooked Mirror debut was *The Evolution of the Theater* (premiere: January 20, 1910), in which he offered four versions of the same subject, written in the manner of Gogol, Aleksandr Ostrovsky, Chekhov, and Andreev.[2] The target was not so much the playwrights themselves but the modernist debate over "the crisis in the theater." His title alludes to Sergey Rafalovich's essay "The Evolution of the Theater," which had appeared two years earlier as the figurehead piece in *"Theater": A Book about the Modern Theater*, a volume of manifestos by Meyerhold, Sologub, Bryusov, Andrei Bely, and other symbolist ideologues. Rafalovich's contribution comprised a potted history of the theater, in which, like the book's other contributors, he spoke of its degeneration from its Greek religious origins and the need for a new synthesis of dance and song to invigorate it. In his view a crucial turning point had been reached: the old theater was dead, and the theater of the future would have to be international, religious, or mystical, with no distinction between the passive spectator and the active performer.[4]

Geyer reduced this fashionable attitude to absurdity by bringing it down to cases. A lecturer explains the episodes as object lessons in the theater's progress from "coarse, primitive, and unintelligible forms to the depiction of the most subtle psychic experiences, the most refined symbols, total intelligibility, and profound thought."[5] It was absolutely novel to offer a play in which the very process of the theater's development becomes the event. This structural principle of modeling a parodic dramatic text would be continued in Geyer's later work.

Similar "variations on a theme" had already appeared in Berlin in Max Reinhardt's Schall und Rauch (Noise and Smoke) cabaret with a parody of Friedrich Schiller's *Don Carlos* in four versions, including the styles of Gerhart Hauptmann and Maeterlinck. A similar approach to Ibsen's *A Doll's House* was offered by Rudolf Bernauer at the Böse Buben (Bad Boys) cabaret.[6] But if Geyer was not the originator of the form, he was a deft manipulator of it. His spoofs of Ostrovsky and Chekhov, singled out for praise by the critics, were masterful because they carefully observed and imitated the pet devices of those playwrights. The Chekhov in particular "was performed, as they say, 'like a grand piano.'"[7] The Andreev sketch was especially apt, since the evening at the Crooked Mirror ended with an Andreev play and skewered the recent Art Theater production of *Anathema*. A version of *Faust* set in a milieu of impoverished Jews, it carried a heavy burden of mysticism. To this Geyer added "Someone in Gray," the Fate figure from *The Life of Man*. The progression from a Gogolian highly colored farce to the obscure woolgathering of Andreev made hash of the modernists' claims to the coming perfection of the drama. Geyer refused to read etiolation as consummation.

Part of Geyer's audacity was in shooting darts at cultural icons. The Art Theater's *Anathema* had gained prestige by being banned, and Chekhov, a mere six years after his death, had already been endowed with a halo. Contemporaries were shocked that Geyer should poke fun at a recently deceased writer whose jubilee had just been celebrated; one reviewer, admitting that the "numerous public" had greatly enjoyed the skit, deplored its "coarse, malicious" mockery of Chekhov, "who is least deserving of mockery," for his heroes, if humdrum, "are still a sign of the times."[8]

Geyer's next offering was equally mirth-raising if less topical: "L'amour d'un cosac russe, a sensational French drama with murder and expropriation from the life of real Russian farmers in 1 act with preface. Adapted from a famous Russian novel by B. Geyer" (premiere: April 8/9, 1910). Ever since Alexandre Dumas père had written of riding in troikas drawn by bears and sitting in the shade of a notorious spreading cranberry bush, French reportage on Russia was a subject for ridicule. A direct target may have been André Antoine's production of *La puissance des ténèbres* at the Théâtre Libre in Paris in 1888.

With Evreinov's advent as artistic director in October 1910 and the evolution of the Crooked Mirror into a distinctly experimental theater, Geyer was able to venture more boldly toward "new forms." Evreinov, in his memoirs, is typically condescending, convinced that Geyer's interest in monodrama was superficial, but was grateful to him for popularizing it in his sketches. "I was never very closely associated with him as a friend, but always considered myself a genuine colleague," giving him the chance to shine onstage that, Evreinov implied, Kugel' had denied him. "In general Geyer was not outwardly as brilliant and clever as, say, Érenberg . . . at first glance, Geyer made the impression of a humble countinghouse clerk," with his limited education, but Evreinov granted he was a steadfast insurgent. His originality lay in a penchant for tragic farce.[9]

Possibly in response to Evreinov's wish to reflect real life in the Mirror's distorting lens, Geyer's next contribution was steeped in undisguised pessimism. In *The Components of Life* (*Élementy zhizni*, December 12, 1910), a latter-day Candide sets out on his journey of discovery. Perhaps with a mocking side-glance at Vorovsky's accusation that the Crooked Mirror had "shrunk from" life (see this book's introduction), the youth explains to an elderly sage, "I am stepping into life . . . I will learn its components . . . I will shrink from neither grief nor joy, hard labor nor idle amusement, nor youthful, beautiful, open, and triumphant love."[10] In short order he runs up against surrogates of these abstract qualities. Joy turns out to be a synonym for Schadenfreude, a writer's glee at the failure of his friend's play. Leisure dwindles into a drunken brawl in a low tavern. Love is an encounter with a prostitute; hatred is petty rage directed against a tailor who forgot to sew on a button. At the end, the youth returns to the old man who points the moral: "Remember this great truth, elaborated over the centuries: to hell with everything and look after your health!" One reviewer noted that it was as if Andreev's *Life of Man*, with its message of indomitable human dignity in the face of ineluctable mortality, has been turned inside out.[11] Once again Geyer was congratulated for compressing a grand and original idea into a very compact space, despite complaints of the "anecdotal" nature of some of the episodes. Then as now, "anecdote" was a term of abuse among critics who disdain specifics for the ineffable.

His next contribution, *Cinema* (*Kinematograf*), was less interesting for its text than for its staging. The actors performed in jerky, angular movements under intermittent lighting fifty years before strobe effects became common. A title-reader stood to one side, melancholically ending each explication with a call to the projectionist: "Miskha, keep cranking!" Of course, it ended in a chase, which proved to be so popular that Evreinov borrowed it later for the final episode in his *Inspector General*.[12]

On the other hand, Geyer drew on Evreinov's theory of monodrama (see the introduction to Evreinov) for his next experiment and created the first play of its kind to be produced. (Evreinov's *A Show of Love* was never performed in Russia, though Geyer may have read it in print.)[13] *The Water of Life* (*Aqua vitae* or *Voda zhizni*), which opened the new season on September 18, 1911, presented not the worldview of a single protagonist but, rather more ambitiously, the changing perspective of a room full of people. It led Kugel' to wonder if "polydrama" might not be a better name for such a play. The scene is set in a cheap, basement-level restaurant whose bartender explains to a new waiter the various stages of inebriation to observe in the customers so that he will learn when to stop serving them.

The play is divided into "four decanters" of vodka, and as each is drunk, the customers pass through those stages. This is in itself unexceptional. What distinguishes the play are the "monodramatic" scenic devices used to enhance the effect. As the first decanter is drunk, the tacky restaurant remains as it is, and one irritated customer even insists that the scratchy gramophone be switched off. With the second decanter, as the characters grumble about work and pick fights over minor issues, the lighting grows brighter, the tables fill up, and the clientele are better looking and better dressed than before. (A curtain is let down between scenes to accomplish this.) The third decanter produces more heated discussion, along with a transition to ribaldry and flirtation. The lighting grows even brighter, so that the scenery sparkles in the glare. All the customers and even the waiters (who have doubled in number) have an improved appearance, and the gramophone's music is amplified by a backstage orchestra. Finally, with the consumption of the last decanter, as the characters grow depressed and speculate about the soul, the lights gradually fade into a dismal gloom and the music turns to a funeral march. The customers depart into real life as the cold gray light of dawn washes over them.

Most of the reviews were highly laudatory, but the originality of this concept was so great that, typically, some of the critics thought it was an unpleasant slice of naturalism saved only by Evreinov's ingenious staging.[14] Evreinov, however, simply implemented what was already in Geyer's stage directions, and the credit for the idea must go to the playwright.[15] After such an imaginative breakthrough, his next effort, *The Baroness's Handkerchief* (*Nosovoy platok Baronessy*, October 20, 1911), seems a step backward, a farcical depiction of a high-society drama as played by provincial barnstormers.

After this retrogression, Geyer's juggling with monodrama was confirmed by a play which, with *The Evolution of the Drama*, was his only work to remain in the Crooked Mirror's repertoire up to its demise in 1931. Writing about *Memories* (*Vospominaniya*; premiere: November 12–13, 1911), Evreinov, who staged it, called it "a masterpiece," while Kugel', a severe critic, went so far as to say, "Geyer's 'Memories' is a remarkable discovery in the realm of drama, the fruits of which will nourish the theater for many years to come."[16] "Geyer is a fresh talent . . . Geyer's ideas (more accurately, his scenic format) are fertile in the highest degree. All art is, in essence, a variant of reality, and this device—a glance into the distance and a reevaluation of reality's manifold observers—promises a new unlimited quantity of such variants of reality."[17] In later life, expanding on his own memory, Kugel' opined:

> Psychologically monodrama presents in itself a multifaceted modification of the same theme, a series of "changes of the beloved face" . . . The late Geyer made some valuable experiments in the spirit of monodrama understood in this sense, having created as it were a stage law of the natural modification of phenomena. Perhaps this isn't a monodrama, but a polydrama, although the name makes little difference. Such, for instance, is the play "Memories." The subject of "Memories" is unusually simple, banal, and even trivial, which is both the play's strength and its weakness.
>
> In execution there are many flaws, but in concept and construction the play is not only talented but in the highest de-

gree original. The artistic perfection of a truly stage-worthy monodrama indubitably belongs to Geyer. Here was an organic merging of form and matter. The idea, put forth by the author, is truly brilliant in its simplicity and importance. The essence, revealed in "Memories" in the form of multiple viewpoints, consists in the fact that we are egotistical, love only ourselves, lie to our own benefit and no one's else, and flatter ourselves: that we dare not believe ourselves, perhaps we should not believe ourselves; that our very life, as we conceive it, is a dream and that in general the fateful question "What is truth?" does not allow for an answer.[18]

For his illustrated "novella" (*povest'*), Geyer once again chose a squalid milieu, similar to the ambience of Dostoevsky's "A Nasty Story" ("Skvernyy anekdot") and Chekhov's *The Wedding* (*Svad'ba*). A lower-middle-class party results in the announcement of an engagement; this banal event serves as a necessary prelude to what follows. The next day, the guests, having drunk themselves sober, recall, each in his own way, the previous night's events. The fiancé, a downtrodden nonentity, sees himself as a gallant champion, a man of action in a crisis. The bride-to-be recalls how cleverly she maneuvered him into making a proposal. A drunken poetaster remembers the evening as an orgy of bacchantes, himself as an honored guest. The pessimistic guest enshrouds the event in funereal gloom, himself the only lively soul there.

Up to this point the critics were delighted.[19] Although they had misgivings about the "anecdotal" nature of the gloomy guest's scenario, they had nothing but praise for the accurate psychology of the wooer's self-delusion and the drunk's bibulous nostalgia. But the greatest praise was lavished on the final episode. Fifteen years later, the mother, fallen into dotage, attempts to remember the event; she considers the couple's happiness her doing. Yet, owing to her senility, her recollections are a series of fragmentary, distorted vignettes emerging from darkness and absorbed back into it. This was a highly ingenious attempt to pictorialize a state of mental debility.

For the most part, the reception was enthusiastic. As usual, there were complaints that Geyer's writing was hasty and unpolished and that the device of a narrator between episodes to cover scene changes was tiresome; but these cavils could not efface the distinction of his achievement. In forty-five minutes, he had packed enough momentous ideas for four hours (Kugel' estimated on reading the manuscript) and had found a viable format for them. The panorama of monodramatic perspectives went beyond Evreinov's desire for audience coexperiencing to make a bigger aesthetic point: since all art is a variant of reality, to reappraise reality through a myriad of views—what we today might call the *Rashomon* principle—offers fresh possibilities for artistic creativity. Capturing the past through the distortion of conflicting consciousnesses was absolutely new to the stage. Without too much overstatement, one might suggest that what James Joyce and Marcel Proust were attempting on broad canvases, Geyer was exploring in miniature.[20]

Geyer's conception of human memory was, however, more Schopenhauerian in its pessimism than Proustian. All of the recollections, informed by vanity and egotism, are essentially mendacious and self-serving. Whether or not there is an objective reality (the preliminary episode was titled "Reality" in the program), the subjective interpretations invariably manipulate "truth" or "facts" to their own advantage. By the time we reach the dim scraps of recall dredged up by the senile old lady, memory has become a symbol for death. Memory has served as life's connective tissue, and as it disintegrates with the passage of each of life's moments, the human fabric crumbles. That memory should be a self-worshipping lie and yet indispensable to the maintenance of human life is a profoundly misanthropic notion. Yet Geyer's means of conveying it richly entertained a cabaret audience. Geyer's "polydramatic" approach seemed so liberating that it was adopted by the humor magazine *Satyricon* when the censorship prevented reportage of the visit of an English delegation to Russia in 1912. V. Azov made up descriptions of the visitors as seen through the eyes of a liberal reformer, an illiterate reactionary, and the mayor of Petersburg.[21]

Pulp Fiction (*Van'kina literatura*; premiere: January 23, 1912) applied the principle of subjective realities to the Russian equivalent of a Harlequin romance. The stage was divided in two: on the left, a comfortable boudoir; on the right, a sordid apartment. On the left, a loving couple reads the latest installment of a new novel whose characters are noble, well-spoken, elegant, and self-sacrificing; the wife keeps interjecting how wonderful the author must be. On the right, the author is seen to be a contemptible penny-a-liner, grinding out his weekly quota while plagued by a shrewish wife, a flirtatious milliner, an alcoholic friend, and a janitor trying to evict him for nonpayment of rent. Each passage read from the novel is ironically counterpointed by the squalid reality underlying it.

COOK [*crude, dirty, enters with the roast*]: Boss, that guy's here about that little matter. He says, when you gonna pay the rent? You owe an awful lot, he says, so the landlord's itchy.

WIFE: Oh, my God . . . Hm, I don't see why he can't wait. Well, tell him we'll pay him tomorrow.

COOK [*on the way out*]: Tomorrow, tomorrow. Nobody'll believe that, you derelict! [*Exits.*]

WRITER: And give him something to eat so he'll leave me in peace for a while. Damn the bastard. [*He writes:*]

HE [*reading*]: "The door opened softly and on the threshold stood the pretty coquette of a parlormaid, bowing respectfully—'Master,' she said, 'the Nutrition Committee for the Poor Children has sent someone to see you . . .' 'Very good,' Roksanov interrupted her. 'I am very busy. Tell your mistress to give them thirty rubles and make my excuses. I am working on an urgent report.' The trim figure was heard to disappear behind the heavy portières and Roksanov plunged back into his papers."[22]

Napoleon and Love (*Napoleon i lyubov'*; premiere: September 13, 1912), a simplistic exercise contrasting great and small occasioned by the centenary of the French invasion,[23] preceded Geyer's next important experiment, *The Dream* (*Son'*; premiere: October 13, 1912).

It should be noted that on this particular bill, Geyer's play immediately preceded Evreinov's important monodrama *Backstage at the Soul*, which came almost a year after Geyer's earliest experiments in the genre. The two complemented one another, since Evreinov's play takes place inside a man's body, while Geyer's takes place inside a man's mind, unconscious in sleep. Whereas Evreinov divided his hero's consciousness into rational, emotional, and eternal selves, Geyer more traditionally presented an undivided psyche. Both playwrights, however, were seeking a way to dramatize subjectivity and subconscious action from within.

Dream's basic motif is Gogolian (after all, *Son* is *Nos* backward): a minor bureaucrat feels aggrieved when his proposal is turned down by a wealthy spinster, a general's daughter. But the treatment was Geyerian. In a subsequent dream, the events the pen pusher has undergone are recreated oneirically: "confused, with unexpected transformations, excursions in the realm of childhood."[24] Strindberg had, of course, already ventured into this field with *A Dream Play* (*Ett Drömspel*, 1901–2, performed 1907), but it was barely known in Russia, and its symbolism relies on personal imagery and Vedantic religion. Most "dream plays" of the period, from Hauptmann's *Hanneles Himmelfahrt* (1893) to J. M. Barrie's *A Kiss for Cinderella* (1916), present the sleep vision as a perfectly coherent if idealized distortion of reality. Geyer's playlet, tailored to the exigencies of a satiric cabaret, is more extreme, garish, and protosurrealist in its depiction of the subconscious.

In a reversal of the situation in *Memories*, the beautiful bride appears as a superannuated gargoyle; the cards the dreamer has been cheating at grow enormous and unwieldy in his hands (shades of Lewis Carroll). The director of his department has become a literal monster, terrifying the wits out of the dreamer; an uncanny Chinaman drifts by holding an ostrich plume; and at the climax, the dreamer loses his trousers. Reviewers, accustomed to seeing visions staged behind gauze, appraised the staging as too realistic for the subject and thereby missed the monodramatic point that the audience was to grant the dream the same credence the dreamer did. Geyer called his piece "a realistic phantasmagoria" and intended the abrupt transitions and unwonted transformations to look as naturalistic as anything in a play by Gorky.

Although this manipulation of what Freud called "dream-work' includes such Freudian items as condensation, displacement, sensory intensity, and absurdity, and culminates in the embarrassment of nakedness, it is unlikely Geyer was familiar with *The Interpretation of Dreams* (first published in 1900), particularly given that he does not adhere to Freud's principal tenet of the dream as wish fulfillment. It is more likely that Geyer subscribed, like Strindberg, to Eduard von Hartmann's *Philosophy of the Unconscious* (1869). For Hartmann, with the dream "all the troubles of waking life pass over into the sleeping state."[25] Since human happiness is unattainable, a dream is most often an unrelieved nightmare, unless mitigated by scientific or artistic enjoyment, the same thing that reconciles a cultured person to life in general. As Geyer's heroes are vulgar boors, this amelioration is impossible; only the enthusiastic Mirror audiences partook of aesthetic pleasure.

The following sketches were largely variations on already visited themes. In *The Legend of the Holy Black Swan* (*Legenda o svyashchennom chernom lebede*; premiere: November 15, 1912), one scene illustrates a tale of artistic creation, and the next shows the grubby truth behind it. It was soon effaced by Evreinov's *Inspector General* two weeks later (see Evreinov introduction), whose success was so great that a play of Geyer's in rehearsal was canceled. His next three offerings were pedestrian, among them a silent-film treatment of *Evgeny Onegin* and an anti-German wartime propaganda piece.

His last two plays, however, attempted to return to the kind of "split-screen" effect he had used before with such success. The title of the "psychological experiment" *What They Say, What They Think* (*Chto govoryat—chto dumayut*; premiere: December 16, 1914) reveals its intention. In part 1, a general's family prepares to welcome and bilk a charitable millionaire; in part 2, their motives and true thoughts are spoken aloud. Geyer made this particularly difficult for the actors by insisting that the characters use the same gestures and facial expressions in both parts.

If speech and thoughts had been directly linked, the contrast would have been both more brutal and more comic. By splitting them into two distinct scenes, Geyer vitiated his effects. Not until 1928, when Eugene O'Neill followed dialogue immediately with spoken thought in *Strange Interlude* (and Groucho Marx lampooned the device in *Animal Crackers*), was a method found to portray this discrepancy. O'Neill, heir to three decades of literary experimentation, was trying to create interior monologues as the dramatic equivalent of the novel's stream of consciousness. Geyer had fewer models to build on. In any case, the critics were undisturbed by the awkward structure; rather, they felt that the subject was too trite.[26] Kugel' later complained that Geyer had misrepresented human psychology, since "our minds hold not one but a multiplicity of thoughts, of which the tongue transmits only a few."[27] This was not so much to denigrate Geyer's achievement as to indicate the complexities Kugel' thought his cabaret capable of dramatizing.

Æolian Harps (*Éolovye arfy*; premiere: November 16, 1915) has a disputed authorship. According to Evreinov, the play was originally credited to Geyer, but Evreinov complained to the management that Geyer had not only appropriated Evreinov's invention, monodrama, but also his basic idea for the play. Eventually the dispute was resolved and they were listed as coauthors. Evreinov was always hypersensitive to what he considered kidnapping of his brain children and insisted that the last scene, which he wrote alone, was the funniest. Most contemporaries regarded *Harps* as Geyer's play, embellished by Evreinov's stagecraft and revisions during rehearsals.

Since the comedy was an attack on reviewers, most reviewers made an effort to be well disposed toward it, although *Rech'* snarled that it was too reminiscent of early Mirror offerings. Actually, the structure has much in common with *Memories*: three newspaper critics attend a saccharine psychological drama saturated with love. An impresario then stages their reviews of that performance. The first, a well-intentioned journalist, views the play as a magnificent symphony; infatuated with a walk-on actress, who, as the maid, says only "Dinner is served," he attributes all the play's success to her "violin-like" reading.[28] With her exit, he loses interest and the stage goes dark. The second critic, hostile to the play, conjures up a series of disasters: the leading man loses his dentures, the door in the flat falls off its hinges, the prompter's voice overtops the actors. The third, who arrives late and drunk, confuses the play with the convivial scene he has just left. The stage is covered in white muslin to represent his muzzy state of mind; the dialogue is garbled, champagne corks pop, and an inebriated voice calls for the bill.

The authors had certainly improved on George Bernard Shaw, who, in *Fanny's First Play* (1911), needed three acts before filling his epilogue with recognizable caricatures of London critics. In *Æolian Harps,* the monodramatic principle is doubled so that the spectator, rather than seeing the stage action through the eyes of the protagonist, sees it through the eyes of another spectator, a rather Pirandellian device.[29]

Geyer went to a mineral springs resort in Samara to treat an ulcer, and there he died of typhoid dysentery in August 1916. He was only forty and, in the opinion of his colleagues, at the height of his powers. The following February a special bill of his plays was presented at the Crooked Mirror in his memory.[30] A list of the theater's parodic specialties[31] that was composed by Evreinov, late in his life, included only three of Geyer's plays—*The Evolution of the Theater* (staged before Evreinov had become artistic director), the relatively minor *Baroness's Handkerchief*, and a post-revolutionary revision of *Cinema*. Significantly, none of Geyer's mono- or polydramatic achievements was mentioned.

NOTES

1. A. R. Kugel', *List'ya s dereva* (Leningrad: Vremya, 1926), 201; Nikolay Evreinov, *Histoire du théâtre russe* (Paris: Éditions du Chêne, 1947), 397. Kugel' also provided a short obituary of Geyer in *Teatr i iskusstvo* 28 (1916): 563–64.
2. Kugel', *List'ya s dereva*, 196.
3. As an émigré in Paris in 1930 Evreinov opened his Strolling Players theater, which lasted only a year; its two programs made up chiefly of his own plays. In the second program he included his revision of *Evolution* retitled *The Evolution of Russian Drama*, the first three parts as in the original, and the fourth a Soviet-style play called "A Difficult Change."
4. Sergey Rafalovich, "Évolyutsiya teatra," in *Teatr: Kniga o novom teatre; Sbornik statei* (Saint Petersburg: Shipovnik, 1908), 219–42. In the same year as Geyer's parody the literary historian V. M. Friche published an essay, "Évolyutsiya teatra i dramy," that cited cabaret as the latest avatar of theatrical development. V. A. Bazarov, ed., *Iz istorii noveyshey russkoy literatury* (Moscow: Zveno, 1910), 61–148.
5. In M. Ya. Polyakova, ed., *Russkaya teatral'naya parodiya XIX–nachala XX veka* (Moscow: Iskusstvo, 1976), 569. It was the only one of Geyer's plays to be published in the Soviet era. Pictures from the original production appear in *Teatr i iskusstvo* 5 (1910): 111.
6. *Don Carlos an der Jahrhundertwende* in Max Reinhardt, *Schall und Rauch* (Berlin: Schuster und Loeffler, 1901), 11–126; *Nora* in H. R. Schatter, ed., *Scharf geschossen: Die deutschsprachige Parodie von 1900 bis zur Gegenwart* (Vienna: Scherz, 1968).
7. S. [Pyotr Solyany], "Krivoe Zerkalo," *Teatr i iskusstvo* 59 (January 31, 1910): 87.
8. Vas. Bazilevsky, *Rampa i zhizn'* 5 (1910): 79–80; *Rech'* 21 (January 22–February 4, 1910): 5. Chekhov's plays had already been less sympathetically parodied by the reactionary journalist V. A. Burenin. See Laurence Senelick, "Stuffed Seagulls: Parody and the Reception of Chekhov's Plays," *Poetics Today* 8, no. 2 (1987): 285–98.
9. Nikolay Evereinov, *V shkole ostroumiya*, ed. Aleksandra Deich and Anna Kashina-Evreinova (Moscow: Iskusstvo, 1998), 278–79.
10. Quoted in Georgy Kryzhitsky, "Vospominaniya: Laboratoriya smekha," *Teatr* 8 (August 1967): 114.
11. A. B., "Krivoe Zerkalo," *Teatr i iskusstvo* 51 (1910): 988; production shots, 988–89.
12. *Rech'* 41 (February 11, 1911): 7; *Teatr i iskusstvo* 7 (1911): 148.
13. Historians have been prone to garble the Crooked Mirror's chronology. For instance, Evgeny Kuznetsov in his *Iz proshlogo russkoy éstrady: Istoricheskie ocherki* (Moscow: Iskusstvo, 1958) writes, "After this monodrama [Evreinov's *Backstage at the Soul*] a series of others followed (*Memories, A Dream, The Water of Life*)" (295). In fact, the first and third of Geyer's plays he cites *preceded* Evreinov's comedy, and the second appeared on the same bill with it.
14. Examples include Evgeny Znosko-Borovsky in *Russkaya khudozhestvennaya letopis'* 15 (1911): 23. His usually harsh critiques of the Crooked Mirror are suspect, since he wrote for rival theaters of miniatures.

15. Geyer's sardonic treatment of alcoholism was adopted by later cabaret authors: "Lecture on the Science of Alcohol" by N. G. Smirnov and S. S. Shcherbakov (1913), for instance, and "Rus's Revel Is to Drink: A Village Comedy" by Fyodorovich (Simon Fyodorovich Saburov) (1914).

16. A. R. Kugel', "Zametki," *Teatr i iskusstvo* 40 (October 6, 1913): 797.

17. *Teatr i iskusstvo* 47 (November 20, 1911): 915.

18. Kugel, *Otritsanie teatra* (Petrograd: Teatr i Iskusstvo, 1922), 198–99.

19. "Great success . . . The play is written very simply and very wittily." P. Yu. [P. M. Solyany], "Krivoe Zerkalo," *Teatr i iskusstvo* 47 (November 20, 1911): 900–901.

20. Contemporary reactions include P. Yu. [P. M. Solyany], "Krivoe Zerkalo," and A. Kugel', "Teatralnye zametki," both in *Teatr i iskusstvo* 47 (1911): 900–901, and 912–15, respectively. For later accounts, see Kugel', *Utverzhdenie teatra* (Petrograd: Teatr i Iskusstvo, 1911), 197–98; Evgeny Znosko-Borovsky, *Russky teatr nachala XX veka* (Prague: Plamja, 1925), 330–31; and V. Polyakov, *Tovarishch smekh* (Leningrad: Lenizdat, 1976), 45.

21. L. Evstigneev, *Zhurnal "Satirikon" i poéty-satirikontsy* (Moscow: Nauka, 1968), 375–78.

22. B. F. Geyer, *Van'kina literature: Protsess tvorchestva v 1 d.* (Saint Petersburg, 1916), 2–3.

23. Pyotr Yuzhny, "Krivoe Zerkalo," *Teatr i iskusstvo* 34 (1912): 738.

24. V. Khovin, "Teatral'naya zhizn': Krivoe Zerkalo," *Vokresenaya vechernaya gazeta* 21 (October 14, 1912): 3; Pyor Yuzhny, *Teatr i iskusstvo* 43 (1912): 817; production shots, 826–27.

25. Quoted in A. A. Brill, ed., *The Basic Writings of Sigmund Freud* (New York: Modern Library, 1938), 217.

26. N. N., "Krivoe Zerkalo," *Teatr i iskusstvo* 51 (1914): 969.

27. Kugel', *Utverzhdenie teatra,* 198.

28. The title *Æolian Harps* alluded to Il'ya Surguchev's sub-Chekhovian *Autumnal Violins* (*Osennie skripki*), which had just made a hit at the Moscow Art Theater.

29. For reportage, see N. N....v, "Krivoe Zerkalo," *Teatr i iskusstvo* 47 (1915), 875; *Rech',* 318 (November 15, 1915): 5; *Birzhevye vedomosti* (November 17, 1915): 6; A. Deych, "Vospominaniya minuvskee," *Zvezda* 5 (1966): 176.

30. *Teatr i iskusstvo* 36 (1916): 77; *Den',* 52 (February 24, 1917): 4.

31. Evreinov, *V shkole ostroumiya,* 40–41.

THE EVOLUTION OF THE THEATER
(*Evolyutsiya teatra*)

by Boris Geyer

1910

CAST

Scene 1: *The Bride Mistook*
   Darya Andreevna
   Marya Andreevna
   Povsekaky Aristakharkovich Cranberry
   Perebeinos

Scene 2: *Drink Your Fill, but Mind the Till*
   Semigromov, a merchant
   Poliksena, his wife
   Nikeshka, the shop assistant
   Zavaldaisky, an actor

Scene 3: *Petrov*
   Petrov
   Lidiya Petrovna, his wife
   Sklyanka (Tippler), her father
   Semyonov

Scene 4: *Visages of a Scream*
   The Invisible One, though visible
   He
   Moishe Rodkin, a gherkin vendor
   Rivkele, his wife

Introduction

LECTURER [*entering through the closed curtains. He is wearing evening dress*]: Kind ladies and gentlemen! Never has there been so much talk and argument about the theater as now. The static theater, the one-dimensional theater, the bas-relief theater, the actor's theater, the director's theater . . . Whither are we drifting? What are we drifting for? Is the theater evolving, is the theater in decline? And a thousand other questions, which make our famous critics cudgel their brains. Hearing all this, I wanted to emulate the many examples and deliver a lecture on the evolution of the theater, but, lacking the gift of eloquence, I decided to demonstrate not by words but by deeds whither the theater is drifting, how much progress it has made over the course of a century, how far we have traveled from coarse, primitive, and obscure forms to the depiction of the subtlest experiences of the soul, to the most delicate symbols, perfect clarity, and profundity of thought . . . Kind ladies and gentlemen! In a moment four plays by four of the most celebrated dramatists of the past century will come before you. I will not name the authors—you will guess them for yourselves. Each author marks an epoch in the theater. And here you shall see with your own eyes whither we are drifting and how far, God willing . . . we shall not get. By an odd coincidence, all four plays are written on the same theme, with remarkable depth and originality. A man makes a declaration of love to another man's wife. The husband comes upon them in the course of the declaration. The consequences of this differ in each writer, but this brings into even sharper focus the evolution of the theater. And so, I crave your attention and hope that after this graphic lecture, you will leave here reassured about the future of our beloved art. [*Exits.*]

The Bride Mistook

[MARYA ANDREEVNA *and* DARYA ANDREEVNA *are sitting at a table and laying out a game of solitaire. They are dressed identically.*]

MARYA ANDREEVNA: Ah, the king of club's turned up again . . . It's definitely Chimpanzinkin . . .

DARYA ANDREEVNA: Not Chimpanzinkin at all, but Cardinkin ...

MARYA ANDREEVNA: No, it's not Cardinkin ... Cardinkin is fair-haired ...

DARYA ANDREEVNA: And I say it is Cardinkin ...

MARYA ANDREEVNA: Cardinkin is the ace of diamonds ...

DARYA ANDREEVNA: Oh, what are you talking about ... the ace of diamonds means a convict. God forbid the ace of diamonds.

MARYA ANDREEVNA: You're still a chit of a girl, you don't understand a thing. When I got married ...

DARYA ANDREEVNA [*interrupting*]: You always dreamed about a cranberry. A red frostbitten cranberry ... And you became Mrs. Cranberry. [*Roars with laughter.*]

MARYA ANDREEVNA: At least I didn't stay an old maid like you ...

DARYA ANDREEVNA [*not listening*]: Ah, my heart is at peace ... The king of clubs again ... And the six of hearts ... Cardinkin and a journey ... I will definitely marry him ...

[CRANBERRY *enters in a dressing gown. Fat. Sobakevich* type.*]

CRANBERRY: And whom, my dear, are you pleased to marry?

DARYA ANDREEVNA [*embarrassed*]: I was just ...

CRANBERRY [*sitting on the divan*]: I was sleeping and dreamed that His Excellency summoned me to his presence and presented me with the order of Andrew the Primeval, and on His Excellency himself, on the ribbon of Anna, hung a bagel ... The most amusing mix-up ...

DARYA ANDREEVNA [*laying out a hand of solitaire*]: The king of clubs for the third time ... Ah-ah, ah-ah ...

CRANBERRY [*slapping himself on the forehead*]: Oh yes, I quite forgot ... Today my former coworker is paying us a visit—Perebeinos. And, to be precise, not so much us as you, my dear.

---

* Sobakevich is the ursine, hard-dealing landowner in Gogol's comic epic *Dead Souls*.

DARYA ANDREEVNA [*embarrassed*]: Me?

CRANBERRY: What's the big surprise? When a spinster's eligible, there's no better time for potential grooms to visit her than the present. You have no father, so I have to look after you. He and I have settled it all by ourselves.

DARYA ANDREEVNA: Ah, sister dear . . .

CRANBERRY: He's a good man: he drinks in moderation, works hard; only one problem—he's a bit absent-minded and near-sighted. But that's the effect of youth and inexperience. It will wear off in time.

DARYA ANDREEVNA: But is he dark?

CRANBERRY: How can I put it . . . yellowish-reddish-brownish . . .

MARYA ANDREEVNA: Congratulations . . .

CRANBERRY: Now get along with you, my dear, and rustle up something to eat. A suitor must be welcomed with respect.

MARYA ANDREEVNA: Is he tall?

DARYA ANDREEVNA: Well built?

MARYA ANDREEVNA: Bearded?

DARYA ANDREEVNA: The king of clubs . . .

[*They both cling to* CRANBERRY.]

CRANBERRY [*beating them off*]: Don't be so fussy, my dear. You're not the one getting married.

DARYA ANDREEVNA: What's his name?

CRANBERRY: I told you—Perebeinos.

DARYA ANDREEVNA: What an odd name . . .

CRANBERRY: Eh, my dear . . . What difference does a name make? You'll be living with a man, not a name. Some names turn up that when you hear them it's as if you choked on a fish bone . . . It's true, his nose is just the slightest bit off-color . . . He says it's hereditary. Oh well, you mustn't pay attention to every flaw. Why, my name is Cranberry.

Why it's Cranberry—no one seems to know. On the other hand, we had an official in our office named Jelly. So His Excellency used to summon us by saying, "Bring me the cranberry jelly." [*He guffaws, deafeningly.*]

MARYA ANDREEVNA: Go get ready.

CRANBERRY: And I'll see to the snacks.

[*They both leave.*]

DARYA ANDREEVNA [*alone*]: A suitor . . . How my heart is beating . . . Mrs. Perebeinos . . . What an odd name, to be sure. [*A bell rings off-stage.*] Ah, good heavens, here he is . . . Run quick . . . [*Whirls about the stage.*]

[*A crash behind the door, then the door flies open with a bang and, having tripped on the threshold and almost fallen,* PEREBEINOS *hurtles in. He is wearing a yellow tailcoat. His hair is of a nondescript color. A big, bright red nose.*]

PEREBEINOS: I tripped on the threshold and banged my nose . . . Confounded myopia. Eh, eh, eh, there's somebody there . . . well, sir, let's inquire . . . Eh, eh, eh, ma'am, I have the honor to inquire, is Povsekaky Aristarkhovich at home?

DARYA ANDREEVNA: He is, sir . . . Really, I'm so embarrassed . . . [*She covers her face.*]

PEREBEINOS [*aside*]: For the life of me, I can't see a thing . . . Is it a woman or a pig's snout? [*To* DARYA ANDREEVNA] And whom, if I may be so bold as to ask, have I the honor of addressing?

DARYA ANDREEVNA: I am Povsekaky Aristarkhovich's sister-in-law. I'm really so embarrassed . . .

PEREBEINOS: 'Tis she. The maid to be married. Now I can see it is a woman . . . I must take her by storm . . . [*To her*] Madam, I am unspeakably happy to make the acquaintance of such a splendid creature . . .

DARYA ANDREEVNA: Ah, my goodness . . . really, I'm so embarrassed . . . Please have a seat.

PEREBEINOS [*sitting beside her, she moves aside, he comes closer, sitting on the very edge. Aside*]: I must broach a conversation. [*To her*] It's very hot in summer, wouldn't you agree?

DARYA ANDREEVNA: Yes . . . I mean, no, I mean, yes . . .

PEREBEINOS: And yet, on the other hand, it was cold in winter . . .

DARYA ANDREEVNA: Yes . . .

PEREBEINOS: I think it must be cold in winter because there's so much ice.

DARYA ANDREEVNA [*aside*]: Ah, what a peculiar way to woo.

PEREBEINOS: The rain is always wet . . . [*aside*] I'm steering this conversation very smoothly . . .

DARYA ANDREEVNA: Ah, don't say that, I'm so embarrassed.

PEREBEINOS: For pity's sake . . . But then again: cocks crow very loudly, especially in the morning, ma'am . . .

DARYA ANDREEVNA [*in embarrassment*]: Forgive me . . . I have to . . . Forgive me . . . [*Runs off.*]

PEREBEINOS: What's wrong, she must been bit by a Spanish fly . . . [*Sneezes a few times, looks for a handkerchief and cannot find one.*] Amazing how absent-minded I am. I left my handkerchief in my winter overcoat . . . [*Goes into the hall and, on the way, knocks over a chair and displaces a table.*]

[MARYA ANDREEVNA *enters by another door.*]

MARYA ANDREEVNA: Silly chit of a girl . . . She was far too easily embarrassed . . . Her suitor must be entertained meanwhile. But he's not here . . . He probably stepped out for a second . . . I shall sit and wait. [*Sits in* DARYA ANDREEVNA'*s place.*]

[PEREBEINOS *enters, blowing his nose, and catches on the doorjamb.*]

PEREBEINOS: I must take her by storm. I shall sit beside her and blurt out all at once that I love her. No fortress can withstand that. [*He comes close, not noticing that it is* MARYA *and not* DARYA *is sitting there.*] Madam, I have come to tell you that I adore you . . .

MARYA ANDREEVNA: Wha-at? . . .

PEREBEINOS: I adore you . . . Be happy till death do us part, be my wife . . .

MARYA ANDREEVNA: Excuse me, my good sir, but I *am* married . . .

PEREBEINOS [*interrupting*]: No one wants to be married at first . . . but later they're overjoyed. Let me kiss your splendid cheek. [*Kisses her.*]

[CRANBERRY *enters, and stops dumbfounded.*]

MARYA ANDREEVNA [*leaping up*]: What an imbrog-lio . . .

CRANBERRY: My dear sir . . . I demand satisfaction . . . By what right, devil take you and 'all your kith and kin to the tenth generation, are you kissing my spouse?

PEREBEINOS: I . . . your spouse . . . What sort of joke . . . I was kissing my betrothed.

CRANBERRY: A betrothed who's been married for two years, sir . . . And you're a fine one, my love . . . Very well, you and I shall discuss this later . . .

MARYA ANDREEVNA: Ah, what an imbrog-lio.

CRANBERRY: I know you, you spendthrifts, ink-slingers, confounded wagtails . . . Milksop, puppy, whelp . . .

PEREBEINOS: My dear sir . . . I am a middle-management civil servant, not a whelp . . . what a delusion. [*Stares at* MARYA ANDREEVNA *in astonishment.*] Now I can see for myself that she is someone else . . .

MARYA ANDREEVNA [*weeping*]: Of course it's my fault that he grabbed me and kissed me . . .

PEREBEINOS: Forgive me, my dear sir. Now I do see that the most amusing mistake has occurred . . . In my myopia, I mistook your spouse for her sister, to whom I had already made my declaration.

CRANBERRY [*roaring with laughter, deafeningly*]: Ha, ha, ha . . . So that's what it's all about . . . Darya! . . . Darya! . . . [DARYA ANDREEVNA *enters.*] Here's your fiancé. Bless you, my children . . .

MARYA ANDREEVNA: What an imbrog-lio . . .

DARYA ANDREEVNA: Now I'm burning with shame . . .

[PEREBEINOS *kisses her.*]

CRANBERRY: And now I ask you most humbly, brother-in-law-to-be, to partake of a little fruit brandy and pickled mushrooms and look over the inventory of the dowry.

PEREBEINOS: The most supernatural of all occasions . . .

CRANBERRY: All's well that ends well. Only, in future, my dearest brother-in-law, try to tell your own children from other people's . . .

[*Guffaws deafeningly. Goes to embrace* PEREBEINOS.]

Drink Your Fill, but Mind the Till

[SEMIGROMOV *in a frock coat and bottle boots is preparing for a journey, stacking coins in a piece of newspaper. He is perceptibly drunk.* POLIKSENA, *a kerchief on her head, sits in a corner.*]

SEMIGROMOV: Y'see how much cash there is. Thirty-five thousand rubles and all in bran' new notes. Your folks never dreamed of sech money in all they lives.

POLIKSENA: What we got to do wi' it . . .

SEMIGROMOV: Shaddap, shaddap, when a person's talkin' to ya. You should 'preciate the way I raised you up . . . Uneddicated iggeramus . . .

POLIKSENA [*quietly*]: Brute.

SEMIGROMOV: Call Nikeshka in here. [POLIKSENA *exits.*] I'll drink another little bottle and already I've got Samovalov over a barrel. He's in urgent need o' thirty thousand, he'd sell his own daughter sooner than that forest.

[*Enter* POLIKSENA *and* NIKESHKA.]

NIKESHKA [*bowing*]: Our best to you, sir, with a cherry on top, sir, Prov sir Melentievich, sir . . .

SEMIGROMOV: Listen here . . . I'm going away on business, so you look after the shop while I'm gone. Get me?

NIKESHKA: How, sir, could I not get you, sir, Prov Melentievich, sir. We'll keep things in tiptop shape, sir, without any mess, sir, sort of like, let's say, sir . . .

SEMIGROMOV: Shaddap, shaddap . . . when your boss is talkin' to you . . .

POLIKSENA [*quietly*]: Brute . . .

NIKESHKA: We'll shut up, sir . . .

SEMIGROMOV: Awright . . . See that you do . . . Don't forget to give short weight and keep your thumb on the scales . . . And don't forget to fob off on somebody that counterfeit note that's lyin' in the cash drawer. Some crook palmed it off on me. Well, you lot, we'll have a sitdown before the journey* . . . [*They all sit down and immediately stand up again.*] Goodbye, Poliksena. I'll be back in three days.

POLIKSENA: Goodbye, Prov Melentievich . . .

NIKESHKA: Our best to you, sir, with a lump o' sugar on top, sir . . .

SEMIGROMOV: Shaddap . . . [*Exits, accompanied by* NIKESHKA.]

POLIKSENA [*alone*]: And how can I go on living, poor little orphan that I am, with such a viper. Ah, if only my poor dear mother could see me now . . . And, ah, if only my dear, dear daddy could see me now . . . And if my dear old granny were to catch sight of me . . . [*Weeps.*] And my old and honorable granddad would take it the same way . . . [*Sobs.*] And my great-granny's all but forgotten me . . .

[*Enter* NIKESHKA.]

NIKESHKA: Sweet marmelady, what're you bawlin' about, ma'am? You missin' your lawful husband?

---

* An old Russian custom is to sit down for a while before embarking on a long journey.

POLIKSENA: Ah, Nikeshka, my lot is a bitter one . . . It is that husband. He's a savage beast . . .

NIKESHKA [*suddenly powerfully emotional*]: And what about me, a dear little orphan, ma'am, an honest, noble lad, ma'am, hangin' around and givin' short measure, ma'am . . . And then there's that counterfeit note, ma'am, to palm off, ma'am . . . And that's a deed that could put me, ma'am, in prison, ma'am . . . [*Wipes away tears.*] And my dear old ma, ma'am . . . and my good old pa, ma'am, don't give me a second thought, ma'am . . . Nor does my old granny, ma'am, remember me, ma'am.

POLIKSENA [*howling*]: Lyin' in the damp earth . . .

NIKESHKA: My dear old granddad, ma'am . . . [*Looks at* POLIKSENA.] Poliksena, ma'am, Nikitishna, ma'am . . . I gaze upon you as I would on fruit caramels, ma'am . . . You are young, like a red baby radish, ma'am, tender as a hothouse cucumber, ma'am . . .

POLIKSENA: Ah, go on with you, Nikifor Pankratievich . . .

NIKESHKA: I love you, ma'am, madly, ma'am . . . I want to be yours till they nail down my coffin, if you'll forgive, ma'am, the expression, ma'am, reg'lar true to the core, ma'am . . .

POLIKSENA: Oy, Nikeshka, take pity on my female frailty.

NIKESHKA: My most brilliant, ma'am, boss-lady, ma'am . . . I'll skip off with the boss's valuables, ma'am, I'll drown your beauty in valuables, ma'am. [*Hugs and kisses her.*]

POLIKSENA [*recoiling*]: Nikeshka . . . stop . . . Who are your kith and kin?

NIKESHKA: What's it to you, ma'am?

POLIKSENA: What village do you hail from?

NIKESHKA: Crooked Ditch.

POLIKSENA: I'm from Crooked Ditch too.

NIKESHKA: So what, ma'am?

POLIKSENA: So don't you remember Polka Zabiyaka?

NIKESHKA: A teeny little girl, ma'am . . . My young sister, ma'am . . . I remember, ma'am . . .

POLIKSENA: Nikeshka . . . Why, that's who I am . . . me . . .

NIKESHKA: Well, ma'am, that takes the cake, ma'am . . . Polka, you're the frosting on that cake, ma'am . . . [*Hugs her.*]

[SEMIGROMOV *suddenly enters. Perplexed look.*
Seeing the couple embracing, he stops.]

SEMIGROMOV: Poliksena . . .

POLIKSENA [*flinging herself at him*]: Prov Melentievich, he's my brother . . .

SEMIGROMOV: Shut up . . . Stop . . . Or I'll kill you on the spot . . . [*Grabs his head.*] Lord, what woes . . . I lose thirty-five thousand rubles on the road, I rush home—my wife is kissing another man.

NIKESHKA: Sir, may I, boss, say, sir . . .

SEMIGROMOV: Shut up. I'll kill you . . . Get on your knees . . . Say your prayers . . . Right now I've got to consider what to do first: go after the thirty-five thousand or kill them.

POLIKSENA: Listen, Prov Melen . . .

SEMIGROMOV: Shut up . . . I'll kill you! . . . [*Takes a knife out of the top of his boot.*]

[POLIKSENA *and* NIKESHKA *get on their knees.*]

NIKESHKA: This escapade, sir, is like a novel, sir, by Mister Mayne Reid,* sir . . .

SEMIGROMOV: Get ready . . . [*Swings the knife.*]

[*The door opens, and* ZAVALDAI-ZAVALDAISKY *enters,*
in a top hat and very shabby suit.]

ZAVALDAI: A tableau . . . A jolly party . . . Say, does the merchant Prov Melentievich Semigromov live here?

SEMIGROMOV: You some sort o' burrocrat? You'll do as a witness. And I'll kill you too . . . Git out, you cur . . .

---

* Thomas Mayne Reid (1818–83) was an Irish author of adventure stories. His novels were translated into Russian throughout the 1860s.

ZAVALDAI: An honorable Russian actor is not to be insulted, you counter-jumper . . . Leave off . . . Listen,—are you Semigromov?

SEMIGROMOV: Well, yes . . .

ZAVALDAI: And you've lost some money?

SEMIGROMOV: I . . . Did you, did you . . . find it? . . .

ZAVALDAI: Oh, you progeny of crocodiles and snakes . . . Oh, you insatiable hyenas and sea lions . . . Leopards, bugbears, and ichthyosauri . . . How greedy you are and how pathetic . . .

SEMIGROMOV: Skip the insults and get to the point . . . Talk like that can land you in court . . .

ZAVALDAI: Forgive me, sir. They're from plays by Mister Shakespeare. Passed unconditionally by the dramatic censor as no. 5211. . . Here's your money. I found it. [*Puts the money on the table.*]

[SEMIGROMOV *rushes to the table and feverishly counts it.*]

SEMIGROMOV: Five, ten, twenty, thirty-five . . . Correct . . . My benefactor, my own father . . . Tell me who you are. We've got to pray to God for you forever . . .

ZAVALDAI: Zavaldai-Zavaldaisky, a Russian tragedian. I have acted with Rossi and Salvini and Zacconi.* He says to me in Italian, "Pal o'mine!". . . And I say to him in Russian, "You know it, pal." And we both weep . . . Got it, you graybeard ribbon-clerk? In your presence talent is an unknown profundity, you wouldn't come up to the heels on Mounet-Sully.†

SEMIGROMOV: Dear old pal . . . Benefactor . . . How am I to thank you? Here . . . here . . . [*Fumbles in his pocket.*] Here's five rubles.

ZAVALDAI [*proudly pushing the money aside*]: An honorable Russian actor needs no money. I ask for only one thing. [*Points to* POLIKSENA *and* NIKESHKA.] Forgive them.

---

* Italian tragedians who had toured to Russia included Ernesto Rossi (1827–96), Tommaso Salvini (1829–1915), and Ermete Zacconi (1857–1948).
† Jean-Sully Mounet (1841–1916) was the leading French tragedian of his time.

SEMIGROMOV: To hell with them . . . I'll send Nikeshka to the woodshed and there's an end to it . . . Get up, I forgive you . . .

POLIKSENA: You won't listen. He's my younger brother.

SEMIGROMOV: Brother?

NIKESHKA: That's, sir, what's so all-fired interestin', sir, about the case, sir. Poliksena Nikitishna, sir, was talkin', sir, about the price, sir, of potatoes, sir . . .

SEMIGROMOV: Shut up . . . If that's so, I kiss you both. And now some vodka . . . Vodka's bracing . . .

ZAVALDAI: That's what I love . . . An honorable Russian actor despises money, but vodka . . . Vodka is only a word, but what a profound idea . . .

SEMIGROMOV: Quite right . . . friend Zavaldai-Zavaldaisky.

ZAVALDAI: Let's go, Kit Kitych* . . . but always remember what the great Goethe said: "Drink your fill, but mind the till."

[*They make their exit, embracing.*]

Petrov

The stage is empty for a while. Then LIDIYA PETROVNA *enters. Dressed in black.*

LIDIYA PETROVNA: All last night the old lindens rustled in the garden . . . The old lindens . . . Which have seen so much of tears and sorrow . . . When we moved here, I felt as if we had been lowered into a grave . . . a grave . . . Moscow . . . Oh, if only I could see Moscow again . . . [*Sits, with her head in her hands.*] Moscow . . . Moscows . . . Moscattle . . . †

[SKLYANKA *and* PETROV *enter. The first is somewhat tipsy.*]

---

* A metatheatrical reference: Kit Kitych (Whale Whaleson) is the obtuse domestic tyrant in Ostrovsky's play *Your Spree, My Hangover* (1856).
† In Russian, Lidiya parses Moscow grammatically—Moskva, Moskvy, Moskvu. When Evreinov revived the play in Paris in the 1920s, he changed Moscow to Kremenchug as a duller, funnier-sounding town to long for.

SKLYANKA: Greetings and salutations . . . Carom from the cushion to the center . . .

PETROV: Why do you always say that? You always say that, whether it's relevant or not. What a lot of rubbish . . . [*Sits down wearily.*]

SKLYANKA: Carom from the cushion . . . When my late wife was alive, she said the same thing to me. [*With tears.*] She used to say, "Sklyanka sweetie-pie . . ." [*His voice breaks; he waves his hand in dismissal, cheering up.*] Greetings and salutations . . .

[*He takes the guitar, sits in a corner, quietly plays. Pause.*]

PETROV: Why, whenever twilight falls, do I start to regret the past? A broken life, monotonously gray, stupid, pointless, mindless, monotonous, and incomprehensible.

LIDIYA PETROVNA: All last night the old lindens rustled in the garden . . . but to go to Moscow . . . Moscows . . . Moscattle . . .

[*Pause.* SKLYANKA *plays the guitar.*]

SKLYANKA: Carom from the cushion to the center . . .

[*Sleigh bells outside the window.*]

LIDIYA PETROVNA [*looking out the window*]: Semyonov is here.

PETROV: Semyonov . . . Goodness, how stupid this is, how vulgar, how pointless, how monotonous . . . And why Semyonov, why Petrov . . . Why invariably these bourgeois sleigh bells . . .

[*Enter* SEMYONOV.]

SEMYONOV [*exchanging greetings with them all*]: Greetings, ladies and gentlemen. Greetings, Sklyanka . . . Foo, chilly, I'm tired . . . Rattling twenty-five miles along a freezing road . . .

SKLYANKA: Greetings and salutations . . . Carom off the cushion to the center . . .

LIDIYA PETROVNA: It's been a long time since we've seen you . . .

PETROV: And why do people who meet invariably say "Greetings" and shake hands. What is this vulgarity, monotony, nastiness . . .

SEMYONOV: A hundred thousand years from now people will be different . . . They will not shake hands, but will only raise their hands . . . [*Ardently*] I firmly believe it . . .

LIDIYA PETROVNA: And in Moscow there won't be any winding and muddy streets . . .

SEMYONOV: Humanity will be beautiful and free . . .

PETROV: But until then we shall rot and be all gray, all nasty, all vile, all stupid . . .

LIDIYA PETROVNA [*wringing her hands*]: All last night the old lindens rustled in the garden . . . And they were remembering Moscow . . . old Moscow . . . Moscows . . . Moscattle . . .

SEMYONOV: A thousand years from now people will fly in the air the same way we walk on earth . . .

SKLYANKA: Greetings and salutations . . .

SEMYONOV: What?

SKLYANKA: No, I just . . . Carom off the cushion to the center. Please, let's go on . . .

PETROV: I'm coming to my senses . . . I want to record in sounds all the foulness, all the vileness, all the vulgarity, all the nonentitiness of our lives. [*Exits, clutching his head.*]

LIDIYA PETROVNA: Poor Vanya . . . He's grieving . . . His talented nature is cramped and bored here . . .

SKLYANKA: Carom off the cushion to the center. I shall go too, greetings and salutations.

LIDIYA PETROVNA [*embracing him*]: Only don't drink . . . Dear papa, don't drink . . .

SKLYANKA: I won't . . . I will . . . not . . . [*Exits.*]

[*Pause. In the distance someone is playing a grand piano. The watchman taps on a board.*]

SEMYONOV: Haven't you guessed why I've come here . . .

LIDIYA PETROVNA: You often stopped visiting us . . .

SEMYONOV: Yes, I often stopped visiting you . . .

LIDIYA PETROVNA: Stopped visiting.

SEMYONOV: Visiting.

LIDIYA PETROVNA: Visiting.

SEMYONOV: Ting. [*Pause.*] What good teeth you have.

LIDIYA PETROVNA: When a woman is unattractive, people always say she has beautiful teeth . . . [*Wipes away tears.*]

SEMYONOV: I didn't say that because . . .

LIDIYA PETROVNA: Tell me why all last night the old lindens rustled in the garden? . . . No, that's not it . . .

SEMYONOV: I understand . . .

LIDIYA PETROVNA: What? Stop . . . I know . . .

[*The sound of the piano cuts off.*]

SEMYONOV: You mustn't, you mustn't . . . A hundred thousand years from now none of this will survive, feelings will be so subtle, so pure, so imperceptible . . . There will be no dirty words . . .

LIDIYA PETROVNA: Stop, for heaven's sake, stop . . . I love Vanya . . .

SEMYONOV: You do?

[PETROV *appears in the doorway.*]

LIDIYA PETROVNA: I do . . .

SEMYONOV: A hundred thousand years from . . . [*Falls silent when he sees* PETROV. *He sits down in confusion.*]

PETROV [*slowly walks down to the footlights*]: I have understood it all . . . They were declaring their love to one another . . . I . . . un-der-stood . . . it all.

LIDIYA PETROVNA: All last night the old lindens rustled in the garden . . .

PETROV [*staring fixedly at* SEMYONOV]: I have understood you . . . But I am not angry . . . It's all too stupid, too vile, too low, too nasty . . .

SEMYONOV: I have to go . . . So strange . . . a peasant wench has taken ill . . . Yes . . . I just have to inspect my instruments. [*Exits quickly, in confusion.*]

LIDIYA PETROVNA [*aside*]: My heart is aching . . . Lord, lord, something dreadful, irreparable . . .

PETROV: I keep wondering are we alive or asleep . . . Tell me . . . are you . . . [*in a whisper*] asleep? . . .

[*A gunshot offstage.*]

LIDIYA PETROVNA: Ah . . .

PETROV: What is it?

[*Enter* SKLYANKA *with a guitar.*]

LIDIYA PETROVNA [*running to him*]: What is it? What's happened? Tell me quickly . . .

SKLYANKA [*calmly*]: The cork popped out of a bottle of Bavarian near-beer.

LIDIYA PETROVNA: Really? Thank God, why, I thought . . .

SKLYANKA [*quietly, to* PETROV]: Go quickly, the doctor has shot himself out there . . .

PETROV [*clutching his head*]: Lord, how stupid this is . . . how savage . . . how clumsy, how vile . . .

[*Exits.*]

SKLYANKA [*sitting and playing the guitar*]: Carom off the cushion to the center . . .

LIDIYA PETROVNA: All last night the old lindens rustled in the garden . . . Father, I feel sad, I feel incomprehensibly ill . . . We are dying . . . Gradually, imperceptibly, lifeless, motionless . . .

SKLYANKA: We shall nap . . .

LIDIYA PETROVNA [*sobbing*]: Yes, yes, you have said the right thing, Sklyanka, sweetie . . . We shall nap . . . [*Kneels at his feet and, yawning, lays her head in his lap.*]

[*The watchman taps.*]

We shall nap . . .

SKLYANKA [*yawning, weeps*]: We shall nap, Lida . . .

LIDIYA PETROVNA [*weeping*]: We shall nap . . .

Visages of a Scream

The INVISIBLE *(though visible)* ONE, *in voluminous draperies, with a half-concealed face, is sitting next to a gong, which he strikes. He speaks monotonously and indistinctly.*

THE INVISIBLE ONE: You naked, tailless apes sitting here, your ears flapping, waiting in avid curiosity for bloody spectacles, I speak to you: behold . . . For here before you the conflict of worlds will take place, which, in your unreason, you call the life of a human being and do not understand with your insignificant brains, circling in a spiral up to heaven itself. Speechlessly I shall speak a loud speech. Behold, hearken, and fail to understand. Here before you is the great featureless struggle. [*He strikes the gong.*]

[HE *enters. Dressed in a jacket. Looks like Anathema.**]

HE: Invisible, though visible, one . . . Here I am at your feet, having come hither to seduce Rivkele and show Moishe how weak and insignificant is his life . . . Utter the truth!

[*The* INVISIBLE ONE *keeps silent.*]

---

* Supernatural antagonist of Andreev's 1909 play of that name, a Lucifer figure. The makeup for him in the Moscow Art Theater production was reptilian.

I address my prayer to you: utter the truth!

[*The* INVISIBLE ONE *keeps silent.*]

You keep silent, in your Satanic twisted pride . . . But for the third time in ophidian guise I ask you: utter the truth!

THE INVISIBLE ONE [*striking the gong*]: Twice two is seven.

HE: So shall it be. [*Wriggles away.*]

THE INVISIBLE ONE: Now Rivkele shall enter. Behold, insignificant ones . . . Here the world of temptation will collide with the world of passion. Behold, hearken and fail to understand . . .

[*Enter* RIVKELE. *Simply dressed.*]

HE: Whom seek you?

RIVKELE: I seek Moishe, my husband, who trades in gherkins there where the accursèd city ends and the wretched plain begins.

HE: Why does he trade?

RIVKELE: He says that gherkins contain a worldview. And everyone who buys a gherkin will discover the secrets of existence.

HE: The gherkin is a three-ply misunderstanding.

THE INVISIBLE ONE [*striking the gong*]: The truth . . .

RIVKELE: Haven't you seen Moishe?

HE: He is coming. I knew that an invisible power compels you to come here to seek him. I waited for you to tell you . . .

THE INVISIBLE ONE: The worlds collide.

RIVKELE: You speak strangely.

HE: An insane passion has inflamed my brain. My arms and legs tremble, and I want to possess you, for therein lies the meaning of the pitiful existence of this insignificant globe called Earth.

RIVKELE [*pensively*]: That's how the army clerks write.

THE INVISIBLE ONE [*striking the gong*]: The truth.

HE: Here, by the will of someone measured immeasurable and unparalleled, I want to possess you, Rivkele, wife of Moishe, for a scarlet glow blazes in my brain and splits my brain like a bottomless abyss.

RIVKELE [*falling into his embrace*]: Let it come to pass!

[*Thunder.*]

THE INVISIBLE ONE [*striking the gong*]: The worlds collide. Burning precipices enliven the ill-omened rainbow.

[*Offstage the heavy measured tread of* MOISHE.]

The world of retribution is drawing nigh . . . Behold, hearken and fail to understand.

[MOISHE *enters with gherkins. Typical poor Jew.*]

MOISHE [*to the* INVISIBLE ONE]: Don't you want to buy a gherkin, which provides immortality and comprehension of the incomprehensible?

THE INVISIBLE ONE: Better look farther on.

[MOISHE *withdraws and turns to* HE.]

MOISHE: Don't you want to b . . . [*Puzzled*] Rivkele . . . And my wife in the arms of some . . . goy. Listen here . . .

RIVKELE [*moving away from* HE]: So it had to be . . .

HE: Moishe Rodkin, who trades in cognition of the world and does not know it himself. The great meaning is hidden in this.

THE INVISIBLE ONE [*striking the gong*]: The Jewish question is solved.

MOISHE: Yet forgive yourself, for pity's sake . . . What kind of meaning do you mean—I understand very well . . . A stranger embracing Rivkele—big meaning . . .

HE: Moishe Rodkin . . . Again I say unto you: this predestination is beyond you.

MOISHE [*throwing away his basket; the gherkins are scattered; a loud bang on the gong*]: I won't . . . I'll scream . . .

THE INVISIBLE ONE: It has come to pass . . . He has scattered the secret of wisdom.

HE: He has lost his mind . . . Moishe, you have released the cold stream of serenity into the lacerated blood of my heart.

MOISHE: I can do nothing—I am split in half. Look, I am alone—I lie on the ground, spilt from the basket in a green mass, while I am another . . .

HE [*interrupting*]: Moishe split in half, I say unto you: stop and the miracle will come to pass . . .

THE INVISIBLE ONE: No more miracles in the noneternal ethers . . . There are only magic tricks . . .

[*Gong.*]

HE: Let the magic trick come to pass.

RIVKELE: I entreat, let the magic trick come to pass.

MOISHE: Magic trick? Am I, a poor Jew, supposed to do magic tricks . . . Oh, our pitiful life . . .

Spend all one's time trading in wisdom so that in the last analysis you are still fools. Farewell, my Rivkele . . .

HE: We are waiting . . .

RIVKELE: We are waiting . . .

MOISHE: I can't . . . [*in despair*] Do you understand, gloomy ones, that I cannot . . .

THE INVISIBLE ONE: You won't?

MOISHE: I am leaving for the predestined cone . . .

RIVKELE: Moishe.

MOISHE: Too late . . . [*He runs offstage.*]

[*Thunder.*]

HE: Where did he go? He blinded my cerebral convolutions with a yellow ignorance. You, entering by all entrances and exiting by all exits, tell me: Where did he go?

[*The* INVISIBLE ONE *keeps silence.*]

At your feet with a hissing cry I entreat you: tell me!

[*The* INVISIBLE ONE *keeps silent.*]

HE: With a stony gaze he penetrates the other side . . . Oh, resolve me too . . .

THE INVISIBLE ONE: It cannot be.

HE: Oh, resolve me.

THE INVISIBLE ONE: Entrance from the side is strictly forbidden.

HE: You won't? Then I compel you by the strong black abyss. [*Rushes offstage, but a bright red flame flares up in his path. He falls.*]

[*Thunder.*]

THE INVISIBLE ONE: In an instant the zigzag of eternity flashed before him, and he is no more . . . Worlds have perished . . .

RIVKELE: Oh Lord . . . What a tragedy . . . How pitiful is our life. Wisdom has awakened, and everything has perished . . . [*Falls to her knees and goes out of her mind.*]

[*Red fire.*]

Now they're laughing with red laughter* . . . Louder, ever louder . . . Ha, ha, ha. [*Lies motionless.*]

THE INVISIBLE ONE: She has gone out of her mind . . . It is dreadful for you, naked and tailless apes. So, you have seen how out of a myriad of worlds three came together and, by colliding, were smashed to bits. Do you understand the simple truth of the symbols? And, poor creatures, you shall question each another and grope about in mindless fear, afraid that you have already gone out of your minds. For there is no boundary between reason and madness. So has it been, so shall it be . . . So has it been, so shall it be.

[*Gong.*]

The end. Curtain . . . Curtain . . .

---

* A reference to Andreev's short story *Red Laughter* (1904).

MEMORIES
(*Vospominanija*)

An illustrated novella in six chapters and one act

by Boris Geyer

1911

CHARACTERS

The Reader

Darya Mikhailovna Krynkina, a widow

Neonila Fyodorovna, her daughter

Ivan Ivanovich Spichkin, a young civil servant

Lakeev, a jolly guest ⎫
Tabachinsky, a gloomy guest ⎭ Spichkin's coworkers

Anechka ⎫
Aganochka ⎭ Neonila's girlfriends

Fyoklusha, a domestic

The curtain is closed. On one side stands a table with two lighted candles and a chair. The READER, *an actor without makeup, enters wearing a frock coat and holding a book; he sits and begins to read in the same voice people use to read in their family circle. He remains seated throughout the act.*

READER: "Memories . . . ," a novella. Krynkina, the poor widow of a civil servant, was going out of her mind. It was plain as day that Spichkin was in love with her only daughter, Neonilochka, but can you imagine! He was so shy that he could not even utter the single solitary words "I love you." Krynkina knew her daughter and had no doubt that if he spoke only one word, the deal would be clinched. Neonilochka herself would handle the rest of the words and deeds required of the least little decent marriage proposal. Krynkina put her head together with the maid Fyoklushka; talked to the neighbor-lady on the back stairs, a remarkably clever and sensible woman, who had once predicted the war twenty years before it broke out; and, finally, hit on a last resort. She decided to throw a party. "When he's tipsy," said the clever neighbor who had predicted war, "words easily trip off the tongue. They even skip. You just keep plying him with drink." To the party they invited the cause for the celebration, without his having a clue that a conspiracy was afoot; two girlfriends of the bride-to-be; and two of Spichkin's coworkers. Between tea, with an abundant outpouring of cognac and rum, and supper the proposal was to take place. Everyone arrived on time and, with the exception of Lakeev, the tea drinking had come to an end and the critical moment had arrived, when the door slammed open and Lakeev entered, already "half seas over."

[The curtain parts.]

Chapter 1

A poorly furnished room. At left a sideboard, beside the door to the kitchen. Straight on, the door to the parlor, where they will dance later to the accompaniment of an ariston (a windup musical disk player); on the right, a sofa and armchair. Center stage, a table covered with a tablecloth, with a samovar. Around the table are sitting KRYNKINA, *the bride-to-be,* SPICHKIN, TABACHINSKY, ANECHKA, *and* AGANOCHKA.

   KRYNKINA *is a stout woman of around sixty, still very lively.* NEONILA *is a perky energetic sort. She speaks loudly and doesn't hold back. Very homely.*

Dressed in a gaudy frock. SPICHKIN, *a tow-haired young man wearing eyeglasses, is very awkward and bashful. He is constantly stumbling, dropping and mislaying things.* TABACHINSKY, *tall and thin, wears a tightly buttoned-up black frock coat and a big black necktie. He speaks in a sepulchral voice, and his whole appearance is suggestive of a funeral. The girls are colorless.*

    LAKEEV *is stout, merry, with a red face and an even redder nose.*

LAKEEV [*entering*]: Looky here now . . . My apologies for being a bit late, but . . . 'tis Fate. Hostess, your dainty hand . . . My most abject bow to the enchanting lady. To the budding splendor, like a painting of caramels, my deepest . . . [*To* TABACHINSKY] Greetings, pal. [*To* SPICHKIN] And greetings to you, although we've already met.

KRYNKINA: You're very late, Sysoy Afanasevich, very late indeed.

LAKEEV: *Mill' pahrdawn.* I happened to be at a business dinner, you know how it is . . . Heh-heh . . . What do I see . . . Cognac, a little rum.

KRYNKINA: Please help yourself.

LAKEEV: *Avek playzir.* [*Pours.*]

TABACHINSKY: And here I was thinking you'd been run over by a trolley.

AGANOCHKA: Oh, you always think the worst.

TABACHINSKY: It's easy enough. One false step and it's all over. Or a motorcar . . . *Crack.* Look, no legs or arms. Or it could even be your head's torn off. Just a for-instance.

AGANOCHKA: Ah, how horrible.

NEONILA [*to* SPICHKIN]: You aren't paying me the least bit of attention . . . Please pass the jam.

SPICHKIN [*stammering a bit*]: I . . . I . . . with pleasure . . . happy to, ma'am . . . [*Hands her the jam and in doing so knocks over his glass.*]

NEONILA: Look what you've done.

SPICHKIN [*embarrassed*]: For you, ma'am.

NEONILA: Have some cognac.

SPICHKIN: Hm, I . . . 'm not used to it, ma'am.

NEONILA: What kind of a man are you, then?

SPICHKIN: The or-di-na-ry kind, ma'am.

KRYNKINA: Now then, dear guests, before the appetizers, don't you want to do a little dancing? The young folks might enjoy it.

LAKEEV [*rapidly pouring himself a shot*]: Because I was late, I can have a double. And dancing *avek play-zir* . . . Kick up one heel and the other will follow.

TABACHINSKY: A heel's a heel, so long as you don't break your leg. A friend of mine was dancing, dancing, and all of a sudden slipped, fell, and now he's a cripple for life.

AGANOCHKA: Ah, how awful.

LAKEEV: Rubbish, don't listen to him. Me and you'll dance the mazurka. Ah . . . [*Drinks.*]

AGANOCHKA: Let's go then.

ANECHKA: Thank you, Darya Mikhailovna.

[*They all thank her.*]

KRYNKINA: Don't mention it. And for your company.

[LAKEEV *downs another shot and goes into the next room with everybody else.* KRYNKINA, NEONILA, *and* SPICHKIN, *held back by* NEONILA, *remain.*]

LAKEEV [*singing in the doorway*]:

> The *pas d'Espagne*'s my delight
> So take your places quick,
> I sure could dance it every night,
> And that's no lie or trick.

Not bad. A poem of my own . . . Made it up just now . . . My, my, my . . .

NEONILA [*to* SPICHKIN]: Wait a minute, Ivan Ivanovich. Please help me with the entertaining.

SPICHKIN: I-I-ma'am . . . I'm at your service. Whatever you say.

NEONILA: Then put the glasses on the tray. Mama dear, we'll clear up here. You prepare the appetizers.

KRYNKINA: All right, my darling girl, my little angel . . . I'm off, I'm off . . . [*Exits.*]

[*In the next room a hurdy-gurdy is playing and* LAKEEV's *stamping and shouting can be heard.*]

NEONILA: Make it snappy, Ivan Ivanovich. One, two, three.

SPICHKIN: R-right away. O-one, two, three. [*Drops a glass and breaks it.*]

NEONILA: Oh, watch what you're about.

SPICHKIN: There, you see. It's always like that. I've got no luck in life.

NEONILA: Never mind, never mind, that's all right . . . Fyoklusha . . . Oof, I'm so tired. [*Runs to the sofa.* FYOKLUSHA *enters.*] Clear away the dishes.

FYOKLUSHA: Right away. [*Takes the tray and exits.*]

NEONILA: Sit beside me, Ivan Ivanovich. Tell me what you do, tell me your life story.

SPICHKIN [*timidly sitting down*]: I-I-ma'am . . . Nothing, ma'am . . . I eat, I drink, ma'am . . . I write at the office . . .

NEONILA: What do you write?

SPICHKIN: Copies, ma'am.

NEONILA: Is it interesting?

SPICHKIN: Very much so, ma'am. Only when you make a blot, it's a nuisance, ma'am.

NEONILA: Why is it a nuisance?

SPICHKIN: You have to copy it out again, ma'am.

NEONILA: And what do you do at home?

SPICHKIN: I-I-ma'am . . . [*embarrassed*] I dream, ma'am . . .

NEONILA: You dream! Ah, how interesting. And what do you dream about?

SPICHKIN: Hee-hee, I'm ashamed, ma'am.

NEONILA: Is that so? So you dream about things you can't say out loud.

SPICHKIN: Hee-hee . . . no, ma'am, that's not why . . . Hee-hee . . . About love, ma'am, and other sublime matters, ma'am.

NEONILA: You're in love?

SPICHKIN [*something goes down the wrong way and he coughs in a squeaky voice*]: K-khee . . . Sort of, ma'am.

NEONILA: Who with? Tell me, if it's not a secret.

SPICHKIN: I don't dare, ma'am . . . K-khee . . .

NEONILA: You promised not to tell anyone.

SPICHKIN: N-no, ma'am . . . that's not why.

NEONILA: Well. Then tell me. [SPICHKIN *wipes sweat off his brow.*] Well . . .

SPICHKIN: I'm af-afraid to.

NEONILA: How come?

SPICHKIN: You'll get angry.

NEONILA: Me . . . Why should I? . . . No, I won't get angry.

SPICHKIN: You will get angry.

NEONILA: How you do go on. Well, let me guess: Is it Aganochka?

SPICHKIN: N-no.

NEONILA: Is it Anechka?

SPICHKIN: N-no.

NEONILA: Could it be me?

SPICHKIN: Yes.

NEONILA [*hiding her face*]: Ah!

SPICHKIN: I . . . I, ma'am . . . that's how it is, ma'am . . . it's not ser . . .

NEONILA [*quickly*]: No, no, no . . . All right, I consent.

SPICHKIN: Neonila Fedulovna.

NEONILA: I love you too. Kiss my hand. [*Extends her hand.* SPICHKIN *timidly kisses it.*] Lord save us and have mercy on us! What bliss . . . [*He kisses her hand a few times, more boldly.* LAKEEV *enters.*] Ah . . . [*Jumps up and runs out.*]

LAKEEV [*standing bewildered*]: Vanka! No, what a rascal! The orphan of Kazan', Astrakhan, and Ryazan'. Kissing a hand.

SPICHKIN: I-I, sir . . . don't think . . . I'm serious.

LAKEEV: I can see you're serious. I came in here, thought I'd have another little shot, and all the while he . . .

SPICHKIN: For heaven's sake . . . We're engaged . . . Don't say a word, please, while . . .

LAKEEV: What the hell do I care . . . After all, I can see you're simply drunk.

SPICHKIN: Me? N-no. You are a bit.

LAKEEV [*pouring a cognac and drinks it*]: Me? . . . That's a lie.

[*From the next room,* AGANOCHKA's *voice: "Sysoy Afanasevich."*]

LAKEEV: I fly. Ladies *gran-ron, le* men *a rosh* . . . [*Does a stunt with his leg and runs out.*]

SPICHKIN: How . . . what . . .

[*Enter* KRYNKINA *and* NEONILA.]

KRYNKINA [*in tears*]: Neonila darling just told me . . . De . . . What next . . . Harmony and love. I'm an old woman and won't stand in your way. Although she is my only child. Be a son to me, Ivan Ivanovich.

SPICHKIN: Ma . . .

NEONILA: Kiss mama dear's hand. [SPICHKIN *cautiously kisses it.*]

KRYNKINA: Well, be happy, my dear children. I'll deal with the guests after supper. Don't be mean to her, Vanechka.

SPICHKIN: Mam-moth . . .

[FYOKLUSHA *enters with a tray and lays out appetizers.*]

KRYNKINA: Now let's call in the young folks. [*Goes into the next room.*]

SPICHKIN: I'm burning up, ma'am.

NEONILA: With love?

SPICHKIN: N-no-ma'am. With shame, ma'am.

NEONILA: But you do love me?

SPICHKIN: Oh-oh!

KRYNKINA [*in the doorway*]: Please, dear guests, come and partake of what God has given us.

LAKEEV [*entering arm in arm with* AGANOCHKA]: Snacks. *Avek playzir.* There's a little vodka, a little herring. You know:

> A herring snack is my delight,
> With vodka on the side.
> I'm bound to have more than one bite.
> And toast as down it slides.

How about that. I just came up with it. My, my, my . . .

AGANOCHKA: So you're a creative type!

LAKEEV: I can knock off a poem. All sorts of 'em . . .

TABACHINSKY [*entering with* ANECHKA]: Some sort of smell keeps swirling around in my nose.

ANECHKA [*flirtatiously*]: Could it be my perfume?

TABACHINSKY: Something of that nature . . . It smells like a corpse, that's it.

ANECHKA: Ah, what's wrong with you?

TABACHINSKY: When a corpse starts to stink, there's something unusual, so they dig it up.

ANECHKA: Ah, how horrid! I won't sleep a wink all night.

KRYNKINA: Please sit down, dear guests. What God has sent, don't stand on ceremony.

LAKEEV [*pouring a drink*]: I know.

KRYNKINA: What do you know?

LAKEEV: To the health of the secret.

SPICHKIN: K-khe.

ANECHKA: Pass me the cheese.

TABACHINSKY: I don't recommend it. Worms make their homes in cheese. Tiny little white worms. You take a bite, and suddenly . . .

ANECHKA: Ah, what's wrong with you . . . No, no cheese. Pass me the herring . . .

TABACHINSKY: But toxic fish is also very harmful. Death in agonizing torments comes within a few hours. Once . . .

ANECHKA: Stop it, stop it . . . I'm not listening to you.

TABACHINSKY [*offended*]: As you please. It's for your own good.

LAKEEV: I am a merry fellow. I can do all sorts of improvisations. Like right now:

> You're a darling, like a rose,
> As a coquette you may pose.
> I shall kiss above your hand . . .

AGANOCHKA: You're being indecent . . . what's wrong with you?

LAKEEV: Poetic license. [*Pours a drink.*] To the health of the secret! Hee-hee.

AGANOCHKA: What's this about a secret?

LAKEEV: A state secret, but I know it.

NEONILA [*looking lovingly at* SPICHKIN]: Ivan Ivanovich.

SPICHKIN: I-I ma'am. What would you like?

NEONILA [*insinuatingly*]: Pass me a sardine.

SPICHKIN: My great pleasure, ma'am.

KRYNKINA: Now then, my dear guests. Because all of you here are close friends of Neonilochka and Ivan Ivanovich, I wanted to tell you the joyful news.

NEONILA: Ah, mama.

SPICHKIN: Embarrassing, ma'am.

KRYNKINA: My innocent children, there's no need to be embarrassed. It's an everyday occurrence. Ivan Ivanovich has proposed to Neonilochka and is to marry her.

AGANOCHKA: Ah, ah!

ANECHKA: Neonilochka, my little angel.

LAKEEV: Vanka, hur-rah! Ah you, a regular Apollo Belvedere!

TABACHINSKY: Congratulations! Although I can't approve. Marriage is in many respects dangerous. Childbirth often ends in the woman's death. Then again the husband may turn out to be a drunkard or a gambler . . .

NEONILA: Ivan Ivanovich is neither a drunkard nor a gambler.

TABACHINSKY: He may turn out to be. People often change.

EVERYONE: Congratulations, congratulations. [*Exchange of kisses.*]

LAKEEV: Vanka! Speech! Give us a speech of thanks for our expressions of enthusiastic sympathy.

EVERYONE: Speech . . . Speech . . .

SPICHKIN [*fidgeting in his chair*]: I-I, lays and gents . . . How, lays and gents . . . I can't, lays and gents, I . . . thank you, lays and gents . . . So happy, lays and gents . . . Mama, your hand, ma'am . . .

KRYNKINA: Very good. Heartfelt.

SPICHKIN: Really, ma'am.

[LAKEEV *pours out drinks for everyone and gets up. By now he is dead drunk and staggering.*]

LAKEEV: Per-permit me to have a word now . . . A poet-ti-cal speech . . . The f-feast is in full swing . . . The hall is radiant and everyone is making merry around the two innocent youngsters . . . Infus . . . I mean, indivi-du-als, whose *amour* has reached out to the heart itself . . . Soon we shall all behold their marriage bed . . .

AGANOCHKA: Ah, what's he saying? . . .

LAKEEV: Which . . . Of course, we shall behold it. And these two innocent subjects will be . . .

TABACHINSKY: Sysoy Afanasevich! There are young ladies present.

LAKEEV: What of it? Very nice too. Don't interrupt me, please . . . Yes . . . The hall is radiant. And I can already see her beneath the sumptuous canopy, in the almost flickering light of little lamps and incense burners. Her wonderful body like a feast . . . mo-ther-of-pearl, shows through the silken air . . .

NEONILA: Ah, good heavens! [*Covers her face with hands.*]

TABACHINSKY: You're drunk. Shut up.

LAKEEV: You're the drunk. I am a poet. I wish to make a speech . . . Her beautiful body . . .

NEONILA: Don't let him do it, Ivan Ivanovich.

SPICHKIN: I-I, sir . . . I won't let you, sir . . . What is all this, sir?

LAKEEV: Don't interrupt for no good reason, if you don't understand . . . Through the incense burners flashes the mother-of-pearl satin . . .

TABACHINSKY [*taking his arm to lead him away*]: There, you see. I told you alcohol leads to madness . . .

LAKEEV: Let me be. The muse is speaking through my lips . . . A mother-of-pearl body . . . [*Exits.*]

KRYNKINA: You can't leave it like this, Ivan Ivanovich . . . In defamation and confusion. Tomorrow you'll have it out with him.

SPICHKIN: I, mama, ma'am . . . I will, ma'am . . . with him tomorrow . . . I'll let him have it tomorrow.

NEONILA: Only no duel.

SPICHKIN: Why should . . . ma'am. I'll . . . with sharp words, ma'am.

KRYNKINA: Well, to the health of the bride and groom!

EVERYONE [*clinking glasses*]: Happiness . . . prosperity . . . Love . . .

NEONILA: Thank you, thank you. [*Exchanges kisses with her girlfriends.*]

[TABACHINSKY *enters.*]

TABACHINSKY: I sent him packing. He's gone. Just as I always said, "A groaning board leads to a yawning grave."

AGANOCHKA: Ah, how horrid!

TABACHINSKY: All gaiety ends in grief. One unseen blow, and sorrow is already at our backs.

NEONILA: Stop it. What's the matter?

SPICHKIN: I, ma'am . . . I, ma'am . . .

AGANOCHKA: Anyway, it's time we left. It's late already.

ANECHKA: It's time, it's time. [*They say their thank-yous and goodbyes.*]

AGANOCHKA: See you soon, Darya Mikhailovna.

ANECHKA: Thank you, Darya Mikhailovna.

AGANOCHKA: Good night, Neonilochka.

ANECHKA: Darling Neonilochka.

TABACHINSKY: I'll escort you. Otherwise these days you might meet with a ruffian at every corner. Just like that! He'd thump you on the head and then who knows what he might do . . .

AGANOCHKA: Ah, don't frighten us.

TABACHINSKY: Worse things happen. Things like Jack the Ripper, disemboweling . . .

ANECHKA: I'm scared . . . Goodbye, Neonila Fyodorovna. [*Goes to the exit.*]

SPICHKIN: Me too, ma'am . . . Goodbye, ma'am, Neonila Fyodorovna.

KRYNKINA: Well, kiss me goodbye, that's the way.

SPICHKIN [*as if kissing a red-hot stove plate*]: Ugh.

NEONILA: You'll come tomorrow?

SPICHKIN: I'll come, ma'am . . . It's a promise, ma'am. [*Turns around, bumps into the cupboard and, having banged the doorjamb, exits.*]

KRYNKINA: Well, now you're a bride.

NEONILA [*bitterly*]: A bride! Nothing but an old overshoe. Well, just you wait . . . As soon as the wedding's over . . . Then I'll show him!

[*Curtain.*]

READER: Reaching the street, Spichkin took his leave of those loitering and walked, nay, more correctly, flew homeward on unfamiliar wings of bliss. Everything that had happened seemed to him a kind of enchanted vision, a fairy tale. "It has all become clear," he thought, with a sigh. "I was afraid I'd be a coward, I wouldn't make up my mind, but it was all so easy." And he approvingly patted himself on the shoulder. Soon his steps slowed and he began to call to mind that wonderful day in his life, the party . . . All the individuals appeared to him in a remarkably endearing light. There still sounded in his ears a kind of gentle music. And the proposal, the congratulations, and the farewell kiss kindled his imagination with a wonderful clarity. Spichkin even stopped under a lamppost and, blissfully smiling into space, began to go over all the details again. "Yes, she dropped a hint to me over tea. How did it go? Neonilochka said so sweetly, 'Pass me the jam.'"

[*The curtain parts.*]

Chapter 2

Everyone is drinking tea. SPICHKIN *is speaking passionately and uninhibitedly.* NEONILA *is very beautiful and very shy. The rest look the same as before. Everything is suffused with a pale pink light.*

NEONILA [*timidly*]: Ivan Ivanovich. Please pass me the jam.

SPICHKIN: Pardon me, I never thought to pass you the jam, probably because I am bedazzled.

NEONILA: What by?

SPICHKIN: Your beauty.

NEONILA: Ah, how can you . . . Would you like some?

SPICHKIN: What is jam to me?! Jam is powerless to rid my life of sorrow.

NEONILA: Are you so unhappy?

TABACHINSKY [*butting in*]: Everyone's unhappy in this transitory world.

SPICHKIN: But I am the unhappiest of the unhappiest.

KRYNKINA: Now then, wouldn't you like to dance, dear guests?

SPICHKIN [*to* NEONILA]: I claim you for all the dances.

NEONILA: Oh, I don't know . . . How can you have all of them? . . . [SPICHKIN *gives her his hand. A backstage orchestra plays a waltz. During the proposal a string quartet will play a serenade.*]

LAKEEV: And I take you. [*Takes* AGANOCHKA *and dances.*]

SPICHKIN: You are as light as a fairy.

NEONILA: You're making me blush.

SPICHKIN: O, I see the first flush of dawn in your crimson cheeks.

TABACHINSKY [*dancing with* ANECHKA]: It's very easy to break a leg when dancing. *Bam*, and it's all over. But I'll risk it.

ANECHKA: Ah, how horrid!

[*Everyone disappears into the next room, dancing, except* SPICHKIN *and* NEONILA.]

NEONILA [*stopping, out of breath*]: Get me some water.

SPICHKIN: Right away . . . [*Gives her a glass.* NEONILA *sits on the sofa.*] Neonila Fyodorovna.

NEONILA: What is it?

SPICHKIN [*sighing*]: You are a goddess.

NEONILA: Ivan Ivanovich.

SPICHKIN [*sitting beside her*]: I know I am a nonentity and a rain-soaked worm compared to you—the dazzling sun of a blazing July day.

NEONILA: Ah!

SPICHKIN: But I am in pain, I grieve, I burn. I already . . .

NEONILA: What are you trying to say?

SPICHKIN [*to himself*]: How shy and how sweet. Neophelia Fyodorovna, do you really see nothing, suspect nothing?

NEONILA: I . . . no.

SPICHKIN: I am in love.

NEONILA: You . . . with whom?

SPICHKIN: Guess. [*To himself*] If her lips were to speak the truth!

NEONILA: Anechka?

SPICHKIN: Listen to me! I am afloat in an ocean of passions and a sea of love. At work I mix everything up and get a dressing-down from His Excellency. At home I run from corner to corner like a hound, beaten with a cudgel. I am overwhelmed by passions, and all that is left to me is one of three things: to achieve my heart's desire, or stab myself with a sharply honed knife, or drown myself in the chilly waters of Markizov pond.

NEONILA: How terrible!

SPICHKIN: That's how it is, ma'am. I am on the verge of an abyss of ruin, and if the hand of my beloved does not stop me, I shall plunge into it like an insignificant microbe.

NEONILA: What can I do?

SPICHKIN: You hold in your hands the fate of my existence. Either send it to the fiery furnace with a curse or take me to the park of paradise.

NEONILA: Ah!

SPICHKIN [*on his knees*]: I love you. I am athirst. Speak . . . speak quickly, for I suffocate from impatience and horror awaiting the critical moment.

NEONILA: I . . . I love you too.

SPICHKIN: My angel! What happiness! What indescribable bliss . . . What enchantment. To call you my own . . . you, Neonilonchik. [*Kisses her hand impulsively.*]

[LAKEEV *enters.*]

NEONILA: Ah! [*Runs away.*]

LAKEEV: Hee-hee. You little Cupids . . .

SPICHKIN [*sorrowfully*]: Were you spying on us? You dared, you contemptible insect, to eavesdrop on us. [*Marches on him.*]

LAKEEV [*frightened*]: For pity's sake, pal. What's come over you . . . gone out of your mind or something? It was an accident, I wanted a little cognac . . .

SPICHKIN: A little cognac . . . Yes, yes, now I'm acting like a madman . . . like King Lear in *Faust*. [*Lays a hand on* LAKEEV's *shoulder.*]

I know you're my friend. So rejoice with me. You're the first to know: she is my betrothed!

LAKEEV: Hurrah! Let's have a drink.

SPICHKIN: That's quite decent of you.

LAKEEV: So it seems to you. Hur-rah!

SPICHKIN: How splendid of you! I love you!

[*The dancers enter.*]

VOICES: What's going on? What now?

[*Enter* NEONILA *and* KRYNKINA.]

KRYNKINA: I must announce the pleasant news. Ivan Ivanovich is getting married to Neonila.

VOICES: Congratulations! How nice! Such happiness!

AGANOCHKA: What a lucky girl you are, Neonila! How I envy you! He's so clever, so good-looking.

NEONILA: Yes.

SPICHKIN [*self-satisfied*]: Hm . . .

ANECHKA: Now you'll get stuck-up, Neonilochka. Such a fiancé!

KRYNKINA: Yes, I can say it without boasting, God has sent me a peach of a son-in-law.

SPICHKIN: For heaven's sake, you are extolling my virtues.

TABACHINSKY: Congratulations, dear Ivan Ivanovich. Heartfelt congratulations. And even though I have my own views on marriage, such a fine young man, such a hero of legend as you are, God grant you won't die prematurely, and you won't take to drink all of a sudden . . . May your children not be born dead either. That happens sometimes . . . You are our eagle.

LAKEEV: The tears are flowing like a fountain from emotion. Vanya, you're my friend, say something. After all, you're quite the orator!

SPICHKIN: Yes, my dear friend! I actually did want to say a few words . . . Yes, I always knew that you were irreplaceable friends of mine, but at this moment I am particularly moved to see your unfeigned and vociferous joy. You know I am modest by nature . . .

TABACHINSKY: Liar, you're a falcon!

SPICHKIN: But I know, I know how to spin the thread of life. Here stands my lawful fiancée, who will be my companion throughout my life, and there stands my soon-to-be kin, my beloved new mama until the gravestone with its epitaph do us part. Please love and care for them as you would me. Heartfelt thanks to you, and to you, mama dear—a low bow with a respectful hand kiss, to betoken a sacred pledge of a son's steadfast and unchanging loyalty and affection. [*He kisses* KRYNKINA's *hand.*]

KRYNKINA: My Vanechka.

LAKEEV: He talks the way he writes. What oratorical talent. You could make a good living defending gangsters.

NEONILA [*quietly*]: How nice you looked when you were speaking!

SPICHKIN: Oh, you!

KRYNKINA: I kindly ask you to come to the table. We must celebrate.

[*Everyone takes a glass of wine.* LAKEEV *is dead drunk.*]

LAKEEV: How about me? I too would like . . . a speech . . . Poetry with the moon, mosquitoes, frogs, and nightingales in the aspen wood.

TABACHINSKY: You're drunk. Shut up.

LAKEEV: Hold on . . . Now what was I . . . Yes . . . On a moonlit night the hall was aglow. The incense burners were gleaming and she . . . [*Points a finger at* NEONILA.] She was superb without any kind of covering . . . I mean . . . sort of, that is, like Eve before the Fall . . .

NEONILA: Goodness, what's all this? . . .

KRYNKINA: A disgrace!

SPICHKIN: Lakeev, do be still . . . Forgive me, ladies and gentlemen, he's my good, kind, old friend, but today his nerves have got a bit unstuck from joy. [*Fondly to* LAKEEV.] Go home, my good old Lakeev. We'll all be going right away. [LAKEEV *goes submissively, escorted by* TABACHINSKY.]

LAKEEV: You don't understand at all. Eve, before the expulsion from the Garden, is a symbol . . . You understand, you Dutch grouch, a symbol. [*Exits.*]

NEONILA [*to* SPICHKIN]: You were magnificent.

SPICHKIN: You have to know how to understand human frailty. Oh, my life! . . .

TABACHINSKY: Ah, Aganochka, we're going.

ANECHKA: It's time, it's time. [*They say goodbye.*]

KRYNKINA: Goodbye. Goodbye, sonny boy, dearie. [*Kisses him.*]

SPICHKIN: So until tomorrow . . . A whole long night.

NEONILA: When will you come?

SPICHKIN: Tomorrow, when a faint light has barely begun to dawn, I shall stand beneath your window to be the first to meet your smile with an airborne kiss.

NEONILA: I love you. [SPICHKIN *kisses her ardently.*] Ah!

SPICHKIN: Goodbye, my Ophelia! [*Exits quickly.*]

READER: Spichkin might still have gone on dreaming a long while, standing under the streetlight, excited by his boldness and resourcefulness that evening, if he hadn't been moved on by a real-life constable, who had been observing him for a long time with great suspicion. "You should go home, mister," he remarked kindly but firmly. "Home's the best place. Especially when you've had a drop to drink." Spichkin, startled and alarmed, moved farther along and, babbling through pale lips, "I-I-sir . . . , never mind, sir . . . I-I, sir . . . right this minute, sir," ran away like a coward at a minor jog-trot, not daring to look back. Meanwhile his fiancée, still seated on the settee, was also recalling what had just occurred. Her face only rarely expressed satisfaction; actually, it was malicious, remembering Spichkin's ineptitude and indecisiveness. "How much that cost me, how much it cost," she whispered, once more turning over in her mind all she had gone through in those few hours.

[*The curtain parts.*]

Chapter 3

Scenery and characters as in the second chapter. Everyone thanks KRYNKINA *for the tea and goes into the next room to dance. Dim lighting.*

LAKEEV [*in the doorway*]: I'm starting my story. Fine. My poem. I made it up just now. For heaven's sake.

NEONILA [*aside*]: Well, thank God, they finally stirred their stumps. Now I've got to buck up this blockhead. [*Tenderly*] Ivan Ivanovich, wait a bit. Help me with the entertaining.

SPICHKIN: I-I, ma'am . . . ye-yes, ma'am . . .

NEONILA [*to herself*]: And he can't make a peep. [*To* SPICHKIN] Here, the glasses have to go on the tray. [*To* KRYNKINA *quietly*] Make yourself scarce, mama, take a turn in there, for heaven's sake. [*Aloud*] We'll clear up in here, mama dear.

KRYNKINA: All right, my little angel . . . I'm going . . . [*Exits.*]

[*A hurdy-gurdy plays dolefully.*]

NEONILA [*to herself*]: Don't be a fool. Take charge, make an effort. [*To* SPICHKIN] Quick now, Ivan Ivanovich. One, two, three.

SPICHKIN: One. [*Breaks a glass.*]

NEONILA [*to herself*]: Oh, the idiot! A brand-new glass . . . Butterfingers! [*To* SPICHKIN] Never mind, never mind . . . [*Quickly cleans it up.*] All done. [*To herself*] Now the moment of truth. [*Sits on the settee.*]

SPICHKIN [*stands at a distance*]: I-I, ma'am . . .

NEONILA [*to herself*]: And why's he standing there like a sign post?! No consideration whatsoever. [*To* SPICHKIN] Ivan Ivanovich, come sit beside me. Tell me what it is you do.

SPICHKIN [*sits timidly*]: I—I, ma'am . . . nothing, ma'am.

NEONILA [*to herself*]: Have to pull it out of him . . . [*To* SPICHKIN] What do you mean, nothing?

SPICHKIN: I write, ma'am . . . copies, ma'am . . .

NEONILA: And is it interesting?

SPICHKIN: Very, ma'am . . .

NEONILA [*to herself*]: Good lord, what a nitwit. If he didn't have a paying job, I think I'd kill him rather than marry him. [*To* SPICHKIN] And what do you do at home?

SPICHKIN: I sleep, ma'am . . . and . . . I dream, ma'am . . .

NEONILA: Well, I think we've got on the right road. I won't waste time . . . [*To* SPICHKIN]

You dream? Ah, that's very interesting. What do you dream about?

SPICHKIN: Heh-heh . . . embarrassed, ma'am.

NEONILA: For pity's sake, he won't say any more. What rotten luck! [*To* SPICHKIN] So that's it. You dream about things you're ashamed to say out loud.

SPICHKIN: N-no . . . on account of, ma'am . . . Heh . . . love, ma'am.

NEONILA [*to herself*]: Thank God, he spat it out. [*To* SPICHKIN] You're in love?

SPICHKIN [*choking up and coughing*]: K-khee, k-khee . . .

NEONILA [*to herself*]: Now he's choking, if you please. This is agony. [*To* SPICHKIN] Well?

SPICHKIN: Sort of, ma'am.

NEONILA: Who with?

SPICHKIN: I don't dare, ma'am. K-kheh.

NEONILA [*to herself*]: It'll take six months to drag it out of him. [*To* SPICHKIN] You've promised not to tell it to anybody?

SPICHKIN: N-no, ma'am . . .

NEONILA: Well then, tell me! [SPICHKIN *mops sweat from his brow.*] Wild horses couldn't drag it out of him. [*To* SPICHKIN] Well?

SPICHKIN: I'm af-afraid.

NEONILA [*to herself*]: I can't stand it. Honest to God, I haven't got the strength. [*To* SPICHKIN] Why are you afraid?

SPICHKIN: You'll get angry.

NEONILA: No, I won't. Well, let me say it: with Anechka?

SPICHKIN: N-no, ma'am.

NEONILA [*to herself*]: I should think not. [*To* SPICHKIN] Aganochka?

SPICHKIN: N-no.

NEONILA [*to herself*]: Now the decisive blow. Will this idiot break down or not? [*To* SPICHKIN] Could it be me?

SPICHKIN: Yes, ma'am.

NEONILA [*covers her face with hands*]: Ah! [*To herself*] He finally came to the point . . . Oof!

SPICHKIN: I-I-ma'am . . . didn't m . . .

NEONILA [*quickly*]: No, no, no . . . All right, I consent. [*To herself*] Almost figured it out, the bastard.

SPICHKIN: Neonila Fyodorovna.

NEONILA: I love you too. [*To herself*] Well, what more is there to do. At least he should have the sense to kiss me. I can't do it myself . . . [*To* SPICHKIN] Kiss my hand. [SPICHKIN *kisses it.* LAKEEV *appears in the doorway.*]

NEONILA [*jumping up*]: Ah! [*Goes to the doorway, to herself.*] This works out all right. Most successful. At least there's a witness . . . Mama dear. [KRYNKINA *enters.* LAKEEV, *splaying his hands to show he's help-less, lies low.*] Mama dear, Ivan Ivanovich proposed to me.

KRYNKINA: What . . . I'm so glad . . . love and harmony. Don't fool an old woman like me . . . After all, she's my one and only, be a son to me, Ivan Ivanovich.

SPICHKIN: Ma-ma.

NEONILA [*quietly*]: Yes, for heaven's sake, don't draw it out, mama. [*To* SPICHKIN] Kiss mama's hand. [SPICHKIN *kisses it.*]

SPICHKIN: Ma-ma.

[FYOKLUSHA *enters and lays out snacks.* KRYNKINA *goes to summon the guests.*]

SPICHKIN: I'm on fire, ma'am.

NEONILA [*to herself*]: Oh, the idiot!

KRYNKINA [*in the doorway*]: Please, dear guests, what God has provided.

[*They all enter and take seats.*]

LAKEEV: *Avek playzir.* Let's have a drink.

NEONILA [*quietly*]: Mama dear, tell them quickly or else he'll change his mind.

TABACHINSKY: It smells of corpses, that's all there is to it.

NEONILA [*to herself*]: What's wrong with mama? Good grief, she isn't talking. What a fool. I'll have to light a fire under her. [*Looks tenderly at* SPICHKIN.] Ivan Ivanovich.

SPICHKIN: I-I, ma'am . . . What can I do for you?

NEONILA [*to herself*]: You might at least squeeze my hand accidentally, you blockhead. But no. [*To* SPICHKIN, *angrily*] Pass me a sardine.

SPICHKIN: Divine, ma'am.

NEONILA [*to herself*] So this is when he gets the hint.

KRYNKINA: So, my dear guests. Because we are all friends here, I would like to tell you some joyful tidings . . .

NEONILA: Ah, mama! [*To herself*] Finally!

SPICHKIN: How awkward.

NEONILA [*to herself*]: And so is he.

KRYNKINA: Ivan Ivanovich proposed to Neonilochka and is going to marry her.

[*Congratulations and kisses all round.*]

LAKEEV: Vanka, speech.

NEONILA [*to herself*]: What the . . . ! He's going to talk . . .

SPICHKIN: I-I, sir . . . I can't, sir . . . thank you, sir . . .

LAKEEV: Hur-rah! . . . So I'll speak instead . . . What's to be said, the bride is a sight for sore eyes . . . a picture of beauty. Word of honor. She should be in a resplendent hall on a luxurious conjugal couch . . .

TABACHINSKY: Lakeev, be careful . . . there are young ladies here . . .

LAKEEV: So what! And her . . . as to her body . . . white as ivory, visible through her nightg . . .

NEONILA: Ah, how embarrassing.

TABACHINSKY: Lakeev, keep it clean! [*Grabs a hold of him and leads him away.*]

LAKEEV: What's wrong . . . Please. I'm giving a speech . . . You get out.

TABACHINSKY: Shut up! [*They exit.*]

NEONILA [*to herself*]: That's a fellow who knows how to talk. I really do have a white body. But where could he have seen it?

KRYNKINA: You can't possibly stay after that, Ivan Ivanovich.

SPICHKIN: I-I, ma'am . . . ma-mama, ma'am . . . tomorrow.

NEONILA [*to herself*]: There you go again. [*To* SPICHKIN, *sarcastically*] Only, for heaven's sake, no duels.

SPICHKIN: No, ma'am . . . I really . . . on my word, ma'am.

NEONILA [*to herself*]: If you do, then make it pistols.

AGANOCHKA: Well, it's time we went. Tabachinsky is already putting on his coat.

ANECHKA: See you soon, Darya Mikhailovna.

NEONILA [*to herself*]: Thank God, they're leaving at last. [*To* SPICHKIN] You'll come tomorrow?

SPICHKIN: I'll be here, ma'am.

NEONILA [*expectantly*]: Well?

SPICHKIN: What, ma'am?

NEONILA: O Lord!

KRYNKINA: Kiss her goodbye.

SPICHKIN [*kisses*]: Ugh!

NEONILA [*surreptitiously wipes her lips*]: And even his kisses . . . Phooey. [*Everyone leaves.* NEONILA *drops on to the sofa.*] God, I'm worn out, totally worn out. Why couldn't he be like Lakeev or something?!

[*Curtain.*]

READER: The following day Lakeev awoke late with a pounding head-ache and therefore decided not to go to the office. He drank three shots of vodka in a row, the fog of the previous night seemed to disperse, and at first hazily, and then gradually more and more clearly everything that had happened took shape in his memory. "Hmm," thought Lakeev, "Yesterday, in truth, I did have a nip or two, but on the other hand the rest was all right. Tabachinsky was dead drunk. And I made them quite a speech. In their enthusiasm they gave me an ovation." And, after downing another shot, he smoked a cigarette and, lounging in an armchair, gave himself over to memories of last night's triumph.

[*The curtain parts.*]

Chapter 4

When the curtains part everyone is dancing a maxixe (an up-to-date Brazilian rumba) to orchestral accompaniment. The lights are up full. The costumes are gaudy and the movements and characters drunken. Very noisy. LAKEEV *enters, stone sober, as he remains to the end of the scene.*

LAKEEV: Excuse me for . . . [*Stops in bewilderment.*] What deviltry is this?

SHOUTS: Lakeev, Lakeev's here. Hurrah!

TABACHINSKY: Lakeyunchik, my sepulchral friend, give us a kiss. [*Embraces him.*]

LAKEEV: Hold on, first let me say hello to my hostess.

TABACHINSKY: What rubbish—say hello! We'd be better off having a drink for the torchbearers.

LAKEEV: Go to hell! [*Pulls away and goes to* KRYNKINA *and kisses her hand*]: Good evening, much-esteemed Darya Mikhailovna. Forgive me for being la . . .

KRYNKINA: What a pity! The night's still young. We've been making merry. Have a drink and dance.

TABACHINSKY [*running up*]: You know, I broke both my legs but never mind, I glued them together with gum arabic, and they move smooth as silk.

LAKEEV: What nonsense.

SPICHKIN: Yes, you're quite drunk, Lakeev.

LAKEEV: And so are you. [*To himself*] That girl over there seems sober. Suppose I make advances to her. [*Walks over to* AGANOCHKA.] Would you care to dance?

AGANOCHKA: Do you know the cancan? Why . . . it goes like this. [*Lifts her leg.*]

LAKEEV: Hee-hee, do tell. Still, you seem in good spirits.

AGANOCHKA: Drunk, you mean? Don't be silly. You should recite something . . . Yes . . . you write poetry, so give us something, improvise.

LAKEEV: I . . . On the spot . . . That's very easy for me.

> Oh, you are beautiful in dance,
> How your eyes so charming gleam,
> But woe, in vain is my fond trance,
> For you star in another's dream.

AGANOCHKA: Ah, you are so po-et-i-cal. So maybe, you would . . . Ah . . . [*Almost embraces him.*]

[*Everyone leaves off dancing and sits wherever they wind up.* SPICHKIN *and* NEONILA *on the settee.*]

SPICHKIN: I love you, Neonila.

LAKEEV [*to himself*]: Right in front of everyone. That's clever.

ANECHKA [*to* TABACHINSKY]: Do you like how my perfume smells?

TABACHINSKY [*sniffing*]: Wonderful. Like a corpse.

LAKEEV: Hee, hee, hee. What fun!

KRYNKINA: Why are you sitting like that? Have a drink, something to eat. [*To* LAKEEV] Would you like to cakewalk with me?

LAKEEV: N-no . . . I prefer cognac.

TABACHINSKY: Don't drink. You're drunk enough already.

LAKEEV: Talking to me? Look at yourself in the mirror.

TABACHINSKY: I swear on a putrid skull that this is poison. [*Drinks.*] *Plop*, man's gone, liquor's gone.

ANECHKA: How horrid!

LAKEEV: It's nonsense.

NEONILA: Ivan Ivanovich!

SPICHKIN: Huh?

NEONILA: Pass me a sardine.

SPICHKIN: Goddess.

LAKEEV: Ha, ha, ha. They don't understand one another. I'd better improvise another poem for you rather than talk rot.

SPICHKIN: Leave off!

AGANOCHKA: Please do, please do.

LAKEEV:

> The table groans with meat and drink,
> And laughter round it loud does ring.
> The merry guests their glasses clink,
> And love to me you sweetly sing.

How about it? Is that all right?

SPICHKIN: Rubbish with French dressing. And you, Lakeev, are making fun . . . Please . . . you understand, don't talk, nobody talk . . . poetry.

LAKEEV: It's beyond him.

AGANOCHKA: Wonderful . . . I'm on your side.

LAKEEV: This one's for you.

> Wait beneath the crimson rose,
> That is most fragrant at the dawn,
> The passion rising in my heart . . .

AGANOCHKA: Ah, don't you dare say another word. Or else I'll fall in love . . .

LAKEEV: With whom? [SPICHKIN *kisses* NEONILA.]

TABACHINSKY: What's going on? . . . Excuse me, but I must protest . . . there are young ladies present.

LAKEEV: So what?

TABACHINSKY: So what!? You're drunk, and she's kissing . . .

KRYNKINA: As if it matters. If it comes to that, I'll tell you a funny joke. Ivan Ivanovich is marrying Neonila.

EVERYONE: Hee, hee, hee. Honest?

SPICHKIN: For heaven's sake, I consent.

LAKEEV: Some joke. Vanka, make a speech!

SPICHKIN: Ee-we . . . anyway . . . what I . . . get out . . .

LAKEEV: I see you are incapable. Let me speak. . . .

TABACHINSKY: Give it up. We'd be better off going home. Or else it'll be dark on the drunken streets. Quite dangerous.

AGANOCHKA: Me too.

ANECHKA: And me.

NEONILA: Hold on, let Lakeev make a speech. He talks . . .

SPICHKIN: Like a gramophone.

LAKEEV: If you wish it, I'm ready.

KRYNKINA: Absolutely.

TABACHINSKY: It's darker when it's hot out, so if a ghost . . .

LAKEEV: What I wanted to say . . .

EVERYONE: By all means. Please . . . Go to it!

LAKEEV: Ladies and gentlemen! Today is a celebration. The hall gleams, the tables groan with food and drink, and we see him and her in our midst. The bride and groom, two angels of heavenly beauty.

ANECHKA: Bravo!

LAKEEV: And in a little while, we shall see them as husband and wife. I believe that their whole life will be the same feasting and joy as today. Their hall will gleam the same way, the incense burners will emit sweet fragrances, and on the luxurious marriage couch . . .

TABACHINSKY: Young persons . . .

LAKEEV: And on the luxurious marriage couch, beneath the magnificent canopy she will glow with the same bewitching beauty, she—Neonila Fyodorovna.

SPICHKIN: Bull's-eye! Quite correct . . .

LAKEEV: Wait, don't interrupt. Day will follow day. The roses on your couch will not fade, and her beauty . . .

EVERYONE: Bravo . . . bravo . . .

LAKEEV: Hold on . . . The incense burners will emit sweet fragrances, and on the couch, glittering almost like mother-of-pearl . . .

TABACHINSKY: Sysoy Afanasevich . . . Poet . . .

ANECHKA: How exciting!

KRYNKINA: The way he speaks . . .

[TABACHINSKY *locks* LAKEEV *in an embrace.*]

LAKEEV: Wait, let me finish.

TABACHINSKY: Friend! Let me kiss you . . .

LAKEEV [*shouting*]: And on the couch, like a goddess of beauty . . .

SPICHKIN: Hoist him up! Hoist him in our arms . . . Such talent . . .

LAKEEV: Hold on, you're all drunk. And I'm a poet . . . Her beautiful body . . . [LAKEEV *is lifted up and carried around.*]

EVERYONE: Hur-rah! . . . Raise him on high . . .

[*Curtain.*]

READER: When questioned by his coworkers as to how he had spent the previous night, Tabachinsky at first maintained a stubborn silence, but then, at last, he related how he had been at Krynkina's party, how they had announced Spichkin's engagement and how they had passed the time. He even got carried away and provided all the details of what had gone on, often even imitating the guests . . . "At first they drank tea and cognac," he related. "Lakeev, of course, was late and got there drunk. He came in with his everlasting free-and-easy manner." And Tabachinsky described how Lakeev made his entrance.

[*The curtain parts.*]

Chapter 5

The room is barely lit by three candles. Everyone is dressed in dark colors. They are speaking quietly, in sepulchral voices. The music is playing something like a funeral march. Everyone is sitting at the tea table. LAKEEV *enters.*

LAKEEV [*gloomily*]: Forgive me . . . I am late . . .

KRYNKINA [*the same*]: What's to be done . . . Man proposes and God disposes . . .

LAKEEV: Good evening.

KRYNKINA: Good evening . . . [*He exchanges greetings with the other guests. Pause.*]

TABACHINSKY: I thought you'd been run over by a trolley.

LAKEEV: Not this time.

TABACHINSKY: Or been killed by accident. It happens these days.

ANECHKA: Of course.

KRYNKINA: Have some cognac.

LAKEEV: Thank you. What more is there to do in life than drink? [*Sighs deeply and drinks.*]

KRYNKINA: Perhaps you'll do a little dancing before the appetizers.

AGANOCHKA: Could be.

LAKEEV: We'll kick up our heels.

TABACHINSKY: So long as you don't break your legs. That's what life is like! Ech!

ANECHKA: Sometimes they don't get broken.

TABACHINSKY: It happens.

LAKEEV [*mournfully sings*]:

> I love dancing, for it numbs
> My sorrow and my grief,
> For there's no guessing what next comes
> And death will bring relief.

A poem of my own. I made it up in my sorrow.

[*Everyone circles around mechanically to the doleful sounds.* FYOKLUSHA *lays out the appetizers.*]

KRYNKINA: Please have a bite to eat. It's humble fare, what can you do.

SPICHKIN [*sighing*]: Everyone's poor, ma'am . . . The only comfort's to be found in the grave, ma'am.

KRYNKINA: Ye-es.

ANECHKA [*to* TABACHINSKY]: How do you like my perfume?

TABACHINSKY: Very nice. Smells of roadkill.

ANECHKA: My favorite. [*Sits down.*] Please pass me the cheese.

TABACHINSKY: It's curdled milk with worms.

ANECHKA: Foo . . . No, I'd rather have herring . . .

TABACHINSKY: Poison in the shape of fish.

ANECHKA: Ah, then the sausage . . .

TABACHINSKY: I can pass it, but I must warn you it's often made of dead pug-dogs.

ANECHKA [*gloomily*]: There's nothing for a person to eat.

TABACHINSKY: Nothing.

NEONILA: Nothing.

SPICHKIN: No-thing . . . [*Pause.*]

LAKEEV [*pouring a drink*]: Sooner or later we're all going to die. Might as well be drunk.

KRYNKINA [*wiping away tears and springing up*]: Dear guest, I would like to inform you that Ivan Ivanovich will be marrying Neonilochka.

EVERYONE [*very faintly*]: Congratulations, congratulations.

TABACHINSKY: Congratulations, although I can't approve. A wife can change, you can take to drink, look, badly brought-up children become criminals and are exiled to a prison colony. Then there's diseases . . . death.

KRYNKINA: Yes . . . yes.

LAKEEV: What can you do! Such is human fate. Vanka, make a speech.

SPICHKIN: What's there to say? . . . [*Depressed.*] Thank you.

LAKEEV: We've got to have a speech. Then I'll do the talking. [*Rises. Speaks in a monotone.*] The lamps had almost flickered out. The feast was in full swing, and everyone there was making merry . . . around the two lovers. But soon we shall see them in a different light. Beneath the canopy of a hearse, led by four horses . . .

AGANOCHKA: Ah, what is this . . .

LAKEEV: What . . . Of course, we shall see. And with shovels at the graveyard . . .

TABACHINSKY: Sysoy Afanasevich, stop it, what are you on about . . .

LAKEEV: Please leave me alone, you're drunk.

TABACHINSKY: You're the one who's drunk.

LAKEEV: And her body, once lustrous as mother-of-pearl, is now . . .

NEONILA [*gloomily*]: Take him away.

KRYNKINA: He's insulting us.

SPICHKIN: I-I, sir . . . protest, sir . . .

[TABACHINSKY *forces* LAKEEV *out.*]

LAKEEV [*gloomily and quietly urgent*]: Wait . . . you don't understand . . . her mother-of-pearl body . . . [TABACHINSKY *slams the door on him.*]

TABACHINSKY: I always said—he'll end up a suicide. That's the lot of a drunkard.

KRYNKINA: Yes! A drunkard.

NEONILA [*quietly*]: A drunkard. [*Pause.*]

ANECHKA: We're going home. It's time.

TABACHINSKY: I'll escort you. Nowadays a dark crime lurks behind every corner. They'll cut open your belly, like Jack the Ripper.

AGANOCHKA: You will protect us.

ANECHKA: We trust in you.

TABACHINSKY: Let's hope for the best. Sometimes things have a happy ending.

SPICHKIN: Goodbye. [*Wipes away tears.*]

NEONILA: Goodbye.

KRYNKINA: Goodbye.

AGANOCHKA: Thanks for the pleasant evening.

ANECHKA: We had a good time and that's enough.

[*Everyone leaves.*]

TABACHINSKY: Go quietly down the stairs. I've heard that on the third floor, it turns out, a general's wife is dying.

KRYNKINA: Come back if you're still alive.

TABACHINSKY: Yes, death is watching at every corner.

SPICHKIN: Cor-ner, sir . . .

[*Curtain.*]

READER: Fifteen years have gone by. Krynkina now has nine grandchildren of various ages. And often, sitting at the stocking she is endlessly knitting, she would recall the evening of the proposal of Spichkin and Neonila and her own innocent cleverness. Much had already been erased from her memory. Some episodes had completely disappeared; some were still clear but not exactly sharp. She quite forgot Tabachinsky, but the look of others appeared dimly before her as in a fog. And beyond the click-clack of the knitting needles there rose before her, like flashes of magnesium powder, pictures of the past.

[*The curtain parts.*]

Chapter 6

Furnishings as in chapter 1. The stage is behind a gauze. There sit KRYN-
KINA, *much aged;* NEONILA, *almost a young girl;* SPICHKIN, *with a big beard;* AGANOCHKA *and* ANECHKA, *as they looked before; and* LAKEEV, *a grizzled drunk. When the curtain parts, absolute darkness. Light gradually seeps in. Along with it only a few separate phrases of the vague whispering of the characters can be heard. Sometimes the light suddenly bursts out brightly, and simultaneously the speech of the characters becomes lively and distinct, then in a moment it completely dies out, and silence ensues. A hurdy-gurdy plays an old waltz by Lanner.*

LAKEEV: I'll have another drink. [*Vague whisper.*]

KRYNKINA: Wouldn't you like to dance, dear guests? The young folk like that kind of thing . . .

LAKEEV: Let's have a dance, while we're still on our feet. And we'll drink to keep up our courage.

[*Music.*]

LAKEEV: I'll have another drink to the health of the dear departed.

SPICHKIN: A herring.

NEONILA: Jam.

[*Blackout.*]

SPICHKIN: I love to make merry by the grave of life.

KRYNKINA: Love me, have pity, for you I . . .

[*Blackout.*]

LAKEEV: Hooray. I'll have another drink. Out . . .

Blackout.

KRYNKINA: Have a bite.

AGANOCHKA: We're going.

EVERYONE: Thank you, thank you, Darya Mikhailovna.

KRYNKINA: Don't mention it.

LAKEEV [*to* KRYNKINA]: Shall you and I trip the light fantastic?

KRYNKINA: It'd be a sin for an old lady.

[*They all leave, except* NEONILA *and* SPICHKIN. *Bright light.*]

NEONILA: Mama dear, Ivan Ivanovich proposed to me.

SPICHKIN [*on his knees*]: I beseech your consent.

KRYNKINA [*to herself*]: It's a slander. What's wrong with you, Ivan Ivanovich? You're still young.

SPICHKIN: I'm praying, ma'am.

KRYNKINA: What the . . . I consent. Bless you, my children . . . [SPICHKIN *embraces her.*]

[*Semi-darkness. Everyone enters.*]

LAKEEV: I love it when the dear departed lurch out at you at night.

AGANOCHKA: Ah, what's wrong with you.

[*Everyone sits down.*]

KRYNKINA: Dead drunk. [*Sudden blackout, then bright light.*] And I wanted to tell you, my dear guests, the joyous news: Ivan Ivanovich is marrying Neonilochka.

EVERYONE: Congratulations, congratulations.

LAKEEV: Hur-rah! [*Embraces* KRYNKINA *and whirls through the room with her.*]

KRYNKINA: What are you doing, what are you doing, dearie.

[*The light dims a bit.*]

LAKEEV [*beginning ardently and rapidly, but ending almost inaudibly*]: I'd like to make a speech. About the marriage bed and Jack the Ripper. Good lord . . . We are feasting here, and soon we'll see the newlyweds on the couch of passion. What are the gleaming halls compared to the bride's body . . . satin skin is not to be feared nor fish poisoning . . . but . . . cheese . . .

SPICHKIN [*in a whisper*]: Out!

[*Blackout. Pause. Light. Onstage only* NEONILA *and* KRYNKINA.]

KRYNKINA: Didn't I manage it all cleverly?

NEONILA: Ah, mama dear, he's a freak and thick as a post.

KRYNKINA: He's a civil servant, and you were an old maid.

NEONILA: I still might change my mind.

[*The light grows brighter.*]

KRYNKINA: They forgot the most important thing. These stockings are all darned. What a disgrace for the bridegroom . . .

[*Blackout*]

[*Curtain.*]

READER: And so year after year the recollections were washed away and finally disappeared entirely from memory. A few more lines and you may close the book, reader. But when one night you're unable to sleep and remember this gloomy story, don't believe that you read it. Perhaps you saw it, you may have heard it, who knows, you may even have experienced it yourself. And if you were to convince yourself that you hadn't read it but had seen it, still don't believe that it was all the way you thought it was, for no one knows just what reality is, and deceptive impressions and memories mean nothing in this world.

[*He closes the book, gets up, and exits.*]

THE WATER OF LIFE
(*Voda zhizni*)*

A play in four decanters

(Monodrama)

by Boris Geyer

1911

CHARACTERS

Ivan Vasilevich, a civil servant

Pyotr Ivanovich, a civil servant

Bartender

Assistant Bartender

Afanasy, a waiter

Karl Karlovich, a sausage maker

Bogdan Andreevich, his friend

Guitarkin, a retired civil servant

Klavishkin, a bank employee

Manya the Polecat ⎫
                          ⎬ young ladies
Black Sasha ⎭

Doorman

Restaurant customers, waiters

---

* *Voda zhizni* is both a translation of the French *eau de vie* (brandy) and a frequent element in Russian fairy tales, capable of bringing the dead to life.

A small, rather neat little restaurant, the kind found amid fruit shops. Left, the full-length bar, stocked with a battery of bottles of various sizes. In front of the bar, an equally long table, fully stocked with snacks and dishes. At right and on the backcloth, small square windows, the kind found in a basement. Through the window can be seen the feet of pedestrians on the pavement. In the right corner, a landing leading to a door.

Near the door behind a low enclosure is a cloakroom, beside which stands the doorman. A drunken look on his face, he wears a green jacket and a peaked cap with braid. Behind the bar stands the bartender, stout and red-faced, remarkably imposing and self-assured. He is wearing a jacket without an apron. Amiable to the customers, strict with the waiters. His assistant, young, pale, fussy, with a sparse goatee, also wears a jacket. Amid the ranks of little tables covered with white tablecloths, the waiters in jackets and white aprons move like sleepwalkers. In the left corner a gramophone is wheezing away. At the little tables the customers are eating and drinking, with frequent change of clientele. Some of them are in overcoats, some without. Customers are constantly coming in from the street, drinking and snacking, standing at the bar; they pay up and go. Up against the footlights, two unoccupied tables, where IVAN VASILEVICH *and* PYOTR IVANOVICH *will sit after they come in. Electric lighting, but dim. On the walls, advertisements for brands of vodka. Near the bar stands* AFANASY, *listening to the bartender. At a table far upstage sits* GUITARKIN *behind a bottle of beer, a bit farther off* KARL KARLOVICH. *The former is badly dressed; his hands tremble, and when he speaks, it's very pedantically. The latter is stout, impassive, and speaks ponderously, like chopping wood.*

1st Decanter

BARTENDER: Since you're new here, I got to tell you this business takes lots of finesse . . . Know what I mean?

AFANASY: I know, Leksandr Vanych! . . .

BARTENDER: What do you mean, you know? You know nothing yet. This ain't no cruddy little tavern where you're working, this is a restaurant. Know what I mean? . . .

AFANASY: Right you are, sir. A restaurant, in short, of the first class, sir.

BARTENDER: Yes, and you better behave nice and quiet here. Besides what I was saying about breaking dishes just now, you also gotta keep an eye on the customers' morials. The regulars you can always size up at a glance. Know what I mean?

AFANASY: I got it, sir.

BARTENDER: If it's someone you don't know, you gotta make sure he don't go past a certain point. Let him get tanked up to that point and then stop . . . But I mean without causing no trouble.

KARL KARLOVICH: Hey, Aleksandr Ivanovich, how much are crayfish today?

BARTENDER: Expensive, Karl Karlovich, sir. Very expensive, sir. Thirty kopeks apiece . . . Would you like an assortment?

KARL KARLOVICH: No, I'm fine . . . [Drinks his beer.]

BARTENDER [to AFANASY]: Now then. In figuring out how drunk each one is, there's a sign. At first they'll talk about their family, the kids and relatives, so you can give 'em whatever they order. Next they start talking about the office and complain about their bosses—no problem, go ahead. Next they start arguing politics and swapping dirty jokes: that's when you start to ease off. Give 'em what they ask for, but take it slow. Know what I mean?

AFANASY: I get the point.

BARTENDER: Now, when they start talking about God and philosophy and all that—that's when you stop. One more shot and that's it. And if you follow my rules, you'll never have no trouble . . . Know what I mean?

AFANASY: Thanks a lot for the tip, sir . . . But can I ask you, Leksandr Vanych, is it the same for everybody?

BARTENDER: Everybody . . . In my time, if I may say so, I've seen more drunks than stars in the sky. And they're all painted the same colors.

AFANASY: Then can I ask another question, What if somebody's alone and doesn't open his mouth? Then what?

BARTENDER: Dope. You start a conversation, and figure out what mood he's in.

AFANASY: I got it down pat, sir.

GUITARKIN [*banging on the table*]: Waiter!

AFANASY: Right away, sir. [*Goes to* GUITARKIN.]

GUITARKIN: Another bottle.

AFANASY: Same as before?

GUITARKIN: Of course.

[AFANASY *takes the empty bottle and goes for a fresh one. In the doorway appear* IVAN VASILEVICH *and* PYOTR IVANOVICH. IVAN VASILEVICH *is dragging* PYOTR IVANOVICH *by the arm. The latter comes reluctantly. Both are about thirty-five or forty.* IVAN VASILEVICH *is wearing a double-breasted civil-service uniform tunic, visible underneath his unbuttoned overcoat.*]

IVAN VASILEVICH: Cut it out, Pyotr Ivanovich, stop messing about. We'll have one little drink and move on.

PYOTR IVANOVICH: I don't care to. I'm fed up with being dragged into this joint day after day.

IVAN VASILEVICH: What choice do you have, it's the only one around. And you can get a bite with your drink, a half-sour pickle . . . Ah . . . Come on, Aleksandr Ivanovich, just one shot.

PYOTR IVANOVICH: Just one shot. [*Walks over to the bar and pretentiously shakes the bartender's hand.*]

IVAN VASILEVICH: Well sir, Aleksandr Ivanovich, just one shot.

BARTENDER: Anything else, sir?

IVAN VASILEVICH: On its own.

ASSISTANT BARTENDER [*pouring a drink*]: There's hot salmon pie, sir, fresh sturgeon, button mushrooms in sour cream.

PYOTR IVANOVICH: No, something quick. Maybe pickled gherkins.

ASSISTANT BARTENDER: Half-sours?

PYOTR IVANOVICH: Of course . . . Your health. [*Clinks glasses with* IVAN VASILEVICH *and drinks.*]

IVAN VASILEVICH: Have another.

PYOTR IVANOVICH: That's enough already.

IVAN VASILEVICH: I talked him into it. [*Emoting.*] "Long time he set his face against it, But at the last he walked right in . . ." Fire up another glass.

PYOTR IVANOVICH: You're a sonuvabitch.

IVAN VASILEVICH: I know you.

BARTENDER: Please sir, the coldest we've got. [*Both drink.*]

IVAN VASILEVICH [*choking*]: K-kha. That's the stuff.

PYOTR IVANOVICH [*glancing over the bar*]: You know, that fish doesn't look half bad. Suppose we have just a little piece . . .

IVAN VASILEVICH: Actually, I wouldn't say no. Come on, take a seat, why not?

PYOTR IVANOVICH: We-we-ll. It's got to be quick. Won't take off my coat.

IVAN VASILEVICH: Suit yourself. [*Sits in front.*] Waiter!

AFANASY [*coming over*]: What's your pleasure?

IVAN VASILEVICH: A decanter of vodka and two pieces of sturgeon, and make it quick . . . we're in a hurry.

PYOTR IVANOVICH: Step on it, pal, I've got loads of work today . . . Still, I'll sit a minute . . . Not so bad.

IVAN VASILEVICH: So don't stop with sturgeon, Lord God Almighty. In five minutes we'll be three sheets to the wind.

KARL KARLOVICH [*to the bartender*]: Hogs have gone way up in price. Nothing but bad news. So many hogs on this earth and they keep going higher and higher.

GUITARKIN: There really are a lot of hogs, mostly ones who walk on two legs.

BARTENDER [*bursting into obsequious laughter*]: That's right, sir. The real ones are in the minority.

KARL KARLOVICH: There are all kinds, but only one kind costs a lot, while the other goes cheap.

PYOTR IVANOVICH: I really can't understand how those people can talk such rubbish and enjoy it.

IVAN VASILEVICH: I'll say. They sit all day, yackety yak. And always the same old thing.

PYOTR IVANOVICH: How about that sturgeon? They're taking their sweet time!

IVAN VASILEVICH [*banging on the table*]: Waiter!

AFANASY [*running over*]: What's your pleasure?

IVAN VASILEVICH: Where's that sturgeon?

AFANASY: Right this minute, sir. They're putting on the garnish, sir.

PYOTR IVANOVICH: They're putting on the garnish. We haven't got time, pal. Get a move on.

[KLAVISHKIN *enters, removes his coat, and sits next to* GUITARKIN. *He's a young man with a curled mustache, dressed elegantly but with the taste of a shop assistant.*]

KLAVISHKIN [*rapping on the table, the waiter comes over*]: The menu.

PYOTR IVANOVICH: But if you look closely, it's a regular dump. Dirty, dark . . .

IVAN VASILEVICH: And a dreary sort of clientele.

PYOTR IVANOVICH: That gramophone is getting on my nerves. How tacky . . . Aleksandr Ivanovich? . . .

BARTENDER: What's your pleasure?

PYOTR IVANOVICH: Could you possibly turn off the gramophone? It's ghastly stuff!

BARTENDER: Some people think highly of it.

PYOTR IVANOVICH: What's to think highly of . . . It's cacophony.

BARTENDER [to his ASSISTANT]: Turn off the machine. [ASSISTANT does so.]

KLAVISHKIN: Pot-a-fesh soup,* roast beef, and ice cream. A decanter of vodka and a hunk of pressed caviar. [The waiter goes off.]

GUITARKIN: Having a meal, are you?

KLAVISHKIN: Yes, after work.

GUITARKIN: I've seen you here a few times, but we never had a chance to get acquainted.

KLAVISHKIN: Delighted—Klavishkin.

GUITARKIN: Guitarkin. So you have a job, do you?

KLAVISHKIN: At the Savings and Loan. A heavy workload, so there's no time to run home.

GUITARKIN: I'm retired, on a pension now, so I make it stretch at this little restaurant.

PYOTR IVANOVICH: When is that sturgeon going to get here at last! Waiter . . .

AFANASY [with the vodka and sturgeon]: Here you are, sir. [Sets them down.]

PYOTR IVANOVICH: You're been long enough about it, pal. Didn't I tell you we got no time?

IVAN VASILEVICH [pouring]: Well, sir, to your health.

---

* Klavishkin means *pot-au-feu,* the traditional French stew.

PYOTR IVANOVICH: And yours. Eh. Dinner's waiting at home. Not bad, Ivan Vasilevich.

IVAN VASILEVICH: How are things? Your wife is pure gold.

PYOTR IVANOVICH: Gold, is she now?

IVAN VASILEVICH: An angel. Honest to God, you don't realize how lucky you are. Fyokla Vasilevna, the one who married Oranzhereikin, always used to say, "That Pyotr Ivanovich is a lucky man."

PYOTR IVANOVICH: Fyokla Vasilevna is a natural-born fool.

IVAN VASILEVICH: She is a fool, all right, but she spoke the truth.

PYOTR IVANOVICH: She's got three false teeth and one of them whistles. She's so stingy with her pennies, the dentist did it to her on purpose . . . "Whistle, sweetheart, so you'll remember me." Honestly, it's not a tooth he gave her, but a police whistle.

IVAN VASILEVICH: Is that so?

PYOTR IVANOVICH: Word of honor.

IVAN VASILEVICH: Well, I've got a mother-in-law. Now there's a brute . . .

PYOTR IVANOVICH: Nags all the time?

IVAN VASILEVICH: Lord God Almighty. She torments the life out of my wife, you see. And she's around my neck too, never fear. She won't go live with her other daughter.

PYOTR IVANOVICH: She doesn't sound like a particularly lovable individual.

IVAN VASILEVICH: She's annoyed I didn't marry the other one. What the hell is she to me . . . She's lopsided—clearly there's something wrong somewhere, and she's got a crooked leg.

PYOTR IVANOVICH: Did you see it for yourself?

IVAN VASILEVICH: How could I! My wife told me about it. As soon as she told me, I made the sign of the cross. I'm thinking, God help me, what if I'd married her, I would have been stuck with that . . .

PYOTR IVANOVICH: And he claims he has no luck. Well, isn't your uncle on his deathbed?

IVAN VASILEVICH: Doesn't look like it. A swindler for ninety years, and he keeps squawking, "I'll live another ninety, and you can sit and lick yourself." Besides, the whole inheritance is barely worth three thousand . . . Pfoo . . .

PYOTR IVANOVICH: The world is full of bastards.

IVAN VASILEVICH: I'll say. And you know, that Nikolay Fyodorovich rides over to his place, starts calling him uncle dear. And he's an uncle to him like a teakettle is an aunt to me.

PYOTR IVANOVICH: Nikolay Fyodorovich. The one in our department?

IVAN VASILEVICH: The very same. Trying it on with him and Gruzdeva. A green kid, wet behind the ears. Gruzdeva's got a dowry, so he's trying for two birds with one stone. An inheritance there and a fortune here. The other day he says to me, "She's a little angel," he says. Meaning that Gruzdeva.

PYOTR IVANOVICH: That tramp a little angel!

IVAN VASILEVICH: The bastard.

PYOTR IVANOVICH: He can go to hell.

IVAN VASILEVICH: Well, how about another. [*Pours.*] Eh-eh-eh . . . say when.

PYOTR IVANOVICH: That's fine.

IVAN VASILEVICH: What do you mean, fine! You want me to drink more than you. No, no, pal, that's not friendly. Wouldn't another little decanter be better?

PYOTR IVANOVICH: Well, finish this one first.

IVAN VASILEVICH: But wouldn't another little decanter be better?

PYOTR IVANOVICH [*hesitating*]: Goodness, that's a lot. And my wife is waiting.

IVAN VASILEVICH: You've got a one-track mind: wife, wife, wife. As if a wife matters.

PYOTR IVANOVICH: But you said yourself she's an angel. How could I leave her by herself?

IVAN VASILEVICH: Some angel. She's a woman like all women. Let's have a drink, all right?

PYOTR IVANOVICH: Just one, for goodness' sake, to please you.

BARTENDER: They've brought out the roast beef with mustard. And cornichons, sir, would you like some?

IVAN VASILEVICH: Let's have it, let's have it.

BARTENDER [to AFANASY]: Two roast beefs for number six.

GUITARKIN: Yes, my dear sir. I look at people, you might say, as gnats. They fly around, they buzz, and, if I may say so, all the same way. Once a louse, always a louse.

KLAVISHKIN: You're a philosophizer.

GUITARKIN: Heh, heh. I'm a spiritualist, dear sir, a spiritualist, and not a philosopher, but not in relation to spiritualism, but in relation to spirits, sir, my dear sir, that's how it is, sir.

KARL KARLOVICH: Why's Bogdan Andreevich so late? Guess he's been held up at the factory . . . Yes . . . there's less call for sausage-making nowadays, Aleksandr Ivanovich.

BARTENDER: It's God's will, sir.

[AFANASY changes the cutlery on the civil servants' table.]

PYOTR IVANOVICH: And let's have another little decanter of the same.

AFANASY: A second, sir.

IVAN VASILEVICH: Who's counting? . . . A second.

KARL KARLOVICH [sighing]: Plenty of hogs, and yet no hogs.

BARTENDER [at the bar]: A second little decanter for number six.

2nd Decanter

The curtain parts after a few minutes. The lighting is somewhat brighter. Better-looking, better-dressed people are sitting around.

AFANASY [*serving the decanter*]: Here you are, sir.

IVAN VASILEVICH: It's awfully hot in here.

PYOTR IVANOVICH: Better take off our overcoats.

IVAN VASILEVICH: But we're in a hurry.

PYOTR IVANOVICH: Who cares, taking off and putting on takes no time at all.

IVAN VASILEVICH: True enough. [*He starts to take off his overcoat.*]

BARTENDER: Doorman, take their coats.

DOORMAN [*running over and helps them*]: Allow me, sir.

PYOTR IVANOVICH [*staring affectionately at him*]: What a wonderful kisser. Honest to God, a noble kisser. If you were in your best bib and tucker—in respectable society . . .

IVAN VASILEVICH: In any drawing room . . .

DOORMAN: Dear me, sir, much obliged.

PYOTR IVANOVICH: And how. Honestly, my young friend . . . As I was saying—to hell with that other fellow.

IVAN VASILEVICH: Yes, he takes home forty rubles but is as arrogant as if it were two hundred.

PYOTR IVANOVICH: What a bastard. I owe him two rubles, so he's snotty with me yesterday . . . That's the word, snotty . . . asking in front of everybody when I'll pay it back.

IVAN VASILEVICH: Son of a bitch. Well, bless us every one. [*They clink glasses.*]

GUITARKIN: Drinking, my good fellow, is a wonderful thing. They may call a man a drunkard. But what of it? A drunkard sees and feels things you wouldn't experience in dreams.

KLAVISHKIN: Even so, there's a lot of harm in it.

GUITARKIN: Rubbish, sir. My father drank for sixty years, and you think he died of drink? No way. He got a splinter in his foot at the bathhouse and died of that.

KLAVISHKIN: Those of us in government, you know . . .

PYOTR IVANOVICH: Snotty's what he was . . . I complained about him to His Excellency today.

IVAN VASILEVICH: Re-al-ly.

PYOTR IVANOVICH: Honest to God. The general called me in. A certain document had gone missing. Well, at first he bawled me out, the old fox, but I says to him, "This," I says to him, "Your Excellency, is because you're not up to date on the facts."

IVAN VASILEVICH: Liar.

PYOTR IVANOVICH: I snapped right at him. "You're not up to date on the facts," I says.

IVAN VASILEVICH: You're such a pussy.

PYOTR IVANOVICH: What, a pussy am I? At times, maybe. But I can . . . I can, it's the gospel truth.

IVAN VASILEVICH: And what about old side-whiskers?

PYOTR IVANOVICH: Didn't turn a hair. "I," says he, "have always appreciated your frankness."

IVAN VASILEVICH: Your health. [*Pours. They clink glasses and drink.*]

PYOTR IVANOVICH: I says to him, "Give me a chance to clean up the department, Your Excellency." I blurted it straight out. "Give me a chance," I says, "and I'll reform the whole place in a jiffy. First, that Nikolay Fyodorovich'll go to the devil and the messenger Sidorenko to the devil's great-grandmother. All he does is take bribes."

IVAN VASILEVICH: Liar! . . .

PYOTR IVANOVICH: Why am I a liar?

IVAN VASILEVICH: You couldn't handle Sidorenko. He'd show you a thing or two, that Sidorenko.

PYOTR IVANOVICH: Well, all right, forget Sidorenko . . . that was a bit of bragging. But on the other hand the vice chairman . . . "Excuse me, Your Excellency," says I, "but your assistant is a rotten egg."

IVAN VASILEVICH: You blurted that straight out?

PYOTR IVANOVICH: Indeed I did . . . a rotten egg . . .

IVAN VASILEVICH: He's a skunk.

PYOTR IVANOVICH: And how.

IVAN VASILEVICH: So what did the general do?

PYOTR IVANOVICH: He shook my hand. "Thank you," says he, "very much. You've opened my eyes to a great deal."

IVAN VASILEVICH: Let's have a drink to the general.

PYOTR IVANOVICH: The hell with him. Do we have to drink to all that trash?

IVAN VASILEVICH: What do you mean, trash! You and he were on the same page.

PYOTR IVANOVICH: So what? He's vulnerable. He's afraid of me. I could play him such a dirty trick.

IVAN VASILEVICH: Something interesting happened to me too. One day I was on my way to this summer place . . .

PYOTR IVANOVICH: I'd take him and . . .

IVAN VASILEVICH: I'm heading for this summer place . . .

PYOTR IVANOVICH: Hold on. I am an upright person. I speak the gospel truth and . . .

IVAN VASILEVICH: Wait, let me tell you. I'm passing this pond . . .

PYOTR IVANOVICH: I says right to his face: "Your Excel . . ."

[*They pound their fists on the table, grab one another by the sleeve, and inter-rupt one another.* BOGDAN ANDREEVICH *enters—a staid, middle-aged Ger-man artisan.*]

BOGDAN ANDREEVICH [*from a distance*]: Karl Karlych.

KARL KARLOVICH: What took you so long?

BOGDAN ANDREEVICH: Those bastards, Schuster, always drunk, typical Russians. Well, how's business, Karl Karlych?

KARL KARLOVICH: Bad. Hogs have gone up again.

BOGDAN ANDREEVICH: A glass of beer. [*The waiter serves him.*]

IVAN VASILEVICH: I pass this pond and I see: His Excellency is sitting in the water.

PYOTR IVANOVICH: Get out, I'd say to the lot of 'em, go to hell . . .

IVAN VASILEVICH: Take it easy . . .

PYOTR IVANOVICH: Right, right. [*Calms down.*]

IVAN VASILEVICH: Awright, sir. Well, I says very politely, "Have you deigned to go in swimming, sir"? He says to me, "Forget the swim-ming, I want you to tell me who wrote that nonsense on the outgoing paper yesterday and screwed up the whole file?" He says that to me.

PYOTR IVANOVICH: From the water?

IVAN VASILEVICH: Obviously.—"Yesterday," says he, "I didn't have time to see to it and ask you."

PYOTR IVANOVICH: What a louse! A viper!

IVAN VASILEVICH: Well, I got the full load of his spite. You know what I'm like: a fiery temper. "Aren't you ashamed," I say, "Your Excellency, to talk business in the lap of nature, so to speak, and in the spitten image of Adam."

PYOTR IVANOVICH: Good for you.

IVAN VASILEVICH: But he slaps the water with the palm of his hand and start shouting in that bass voice of his, "I am an official wherever I am. When I'm dry and when I'm wet." Just like that.

PYOTR IVANOVICH: So what did you do?

IVAN VASILEVICH: So I picked up his clothes and says, "If that's how it is, I'm taking all this away and then try and prove you're a general, bub."

PYOTR IVANOVICH: Bub?

IVAN VASILEVICH: Bub!

PYOTR IVANOVICH: Good for you. Let's drink to your health. That's the kind of friend I like.

IVAN VASILEVICH: Then he starts pleading. "Don't ruin me," he says. "I'll get you the order of St. Stanislas third class." So I gave him back his clothes, and he made an effort to get me the Stanislas.

PYOTR IVANOVICH: Liar. You haven't got the order of Stanislas third class.

IVAN VASILEVICH [offended]: Not now, maybe. It's on its way. He promised.

PYOTR IVANOVICH: Well, if he promised.

KARL KARLOVICH: There are all kinds of hogs. Some are fatter, some are not so good, but there's a lean one that's got plenty of fat.

PYOTR IVANOVICH: What's all this about hogs? Are they referring to us?

IVAN VASILEVICH: Damned Krauts.

PYOTR IVANOVICH: I'll go and ask.

IVAN VASILEVICH: Let it go . . . To hell with him.

PYOTR IVANOVICH: What do you mean, to hell? . . . He's calling me hog after hog, so what am I supposed to do? You saying I'm not up to it?

IVAN VASILEVICH: Let it go, I'm telling you.

PYOTR IVANOVICH: And you call yourself a friend? Instead of standing up for me . . .

IVAN VASILEVICH: I'd put my hand in the fire for you . . .

PYOTR IVANOVICH: Listen here, you sausage . . .

KARL KARLOVICH: What's the matter?

PYOTR IVANOVICH: You German sausage, I say. Why are you calling us hogs, may I ask?

KARL KARLOVICH: Get away from me.

PYOTR IVANOVICH: Get away? First it's hogs and then it's get away. I'm a civil servant, my good sir . . .

IVAN VASILEVICH: I'm a witness that you were calling us "hogs," yes, "hogs."

BOGDAN ANDREEVICH: *Aber was ist das?*

IVAN VASILEVICH: There they go again. I don't understand German or whatever it is . . . What did you say . . .

BARTENDER [*coming out from behind the bar*]: Stop it, gentlemen. What's all the fuss about?

PYOTR IVANOVICH: No, Aleksandr Ivanovich, how can this be? We're your guests, and these Krauts are calling us hogs. You should apologize, sir.

BARTENDER: They happen to be in the sausage-making business, so they're talking about the price of hogs. You didn't hear them properly.

IVAN VASILEVICH: That's a lie. Just now I heard for myself, that one said "hogs" in German.

BOGDAN ANDREEVICH: Well, I did say it. We were talking business, and you creep over to us with your "hogs.". . . What got up your nose?

KARL KARLOVICH: They've been drinking.

BARTENDER: They pleased to mishear. They're regulars of ours, excellent backgrounds, sir, only just now they made a mistake.

IVAN VASILEVICH: Petya . . . Friend . . . Seems we've made a mistake . . .

PYOTR IVANOVICH: I . . . don't know . . .

IVAN VASILEVICH: Well, to hell with them. Let's drink vodka.

KARL KARLOVICH: Dot's bedder.

BARTENDER: A simple misunderstanding, sir . . . It happens . . . Afanasy! [AFANASY *comes over.*] What were they talking about at number six just now?

AFANASY: They were badmouthing their boss.

BARTENDER: Well, that means things're still all right . . . O Lord Jesus Christ. [*Yawns.*]

IVAN VASILEVICH: And the bartender is a bastard. A sly fox. I can't stand that greasy kisser of his. He's got his hand in the till.

PYOTR IVANOVICH: He's obviously a thief.

GUITARKIN: There's bound to be a blowup. I'd like to go over there right now and say that, if they like, I can be an objective witness.

KLAVISHKIN: Stay put.

GUITARKIN: I can't. My noble blood is up. [*He walks over to the civil servants.*] Forgive me, sirs, colleagues, I wanted to say . . .

IVAN VASILEVICH: Delighted . . .

GUITARKIN: Guitarkin, retired civil servant, third class. In case there's an altercation I can be an objective witness.

PYOTR IVANOVICH: Delighted. Please have a seat.

GUITARKIN: *Merci*, I heard there was a misunderstanding.

IVAN VASILEVICH: Yes, it was a trifle, it's over now. Would you like a little vodka?

GUITARKIN: No, I'm on beer . . . Waiter! A bottle of lager!

PYOTR IVANOVICH: Where did you please to work?

GUITARKIN: In the Bureau of Untraveled Roads.

PYOTR IVANOVICH: So, you qualified for a full pension and now you're retired.

GUITARKIN: No, I sort of left. There was a difference of opinion.

IVAN VASILEVICH: So that's it.

GUITARKIN: You mustn't think it was anything like . . . Embezzlement or some such . . . Here's how it was. I once handed a document to the department head, well, the usual style, "In answer to your letter of such and such a date" and so on. But he says to me, "What year."— "Why," says I, "this year." "Meaning, the present year." "The present year," I answer. "And where does it say present?"—No present time, but quitting time. Well, he tore me a new one and tore up the paper. I got mad and put down "on such and such a date of the present 1911 Anno Domini."

IVAN VASILEVICH: Ho, ho.

GUITARKIN: They wanted, dear sirs, to give me summary dismissal. I barely managed to worm out of it. And for what? Hadn't I suffered enough?

IVAN VASILEVICH: If I run into the little creep, I'll tell him: you fired a man of pure gold.

GUITARKIN: Gold is right. I was his good right arm, if some important paper had to be mislaid, right away, done that very minute. I would write so you could think for a whole year and not figure out a single detail. Sort of like this: "In reply to your letter sequence number, we have the honor to inform you that, taking under advisement the memorandum of such-and-such a date, sequence number, and with reference to the latest directives of the minister of such-and-such a date, sequence number, in accordance with the instructions, subsequent to such-and-such a date, which, having stipulated the aforementioned occasion and based on the regulations of such and such a year, he has determined in the aforesaid events to be guided by the law governing the situation . . ." And three pages in that style without a full stop. So there, my dear fellow, you can put on your thinking cap, but in the end you'll spit and stop pestering us for an answer. That's what I could do. And for some trivia he wanted to leave me high and dry.

IVAN VASILEVICH: Here's to your talent.

PYOTR IVANOVICH: Hur-rah . . .

[BLACK SASHA *and* MANYA THE POLECAT *enter. They are both dressed rather poorly, but garishly. They modestly sit down in a corner and order tea.*]

GUITARKIN: Beautiful ladies have come on the scene.

PYOTR IVANOVICH [*taking a look*]: Tramps.

IVAN VASILEVICH: All the same, it's cozy here, honest to god. Warm, bright.

PYOTR IVANOVICH: A good restaurant.

KLAVISHKIN: Hem . . . hem . . .

BLACK SASHA: Looky there, Manka . . . There's doings over on the left.

KLAVISHKIN: Hem . . . Permit me to drink a sip of wine, eh-eh-eh, to your health.

MANYA THE POLECAT: You may.

KLAVISHKIN: May I sit beside you?

BLACK SASHA: Please do.

KLAVISHKIN [*with a gallant bow*]: Gromoboev.

MANYA THE POLECAT: Ever so pleased . . . [KLAVISHKIN *sits down.*]

GUITARKIN: So I moved on.

IVAN VASILEVICH: Here's to "the present year," gentlemen, let's have a drink.

PYOTR IVANOVICH: Let's have another.

IVAN VASILEVICH: Here's to all the rats in the department.

GUITARKIN: Hear, hear. [*They clink glasses.*]

IVAN VASILEVICH: That little decanter seems to have dried up.

PYOTR IVANOVICH: Should be enough.

IVAN VASILEVICH: But we have to drink to the downfall of generals.

PYOTR IVANOVICH: Should we . . .

IVAN VASILEVICH: Waiter!

AFANASY: What's your pleasure?

IVAN VASILEVICH: A fresh one.

KARL KARLOVICH: And if that's the way hogs are going, Bogdan Andreevich, then I have to stop coming here.

BOGDAN ANDREEVICH: But why should they go up in price . . . After all, there's no shortage of hogs.

CHAIRMAN: A third little decanter for number six.

3rd Decanter

The stage is brightly lit. All the characters, except for the two civil servants, are good-looking and well dressed. When the gramophone begins to play, an unseen orchestra will play along with it.

GUITARKIN: Yes . . . and that boss of mine went on living hale and hearty. He's a rich man now.

PYOTR IVANOVICH: Where is he?

GUITARKIN: Could be the war department. He got all sorts of per diems, travel grants, meal allowances, a bit of this and a bit of that . . .

IVAN VASILEVICH: Yes, war. And soon there'll be a war.

AFANASY [*walking over quickly*]: Allow me, sir. [*Puts the decanter on the table and surreptitiously makes a note on a slip of paper.*]

PYOTR IVANOVICH: And where are you hurrying off to? What's the rush? You're not running to a fire.

AFANASY: A while ago you pleased to ask me to hurry up . . .

PYOTR IVANOVICH: Hmm . . . What's the difference? . . . There's a time to hurry and a time not to. Shoo! And there won't be any war.

IVAN VASILEVICH: You'll see, there will be.

PYOTR IVANOVICH: Who with?

IVAN VASILEVICH: China.

PYOTR IVANOVICH: The Germans won't allow it.

IVAN VASILEVICH: And America will stand up for China, and the Japs will march against the Americans.

PYOTR IVANOVICH: Why should they get mixed up in it?

IVAN VASILEVICH: Why should they get mixed up in it! No, pal, don't argue. I've got reliable information. The assistant station master told me that they received the kind of notification that, oy-oy-oy. Wait and see.

GUITARKIN: Oh, I get it! . . .

PYOTR IVANOVICH: Then they'll be back in the soup.

IVAN VASILEVICH: It's not known yet.

PYOTR IVANOVICH: Sure thing. On our side we got one, the French, two, the Germans, three, the English and four, the Japs. And they've got America—their only cover.

IVAN VASILEVICH: Wait a minute. How's that? Why have we got the Germans?

PYOTR IVANOVICH: Plain and simple. What are they waiting for? For us to catch fire. [*Shows it on the table.*] Here are the French, here the Germans, over here the English, on that side the Japs, and we're way over here, at the top, at the top.

IVAN VASILEVICH: Hold on, that's not right. The English are over here, the Germans are over here, why stick 'em over there. They've got a navy. Picture this . . .

PYOTR IVANOVICH: What navy? It'll be close to there.

IVAN VASILEVICH: Wait a minute. I know about these things. I was a noncom in the volunteers. The French are on this side . . . Where's China?

PYOTR IVANOVICH: Here's China . . . This napkin.

GUITARKIN: So the Japs are on this side and the Germans on the other . . .

IVAN VASILEVICH: The Germans won't be coming.

GUITARKIN: They will . . .

IVAN VASILEVICH: They won't. Why the hell should they get involved?

PYOTR IVANOVICH: And I say they will. They care a lot for their own skin.

GUITARKIN: Let's ask the Germans.

IVAN VASILEVICH: Right you are . . .

PYOTR IVANOVICH: Herr . . . Ah, Herr . . . Excuse me please, may I ask you a question . . . We're having a debate. If there's a war with China, would you side with us?

KARL KARLOVICH: What do you mean, with you?

PYOTR IVANOVICH: Germany for Russia or against?

KARL KARLOVICH: War with China . . . We'd be with you.

PYOTR IVANOVICH: Hur-rah! . . . What did I say?

IVAN VASILEVICH: Attaboy, Germans . . . Here's to Germany, pals.

KARL KARLOVICH [*very pompously*]: *Danke.*

BOGDAN ANDREEVICH: *Prosit!*

IVAN VASILEVICH: I saw at once that you are decent people, clever fellows.

PYOTR IVANOVICH: Come and sit over here with us . . .

KARL KARLOVICH: But we're here on business . . .

PYOTR IVANOVICH: Drop it . . . Let's talk about the war.

KARL KARLOVICH: All right, let's go, shall we, Bogdan Andreevich.

BOGDAN ANDREEVICH: *Gut.* [*They change their seats.*]

IVAN VASILEVICH: This is what I like. Waiter, turn up the gramophone, make it louder. [*The gramophone plays along with the orchestra.*]

PYOTR IVANOVICH: What a charming instrument . . . Honest to God, it plays and you listen spellbound.

GUITARKIN: And the Germans invented it all.

IVAN VASILEVICH: The gramophone is American.

KARL KARLOVICH: The gramophone is ours . . .

PYOTR IVANOVICH: I love Germans. Let's drink to the health of Germans . . . You're businessmen . . .

KARL KARLOVICH: I own a sausage factory.

PYOTR IVANOVICH: That's just what I heard, you were having such an intelligent and well-informed conversation. Hogs, you were saying, yes, hogs . . . So they've gone up in price.

KARL KARLOVICH: Oh, quite a lot.

PYOTR IVANOVICH: Who would have thought it. To hell with them . . . Word of honor. The hogs're acting just like swine. N-no, Ivan Vasilevich, take a look at the bartender . . . What a magnificent kisser . . .

IVAN VASILEVICH: Mm-yes, I'm fond of the fellow.

PYOTR IVANOVICH: Aleksandr Ivanovich . . . Please come over here. We'd like to drink to your health.

BARTENDER [*walking over*]: I thank you kindly.

PYOTR IVANOVICH: A little shot.

BARTENDER: I don't drink, sir.

PYOTR IVANOVICH: Liar . . . Just one . . .

BARTENDER: I can't, sir. Forgive me. I wish you your very good health.

IVAN VASILEVICH: To the prosperity of this establishment . . .

EVERYONE: Hur-r-r-rah . . .

PYOTR IVANOVICH: Aleksandr Ivanovich, will there be war with China or not?

BARTENDER: Let's hope not, otherwise what would they do with all that tea? They'd have to lower the price . . .

IVAN VASILEVICH: What's tea got to do with it? We'll take it all, lower price or not . . .

PYOTR IVANOVICH: Don't you get it, China's over there and we're here. There's the Germans, there's the French. We're out in front, and they'll hold up the rear . . .

BARTENDER: It may be so, sir . . .

PYOTR IVANOVICH: I am so fond of you, Aleksandr Ivanovich . . . You're a darling of a man . . . Let's have a kiss.

BARTENDER: Good gracious, what for, sir.

PYOTR IVANOVICH: You don't want to. All right, I'll remember that.

BARTENDER: For pity's sake, if it'll make you happy.

PYOTR IVANOVICH: I'm so fond of this fel . . . [*Hugs and kisses him.*]

KLAVISHKIN: Well, ma'am, I have to go, my lovely ladies. [*Pays up and exits.*]

MANYA THE POLECAT: What a tightwad. Wasted all our time and treated us to a penny's worth.

BLACK SASHA: The riffraff's gone now.

KARL KARLOVICH: Germania will march from here.

GUITARKIN: And the Japs from here.

IVAN VASILEVICH: And we'll have a cute little canteen over here, we'll set up a cute little canteen.

GUITARKIN: That's no place for a little canteen. Over here is better . . . It has to be . . . When I was a volunteer noncom . . . We set one up on maneuvers, and there—the business was run by the Shavlyas—one of them was a Jewess—re-a-l-ly pret-ty little thing . . .

IVAN VASILEVICH: All right, all right . . .

GUITARKIN: The way she used to handle the sales . . . hm . . . you know, all sorts of sweet talk.

PYOTR IVANOVICH: Ho, ho, ho . . .

GUITARKIN: Ah yes . . . To some she sold wine, know what I mean, and tobacco . . . But to some . . .

IVAN VASILEVICH: Ha, ha, ha . . .

GUITARKIN: Hee, hee . . . And she says, you follow me, "I got all sorts of wares, Mister Officer. You can get whatever you like . . ."

PYOTR IVANOVICH: Ho, ho, ho . . . Is that what she used to say . . .

GUITARKIN: She used to say, "An officer needs three things: wine, cards, and a woman."

IVAN VASILEVICH: Ready for anything just for the fun of it.

PYOTR IVANOVICH: No, that's something, but somebody told me . . .

IVAN VASILEVICH: Hold on, there's this thing happened to me . . . Picture this, I'm walking down the street once, in a new jacket, mustache twirled, and suddenly this little lady runs into me with such a look in her eyes—wink, wink . . .

PYOTR IVANOVICH: Stop . . . I've got a funny story. A gent walks up to a girl and says, "Mademoiselle, may I". . . [*Glances at the other tables and whispers in their ears.*] Ho, ho, ho . . . No, listen to this . . . [*Whispers. Everyone bursts out laughing.*]

GUITARKIN: That's something, but that canteen woman once pulled off quite a stunt. [*He tells it in an undertone, leaning over the table, while* IVAN VASILEVICH *stares at* MANYA *and* SASHA.]

IVAN VASILEVICH: Those are real good-lookers . . . Petya, hey, Petya . . . Honest to God, never mind that . . .

PYOTR IVANOVICH: Stop it, come and listen.

IVAN VASILEVICH: Honest to God, Petya, you were wrong to call them tramps. Word of honor.

PYOTR IVANOVICH: Wait.

IVAN VASILEVICH: I'll call them over. You can get a look at 'em close up. Honest to God, beauties.

PYOTR IVANOVICH: All right, call them over. [IVAN VASILEVICH *goes to the girls, bows and starts talking. Loud guffaws at his table at* GUITAR-KIN's *stories.*] Your very good health . . .

BOGDAN ANDREEVICH: *Sehr schön.*

GUITARKIN: Now then, Karl Karlovich, are we going to war?

[IVAN VASILEVICH *and the girls come over.*]

IVAN VASILEVICH: May I introduce my beautiful canteen ladies, ready to go not only to war, but to whatever you like.

GUITARKIN: Ho, ho . . . Delighted.

PYOTR IVANOVICH: Please have a seat.

BLACK SASHA: So you're going to war?

KARL KARLOVICH: Soon as we leave here.

IVAN VASILEVICH: We'll show 'em.

MANYA THE POLECAT: What elegant company! . . .

IVAN VASILEVICH: Wai-der . . .

AFANASY [*running over*]: What's your pleasure?

IVAN VASILEVICH: A decanter, a little bigger one, and an assortment of snacks.

PYOTR IVANOVICH: And while we're waiting, single shots to toast the coming war.

IVAN VASILEVICH [*nudging* MANYA]: Going to war's not scary with someone like her.

EVERYONE: Hur-rah . . .

KARL KARLOVICH [*good-naturedly*]: And then I'll turn my back on hogs.

AFANASY [*at the bar*]: For table six—a fourth decanter.

4th Decanter

Lights full up. The gramophone is playing its loudest.

PYOTR IVANOVICH: Gramophone, make it hot . . . Show what you can do . . .

IVAN VASILEVICH: "The Marseillaise". . .

BARTENDER [*walking over*]: You're not supposed to shout such things.

IVAN VASILEVICH: But if I wa-want . . .

BARTENDER: You're not supposed to, Ivan Vasilevich, it's wrong, sir, and not allowed.

IVAN VASILEVICH: Good Lord . . . The French, they're friends of ours, right, and all of a sudden . . .

BARTENDER: It's good advice, sir . . .

IVAN VASILEVICH: I'm fond of you, Aleksandr Ivanovich, honest to God . . . [*Wants to embrace him. The* BARTENDER *goes behind the bar.*] You don't want to, then to hell with you and your moronic kisser.

[PYOTR IVANOVICH *suddenly becomes gloomy and sits silently to one side, from time to time shaking his head pensively.*]

MANYA THE POLECAT: You should treat us to a cordial.

IVAN VASILEVICH: Wait a bit. First let's finish the vodka.

[AFANASY *brings vodka and snacks, changes the glassware.*]

GUITARKIN: I'm in love . . . Beautiful lady, let me kiss you . . . [*Tries to kiss* SASHA.]

BARTENDER [*walking over*]: Get a private room, sir.

GUITARKIN: What?

BARTENDER: Get a private room, sir.

GUITARKIN: I'm full of poetry, love, and moonlight, and you start talking about your sleazy private rooms. Beat it . . .

BARTENDER: There's a time and a place for everything. Some things belong in a public space, sir, some in a private room, sir, and you are powerless to change that law of nature, sir.

GUITARKIN: Can't you understand, my soul is aflame and overcome with emotion, while you and your talk . . .

BARTENDER: I can't help it, sir. [*Walks away.*]

IVAN VASILEVICH: To beauty and li-life, gentlemen . . . Let's have a friendly drink . . . [*Everyone clinks glasses.*]

KARL KARLOVICH: *Gut.* Awfully hot in here, I'm even coming out in a sweat.

IVAN VASILEVICH: Petya, why, Petya, why aren't you drinking?

PYOTR IVANOVICH: Quit it, I can't stand to look at your abominations.

IVAN VASILEVICH: You're off your rocker.

PYOTR IVANOVICH: There you are laughing your heads off . . . while in the cemetery, do you follow, in graves lie the dear departed dead, while in the steeple the church bell tolls. So dolefully they remind us of the immortal soul.

IVAN VASILEVICH: Rubbish.

PYOTR IVANOVICH: What do you mean, rubbish! . . . The soul is rubbish?

GUITARKIN: Qu-quite correct . . . I always say, my soul thirsts for alcohol . . .

PYOTR IVANOVICH: Hold on. Tell me: Is there a soul or not?

IVAN VASILEVICH: What kind of soul?

PYOTR IVANOVICH: Well, you tell me if your soul's that of a chicken or not. If you've got a spirit, that's what you call . . . metaphysics . . . which without chemistry . . .

IVAN VASILEVICH: Go to hell.

PYOTR IVANOVICH [*almost weeping*]: Well, all I'm saying is . . . Transmigration of souls is . . . reassuring . . . I used to be a crocodile, and suddenly I'm a human being. V-Vanya, don't you get it . . . I was a crocodile . . . How can I stand it?

IVAN VASILEVICH [*sympathizing*]: It's hard.

PYOTR IVANOVICH: And a world of infinite stars is shining . . . And how . . . Don't you get it . . . infinity . . .

IVAN VASILEVICH [*puzzled*]: Yes . . . It means, endless.

GUITARKIN: I studied this psychology. There're different kinds of infinity . . . Em . . . embyr . . . embryonality . . . no . . . that's not it. Something like vibryons . . .

BLACK SASHA: Quit this cholera stuff. Better drink.

PYOTR IVANOVICH: Can't you understand? There's a great transmigration of souls from a crocodile, and you're on about cholera . . . I'm going to go ask Aleksandr Ivanovich. [*He goes to the* BARTENDER.]

GUITARKIN: I understand, sir. Infinity is just like this decanter. No matter how much you pour, it'll end up empty. That's what infinity is, that is.

PYOTR IVANOVICH: Aleksandr Ivanovich . . . Do you realize how offensive I find this . . . Philosophy is a kind of science, and they don't understand. Now tell me, does the soul exist or not?

BARTENDER: Of course it does. There are different kinds of soul. One guy has a bastard's soul, and another guy has, let's say, a dove-like soul.

PYOTR IVANOVICH: And is there a crocodile type?

BARTENDER: I couldn't say for certain, but I'll bet there isn't.

PYOTR IVANOVICH: So, that means I don't have a soul . . . I didn't expect such a dirty trick, Aleksandr Ivanovich, from you. Honest to God, I didn't.

BARTENDER: For heaven's sake, sir . . .

PYOTR IVANOVICH: I don't want to have anything more to do with you. You can go to hell, if that's how things stand . . . Listen to this, if you please: crocodiles don't have souls . . . [*Insulted, he walks back to the table.*]

AFANASY: They're on about the soul, sir, Leksandr Ivanych.

BARTENDER: Which means, it's all over. Mineral water and nothing else. [*The customers gradually leave, and the light grows a bit dimmer. The gramophone plays without the orchestra, then stops.*]

GUITARKIN: I w-want to make a sp-speech . . .

PYOTR IVANOVICH [*weeping*]: I've come down to this . . . To this, good God Almighty, I've come down to this . . . Dar-win and Schopen-hauer . . . I'm a lowlife. The gramophone . . . Strike up a funeral march . . .

GUITARKIN: Gentlemen . . . I w-want to make a philosophical speech . . .

IVAN VASILEVICH: Give it a whirl . . .

GUITARKIN: Just a second . . . Now we've all been drinking . . . Yes . . . But what we're drinking and why we're drinking . . . That is the question. There is a temperance society . . . that's all rub-rubbish . . . A man has to drink, gentlemen, that's the point . . . Vodka, it gives us new life. Look at us sitting here, having intelligent conversations, and you are like brothers to us . . . and dear sisters too . . . And that is because it is not vodka, but water. Yes, the water of life, as our French-men say. A transformation, in the words of learned philosophers, is taking place . . . And you've got to understand it. And so here's to vodka . . . phooey . . . to the water of life. Hur-rah . . .

EVERYONE: Hur-rah . . .

IVAN VASILEVICH: Waiter . . . coffee and a liqueur . . .

AFANASY: Excuse me, sir, we're closing, sir.

IVAN VASILEVICH: What do you mean, closing? . . .

AFANASY: It's time, sir. If you please, the bill. [*Gives him the bill. The Germans and* IVAN VASILEVICH *hand over money.*]

IVAN VASILEVICH: What a blow! . . . What if I don't want to?

AFANASY: You've got to, sir.

IVAN VASILEVICH: This is an outrage!

BLACK SASHA [*to* GUITARKIN]: Let's go, old-timer. [*They get up, say goodbye, and head for the door.*]

BOGDAN ANDREEVICH: Well, let's be off, Karl Karlovich . . .

KARL KARLOVICH: Goodbye, gentlemen. [*Laughs.*] You know what, Bogdan Andreevich, now I'm thinking hogs have gone way down in price.

AFANASY [*taking the money*]: Thanks a lot.

BOGDAN ANDREEVICH: *Gut getrunken.*

KARL KARLOVICH: *Sehr gut.*

[MANYA THE POLECAT *latches on to him. It's almost fully dark.* PYOTR IVANOVICH *is asleep, leaning on the table.* IVAN VASILEVICH *is nodding off. Pause.*]

AFANASY [*going over to them*]: We're locking up, sir. If you please. [*He shakes* PYOTR IVANOVICH.]

PYOTR IVANOVICH: Leave off . . .

AFANASY: If you please . . .

PYOTR IVANOVICH [*muttering*]: N-yes . . . the water of life . . . N-no, the way he insulted me: no, says he, there's no crocodile soul . . . But . . .

AFANASY: We're closing up, mister.

PYOTR IVANOVICH [*looking around and suddenly sobering up*]: Huh . . . what? Well, well . . . Ivan Vasilevich . . .

IVAN VASILEVICH [*drowsily*]: We're going, I guess. [*Gets up.*]

BARTENDER: I wish you the best of health.

PYOTR IVANOVICH [*dryly*]: Goodbye.

IVAN VASILEVICH: This place is a dump. Swear to God . . .

PYOTR IVANOVICH: And those Germans are crooks . . .

IVAN VASILEVICH: And those tramps . . . Phooey.

PYOTR IVANOVICH: And the bartender's a thief. Probably overcharged us. Bunch of swindlers . . . [*Puts on his overcoat.*]

IVAN VASILEVICH [*looks at the* DOORMAN]: That one's the only decent fellow in the place, and he's probably a swine too.

PYOTR IVANOVICH [*with conviction*]: Swine. [*He stumbles his way out.*]

BARTENDER: So now do you understand how you have to handle our noble guests?

AFANASY: I got it, sir.

BARTENDER: Just so's you know. For them, it's "rotgut," and for us, "the water of life." Because everything's first class, pal . . . before three o'clock in the morning . . .

WHAT THEY SAY, WHAT THEY THINK
(*Chto govoryat—chto dumayut*)

A psychological experiment in one act and two scenes

by Boris Geyer

1914

CHARACTERS

General

General's Lady

Daughter

Secretary

Capitalist

Lady

Tramp

Butler

Scene 1. What They Say

A drawing room. A big table center, covered with a green cloth. The BUTLER, *old and decrepit, is arranging an inkwell, pens, and paper.*

BUTLER: Oh me oh my. Lordy, when's this gonna end? If it don't, the master's affairs is in an awful bad state. Ain't paid my wages for three months. Only hope is getting her married off. He knows what he's doin'. Sometimes you stop and think, what if everybody said out loud what they was thinkin'. What a mess that would make! . . . Ah, that'd be somethin' awful . . . They all been lyin' to beat the band . . . In league with the devil and no mistake . . .

247

[*Enter the* DAUGHTER, *already halfway to being an old maid, but dolled up to the nth degree.*]

DAUGHTER: What are you stealing over there, old man?

BUTLER: Nothing, ma'am, Your Excellency. Just settin' things up, ma'am. Seein' as how today's an important meeting of our charity society.

DAUGHTER: Look, does everything seem all right from the back? [*She turns around in front of him.*]

BUTLER: It'll do, ma'am . . . [*She walks over to the mirror.*]

DAUGHTER: Ah, there's a pimple on my nose . . . A downright horror . . . It all comes from overexcitement. Nikita, that gentleman, you know the one, the millionaire, has he come yet?

BUTLER: Twice today by 'phone he was pleased to confirm it. And asked after you too, ma'am.

DAUGHTER: Ah. Good heavens, Nikita, go quick, get some powder from Liza. This pimple is a total disaster.

BUTLER: Right away, Your Excellency. [*He exits. In the doorway he runs into the* SECRETARY, *a sleek young man who trips, but immediately recovers and grovels lovingly.*]

SECRETARY: Nadezhda Pavlovna, you flourish as ever. I look and I admire. It's still morning, and already you're bustling about . . .

DAUGHTER: Ah, is that you, Evgeny Nikolaevich. Please take a seat. You're right on time. The meeting should be any minute now. You've heard that Polunov is coming in person . . .

SECRETARY: You know him?

DAUGHTER: I met him at a ball.

SECRETARY [*grasping his foot*]: Ow-owy . . .

DAUGHTER: What's the matter?

SECRETARY: Absolutely nothing . . .

DAUGHTER: But you're wincing? Are you unwell?

SECRETARY: Oh, it's nothing, nothing at all . . . An old adventure . . .

DAUGHTER: An old adventure? Ah, that sounds terribly interesting. Tell me about it right now.

SECRETARY: But, Nadezhda Pavlovna, it's such a trifle . . .

DAUGHTER: No, no, you have to tell me right away . . . You must . . .

SECRETARY: M-m-m . . . all right . . . m . . . m . . . you see, once I fought a duel and got shot. In the foot, right there . . .

DAUGHTER: You fought a duel?

BUTLER [*enters*]: The powder, please, Your Excellency.

DAUGHTER: *Mursee.* Put it down here.

BUTLER: Yes, ma'am . . .

SECRETARY: Do you really need powder? For your smooth, pale, pensive face . . . Ow-ow-ow . . .

DAUGHTER: Shame on you . . .

SECRETARY: Nadezhda Pavlovna, how can you doubt me for a minute? I was about to say . . . I was about to say . . . [*Grasps his foot.* BUTLER *exits.*]

DAUGHTER: It's back again . . .

SECRETARY: Yes, when the weather's like this, it always twitches.

DAUGHTER: And that duel . . . was it . . . over something romantic?

SECRETARY: Oh, Nadezhda Pavlovna, let's not probe old wounds . . . Rather, let us speak of future happiness, which is in your hands.

DAUGHTER: I don't understand what you mean.

SECRETARY: Nadezhda Pavlovna, how can you not see, not guess . . . ow . . . ow . . . [*Grasps his foot.*]

[*Enter the* BUTLER *and the* TRAMP.]

DAUGHTER: Stop. You and I will discuss this later. [*Rises.*]

SECRETARY: I shall await your answer . . .

BUTLER: Stand here . . . Got it?

TRAMP: What's not to get?

DAUGHTER: Ah, this is the fellow, the little peasant from the village. [*Looks him over.*] Poor, poor man . . . You're so skinny . . . Never mind, never mind, little peasant, we'll help you. We'll help you and we'll help your chickens and your pigs . . .

SECRETARY: We shall "re-hab-il-i-tate" you . . .

TRAMP: Thank you kindly . . . That's awfully nice of you . . .

DAUGHTER: Let's go, Evgeny Nikolaevich, you still have to finish your story about the duel, I find it so exciting . . .

SECRETARY: Oh, Nadezhda Pavlovna . . . [*He raises his arms, but immediately grasps his foot. They both exit.*]

TRAMP: Who's that?

BUTLER: The young mistress, their excellencies' daughter.

TRAMP: Izat so? . . . Still single. What a babe! . . . And what's your gen'ral like?

BUTLER: He's coming now. Have a word with him . . .

TRAMP: Sure thing. I'm a bit peckish. So let's split a bottle, so the tears will flow . . .

GENERAL [*entering; grizzled, in a dress uniform*]: Aha . . . Here already! . . . Well? got the petition?

TRAMP: Just so, Your Wuship, seeing as how I'm a peasant from the village of Dogshire, Onuch district, an' we ain't got the strength to go on much longer.

GENERAL: Name?

TRAMP: Say again please?

GENERAL: What's your name?

TRAMP: Uncle Kovylyay's what they call me. Uncle Kovylyay's my handle in the village. With a petition, y'see, from the council, on account of food, y'see . . .

GENERAL: All right, all right . . . Remember what your name is—and keep your mouth shut . . . Though if they ask a question, answer it . . . Got it?

TRAMP: Got it, Your Wuship . . .

GENERAL: Make an effort, my dear fella . . . and by all means don't overdo it.

[*Enter the* GENERAL'S LADY, *a middle-aged woman who acts younger than her age . . . She inspects the* TRAMP.]

GENERAL'S LADY: Is this the one?

GENERAL: A petition-bearer from the peasant elders . . .

GENERAL'S LADY [*sniffing*]: He smells . . . He smells dreadful . . .

GENERAL: Oh, that's nothing . . .

GENERAL'S LADY: Straight from the barracks . . . the stables . . . Nikita, take him away. Have him sit in the servant's hall. And fumigate the room with something.

BUTLER: Yes, Your Excellency . . . [*The* TRAMP *and the* BUTLER *exit.*]

GENERAL'S LADY [*staring long and hard at the* GENERAL]: So last night you sat up again at the meeting until dawn?

GENERAL: Business, my dear, business. The count was there, General Vernoboev, from the Ministry, then someone else . . . someone else . . . [*Hesitates.*]

GENERAL'S LADY: Who else?

GENERAL: Okonadze was there. You know, the one with the oil well in Baku, not a well, but a whole gusher.

GENERAL'S LADY: All right, darling, here, let me kiss you. My old dear . . . [*Kisses and sniffs.*] So you sat up till five in the morning?

GENERAL: Five, my dear, till five. This charity work keeps me sitting wherever.

GENERAL'S LADY: I suppose so. So long as it doesn't affect your health? You're so stout.

GENERAL: What can I do, what can I do? The times demand it . . . Our obligation, our duty is to sacrifice ourselves for the welfare of our fellow man. But you got all dolled up? Hee, hee, hee . . . Could it be that Polunov is starting to take an interest in you and not Nadya?

GENERAL'S LADY: So what? Am I so old? But where is Zhenya? I mean, Evgeny Nikolaevich, our secretary. I always call him that behind his back.

GENERAL: Very nice.

GENERAL'S LADY: You're jealous?

GENERAL: But I can't just ignore him.

GENERAL'S LADY: So the meeting lasted till five in the morning, did it?

GENERAL: My dear, let me explain . . .

[*Enter a* LADY *in an extremely low-cut dress and heavily made up.*]

LADY: Am I late? Has it started already? My dear . . . *Mah sheree* . . . General, *Toujours comme un brave soldat.*

GENERAL: Enchantress. Always full of energy and high spirits.

GENERAL'S LADY: Your new dress is so becoming. It's delicious.

LADY: Oh go on! It's the simplest thing, homemade.

GENERAL'S LADY: It's obviously very expensive. Oodles of taste.

LADY: My own invention.

GENERAL'S LADY: You're a regular fashion designer . . .

LADY: Yes, everyone says I've got an artistic flair. Most women dress in such poor taste it's simply appalling. [*Looks the* GENERAL'S LADY *up and down.*]

GENERAL'S LADY: Of course. My sincere congratulations. But for now forgive me, I have to go and make arrangements. After all, I am only the hostess. Yes, ma'am. [*Exits, slamming the door.*]

LADY: Is your lady-wife very busy?

GENERAL: Yes. A beautiful woman . . .

LADY: So you and she are still in love?

GENERAL: Well, in love . . . That's such a sinful concept. Our concern is doing good, consideration for our fellow man. Do have a seat, dear lady, why are we standing, sit here, on the settee.

LADY: *Mursee* . . . [*Sits. The* GENERAL *sits very close beside her.*] Oh, what are you . . .

GENERAL [*squeezing closer*]: Your snow-white throat is so lovely . . . and the cameo on it . . .

LADY: Oh-oh-oh . . . An old keepsake . . .

GENERAL: Allow me, allow me to inspect it. The art of an Italian master. Venetian period . . . Oh-oh-oh . . . [*Makes ready to kiss her neck.*]

LADY [*moving away*]: General, you're obviously a great lover of beauty . . .

GENERAL [*choking*]: Oh yes . . . allow me just once more . . . [*He stoops over. Just then the* GENERAL'S LADY *enters. She casts a suspicious glance, but speaks casually.*]

GENERAL'S LADY: A pleasant *koh-zeree*? . . . What were you discussing?

GENERAL: The haves and have-nots.

LADY: Your husband is so devoted, such an enlightened soul.

GENERAL'S LADY: Indeed he is. But, Pavlusha, go and greet our guest. Polunov has arrived.

GENERAL: He's here? Ah, glad to. [*He is about to go. The capitalist Polunov enters; middle-aged, in a frock coat, with a blond beard. Looks shrewd.*] Panteley Ivanovich . . . Our benefactor . . . I don't know how to thank you.

CAPITALIST: Don't mention it . . .

GENERAL: Allow me to introduce: my wife, and this is our colleague, a tireless activist and comforter of the poor, Avrora Sergeevna.

CAPITALIST: Delighted.

GENERAL'S LADY: I have heard so much about your good works . . .

CAPITALIST: For pity's sake . . .

LADY: The whole town is talking about you . . .

CAPITALIST: The rumors are exaggerated, ma'am . . .

GENERAL: You've dropped in right on cue. Today a petition-bearer arrived from the elders of a certain village . . . So he can tell it all to you directly. You will be personally convinced and will see how much help is needed.

CAPITALIST: I am always ready.

GENERAL: I know, I know. And in that regard let's have a word in private. [*Takes him by the arm and leads him to one side.*] You understand? Our society has powerful connections. When the sacrifice is great, many others are to be counted on.

CAPITALIST: Oh, I will gladly . . . I am always ready on behalf of the poor . . . How much do you need?

GENERAL: I know you'll be generous . . .

CAPITALIST: All the same?

GENERAL: Fifteen, twenty thousand . . .

CAPITALIST: So what, for an act of charity I don't begrudge money. How is it to be paid?

GENERAL: Through me.

CAPITALIST: So, so . . . [*The* DAUGHTER *and* SECRETARY *enter.*] And here is your dear heiress.

DAUGHTER: I'm so happy to see you.

GENERAL: Our secretary.

SECRETARY: Delighted.

DAUGHTER [*to the* CAPITALIST]: Now you're in my power. I shall be *your* secretary . . .

CAPITALIST: That's all I could ask for.

LADY [*languidly*]: Evgeny Nikolaevich, come over here to me. I shall also help you do your secretary stuff.

GENERAL'S LADY: Evgeny Nikolaevich, over here. I will probably be presiding, so you have to . . .

SECRETARY [*smiling*]: Madam, I am entirely at your service. This very second. Your Excellency, shall I begin?

GENERAL: Yes, yes. Please sit down, ladies and gentlemen. Panteley Ivanovich, please take the chair.

GENERAL'S LADY: Ah, isn't this nice . . .

CAPITALIST: Where should I . . .

DAUGHTER: Please, please . . . [*Sits at the table. The* CAPITALIST *next to the* DAUGHTER, *on the other side the* GENERAL *and the* LADY. *The* SECRETARY *near the* DAUGHTER, *but next to the* GENERAL'S LADY.] *Mammaw*, aren't you getting a draft from the door?

GENERAL'S LADY: Never mind, my dear little child.

SECRETARY [*to the* DAUGHTER]: Won't the responsibilities of a secretary be too burdensome for you?

DAUGHTER: You can help me in future.

GENERAL [*ringing, the* BUTLER *enters*]: Call in the emissary from the village elders.

CAPITALIST: I'm not looking for honors. I am ready to give my all for the people . . . my all . . . my all . . .

DAUGHTER: How noble!

[*Enter the* TRAMP.]

TRAMP: I bear a petition from the elders, y'see, of the village of Dogshi . . . shire . . . Uncle Kovalyey's what they call me. We got heaps o' trouble. The huts fell down, the livestock ate the straw off the roofs.

GENERAL: Dreadful . . .

DAUGHTER: Such a tragedy . . .

CAPITALIST [*looking him over*]: Hold on . . . You, pal, didn't you work in a factory?

TRAMP [*looking at him*]: No, never happened. I push a plow.

CAPITALIST: Hm . . . All right. I'm ready. Ladies and gentlemen, I will make a sacrifice. I have hope. That I will become a member of your committee . . .

GENERAL: Most esteemed . . .

DAUGHTER: And I'll be your secretary. Won't I?

GENERAL: You won't refuse to join us more often?

CAPITALIST: Of course. To help the people I am ready for everything . . .

GENERAL: So how do we do this? May I have a check?

CAPITALIST: N-no. I'd rather give you shares in my factory.

GENERAL: Fac-tory? All right, shares will do. [*Disappointed.*] Ladies and gentlemen, it's time to adjourn the meeting. We'll be looking for you, Mister Polunov.

CAPITALIST: In the near future. The very near future. My general greetings to all. Goodbye. [*He bows and exits.*]

GENERAL: A million . . . and up the spout . . . Well, wait . . . I'll get you in my clutches yet.

DAUGHTER: Oh, what a darling . . .

GENERAL: A darling! Of course. You made an impression on him. Let's see what'll come of it.

GENERAL'S LADY: You're tired, poor man . . .

TRAMP: Lemme have what you promised.

GENERAL: Later, later. Nikita. take him away, feed him in the kitchen. Maybe business isn't so bad after all, my friends.

Scene 2. What They Think

The same stage set. The same characters, in the same costumes and makeup. The characters' situation and acting are the same as in scene 1, independent of the meaning of the lines they speak. The BUTLER *is arranging paper, pens, and ink.*

BUTLER: Oh me oh my. Now the swindle's back in business. As sure as I'm a retired master sergeant, we'll all end up in court one of these days. It's a clear case: they're cheatin' people. They're extortin' money. A regular jailbird with a ball and chain. Phooey . . .

[*Enter the* DAUGHTER.]

DAUGHTER [*caressingly*]: Rooting in our things, you old baboon?

BUTLER: Readyin' things up, ma'am. Soon there'll be a meeting of the swindlers and conmen, those magnificent parents of yours. Then there'll be doin's.

DAUGHTER: Have you stolen everything yet? Look here, I know what you're up to. Oh dear, I think my dress has come undone in back. Hey you, have a look. [*Turns around.*]

BUTLER [*servilely*]: So I got to look at you again. [*Looks at a corner.*] Fine and dandy . . . [DAUGHTER *goes over to the mirror.*]

DAUGHTER: It's simply shocking. A wart, right on my nose. And all on account of cheese. Whenever we have cheese, I get a wart. And I know I shouldn't eat it, but I eat and eat. How am I going to talk to this idiotic millionaire today? Hey you, old baboon, do you know if that Mister Money-bags is coming . . .

BUTLER [*submissively*]: Why shouldn't he come, when they've pestered him three times on the 'phone. Not a moment's peace, ringin' him and ringin' him. Once he even told me to go to hell.

DAUGHTER: Ah, run quick to that slut Liza, bring me some powder. I think I'm going to burst with spite because of that cheese. Well, get a move on . . .

BUTLER: You won't die of it. You'd think the house was on fire. [*Exits. In the doorway he runs into the* SECRETARY, *who trips, then bows.*]

SECRETARY [*with a less than cheerful expression*]: Damn these throw rugs. I suppose they're eager to look fashionable . . . Is that gargoyle still here? What a kisser, honest to God. She gives me no peace day or night. It's still morning, and she's already dolled up . . .

DAUGHTER [*flirtatiously*]: Ah, is that you? Your face looks especially stupid today. You probably spent all night getting drunk and playing cards.

SECRETARY: Did you see, your respected papa found himself a worthy accomplice, some thug? We'll all get into real trouble one of these days.

DAUGHTER: He'll probably propose to me today. Only I won't give him an answer whatever he does. Not if I know it, my good sir. First I'll try for the millionaire.

SECRETARY: Taking your time? Savoring the moment? Making your choice? I see it all . . .

DAUGHTER: Well, say something, don't mumble . . . Let's sit over there on the settee.

SECRETARY: Should I make my proposal now? Should I risk it? [*Grasps his foot.*] That ankle boot . . . It's too tight, it pinches . . . A real torture . . .

DAUGHTER: Why are you wriggling? Aren't you well?

SECRETARY: It had to start up . . . If I say it's to do with my shoe, it'll spoil the mood . . . Ow . . . ow . . . I'll try to slip it off gently.

DAUGHTER: He's in pain. How stupid. I'll have to encourage him. What's wrong with you?

SECRETARY [*speaking to her as if on the telephone*]: I told you. Don't hold your breath. Ow-ow . . . What can I come up with? Yes . . . that'll probably do the trick. A duel . . . A duel, Nadezhda Pavlovna . . .

DAUGHTER: A lie, a stupid, impertinent lie. The fellow's incredibly thick. [*The* BUTLER *enters.*]

BUTLER [*in the tone of an announcement*]: I broke my whole back lookin' for it. You tossed your powder under the bed . . .

DAUGHTER [*very affectionately*]: Blockhead, idiot . . . Why give it to me in front of him? Ah, I wish you'd . . .

SECRETARY [*lyrically*]: Thought you'd powder yourself? Figure that'll make your kisser any slicker? Silly goose. Yes, it doesn't matter, though. The main thing for me is the dowry. The old man is bound to have lots tucked away, one way or another. I'll propose right now . . . Nadezhda Pavlovna . . . Ow, ow . . . My foot, my foot . . . And my pet corn too . . . Well, can I get away with it? . . .

DAUGHTER: Don't drag it out, for heaven's sake. Say what has to be said quickly . . . These men are such impossible contraptions . . .

SECRETARY [*passionately*]: Nadezhda Pavlovna, if it weren't for this damned boot, I might propose on the spot, but it's impossible now. I have to take it off first, and then . . .

DAUGHTER [*embarrassed*]: You're a prize idiot . . . He drags it out, makes a fuss about his foot. I'll have to forget about marrying you . . . Oh well. [*The* BUTLER *and the* TRAMP *enter.*] Anyway, it's too late now . . . What a stupid lump . . .

BUTLER: Stand here and look around . . . Don't pinch anything.

TRAMP: This is a fine mess I'm in.

DAUGHTER [*with curiosity*]: Phooey, how disgusting. A drunkard, I suppose, some sort of thief. Maybe even contagious . . .

SECRETARY [*familiarly*]: I suppose the chain gang's been missing you for a while.

TRAMP: Why're they googlin' their eyes at me? I'm s'posed to thank them, or what? I been hired, but what for I dunno.

SECRETARY [*amiably*]: We'll make it hot for you around here, pal . . .

DAUGHTER: I've got to make him propose at last. I'll take him to my room. Evgeny Nikolaevich, let's go to my room. You oaf . . .

SECRETARY [*choking with emotion*]: Your room? Oh no. Not on your life . . . I've almost got the boot off. I won't stay on my feet for anything . . .

DAUGHTER: Your story about the duel excites me. [*Drags him.*] Let's go . . .

SECRETARY: Good Lord . . . How'm I going to walk? Hold on . . . [*Adjusts his boot and limps off.*]

DAUGHTER: Well, I'll remind you . . .

TRAMP: Now there's a bimbo . . . Never in all my born days seen one like that . . . How's about this crib here . . . You, pal, it's clear you been fillin' your belly on the boss's grub too?

BUTLER [*benevolently*]: I should be goin', but I can't leave you here, because you're bound to swipe something off the table . . .

TRAMP: If this guy was human, he'd bring a flask o' somethin'. But it's just yap, yap, and what's the point?

BUTLER: I'll bet you were in prison, maybe even for murder . . .

TRAMP: "I put on this bobtailed jacket and act highfalutin, but at home, mind you, I used to eat cabbage soup with noodles." Where the blazes did your general get to?

BUTLER: Here comes our big noise now, as you see. He'll put you straight.

[*Enter the* GENERAL.]

GENERAL [*inspecting him*]: A poor specimen . . . He's like a peasant the way I'm like the pope of Rome. Some sneaking snitch. Look at me, you . . .

TRAMP: Now I'm stuck with the big shot, look at him, look at him till he bursts . . .

GENERAL [*sternly*]: If he pulls some kind of boner, the whole scheme's shot to hell . . . Hey, you, lie the way you were told to lie.

TRAMP: I'm Uncle Kovylyay . . . that's right anyways. And from . . . there, damn, I forgot, the village flew out of my head. Dog Sh . . . not, that's not it . . . Seat . . . shot . . . shire . . . Dogshire, Your Wuship.

GENERAL: Bad, very bad, not worth three rubles. They foisted some old jailbird on me . . . Should have dumped him long ago.

[*Enter the* GENERAL'S LADY.]

GENERAL'S LADY [*squeamishly*]: Oy, saints in heaven . . . what kind of highway robber have we here? I think the old man must have gone out of his mind.

GENERAL: You should at least have washed properly. You're still flushed from last night and your ears are full of dirt. Incredible . . .

GENERAL'S LADY: It's obscene the way he stinks . . . I'm surprised at you, what will you think of next?

GENERAL: Don't I have to find you money for your glad rags? Who's the first to complain?

GENERAL'S LADY: Kick him out, kick him out at once and perfume the air. You, you old dummy, look sharp.

BUTLER: Looky there, their high-class habits kicked in. Their noses can't take the smell. Phooey . . . [*Exits with the* TRAMP.]

GENERAL'S LADY [*very affectionately*]: Now I'll have it out with you, my dearest darling. I'll make you confess. Tell me, where were you hanging around until five in the morning?

GENERAL [*casually*]: I see, I see where this is heading. Now you'll start nagging, nagging like a rusty saw. Well, crucify away . . .

GENERAL'S LADY: Sitting up with all kinds of Mashettas and Nashettas? Throwing away good money? What a lowlife. He doesn't even show it.

GENERAL: Damn you, what's the best thing to tell you? It's not exactly an oil well, more like a gusher . . . That's a clumsy, clumsy lie . . .

GENERAL'S LADY: Make things up, make things up, you blockhead. No, you won't get around me. Now I'll kiss you, my friend, and find out what liquor you smell of. [*Kisses him.*] Oh, oh . . . and he smells of perfume . . . I knew it . . .

GENERAL [*speaking directly to her face, smiling*]: If only that little music-hall singer could see me now. She'd die laughing. A sweet little tease . . . Well, you old crow, carry on with your usual routine. Go into hysterics according to all the established rules.

GENERAL'S LADY: What's wrong with you? You take all sorts of women to all the restaurants at night? Fine, I'll take up with our secretary Zhenka. Now I've got no reason to hold back . . .

GENERAL: She calls him Zhenka? Right to my face. No, this is some kind of impudence and impertinence. Just to spite you I won't argue, you old harpy, just to spite you . . .

[*Enter the* LADY.]

LADY [*cheerfully*]: Bickering already? Here's happy family life for you.

GENERAL'S LADY [*smiling sweetly*]: Why did you have to turn up, right on cue, you gadabout? Shameless hussy . . .

LADY: All gussied up, dearie, like a scullery maid . . . That's what I call taste . . .

GENERAL'S LADY: You should strip even more naked. What's holding her back . . . That's what some people find attractive. Very nice . . .

LADY: If you keep on looking at me with that look, I'll call you such a name you'll burst with spite.

GENERAL'S LADY: Please do. Prides herself on her brains. An utter fool, nothing but a fool. And I have no wish to converse with you. Sit over there with my beauty. It'll make him happy. [*Exits, slamming the door.*]

LADY [*lovingly*]: That's quite a wife you've got . . .

GENERAL: My life is cursed. Still, it's nice from time to time when fate sends me such pretty little things as you. It's my only consolation . . .

LADY: After all, the little old fellow is pretty well preserved.

GENERAL: You should sit closer, closer . . . Oof . . . Such a little neck . . . God willing. Should I risk it or not? Suppose I invited her to supper somewhere, hm . . .

LADY: Well, well, he doesn't waste time . . . So slippery . . .

GENERAL: I'll kiss her . . . I'll take her and kiss her . . . To let such a wonderful moment pass . . . [*He stoops over; the* GENERAL'S LADY *enters.*]

GENERAL'S LADY: Playing love games? I can see it in his face.

GENERAL: I'll be paying for this sooner or later . . .

LADY: She snatched him away at the critical moment. Yet, who knows, she may have been spying . . . Such dignity . . .

GENERAL'S LADY: Go on, go on. Mr. Money Bags has arrived. This is what matters most.

GENERAL: Good heavens. Get thee behind me, Satan . . . What if I don't manage to put through the deal. [*The* CAPITALIST *enters.*] I've started quaking in my boots. Pa-pa-pa . . . Panteley Ivanych . . . Benefactor . . . Please. Unspeakably delighted. Lord, you look like a junkyard dog. God bless such a fool.

CAPITALIST: I must say I'm pretty fed up with your constant reminders. What sort of emergency is this?

GENERAL: A regular Rothschild . . . Vanderbilt the American . . . What a way with him . . . A big shot, no question . . . I have to introduce him to my crocodile. This model wife is bound to pull some stunt any minute . . .

GENERAL'S LADY: Delighted, quite delighted. The man's not half bad. Just the thing for our Nadenka . . .

CAPITALIST: Look at that. Ready to eat me up.

LADY: If I had a hubby like that . . .

CAPITALIST: Oho-ho . . . there's something doing there . . . It seems my visit isn't a total waste of time.

GENERAL: If you only knew what my situation is, you'd clear out this very minute. As for the Association . . . Devil take them, those clumsy idiots. And for me, for me, the chairman, the donations aren't enough to pay a salary. Not enough for a secretary, not enough for an inspection committee . . .

CAPITALIST: A sharp fellow, the way his eyes dart back and forth. Well, pal, you won't pull the wool over mine. I don't make this kind of deal.

GENERAL: What about the peasant? Phooey, that's dealt with. But how will I manage? Do you understand this, do you read my mind—you sack full of greasy banknotes?

CAPITALIST: Shall I give you something or not?

GENERAL: I've got to show you that jailbird. Maybe it'll work.

CAPITALIST: I don't like your face or your self-importance . . . What makes you so worried if you haven't got a stake in this? . . .

GENERAL: Now I'll play my trump card . . . Let's see if you falter. [*Leads him aside.*] I'll finally be awarded a medal. You understand, a medal . . .

CAPITALIST: Well, this old woman has bet on a dark horse.

GENERAL: He doesn't believe me. You don't believe me, you muttonhead? . . . I've run up against the devil. What the hell more do you need?

CAPITALIST: If the price is right, I might strike a bit of a bargain, I'm not against your Association, if that little lady is in it.

GENERAL: Why hesitate? Fifteen thousand and it's in the bag.

CAPITALIST: Right now, no matter what. [*The* DAUGHTER *and* SECRETARY *enter.*] Ah . . . And here's your overripe virgin . . .

DAUGHTER: Well, I'll try casting my line at him.

GENERAL: Our secretary, to be honest, as thick as a plank.

SECRETARY [*bowing*]: I despise capitalists . . .

DAUGHTER: I won't leave your side.

CAPITALIST: Now she's clinging to me. I'd much rather be with the . . . other one . . .

LADY: No one's paying me the least attention . . . That trashy old maid was laughing at me . . . Ah, the good-for-nothing. Well, let's see . . . Evgeny Nikolaevich, I'll go for you, at least I can't let such an idiot girl get away with it . . .

GENERAL'S LADY: I'll show up my loving hubby at the meeting . . . I'll hang round the neck of that curly little poodle . . . Evgeny Nikolaevich . . .

SECRETARY [*very affectionately*]: Ah, go to hell . . . I'm being pestered by gargoyles from both sides . . . Leave me alone, for heaven's sake . . .

GENERAL: It's time to pick our chairman . . . For want of a better. Panteley Ivanovich, take the top spot. It serves you right . . .

CAPITALIST: Thank God, they've had the sense at least to offer us seats. No, this is clearly a shady business.

DAUGHTER: Let's see how you stand up to my languorous gaze. Only it's a nuisance about that cheese wart. And mama dear over there is shameless . . . Hanging round Evgeny Nikolaevich's neck.

SECRETARY [*to the* DAUGHTER]: And you're not leaning heavily on that millionaire, are you? I may be a nobody, but I'm more to be trusted, and how!

GENERAL: Well, now I'll play my trump card. Will it bowl you over or not? [*Rings.* BUTLER *enters.*] Show in that jailbird. [*Emotionally.*] You know, it's impossible to look at that godforsaken face without disgust.

CAPITALIST [*agreeing lovingly*]: Obviously, a gang of swindlers, got to keep a sharp lookout.

GENERAL [*affirmatively*]: Quite so. Here's the little wonder. Only for such as you are medals awarded.

[*Enter the* TRAMP.]

TRAMP: Oho-ho . . . Now's when I'm s'posed to do my stuff, I guess. Oh Lord, I stole a samovar from his factory . . .

CAPITALIST: Eh . . . still . . . so that's the emissary from the elders . . . I know that face. My dear fellow, didn't you used to work in my factory?

TRAMP [*firmly*]: I'll spill the beans right now. There's no point in waiting . . .

CAPITALIST: Clearly a gang of confidence tricksters . . . I'd better pull out.

GENERAL: Well, it's time to hand over what was asked of you, moneybags.

CAPITALIST: I am ready to donate shares in my factory. It doesn't matter, I'll be closing it soon, and they won't be worth a tinker's damn.

GENERAL: Eh-eh-eh . . . Don't try to worm out of it . . . Give us cash money . . .

CAPITALIST: There you have it. If you want it, please go and look for it.

GENERAL [*disappointedly*]: A cheater, you cheater, who the hell needs your shares? Though I'll take 'em, you can get a hank of hair even off a mangy dog . . . Hand over the shares.

CAPITALIST: We've yet to settle this, stop by, we'll talk it over. But now I'm off. Goodbye, speculators. [*Bows, exits.*]

GENERAL: Scum of the earth . . .

DAUGHTER: That repulsive individual did not deign to cast a look my way.

GENERAL: Of course . . . who could be tempted by such a kisser?

GENERAL'S LADY: He yawned in our faces, you fool. I expected as much . . .

TRAMP: And what about me? I was promised three rubles.

GENERAL: Three rubles? Would you like it round the neck? Nikita, throw him out . . . The scheme's a bust.

NIKOLAY EVREINOV

INTRODUCTION

Everything about Nikolay Nikolaevich Evreinov (1879–1953) cried aesthete: his pageboy haircut, his beardless face at a time when only actors and non-Orthodox clergy were clean-shaven, his impeccable footwear, his tendency to inject himself into every literary controversy going. He was eager for the world to see him as an "admirable Crichton," capable of anything in the artistic line. It had started early. From the age of five, this son of a distinguished engineer was taken to the theater by his mother, a Russian of French descent. At seven he wrote his first play, a parody based on Ivan Turgenev called *Luncheon with a Minister of State*. In his teens, living in Pskov, he mounted a puppet theater and studied piano, violin, cello, flute, and piccolo. Like so many of his contemporaries, he entered the law curriculum at Saint Petersburg University, enrolled by his parents, but in the summers he performed conjuring and played Pierrot in the Moscow suburbs. The white-faced mime became his alter ego.

Meanwhile, Evreinov was writing plays with *commedia* characters and studying Nietzsche and religious philosophy. He earned his law degree with a dissertation on corporal punishment in Russia and made a living as a civil servant in the Ministry of Roads and Communication. He now embarked on a serious musical education, four years under Nikolay Rimsky-Korsakov and Aleksandr Glazunov, composing for theatrical productions. He became a familiar figure at fashionable salons and vernissages, posing for such prominent artists as Yury Annenkov, Serge Sudeikin, and Nikolai Kul'bin. Typically, he published a volume of portraits of himself with commentary. From 1902 Evreinov's plays began to be staged in leading Saint Petersburg theaters with uneven success.

In 1907, along with the historian and censor Baron Nikolay Drizen (Osten-Driesen), he created the Antique Theater (Starinny Teatr), where he attempted to reconstruct the performance styles of the past. Its first season of medieval French plays was well received, but not until 1911–12 could it produce another set of reconstructions. That one, devoted to the Spanish Golden Age, was performed with an onstage audience of peasants and sets changed in full view of the audience, blurring the line between theater and life. A third season devoted to *commedia dell'arte* was aborted by the outbreak of the war.[1]

Another sign of recognition came in 1908, when Russia's most celebrated actress, Vera Kommissarzhevskaya, engaged Evreinov to join her brother Fyodor in codirecting her theater. She had just dismissed Vsevolod Meyerhold for overindulgence in stylized experimentation, and from then on Evreinov and Meyerhold would be rivals, keeping a cautious distance while accusing one another of plagiarism.[2] Evreinov's elaborate production of Oscar Wilde's *Salome* was prevented from opening by the Holy Synod, leading to the theater's bankruptcy. So, with Kommissarzhevsky, he founded the Merry Theater for Grown-Up Children (1909) chiefly to stage his symbolist harlequinade *A Merry Death* (*Vesyolaya smert'*, 1909), in which Death appears as a pretty girl. "Success made me self-confident," he later wrote, "and publicity made me famous."[3]

Fame also derived from his theatrical manifestos. One of Evreinov's central theses was *teatral'nost*, or "theatricality." Bolstering his argument with references to zoology, ethnography, behaviorism, and a wide sphere of knowledge, he maintained that all aspects of creation were endowed with a pre-aesthetic instinct for performance, as fundamental as sex, hunger, or self-preservation. Make-believe, acting out, and dressing up are basic needs of human psychology. The world is an arena for role- and game-playing. Play exists to project the drama of the inner self. Revealing this inner drama requires such techniques as distortion, exaggeration, and grotesquerie. The desire to perform, to assume a persona, to act out in everyday life is a basic instinct. The human race is ruled by a "theatrocracy," therefore the theater is an essential component of life, deserving of respect and close attention. Evreinov clearly foreshadowed Johan Huizinga's *Homo Ludens* (1938); his writings propagated ideas that gained wide currency only years later through Erving Goffman's *Presentation of Self in Everyday Life* and Judith Butler's doctrine of gender as performance. (His three-volume theoretical treatise *A Theatre for Oneself* [*Teatr dlya sebya*] was written in 1915–16, while he was working at the Mirror.)

The theater, which arises from this faculty, must not try to copy "life" but must be colorful, artificial, flamboyant, to fulfill these needs. What goes on onstage must create an alternative world to the world outside the theater, at least until the outside world becomes fully theatricalized. The only ethics in the theater, Evreinov insisted, is the right to receive impressions and an obligation to produce them. Paraphrasing Verlaine, he rejected messages: "All the rest is metaphysics."[4]

Evreinov shared with Gogol the belief that a comic author's task was a noble one: to evoke intelligent, socially committed laughter and to pour scorn on the negative elements of life. One of Evreinov's favorite words was "merry" (*vsyoly*), and like Wilde and Shaw, he found that the best way to convey his ideas was in a flippant tone of voice. "The aim of parody," Evreinov wrote, "is to render comic those things that are taken seriously." As a panacea, it goes beyond simple caricature if one flays abuses by spotting their essential foible and exploiting it. This involved the grotesque, which "consists in acting as if the object mocked is subject to no taboo, as if morality not only authorizes that it be turned to derision, but has somehow condemned it to undergo the punishment of laughter and even profanation."[5]

It was at this point that the mercurial Evreinov was invited to take over the artistic direction of the Crooked Mirror. He accepted with conditions: he wanted an assistant director and a designer, both chosen from progressive art movements; the move from a cabaret space to a full-fledged theater building; and a decent salary. This last remained a bone of contention, and he and Kugel' often locked horns over matters artistic and material. Kugel' was the more pragmatic, looked down on by Evreinov for never enunciating a theory or a manifesto. Still, Evreinov maintained his association with the Mirror until 1917. He claimed to have been involved in one capacity or another (author, director, composer, translator, consultant) in over a hundred plays there.

Evreinov's first works for the Crooked Mirror were very much rooted in the world of theater. *Living Statues* (*Ozhivayushchie statui*, January 24, 1911) lampoons a popular variety act. More ambitious, *The School for Stars* (*Shkola étualov*, November 13, 1911; Evreinov puts the French *étoile* into Cyrillic letters) aims its shafts at several targets. First of all, there is the European-style variety theater, with its song-and-dance acts and exotic attractions. This was precisely the kind of entertainment the Crooked Mirror was devised to counteract. Next there is the absurd notion of a school to train for such an amusement, with pretensions to art and the ideal. Stanislavsky's studios may also be slated for ridicule. And, not least, Evreinov has in his sights the Russian fashion for "folkloric" performance. When the Variety Manager goes into ecstasies over an untutored scullery maid singing a common folk song, the butt is those performers who gave up evening dress for peasant blouses and lieder recitals for gypsy ballads, along with the audiences that acclaimed them.

It was not until the fifth season (1912–13) that Evreinov set his stamp on the program as a playwright. Back in 1908, he had published "Introduction to Monodrama," and by March 1909 he had delivered it three times as a public lecture. Behind Evreinov's elaborate fan dance of erudite citation, convoluted syntax, and wide-ranging allusion, the idea is essentially straightforward. The audience is to identify and empathize with only one character onstage: the *deystvuyushchee litso*, or active participant ("protagonist" is an alternative translation). Everything in the play is to be staged from that character's point of view, and all scenic means are to be employed to portray his state of mind at any given moment. If the presentation is successful, the spectator will serve as alter ego and undergo a coexperiencing (*soperezhivanie*) with the protagonist. The onstage drama will become entwined with the personal drama of the spectator, and the divisive split between stage and auditorium will be obliterated. This last point brought Evreinov close to the symbolist desideratum of the integration of audience into the performance, but without the sacerdotal trimmings.[6] His prime concern was to give the spectators the illusion that they themselves are acting, not so that they can commune with a higher truth but so that theatergoing will become a meaningful experience for them.

As it happened, in the monodramas produced at the Crooked Mirror the technique was often to fragment the central character into several facets played by several actors, creating a dialogue within a monologue. Although Boris Geyer and Evreinov himself were the chief practitioners of the form, some actors played their own monosketches, and Geyer's *The Water of Life* is a reductive parody of the monodramatic idea. It always galled Evreinov that his first attempt at a monodrama, *The Presentation of Love* (*Predstavlenie lyubvi*, 1910), was produced not in Russia but in Vienna and Budapest and that the Crooked Mirror's debut monodramas—*The Water of Life*, *Memories*, and *The Dream*—were by Boris Geyer. (See the Geyer introduction.) It was important to Evreinov's ego to be recognized as the "onlie begettor" of ideas and devices; his memoirs teem with claims to primacy in many fields.

To reclaim ownership of monodrama as a playwright, at the end of the 1911–12 season Evreinov proposed *Backstage at the Soul* (*V kulisakh dushi*) to his colleagues. Kugel', Khol'mskaya, Urvantsov, Geyer, and Érenberg were all taken aback by this one-act, set in the human psyche. They thought an equally bewildered audience would reject it. In autumn 1912 Evreinov offered them a model of the set as well as his composition "Hymn of Love," to be strummed on the nerves. Khol'mskaya now endorsed the play, though Kugel' suggested changes, writing a prologue that served as both a satire of academic lectures and a guide to the outlandish play to come.

The designer Mikhail Bobyshev found ingenious means to realize Evreinov's model, lighting it in an oxblood–violet range, giving the internal anatomy a mystical character. On the gigantic spinal column at the back of a wide stage, pale blue gaps appeared between the vertebrae, painted on the kind of transparent scrim used by draftsmen. A large heart, naturalistic in form, expanded and contracted at a rate corresponding to the feverish intensity of the dialogue and action; it glowed in crimson tints. Spongy lungs of a bluish hue inflated and deflated like sails on a boat in bad weather. The dark crimson diaphragm, on which the monodrama was played out, was carpentered to be anatomically correct. When the curtain rose on this never-before-seen picture of a human inside, some of the spectators later reported to have felt queasy. The mother of the matinee idol Vladimir Maksimov became so ill that she had to be carried out of the auditorium.[7]

The play's success exceeded expectations. It was eventually staged in Vienna, Berlin, and even England (the Little Theater, 1915, codirected by Gordon Craig's daughter Edith).[8] Evreinov claimed that Freud not only mentioned it in *Ich und Es* but also based his concept of Id, Ego, and Superego on it. He quoted the Austrian playwright Franz Csokor as calling it a forerunner of expressionism and cited the English critic Allardyce Nicoll's description of it as "the art-form of the immediate future."[9]

As an illustration of Evreinov's monodramatic theory, *Backstage at the Soul* doesn't quite work. The individual himself, whose psychic workings we observe, is personally unaware of what's going in behind the scenes of his mind. We see not through his eyes but as an omniscient observer, with the fourth wall—that is, flesh, blood, and bone—stripped away. Nevertheless, the dramatization of a divided self, the transformation of the scenic elements to depict a character's state of mind, and the mechanistic presentation of psychological factors are all ingeniously innovative and "modern" in their application.

The three other Crooked Mirror plays Evreinov chose to include in his collected works all refer directly to the contemporary theater. For him, *The Inspector General* (*Revizor*), which opened on December 2, 1912, was a "synthetic parody," since it ridiculed not Gogol's text but the mishandlings of his text by overweening directors imposing them on credulous audiences. The self-importance of those tin gods had to be undermined if the theater was to remain healthy.

The Crooked Mirror's *Inspector General* was meant to ridicule the whole trend toward directorial reinterpretation of the classics. Kugel' wrote the speeches of the official who explains matters to the audience, and Sergey Ivanovich Antimonov composed the verse in the Reinhardt sequence. Once again, Bobyshev supplied the scenery. Evreinov's contribution was to devise the most salient and ludicrous ways of staging the classic comedy, in order to draw attention to the stylistic absurdities of certain well-known directors. Excerpting a couple of scenes from act 1 of Gogol's play, he limited himself to the types most in the public eye at the time.

The "ordinary" staging of *The Inspector General* was meant to be a norm by which to measure the deviancy of what followed. Despite its naive conventions, Evreinov admires its straightforward presentation of the text and its refusal to pretend that the stage is anything but a stage. Gogol's comedy was the most frequently performed play on provincial and amateur stages, and the average Russian theatergoer knew its standardized stage pictures and pieces of business by heart.

The second version in the style of Stanislavsky was a well-aimed swipe at a man whom Evreinov admired personally but whose avowed principles were diametrically opposed to his own. The Moscow Art Theater, with its adherence to psychological naturalism—its endless table rehearsals and discussions; its elaborate subtexts, understated acting, and pregnant pauses; its pursuit of historical accuracy in classical drama—was a ripe target for satire. Nemirovich-Danchenko, its cofounder, had been quoted as saying, "Before we begin rehearsals, we read the play to distill, so to speak, the Mood."[10] For Evreinov, however, the mood was a dingy haze that obscured the sharp contours of theatricality, and he mocked its pretensions unmercifully. As a matter of fact, the Art Theater had staged *The Inspector General* in 1908 in a production that sought to reproduce in detail small-town Russian life in the 1830s; the consensus was that the carefully researched props and costumes were an unfunny reversion to the antiquarianism of the Saxe-Meiningen troupe. So when Evreinov's Mayoress and her daughter subside into Chekhovian gloom as the rain patters down, he is illustrating the pointlessness of the Art Theater method when applied to classic comedy.

The third version, in the style of Gordon Craig, was another potshot at the Art Theater. From 1909 to 1912, Craig, the apostle of Übermarionettes and kinetic screens, had worked sporadically with Stanislavsky on a production of *Hamlet*. It was a fertile source of gossip in theatrical circles, and the production's delays and setbacks were fodder for the Art Theater's opponents. Craig had envisaged a monodramatic tragedy, the events and characters seen through the eyes of the Prince, a hypersensitive reformer accompanied by an androgynous Death figure. The milieu was to be an undefined stage space, created by massive, reversible screens. Craig's idealized vision collided with the Art Theater's aesthetic practice and policy, and the result was a sorry compromise between the two. The settings wavered between symbolism and vagueness; the actors were incapable of relinquishing their nuanced psychologies, and it turned out, as Gogol might have put it, "neither fish nor flesh nor good red herring." In his parody, Evreinov scores off the Art Theater's pretentious publicity about keeping Craig's methods secret, the lugubrious music by Il'ya Sats, and the whole portentous mysticism in which Shakespeare's tragedy had been steeped.

The fourth version, as if directed by Max Reinhardt, is perhaps the least pointed, since the least indigenous. Reinhardt toured his production of *Oedipus the King* to Saint Petersburg in 1912, but the Crooked Mirror was hardly equipped to parody the massive crowd scenes. Instead, Evreinov goes after Reinhardt's dependence on recensions of classical drama by the Austrian poet Hugo von Hofmannsthal. The joke ran that Hofmannsthal's febrile reworking of *Electra* and *Oedipus* caused "Neu-Romantik" to be spelled "Neuro-mantik." The German love for abstraction (and proverbial inability to see a joke) are suggested by the allegorical figures of Satire,

Laughter, and Humor. The garish colors of the Munich Secession school of painting appear in the stage design, and Evreinov teases the European penchant for staging Russian plays in gaudy Ukrainian peasant costume and comic-opera uniforms.

Finally, the silent-film version protests the violence done to a play by reducing it to the basic elements of slapstick. By 1912, Max Linder was a much-loved comedian on Russian screens, and audiences had found a popular native clown in their own, V. Avdeev, a buffoon of elephantine proportions billed as Dyadya Pud, or Uncle Tonnage. Astutely, Evreinov is already pointing out that the chase scene is the *ne plus ultra* of cinematic comedy.

From the parody's opening night, the Crooked Mirror audiences fell in love with it and made it one of the theater's most abiding hits. At Imperial command, a special performance was given at Tsarkoe Selo in 1913, along with *The Guest Artist*, for the imperial family. Every member of the cast and crew received a gift, except for the uninvited Kugel', who was a Jew.

One of the butts of Evreinov's satire took offense. Stanislavsky, notoriously thin-skinned about criticism, resented both the gibes at the *Hamlet* on which so much time and energy had been expended and the reference to his poorly received *Inspector*. For years afterward, Evreinov and Stanislavsky sedulously avoided one another. When Evreinov later claimed that his parody was responsible for Stanislavsky's restaging of *The Inspector* in 1922, the latter was incensed.

Over the years the play was updated to reflect changing fashion in directing. In the early 1920s, a constructivist *Inspector* was added, aimed at Meyerhold, Eisenstein, and left-wing artists in general. After Meyerhold staged his own *Inspector*, Kugel' made a few additions directed against it. Evreinov also replicated his success with *Hand Over Hamlet*, Shakespeare's play as staged by the leftist avant-garde. (The title refers to Meyerhold's *D.E.* [*Daesh Evropy*, or *Hand Over Europe*]).

A peripheral effect of the Crooked Mirror *Inspector General* was an innovation in Russian copyright law. Since most of the lines in the play itself were by Gogol, Evreinov, in obtaining an author's fee from the Union of Dramatic and Musical Authors, proved "the possibility of protecting the *director*'s authorial rights" over his own staging. After the fact, Evreinov claimed that he had, in part, written the parody to test the point. Kugel', who had intended to blast directors, must have been chagrined to find directorial creativity sanctioned in this manner. In the US an unsuccessful attempt was made in the 1980s to copyright specific productions, without reference to Evreinov.

Evreinov's *Inspector General*, by turning the spotlight on staging abuses, brought what had been an exclusively professional question of technique before a wider public and made it aware of the ongoing debate in the Russian theater. Moreover, he originated the "in the style of" format, which became a regular feature of revues and cabaret theaters for decades. Unwittingly, Second City, the Premise, the Proposition, and scores of other satirical troupes have perpetrated Evreinov's innovation.

On October 23, 1913, Evreinov offered *The Laughter Kitchen: A Worldwide Humor Competition* (*Kukhnya smekha: Mirovoy konkurs ostroumiya*), a parody in four caricatures. The alleged occasion for the contest is a theater's need to fill its repertory with contemporary comedies in translation. Each of the winning plays is supposed to constitute the quintessence of the national sense of humor. The German entry, *Die Bienenliebe oder Was soll es bedeuten* (*Bee Love, or What's This Supposed to Mean*) by Georg Meyer, is a heavy-handed sketch with Prussian officers, a stutterer, and sentimentality. *Les Boutons d'amour, ou Oh–la–la ou Un quart d'heure avec Georgette* (*The Buttons* [or *Nipples*] *of Love, or Fifteen Minutes with Georgette*), by Jules Corbeau, is a typical bedroom farce. The American winner, *The Betting of the Two Red Devils, or Time Is Money* by William Mudge, is a "hyperbolic grotesque, neo-publicity, trans-comedy, super-caricature" of "typically Anglo-Saxon features" such as an exchange of slaps, a scene in a toilet, and a checkered handkerchief into which a big red nose is blown. Finally, we are treated to the Russian entry, *Troglodytov's Happiness* (*Shchast'e Trogloditova*) by Osip Arkadchenko (a merging of the humorists Arkadiev and Averchenko), whose cast includes such familiar types as a drunk, a mother-in-law, a "dacha husband," and a Jew speaking in the Odessa dialect.[11]

Evreinov responded to the lukewarm reviews by saying he was more interested in form than content. Even so, the play represented his abiding interest in comedy and why something is funny. The stale jokes and clichés he parodies remain valid for most audiences, and the caricatures of national character are long a-dying.

If we set aside a ballet parody, *A Columbine of Today* (*Kolumbina segodnyay*, 1913), and the disputed *Æolian Harps* (see the Geyer introduction), Evreinov's last contribution, first performed on December 21, 1915, was *The Fourth Wall* (*Chetvyortaya stena*). The objects of the satire were threefold. First, as usual, Evreinov had in mind the Moscow Art Theater, famous for its "striving for archeological historical specificity, ethnography, true-to-life naturalism and, finally, for 'the fourth wall,' trees planted center stage, chairs and actors turned backs to the audience."[12] Ironically, that quotation comes from Evreinov's second target, his former colleague Fyodor Komissarzhevsky. Komis (as he was later known to English actors) had become a prominent director who advocated staging each play in accordance with its author's idiosyncratic style. He had mounted a production of *Faust* at Nezlobin's Theater in Moscow in September 1912 and had written, "Mephistopheles in Goethe's tragedy *Faust* is for me Faust's 'alter ego.' He is the devil but a special devil, namely a Faustian devil . . . I would even like it if the face and figure of Mephisto as depicted onstage reminded me of Faust."[13] He had in mind Vasily Kachalov's performance as Ivan Karamazov in the Art Theater's adaptation of *The Brothers Karamazov*. In the scene of Ivan's nightmare, his colloquy with the Devil, Kachalov had taken both parts.

Evreinov was amused to push this idea to its logical conclusion and envisage a production of Gounod's opera in which the tenor has to sing both roles. Using Gounod rather than Goethe enabled him to include in his mockery attempts to reform the staging of opera in the early twentieth century. He had in mind particularly the *Faust* staged at the Theater of Musical Drama. Its founder, Igor' M. Lapitsky, wanted to adapt Art Theater principles to opera production and went overboard in his aspiration to "realism." In *Carmen*, for instance, he had an ambulance park outside the bullring in act 5 in case Escamillo was gored. In *The Fourth Wall*, the Artistic Director employs every means at his disposal—lighting effects, props, smells, the performer's living the role—to create "realism." In a bit of Evreinovian metatheater, he condemns traditional operatic conventions as *Vampuka*. Ultimately the would-be reformer's efforts result in the abolition not only of opera but of spectacle in general, by constructing a brick-and-mortar fourth wall. Evreinov claimed that his play enjoyed a success equal to that of *Vampuka*,[14] but it had less effect in extirpating artistic abuses.

During the war years Evreinov helped create the literary cabaret the Stray Dog and its successor, the Comedians' Rest, where he improvised on the piano and sang his lyrics. In fall 1917 he left Petrograd, worked in Kiev, and in Tiflis, the capital of Georgia, organized yet another cabaret, the Chimerion. After the Civil War, although he was essentially apolitical, to celebrate the third anniversary of the October Revolution he headed a ten-man team, including Kugel', to devise the mass spectacle *The Storming of the Winter Palace* (*Vzyatie zimnego dvortsa*), which involved eight thousand performers. It took place in 1920 in the open air on two stages, one white and the other red, to symbolize the struggle between the tsarist forces and the revolutionaries. For an artist whose preferred format was the miniature, this was an unusual change of (s)pace.

In 1921 Evreinov married a commonsensical young divorcée who would provide him much-needed emotional stability for the rest of his life. He also published his most circulated play, known in English as *The Chief Thing* (*Samoe glavnoe*; a better translation would be *What Matters* or *What's Important*). This somewhat Pirandellian comedy was performed all over the world and helped support Evreinov and his reputation during hard times. The following year the newlyweds toured to Berlin and Paris, fully intending to return so that Evreinov could honor a contract directing Mirror plays at the Crooked Jimmy cabaret in Moscow. The same intention held when he joined the Mirror's tour to Warsaw in 1925, but its disastrous outcome caused a definitive break with Kugel'.

A review by a Soviet critic of a revival of *Backstage at the Soul* reveals how irrelevant Evreinov had become in the new order:

> *Backstage at the Soul* . . . seems nowadays something exceptionally vulgar. For its time and its circle of spectators, perhaps, it was appropriate fare; nowadays such a spectator is quite on the decline, and for the new one mysticism and bourgeois morality, even if concealed behind an ironic smile, are quite unnecessary. However, "Backstage at the Soul" is performed very decently, probably because the theatre has long been thoroughly familiar with it.[15]

The Evreinovs saw the futility of return and moved to Paris. There he became a major player in Russian émigré theater, helping to found an epigone of the Crooked Mirror, the Strolling Players (Brodyachie Komedianty); heading the Theater of Russian Drama; and turning out more plays, memoirs, radio broadcasts, and a history of Russian theater.

Constantly regarding himself as unappreciated and undervalued, he took every opportunity to publicize his past achievements. During the Nazi Occupation, he was under scrutiny by the Gestapo for being a Freemason and was wrongly suspected of being Jewish. His last years were burdened with illness and privation. When he died in 1973, he was buried in Sainte Geneviève de Bois cemetery in Paris, but his widow donated his papers to the literary archives in Moscow. After the collapse of the Soviet Union, his plays and theoretical writings and even unpublished manuscripts were finally made available in his native land.

NOTES

1. Evreinov's provocative directorial experiments elsewhere include Schiller's *Maid of Orleans* with a male Joan of Arc and a *Francesca da Rimini* staged in the round.
2. For a full exploration of this prickly relationship, see Anthony G. Pearson, "Meyerhold and Evreinov: 'Originals' at Each Other's Expense," *New Theatre Quarterly* 8, no. 32 (November 1992): 321–32.
3. Nikolay Evreinov, *V shkole ostroumiya*, ed. Aleksandra Deich and Anna Kashina-Evreinova (Moscow: Iskusstvo, 1998), 125.
4. Evreinov, "Teatral'nye inventii," *Maski* 1 (1912): 77.
5. Evreinov, *V shkole ostroumiya*, 125.
6. A translation of *Vvedenie k monodramu* appears in Laurence Senelick, ed. and trans., *Russian Dramatic Theory from Pushkin to the Symbolists* (Austin: University of Texas Press, 1981), 183–99.
7. Evreinov, *V shkole ostroumiya*, 283–88.
8. He also boasted that when the Lord Chamberlain's Office tried to ban it, Lady Randolph Churchill intervened.
9. Nicoll also said "whether we like it or not." Allardyce Nicoll, *British Drama: An Historical Survey from the Beginnings to the Present Time* (New York: Thomas Y. Crowell, 1925), 403.
10. Quoted in *Rossiya* 238 (1899).
11. In the Soviet era this was replaced by *Gorderdergor ili Ugukusmekh* (*Townencountryton*), allegedly written by a collective, to be played in the open air with infantry, cavalry, artillery, air force, war elephants, and performers from the theater, opera, ballet, and circus organized by a staff of directors who wigwag signals to each other by telegraph, spotlights, and flags. Co-authored by Evreinov and Vladimir Azov, it spoofed the very mass spectacle that Evreinov became known for.
12. F. F. Komissarzhevsky, *Tvorchestvo aktyora i teoriya Stanislavskogo* (Prague: Svobodnoe iskusstvo, n.d.), 86.
13. F. F. Komissarzhevsky, *Teatral'nye prelyudy* (Moscow: A. P. Korkin, A. V. Beydemon & Ko., 1916), 47.
14. Nikolay Evreinov, *Histoire du théâtre russe* (Paris: Éditions du Chêne, 1947), 399.
15. S. Voskresensky in *Krasnaya gazeta* (Leningrad), February 18, 1927.

THE SCHOOL FOR STARS
(Shkola étualov)

Grotesque parody in one act

by Nikolay Evreinov

1911

CAST

The Headmaster of "The Music Hall School of Vocalizing"

Instructress

Music-hall Manager

*First, Second, and Third Baby, a trio**

Servant

Apache[†]

Apache Girl

Duncan Dancer[‡]

Music-hall Singer

Annushka

---

* Babies, young women in bonnets and pinafores, performed double-entendre routines. (See Toulouse-Lautrec's poster of May Milton.) The famous Danish ensemble the Barrison Sisters would hold black kittens below their waists and sing of how they loved their pussies.

† *Apache* (pronounced "ah-*pahsh*") derives from the native American tribe considered especially fierce. It was a term both derogatory and admiring that French journalists bestowed on thugs and pimps who haunted the outskirts of Paris. The *apache* dance, launched in 1908, involved a pimp and his moll in a brutal display of contortions and violent actions. It became immensely popular in nightclubs and on the variety stage.

‡ The American Isadora Duncan (1877–1917), famous for her barefoot, uncorseted expressive dances in flowing drapery, toured to Russia in 1904–5 and 1907–8. She was highly influential, counting Konstantin Stanislavsky among her admirers.

*A mass of eye-catching, garish posters and photographs of stunning balleri-
nas. Downstage a platform stage. Left, by the upright piano, a tiny orchestra
of "seedy-looking musicians." The "coeds" cluster right. On the platform is the
"*BABY TRIO.*" Before the platform stands the* HEADMASTER *himself and an*
INSTRUCTRESS. *The orchestra leader who accompanies them at times on the
fiddle, at times on the piano, is much out of sorts and often utters bitter truth
to the musicians, whose faces show that they make an effort but are definitely
underpaid. When the curtain rises, the* HEADMASTER *is beside himself. He is
a very proud man, not devoid of "exoticism" in appearance; he speaks in a foreign accent and, like all poetic and talented natures, has boundless impatience.*

HEADMASTER [*yelling*]: Not like that, not like that, damn it! . . . How
many times do I have to tell you, you confounded devils? A one-
year-old would understand that when you lift your right foot, you
have to go down on your left. Did you study in your laundry?—then
why bother coming to my school? I won't be compromised. [*Claps his
hands.*] From the top! . . . [*To the musicians*] Hey! . . . [*To the* BABIES]
Now let's have a smile, damn you! . . . Smile! You're not going to a
funeral. If your auntie or your granny died, then go and pray, but don't
try my patience.

INSTRUCTRESS [*to the* BABIES]: That's it, nice big smile! I said: smile.
Lightly on the right foot! Nod your heads!

HEADMASTER [*yelling, clapping his hands*]: From the top. [*The music plays.*]

BABY RIO [*singing and dancing*]:

> With cakewalks and maxixes,* we soon were bored to tears,
> But now a new dance craze appears.
> The Pola-pola's really blazing, the Pola-pola's just amazing.
> Everybody, small and tall, does this dance at every ball,
> It's the greatest fun of all . . .
> The Pola-pola sets you free, drives you into ecstasy.
> Don't we always take the tone set by modern Babylon?

---

* The cakewalk was a high-stepping dance performed by slaves on plantations in the US South,
later popular on the minstrel stage and in vaudeville. It was introduced into Russia around 1900.
The maxixe (pronounced mah-*sheesh*) is a Brazilian tango, which became popular both with
adagio dancers onstage and in ballrooms at the same time as the cakewalk.

That must be the reason why we all give this dance a try.
The Parisian's a patrician, 'cause dancing's his strong suit.
He wins ev'ry competition and thinks he's awful cute!

[*They dance to the music between the verses.*]

HEADMASTER [*stopping them*]: Stop! First, I can see you don't understand a word of what you're singing. [*To the* INSTRUCTRESS] Klavdiya Ivanovna, did you explain to them what it means?

INSTRUCTRESS: Good grief, Henrik Oskarovich, at least a thousand times. You know how devoted I am to my work.

HEADMASTER: Yes, but they sing it as if it had nothing to do with them.

INSTRUCTRESS [*to the* BABIES]: Where is your phrasing, you godless heathens? . . . Didn't I show each of you individually that . . .

HEADMASTER [*interrupting*]: I simply don't know what to do . . . The manager of the Variety Theater will be here any minute—I promised him the trio would be ready—he got at most two numbers for the closing. He'll say I'm a fraud.

INSTRUCTRESS [*in tears, to the* BABIES]: I'm asking you, where is your phrasing?

HEADMASTER: You should have asked that before, not now with a debut staring us in the face.

INSTRUCTRESS: Henrik Oskarovich, I really don't spare my energy.

HEADMASTER [*to the* BABIES]: Do you or do you not realize that you're singing like cows? [*They remain silent.*] What is this music-hall ditty about? . . . Answer me . . . [*They remain silent.*] Zhiguleva! . . . What's it all about?

ZHIGULEVA [*one of the* TRIO, *timidly*]: Uh . . . well, pola-pola means like it's sort of a trendy dance, and the French do it, I mean, the pola-pola, they win contests with it . . . and think it's cute, I guess.

HEADMASTER: And that's all?—Very clever. Outstanding. I see you don't understand a single word of what you've learned by heart—your sacred duty.

ZHIGULEVA: For heaven's sake, Henrik Oskarovich. "With cakewalks and maxixes we soon were bored to tears" [*Recites it to the end.*]

HEADMASTER [*exceptionally instructive*]: "With cakewalks and maxixes we soon were bored to tears"—then show you're fed up with them, you're bored to death, you're longing for something . . . "And now a new dance craze appear!"—Surprise!—act as if you're happy. Or, for example, "Don't we always take the tone set by modern Babylon?" What's Babylon? Answer me. [*They remain silent.*] Sidorova . . .

SIDOROVA [*one of the* TRIO]: It's a city.

HEADMASTER: What kind of city?

SIDOROVA: Babylon.

HEADMASTER: Well, what exactly is Babylon?

SIDOROVA: I just said—a city.

HEADMASTER [*laughing in contempt*]: It's Paris! . . . [*They are amazed.*] Paris. Paris is called "The Modern Babylon."

SIDOROVA: I never heard that. How was I supposed to know?

HEADMASTER: Then you should have figured it out. Why did God give you a brain? Answer me.

SIDOROVA: Paris. Now I know.

HEADMASTER: Well, and what is Paris?

SIDOROVA: It's the modern Babylon.

HEADMASTER: Do you understand now?

BABY TRIO: We understand, Henrik Oskarovich.

HEADMASTER [*to the* INSTRUCTRESS]: Why didn't you explain it to them?

INSTRUCTRESS: I did explain it to them, but they forgot.

BABY TRIO: No, Klavdiya Ivanovna, you never said a word about modern Babylon.

INSTRUCTRESS: You bare-faced liars! I even mentioned the Whore of Babylon.

BABY TRIO: You did mention whores, you were wondering which of us was a whore, but nary a word about Babylon.

HEADMASTER: Let's proceed! . . . "Don't we always take the tone set by modern Babylon! That must be the reason why we all give this dance a try." Understand?

ZHIGULEVA: Sure, because it's Paris.

HEADMASTER: God be praised. Then comes a full stop, but you go on singing as if it were a comma. Klavdiya Ivanovna, did you explain to them the difference between a full stop and a comma?

INSTRUCTRESS: Not in the first verse, but in the second I even drew them and made them draw them.

HEADMASTER: Yes, but you're always too theoretical, Klavdiya Ivanovna. We don't intend to create a chair of grammar and punctuation. From the top! And legs higher, higher!—I won't be compromised . . . Let's begin ! And smile, damn you . . .

[*The* BABY TRIO *sings and dances.*]

HEADMASTER [*interrupting the finale of the interlude music, leaps on the platform angrily*]: Sidorova!!! Gone wrong again? How many times do we have to rehearse this?! And why the hell are your shoulders always up in the air? Get 'em down, what an idiot! [*Pushes down her shoulders so that she screams and howls.*] Damn you! You want to lay me in my grave. I won't be compromised. [*Comes off the platform and wipes the sweat off with a handkerchief as he toys with a multicarat diamond.*]

INSTRUCTRESS [*consoling* SIDOROVA]: There, there, what a cry-baby! Foo! So touchy! It's your own fault, getting all weepy over this.

SIDOROVA [*crying*]: I'm not an idiot, I can't help it if my shoulders are made this way . . .

ZHIGULEVA [*to* SIDOROVA]: Oh, stop bawling! You gotta put up with a lot for your art. Art demands sacrifices.

HEADMASTER [*clapping his hands*]: Interlude music! [*The orchestra plays the music; the* BABIES *dance. At the end of the number:*] Zhiguleva! . . . Hmmm . . . you said you had a sharp pain in your armpit?

ZHIGULEVA: Yes . . .

HEADMASTER: Klavdiya Ivanovna, be sure you tell 'em in wardrobe . . . what kind of fitting did she have? I'm fed up to here with those kinds of measurements . . . Yes, Zhiguleva! [*He beckons with his finger, she comes off the platform. In an undertone:*] Don't come tonight; my stomach's upset.

ZHIGULEVA: That's because you refused to put on your truss last time, you were being vain . . .

HEADMASTER: No, it's just some fish I ate. Arepina always crams me with all kinds of rubbish at dinner.

ZHIGULEVA: The bitch!

THE OTHER BABIES: Can we go?

HEADMASTER: Go on. Next!

INSTRUCTRESS: Urykina!

[*The* BABY TRIO *exits. A seriocomic* in traditional costume comes onstage.*]

HEADMASTER: Fixed it?

URYKINA: Yes . . .

HEADMASTER [*to the musicians*]: All right!

URYKINA [*sings*]:

> Once beautiful Katrina
> Was walking down the track.
> As soon as folks had seen her
> They laughed behind her back.
> Through the dress she wore

---

* In English variety and music hall, a seriocomic was a female singer whose repertory consisted of both ballads and comic songs, often tinged with sexual innuendo. A large plumed hat and tight corseting were standard features.

Stockings showed their traces,
So did ribbons and laces,
And something more.

A gay blade having seen her,
His admiration grew,
For beautiful Katrina
His passion was true blue.
On the spot he swore
Katrin he did adore,
For her his heart was sore,
And something more.

SERVANT [*entering*]: The new girls are here.

HEADMASTER: Klavdiya Ivanovna, see to them, angel!

INSTRUCTRESS: Right away. [*She hurries off left, followed by the servant.*]

HEADMASTER [*to* URYKINA]: Do you have a sharp pain anywhere?

URYKINA: No, nowhere.

HEADMASTER: Your feet are free?

URYKINA [*lifting her feet*]: Yes.

HEADMASTER: Then come over here! [*She does so. In an undertone:*] I'm
free today too. Come by this evening.

URYKINA: Yesterday you said your stomach was upset? . . .

HEADMASTER: Nothing wrong with it now . . .

URYKINA [*laughing*]: Ah, what a sly fox!

HEADMASTER [*sternly*]: Now don't forget!—The school is a temple! . . .

[*The* INSTRUCTRESS *enters with two new girls: one is flashily dressed, the
other wears a kerchief on her head. The* HEADMASTER *looks them over
pompously.*]

HEADMASTER: Third verse! Music! . . . Introduction! [*Claps his hands.*]

URYKINA:

> Beautiful Katrina's
> Agreed to be his wife,
> But soon her misdemeanors
> Have poisoned his young life.
> Three fellows pop indoor,
> And hubby, oh alack!
> Hears one smack, second smack,
> And something more.

HEADMASTER [*self-importantly*]: The treatment is, by and large, correct. Evidently you've been working on what I told you to. However, certain minor details in the phrasing of the refrain are too crude. More psychology! I exhort you by all that's holy: more psychology! Don't skimp on the psychology! Don't spare it! It's the most important thing. And then the rhythm. Rhythm, rhythm, and more rhythm. When you sing a music-hall ditty you must perform it as a religious ritual. Just what is a music-hall ditty? [*Addressing himself more to the others than to her.*] Many people think a music-hall ditty is something like . . . Rooty, tooty, one, two, three . . . Not at all. The audience that comes to hear a music-hall ditty demands aesthetic relaxation. Businessmen, bankers—after a hard day at the office do they come to see some Shakespeare, Uriel Acosta,* and the like? Never. They see too much drama all day long. They don't need drama. Do they go to see comedies?—no again. Where does such an audience go? They go to a cabaret. [*Laughter.*] And that's no laughing matter, because here they get a well-deserved rest, here they can recover their strength for the morrow, here they see grace, wit, good clean work, in short everything they never see at the office! . . . I implore you in the name of the highest goals, give them something first rate! Take your business seriously. I beseech you not for your own sake, but for the welfare of the nation! [*The bystanders applaud.*] To be specific, Miss Urykina, you must make the refrain more racy, and the interlude more rollicking.

---

* *Uriel Acosta* is a verse tragedy by Karl Gutzkow (1847) about a seventeenth-century Portuguese Jewish philosopher who was excommunicated by the Amsterdam synagogue for heresy. Every nineteenth-century Central European or Russian tragedian felt obliged to undertake the role sometime in his career.

[*Leaps onto the stage.*] Music! [*The musicians pull themselves together.*] What's more, you don't sing the verse about Katrina's lover comically enough. You perform it like this. [*He sings.*] "Three fellows pop indoor and hubby, oh alack! Hears one smack, second smack." That's not funny. But like this it is funny. [*He shows her. Everyone utters a forced laugh.*] The audience will die laughing. Understand?

URYKINA: I do. Thank you, Henrik Oskarovich.

HEADMASTER: That's right. Now, make me an exit to applause. [*She does so.*] Hmm . . . W-well, if you want to get spotty applause, that's the way to make an exit! But if you want the whole house to shake with the thunder of the plaudits then you should do it like this! [*He shows her.* URYKINA *thanks him and exits.*]

INSTRUCTRESS: Headmaster, please meet the new girls.

HEADMASTER [*self-importantly*]: Do we have a vacancy?

INSTRUCTRESS: Just two.

HEADMASTER [*to the new girls*]: What genre do you perform? [*They remain silent.*] What do you wish to specialize in? [*They remain silent and ponder.*]—Seriocomic singer, lyrical soprano, quick-change artist, tramp comic, eccentric dancer, flamenco, living picture, gypsy ballads, babies, Isadora Duncan style . . .

DUNCAN DANCER: That's the one.

HEADMASTER: Duncan style?

DUNCAN DANCER: Duncan or an American dance with my own Negroes.

HEADMASTER: All our "my own Negroes" have already been handed out. But if you're willing to go on without "my own Negroes". . .

DUNCAN DANCER: No. Then Duncan.

HEADMASTER: Fine. [*To the shy one*] And you?

ANNUSHKA: I don't know diddlysquat, sir. But I heard tell if a body gets in the show business, you just sing and dance and make good money at it—I mean, that's what Cook read me outa the papers—I'm working my way up as scullery maid in a restaurant—that they learn you that kinda stuff here, and give references besides and recommend a body for a job, so I came to give it a look-see and learn something too, check out the odds.

HEADMASTER [*thoughtfully*]: You read about it in the papers? [*Smugly*] Yes, yes, lots of papers mention our establishment.

ANNUSHKA: In the ads, I mean . . .

HEADMASTER: Ah yes, well, it's the same thing. Now then, let's see, the lessons will begin at once. Two hundred for the course and 25 percent of your salary when you go on the stage. Only you'd be wrong to think it's easy to become a music-hall star! You need long schooling, serious work, inflexible principles. On the other hand, of course, a successful star can live like a millionaire. [*Points at one poster after another.*] These are students of mine who graduated with a degree!— Fanny Edward!—international dances!—has fifty thousand in gold in the World Bank, not to mention gowns, jewels, and so on. Eleonora Tremblinskaya! the Polish diseuse,* has an estate, foreign currency, a sealskin cape; and so on. Olya Lastochkina!—Russian seriocomic— kept by the oil industrialist Galkin—plans to go to America and has already paid twenty gold rubles for a passport. Clara Fisher!—quick-change artist and music-hall song-stylist—she died recently, the funeral alone cost over two hundred silver rubles . . . Others of that ilk . . . So you go and register at the office—three-ruble fee, and we'll give you trial lessons immediately. [*Starts to exit left.*]

APACHE [*rushing up to the* HEADMASTER]: But when do we do our *apache* dance? You promised you'd look at it onstage soon.

HEADMASTER: Right away, right away. Just give me five minutes, [*whispers in his ear*] nature calls. [*He is gone, with the* APACHE *behind him.*]

INSTRUCTRESS [*to the flashily dressed one*]: If you please! [*Points to the platform.*] You want to dance like Duncan? The most important thing for that is to take off your shoes.

---

* A diseuse is a female performer who recites monologues or spoken songs; the most famous is Yvette Guilbert.

DUNCAN DANCER [*simpering as she sits down*]: Ugh, that's awful. [*Takes off her shoes.*] Stockings too?

INSTRUCTRESS: How else? If you want to move like Duncan, away with stockings. It's a convention.

DUNCAN DANCER [*removing them*]: Ugh, it's cold!

INSTRUCTRESS [*going on to the platform with her*]: Please, here's a pin, tuck up your skirt and do what I show you. [*Suddenly stares at her feet.*] Have you got corns?

DUNCAN DANCER: It's my shoemaker's fault.

INSTRUCTRESS: Yes, but if you've got corns, you should get a pedicure first. Give me your word of honor you'll see our pedicure this very day. 24 Marat Street—say you're from our school.

DUNCAN DANCER: Yes, ma'am.

INSTRUCTRESS [*demonstrating "beauty"*]: First pose—"striving for the ideal.". . . Pull in your elbows. Weaker in the knees. That's it. Second: "I will not accept this sacrifice." Pull back. You have localized obesity. Better get a massage. It's indispensable. Third pose: "I adore you, my beloved." More expression. Personify beauty. Arms down. God, what bunions. Don't forget: 24 Marat Street. From the top. "Striving for the ideal." That's it. "I will not accept this sacrifice." "I adore you, my . . ."

HEADMASTER [*entering with the* APACHES]: But if you dance against the beat again, I'll tell you again you're dancing against the beat.

APACHE GIRL: What about me?

HEADMASTER: You? . . . Ah, there was something I wanted to tell you. [*Takes her aside, in an undertone:*] For heaven's sake don't come today; for the last two days, Lord knows what's up with my stomach—aches, pains. The doctor said, "Absolute rest."

APACHE GIRL: If that's what you want.

HEADMASTER [*clapping his hands*]: Klavdiya Ivanovna, let us have the stage. [*The* INSTRUCTRESS *and Duncan Dancer step off the platform.*] Music for the "Apache Dance."

[*The* APACHES *dance their dance. The* HEADMASTER *marks the tempo with his foot and shouts:*] Cleaner! More precision! More sadism! Sadism! I beseech you, more sadism—that where's all the impact is . . . Expression! Psychology! Don't forget the psychology.

APACHE GIRL [*screaming*]: Ay! He's pulling out all my front hair!

HEADMASTER [*to her*]: Don't lose your balance. Keep in time. One, two . . . Psychology. [*As the dance ends:*] If I tried to show you all your mistakes, the list would take a full week . . . First, dear girl, you have far too little shamelessness. If you want to pose as an innocent, get thee to a nunnery, but don't get on my nerves.

APACHE GIRL: Just what kind of shamelessness do you want?

HEADMASTER [*to the* INSTRUCTRESS]: Did you explain in class what kind of shamelessness is required here?

INSTRUCTRESS: For heaven's sake, you know perfectly well, Henrik Oskarovich, how devoted I am to my work!

HEADMASTER: I judge by results.

INSTRUCTRESS [*to* APACHE GIRL]: Do the splits with more enthusiasm! You're nothing but a troublemaker. [*The* APACHE GIRL *does it.*]

HEADMASTER: Yes, that's shameless, but it's obscene. You've got to do it so that the audience doesn't take it the wrong way. I seriously advise you to give this some thought, if you mean to devote yourself to art . . . Yours is a rudimentary shamelessness. On the other hand, if you're such a prude that people mustn't pull your hair or touch your waist, then crawl into a jar full of cotton, but don't study *apache* dancing. [*To the musicians, who are conversing loudly, playing cards on the piano keyboard.*] Are we disturbing you? [*They quiet down in embarrassment.*] This is a school, not a tavern! [*To the* APACHE GIRL] What is an *apache* dance? An *apache* dance is when he beats her and she likes it, he pulls her by the hair and she smiles, he starts to strangle her and she falls in love. That's what an *apache* dance is. It's pure, unadulterated psychology. [*To the* APACHE]. As for you, Merinov, there's nothing uninhibited about you.

APACHE: How so?

HEADMASTER: Here's what I mean. Make me an entrance like an uninhibited thug, but so your lack of inhibitions comes across the footlights. [*The* APACHE *makes an entrance as an uninhibited "thug."*] All right, now I'll show what uninhibited means. (*He shows him, smugly.*) You understand the difference? Did you understand that, Merinov? That's one. And two, you aren't enough of a thug, you aren't convincing.

APACHE [*offended*]: As for being uninhibited—that's as may be, but when it comes to being a thug, I not only know a lot of thugs, but in my own lifetime I smashed a hundred streetlights, ripped up the overcoat of a citizen like you with a knife, and gave a certain lady . . .

HEADMASTER: Yes, but it doesn't show when you dance. You're concealing your temperament somewhere.

APACHE [*exploding*]: You really want me to knock the living daylights out of her?

HEADMASTER: That's a bit extreme.

APACHE [*seriously*]: I don't know about extreme, not extreme, but I'm telling you for the last time if you don't arrange for my debut in a theater here this week I'm liable to do anything—I ripped up the overcoat of a citizen like you with a knife—got three months in stir.

HEADMASTER: Good heavens, Pyotr Ivanovich, you're behaving, excuse me please, like a child. I'm doing this on your behalf!

APACHE: This course costs two hundred rubles!

HEADMASTER: Hmm! . . . What a hot-headed fellow . . . Well, all right, let's do it your way, I don't hold grudges. You'll make your debut tomorrow, if the time is ripe. I have heaps of grateful testimonials. Music! . . . Let's begin.

[*Frenzied "Apache dance."*]

SERVANT [*running in*]: Gennady Potapovich is here.

[*The music breaks off. The* HEADMASTER *hurries left to meet the* MANAGER *of a music hall. The* APACHES *go off right.*]

VARIETY MANAGER [*a stout, shrewd bar owner, with pretensions to being a Western European*]: Am I late?

HEADMASTER: Of course not, for goodness' sake. Right on time.

MANAGER: Is the Baby Trio ready?

HEADMASTER: Not quite, Gennady Potapovich, they need more polish.

MANAGER: What are you doing to me, you cutthroat?! . . . I've got to have three acts for the finale.

HEADMASTER: Of course, if it's urgent . . . You did say that . . . [*To the* INSTRUCTRESS] Klavdiya Ivanovna, detain the Babies! Look sharp! [*She flies backstage.*] Only be a little indulgent, because . . .

MANAGER: I'll be the way the audience is.

HEADMASTER: Day after tomorrow I'll have the *apaches* so ready for you, you'll smack your lips over them.

MANAGER: Give me a break, kiddo. I've already got some. Who needs 'em?

HEADMASTER: These're are something out of the ordinary. [*In a whisper*] You'll give me back that little IOU! For heaven's sake, I'm making an effort!

MANAGER: We'll discuss that later. [*Points at* ANNUSHKA.] Who's that character?

HEADMASTER: A new girl.

MANAGER: Funny?

HEADMASTER: Haven't tried her out yet.

MANAGER: Don't be so shy! While the babykins are getting into costume, let's give her the once-over.

HEADMASTER: If you're interested . . . [*To* ANNUSHKA] If you please, Miss. [*She climbs up onstage. To the* MANAGER] I'm actually rather glad you'll see what she is now and what I'll make of her in three months. [*To her*] Show us what you can do!

ANNUSHKA: I sing, sir. But only just silly stuff, sort of . . .

HEADMASTER: Whatever you like. [*To her*] Now then! Don't be embarrassed. Mister Maestro will accompany you. Maestro, a few encouraging chords!

[ANNUSHKA *sings "Dear Little Cap"* with piano accompaniment.*]

MANAGER [*jumping up in indescribable excitement*]: Now that's what I call brilliant! She's a world-class hit! Damn me if she ain't! She tops 'em all! Every one of 'em! I was telling you I needed something with punch, just now . . . Something earthy, something that's got juice, spontaneity! And here she is, here she is! Eureka, sir, eureka!

HEADMASTER: Not bad . . . she still has to study . . . acquire polish, so to speak.

MANAGER: To hell with polish! Nobody wants that nowadays. You got no nose for what the public wants! Nowadays you need something that smells of sweat! That makes you feel the calluses on her hands! What's your name, my dear?

ANNUSHKA: Annushka.

MANAGER: Brilliant! A personal appearance by Annushka in her own repertoire! She's purer than Plevitskaya,† my boy! Think of all the imitators she'll have! My God! My head's spinning! Let's go to the office—draw up a contract!

ANNUSHKA [*coming off the platform*]: I can't read or write, sir.

---

* "Shapchishche" (a cap with earlaps) is actually a Bulgarian folk song.
† Nadezhda Vasil'evna Plevitskaya (1884–1940), a Russian mezzo-soprano of peasant origin, became a leading concert singer of both folk songs and urban ballads from 1909. She was probably the most celebrated nonoperatic female Russian singer of her time.

MANAGER: Nonsense!

HEADMASTER: Yes, but excuse me, Gennady Potapovich, what about me? After all, she did come to my school!—And suddenly without a lesson . . . so . . . simply . . . where's the ethics in that? Where's the ethics?

MANAGER: In your IOU! [*Gives it to him. To her*] Let's go! . . . She doesn't even wear shoes.

[*He leads her by the hand to the office, humming "Dear Little Cap." Appearing on the platform the* BABY TRIO *watches them go in bewilderment, the same bewilderment as the* HEADMASTER's, *as he holds the IOU in his hand, trying to figure out whether he has won or lost. Finally, the* HEADMASTER *recovers, puts the IOU in his wallet, and claps his hands.*]

HEADMASTER: From the top! Music!

BABY TRIO [*singing*]: "With cakewalks and maxixes we soon were bored to tears, etc. . . ."

BACKSTAGE AT THE SOUL
(*V kulisakh dushi*)

A monodrama in one act and a prologue

by Nikolai Evreinov

1912

CHARACTERS

Professor

S1, the rational aspect of the Soul

S2, the emotional aspect of the Soul

S3, the subconscious aspect of the Soul

Wife Image No. 1

Wife Image No. 2

Chanteuse Image No. 1

Chanteuse Image No. 2

Train Conductor

The action takes place within the Soul. The duration of the action is half a minute.

A blackboard and chalk stand in front of the closed curtain.

PROFESSOR [*entering from the side, stopping by the board, bows, and picking up a piece of chalk*]: Ladies and gentlemen! Some days ago the author of "Backstage at the Soul," the work presented to you today, came to see me. I must confess at first I regarded this work with some suspicion, supposing it to be—as is often the case in the theater—some vapid farce, devoid of any creative concept or moral significance. So I was all the more pleased to be persuaded that "Backstage at the Soul" is a strictly scientific work corresponding to the latest developments in psycho-physiology. The researches of Wundt, Freud, Théodule Ribot,* and others demonstrate that the human soul is not something indivisible, but consists of several "*Selves.*" Is that clear? [*Writes:* $S_1 + S_2 + S_3 = S_n$.] Now Fichte[†] argues that if the "Self" is the "Self," then the world is not the "Self." Is that clear? All right, then . . . But, according to the latest data, while the world is not the "Self," the "Self" itself is not the "Self." Is that clear? The "Self" is not the "Self," because there are several "Selves" in the "Self." In fact, the "Self" consists of three "Selves." [*Writes on the board:* $S = x/3$.] Therefore, the primary Self, the central Self—what we used to call the "Soul"—may be broken down into three parts: Self 1, the rational self, the thinking self (what we used to call Reason); Self 2, the emotional self, the passionate Self (what we used to call Feeling); and Self 3, the subconscious Self, the psychical Self (what we used to call the Eternal). Is that clear? These three "selves" together make up a larger entity, the Self. [*Writes:* $s + s + s = S$.] The ancients assumed that the "Self" was located in the liver. Descartes speculated that it was in the brain,[‡] but the author of the present work quite reasonably supposes that the soul is contained in our body up against that spot on our chest that we strike instinctively when we assert our innocence or say things like "my heart is sore". . . "My heart is filled with joy". . . "My breast boils with indignation!" and so on. In accord with this, the backstage of the soul may be outlined as follows. [*With multicolored chalks he draws a diagram, which he then explains.*] Above the prominent barrier of the diaphragm, there is a large heart suspended from the aorta and the upper vena cava, beating at a rate of 55 to 125 throbs per minute, and framed, right and left, by the curtains of the lungs, inflating and deflating at the rate of 14 to 18 times per minute. At the back, representing the spi-

---

* William Wundt (1832–1920), the "father of psychology," promoted the self-interrogation of one's thoughts. Sigmund Freud (1856–1939) was known in Russia by 1909, and a journal *Psychoanalysis* ran from 1910 to 1913. Théodule Ribot (1836–1916) of the Nancy school is often cited as the inspiration for Stanislavsky's theory of emotional memory.
† Johann Gottlieb Fichte (1762–1814) was a German philosopher who explored subjectivity and self-consciousness.
‡ René Descartes (1596–1650) believed that the pineal gland was the connection between the soul and the body.

nal column and its ribs, is a small, jaundice-yellow telephone. Some straw-colored threads of nerves quiver upward from the diaphragmatic barrier. There you have, so to speak, a model "theater of action" for the deconstructed "Self." Now science, ladies and gentlemen, not only offers explanations, it also provides relief; for instance, it is not enough to say that the "Self" has behaved stupidly! One has to determine which "Self" was the stupid one. If the stupid "Self" was the emotional one—it doesn't mean a thing. The subconscious isn't worth bothering about either. Do be concerned if it's the rational Self acting stupidly. But, esteemed ladies and gentlemen, whose "Self" can be clearly expressed in our frantic era? . . . At this point, my lecture has come to an end and I yield the floor to the author, the performers, and you, worthy judges of this unusual work.

[*The* PROFESSOR *exits; the blackboard is taken away; the curtain rises, revealing a picture of the soul very much as the* PROFESSOR *described and outlined it. Onstage, that is, on the diaphragm barrier, are all three* "SELVES." *They resemble each other, all in black, but dressed differently.* S1 *wears a frock coat,* S2 *wears an artist's smock and a red bowtie,* S3 *wears a car coat. Further distinguishing features are that* s1 *has gray, neatly combed hair, eyeglasses, a pale face, thin lips, and staid manners.* S2 *has tousled hair, seems very young, with crimson lips and sweeping gestures.* S3, *in a black half-mask, is sleeping on the forestage with one arm around his suitcase in the pose of an exhausted traveler.*]

S2 [*on the telephone*]: What? Hello! You can barely hear me? But I'm speaking loud enough . . . There's a loud humming? That's because your nerves are stretched extremely taut . . . Well, all right . . . Vodka! . . . I tell you, more vodka! . . .

S1: Bear in mind you're the one forcing him to drink the third bottle for your own pleasure. The poor heart! . . . Look how it's beating!

S2: And so according to you it ought to be napping all the time like Subconscious over there? . . . A nice sort of way to spend one's time . . .

S1: If the heart keeps beating that hard, it won't go on much longer.

S2: So what—sooner or later it's bound to stop.

S1: Just what I'm always saying.

s2: Well, you don't always talk rot.

s1: Don't strum the nerves! . . . Haven't you been told . . . [*The nerves hum whenever they're touched.*]

s2 [*flaring up*]: Who told me? Who was told? . . . What am I around here, a flunky or something? I'm a poet! . . . I'm love! . . . I'm passion! . . . If it weren't for me this place would be mold and cobwebs . . . a lecture hall, a graveyard! Because where there's no passion, there's a graveyard . . .

s1: Talk is cheap . . .

s2: I'm speaking the gospel truth . . . Whose fault do you think it is he drinks?

s1: You're the one calling for vodka!

s2: Sure I am, because you could drive him to hang himself.

s1: Talk is cheap . . . I think it's the other way around, all his unhappiness and misfortunes occur because you, the emotional Self, are, for the most part, so lost and misguided! Couldn't you take the faintest interest, well, let's say, in intellectual pursuits, in the noble work of the mind, don't you ever entertain thoughts about moral values?

s2: I've had it with you! Your damned copybook morality, your miserable sermonizing!

s1: I despise you, emotional Self! . . .

s2: And I despise you, rational Self! [*With his sweeping gestures he brushes against the nerves.*]

s1: You roughneck! Don't strum my nerves!

s2: Shut up! . . . May I observe, Mr. Rational Self, that we possess our nerves in common, and when I strum your nerves, I'm also strumming my own, and when, thanks to you, my nerves go numb, then I get dull as ditchwater, a lot like you. If I feel like strumming my nerves, I will . . . In fact, I'm glad they're strained so tight—it gives me a chance to play a rhapsody of love and freedom on them! . . .

[*Plays his rhapsody, after which the heart begins to beat even faster. On the telephone:*] More vodka!

s1 [*tearing away the receiver*]: Aspirin!

s2 [*tearing it back*]: Vodka!

s1 [*tearing it back and holds off* s2]: Aspirin! . . . You hear! . . . None left? . . . Look in the medicine cabinet . . . Aspirin! . . . Two tablets with a glass of water. [*Leaves the telephone . . . Both pace back and forth. They meet face to face.*] Have you calmed down?

s2: Have you?

s1: As you see. [*Goes over to* s3. *Pause.*]

s2: What's Subconscious up to?

s1: Same as ever . . . Utter serenity . . . Don't disturb him! . . . It'll be worse for you . . . [*On the telephone*] Did you take the tablets? Fine, I'll try one more time to reason with him. [*Takes* s2 *by the arm and walks around with him.*] Basically I don't understand the underlying cause. Well, all right, this woman has captivated you with the so-called originality of her talent, if we can call it talent, but for a man to abandon his wife and children on that account—excuse my saying so—is not exactly a way out of the predicament . . . at least not unless we adopt the view of polygamists, that is, savages for whom curvaceous thighs or the slope of a backside are more precious than a temple such as this, I mean the soul . . .

s2: Oh, viewpoints again! . . . What do I care for all of that?! She's beautiful! . . . What's there to reason about?

s1: Animals don't reason either, but human beings, in whom a glint of logic should inhere . . . [*Into the telephone as he goes by*] Smoke a cigarette!

s2: God, you bore me to tears! . . . It's awful to be eternally linked with a creature as tiresome as your reverence.

s1: You didn't always talk this way.

s2: On the contrary, I was even very fond of you, when you and I would stroll arm in arm. For instance, I'll never forget the favor you did me when I was ablaze with love for Anyuta. Winning over a distrustful girl and lulling the vigilance of her parents . . . When you feel like it, you can be a very shrewd operator! But since then you've not only failed to get sharper, but you've turned quite dull, my dear friend, like a rusty razor . . .

s1: *Merci* for the compliment . . . I'm not offended. Besides, your judgment is clouded by your overexcitement.

s2: Ah, but she's beautiful . . . Ye Gods! . . . You've forgotten how beautiful she is, how exceptional she is, so refined, so racy! . . . Sure, she's a music-hall singer, but what does that prove? . . . You've forgotten about her form and figure . . . You've forgotten her image! I'll call her. [*He leads out from the right an image of the music-hall singer, an exceptionally attractive one. To her*] Sing, sing, the way you sang yesterday, the day before, last week, on that Sunday. *Chantez, je vous prie!* I beg you! . . . [*To* s1, *who turns away from the summoned image*] Please bone up on your French!—I really need it.

CHANTEUSE IMAGE NO. 1 [*singing and dancing in time to the joyously beating heart*]:

> Est-ce vous le p'tit jeun'homme
> Qu'était l'autre jour tantôt
> Près d'moi dans l'métro?
> A la station
> De l'Odéon?
> Je n'ai pas pu vous voir
> Car il faisait trop noir
> Mais j'voudrais savoir
> Est c'vous? est c'vous?
> Dont mon baiser si doux
> M'a rendu amoureux fou?
>
> L'autre jour j'étais dans le métro
> Un monsieur s'assied près de moi,
> Je le regarde aussitôt.

> Mais la lumière juste à ce moment
> S'éteignit subitement.
> Mon voisin effrayé s'jette dans mes bras!
> Affolée je l'embrasse et depuis c'jour-là
> Je le cherchais en vain et plein d'émoi.
> J'dis à chaqu' homme, que j'aperçois:
> Est c'vous le petit bon homme, etc.*

s2 [*in raptures*]: Enchanting! . . . Such joy is worth more than the whole world! And those feet! . . . My God, is there in this world a carpet worthy of those tootsies, so dainty they make you want to cry . . . Dance on me! . . . Dance in me! . . . The sweet-smelling incense of an angel! . . . [*Kisses her feet, then her hands and lips.*]

s1: Oh, delusion! . . . Leave her alone! . . . leave her . . . It's only your imagination! . . . She's not like that at all! You're kissing her rouge, you're caressing her wig . . . She's forty years old . . . Leave her . . . It's all fake . . . Here's the reality. [*As he begins speaking* CHANTEUSE NO. 1 *disappears left, whence* s1 *leads in* CHANTEUSE IMAGE NO. 2, *a god-forsaken caricature.*] Look, if you want to know the truth . . . Ingrown toenails on those divine feet and those "beloved" corns . . . Calf's head *au naturel*—without wig or rouge. [*Lifts off her wig, revealing a bald head underneath.*] Off with your bust now! [*She removes her false bosom.*] Out with your teeth now! [*She removes her dentures.*] Now sing! [*She sings, mumphing and off-key, prancing about with the grace of an old nag sent to the boneyard.*]

s2 [*shouting*]: It's not true, it's not true! . . . She's not like that! [*To her*] Get out of here!!! [*Chases her off.*]

s1: "Jove, thou art angry . . . therefore thou art in the wrong."†

---

* "Is that you, the little young man / Who sat beside me / just the other day on the subway?/ At Odeon / Station? / I couldn't see you / Because it was too dark / But I would like to know / Is it you, is it you / Who my so gentle kiss / Made me madly in love? / The other day I was in the subway / A gentleman sits next to me / I look at him at once. / But just at that moment / The light goes out. / My frightened neighbor throws himself into my arms! / In my panic I kiss him and ever since that day / I've been looking for him in vain and full of emotion. / I say to every man I see: / Are you the nice little man, etc."

† The Latin adage "Iuppiter iratus ergo nefas" was a commonplace in Russian, quoted by Dostoevsky, Chekhov, and Lenin, among others.

s2: Rot.

s1: Oh, you know perfectly well the source of your passion is unworthy to unlace the sandals of the woman you're prepared to betray . . . And for what? For what? [*Leads out from left a beautiful image of a* WIFE, *cradling a baby.*] For always being so modest, for coddling you, nursing your baby? . . . Oh, of course, her singing can't match what you hear in a music hall, but just listen to how she sings a lullaby, if you still have ears for pure sounds. True, she sings in a low voice, but she's been singing without sleep the last three nights . . . She's been waiting up for you . . .

WIFE IMAGE NO. 1 [*singing softly*]:

> Go to sleep, my darling boy,
> Sweet dreams come and be your joy . . .
> Sleep, my darling, don't you cry,
> Lulla, lulla, lullaby . . .

Sleep, my little one, go to sleep . . . Do you hurt? Is it a booboo?— It'll go away, it'll go away, sweetheart . . . Just wait, my precious . . . What? . . . Papa? . . . Where's Papa? Papa'll be here soon. Papa's working now, but soon he'll buy you a nice new toy. You'd like a horsie? Clippity clop . . . You'd like a horsie? . . . Papa's so kind . . .

s2 [*rudely*]: Enough of this farce! . . . That's nothing like her . . . It's a crude idealization . . . [*Chases her off.*] Get out of here! . . . Imagine, some heroine! . . . A total exaggeration . . . She's not like that at all . . . I know her . . . She's poisoned my whole life . . . No poetry, no joy, nothing but prose and posing as a martyr . . . A short-order cook! . . . Here's what she's like . . . [*In place of* WIFE IMAGE NO. 1 *he leads in* WIFE IMAGE NO. 2, *to wit, a sharp-tongued lower-middle-class housewife, her hair in a sloppily twisted bun, wearing a housecoat spotted with coffee stains.*]

WIFE IMAGE NO. 2 [*shrilly*]: And to think, just my luck, a bookkeeper! . . . If my parents only knew how I suffer with that damned creature . . . I'm surprised he hasn't been fired from his job by now! . . . The drunken sot! . . . His rotten brain won't make a move without vodka . . . Stuck me with all these kids, and now it's the kiss-off . . . I'm in love, he says, art, theater . . . That music-hall singer a theater! I wouldn't touch greased-up sluts like that with a ten-foot pole! He'll infect all the kids yet! Lowlife pervert . . . What can you get from him? . . . If it hadn't been for me he'd have hocked the kids' undies . . . Won't make the sign of the cross neither, the atheist . . . Crazy as a loon, but always philosophizing . . . Freedom, he says, is a civic duty . . . So he can guzzle vodka? . . . I'll give you freedom! . . .

s2: There she is, your heroine . . . That's the one I dare not leave for [*leads in from right* CHANTEUSE IMAGE NO. 1] this one, who, like some magic potion intoxicates me, makes sense of my existence . . . [*The* CHANTEUSE *sings and dances the cancan, forcing* WIFE IMAGE NO. 2 *left into the shadows, but then steps back, falls silent as* WIFE IMAGE NO. 1, *replete with majestic nobility and grief, advances on her.*]

WIFE IMAGE NO. 1: Begone, I implore you, there is no place for you here.

s1: Quite right.

WIFE IMAGE NO. 1: You don't love him anyway . . . You wouldn't sacrifice a thing for him. You've known lots like him before . . . Don't get him excited if you have the slightest shred of decency left. I need his presence, his support . . . Don't distract him . . . Don't take him away from his family! . . .

CHANTEUSE IMAGE NO. 1 [*with a silvery laugh*]: Ha, ha, ha, ha! [*In a foreign accent, rolling her* r's] Such threatening words! . . .

WIFE IMAGE NO. 1: Go away, I repeat, don't force me to extremes . . .

CHANTEUSE IMAGE NO. 1: Are you threatening me? And what for? Because I have beautiful legs, perky breasts, and cheerful words fly from my mouth like doves . . . like champagne corks! . . .

s2 [*applauding*]: Bravo, bravo . . .

WIFE IMAGE NO. 1 [*to her*]: All you care for is money, you two-bit baggage!

CHANTEUSE IMAGE NO. 1: What? I'm a two-bit baggage, am I? . . . You take back that insult this minute . . . [*Advances on her.*]

WIFE IMAGE NO. 1: Get out of here! . . .

[*They grapple with each other and battle furiously, to the loud beating of the heart quivering as if in its death throes. We also hear curses and threats, full of irrepressible malice: "shameless hussy . . . baggage . . . skank . . . birdbrain, trollop . . . slut . . . jezebel." They disappear into a dark corner, then come out again even more frenzied, but now in the form of* IMAGES NO. 2. *The* WIFE *has the* CHANTEUSE'S *wig in her mouth, the* CHANTEUSE *has her hands on the* WIFE'S *braid. They switch back again to their positive images and reveal the* CHANTEUSE'S *victory over the* WIFE. *The* WIFE *is held flat on the floor by the* CHANTEUSE'S *resilient knee. The unfortunate* WIFE *then runs off left with a wail, accompanied by the* CHANTEUSE'S *loud laughter and* SELF 2'S *applause. Meanwhile, an outraged* SELF 1 *sends the* CHANTEUSE'S *face a resounding slap, and she yelps pitifully as she withdraws upstage like a stepped-on lapdog.* S2 *is not going to stand for that! He strenuously hurls himself at* S1 *and strangles him to death. The heart stops for an instant; two or three overstrained nerves snap.* S2, *having made sure that his opponent is dead, throws himself at the* CHANTEUSE'S *feet.*]

S2: You are now the queen here! . . . My queen! . . .

CHANTEUSE IMAGE NO. 1: Oh no, darling, no indeed . . . I was just kidding . . . First money, then love . . . And you don't smell much like money . . . Where are you going to get it? . . . No, no, I'm not for you . . . I was just kidding.

[*She disappears left.* S2 *freezes in a pose of despair. From the right, far, far away, echoes the catchy tune of the music-hall ditty, and from the left, filled with infinite sorrow,* WIFE IMAGE NO. 1, *inseparable from her sick baby, fixes her enormous eyes on* S2. *She seems at times to be rocking her baby, and at times nodding her head reproachfully in* S2's *direction.*]

S2 [*unable to bear it any longer, rushing to the telephone*]: For heaven's sake . . . quick . . . it's all over . . . I'm exhausted . . . The revolver's in the right back pocket . . . Hurry! . . . Hurry! . . . It's too much for me . . . Don't miss! . . . Between the third and fourth ribs! Go on, go on! . . . What are you afraid of? . . . It only takes a moment. Quick! . . .

[*A pause.* S3 *awakes and uneasily looks around as if in agonizing suspense. A shot rings out, very loud, as if from a cannon, and the blast reverberates beneath the vaults of the soul. An enormous gaping hole appears in the heart, out of which blood-red ribbons unfurl. Darkness descends.* S2 *falls convulsively to the floor beneath the heart, drowning in a sea of red ribbons. The heart stops beating. The lungs stop breathing.*

A pause. S2 *trembles and stretches uneasily a few times. The* TRAIN CONDUCTOR *enters with a lighted lantern.*]

TRAIN CONDUCTOR: New Manville . . . Who's getting off here? . . . Mr. Subconscious, hey, Mr. Subconscious! . . . Here's where you change . . . New Manville . . .

S3: New Manville? All right . . . If it's New Manville, then New Manville it is! . . . [*Puts on his hat, picks up his suitcase and yawns as he follows the* TRAIN CONDUCTOR.]

THE INSPECTOR GENERAL
(*Revizor*)

A directorial buffoonery in five interpretations of one excerpt

by Nikolay Evreinov

1912

CHARACTERS

Official on special assignment to the Crooked Mirror

Anton Antonovich Shvoznik-Dmukhanovsky, the mayor

Lyapkin-Tyapkin, the judge

Zemlyanika, the welfare commissioner

Huebner, the district doctor

Khlopov, the school superintendant

Anna Andreevna, the mayor's wife

Marya Antonovna, the mayor's daughter

Ukhovertov, the chief of police

Svistunov
Derzhimorda } constables

Laughter

Satire

Humor

OFFICIAL ON SPECIAL ASSIGNMENT TO THE MANAGEMENT OF THE CROOKED MIRROR:

[*Appears before the curtain*]: Kind ladies and gentlemen! . . . Through a printer's oversight your programs do not indicate that tonight's performance of *The Inspector General* is nothing less than a competitive contest among certain directors, invited here as guest artists by the management.

Ladies and gentlemen, that there is a crisis in the theater is a long-standing proposition; the cry goes up in unison—"There are no plays . . ." We are counseled to turn to the classical repertoire. But is the finite number of classical plays sufficient to all theaters and all reportorial needs? . . . This is what the Crooked Mirror, which set itself the goal of exploiting all means of theatrical accomplishment, has decided to put to the test, a test which, we hope, will have some effect. To wit: we have deliberately picked out a number of classic plays and staged them in five distinct interpretations so that each play will yield five separate plays.

I refrain from mentioning the names of those directors invited for this purpose, in order to prompt the audience met here to a completely impartial verdict on their creative endeavors. In any case, it is not a question of names, but of the rivalry between methods of staging, each sharply distinct from the other, and at the same time similar in one very important respect: *each of these methods renders the author's work uniquely unrecognizable.*

Consequently, if the experiment we offer to our respected audience succeeds—which you will testify to by your applause—we will be able to acquire five *Inspectors General*, five *Woes from Wit*, five *Krechinsky's Weddings*, five *Thunderstorms*, and so forth. Not to burden you with figures, I may remark that the ranks of the Russian theater will burgeon with, approximately, 120 completely independent classical works by five Gogols, five Ostrovskys, five Griboedovs, five Sukhovo-Kobylins, and ten Tolstoys—five Lyovs and five Alekseys. And this bumper crop of classical works will be harvested with the help of talented and inventive directors.

To prove to this most respected audience that there now really will be excerpts from *The Inspector General* performed onstage and not some other play that has nothing in common with *The Inspector General*, we shall first present *The Inspector General* in the guise in which it has been ordinarily performed before the crisis in contemporary theater occurred. After that, the audience will fully understand the progress contemporary directors have made and what progress they may continue to make, if, of course, nobody stops them.

As to the following interpretations, to elucidate to the audience the way it is to respond to what ensues onstage, and, at the request of the management, I will set forth, prior to each new staging, a compact summary of those assumptions on which the directors have based their creations.

And so—first of all the traditional staging, which requires no explanation and no commentary.

1. Classic Staging

A yellow room with a door center, a window at left, and a door at right. Overhead, sky-blue teasers with details painted on. All the characters in the scenes of The Inspector General *are seated on chairs near the footlights, the* MAYOR *in the center. The usual costumes, although verging on fancy dress; the wigs are rather crude and obvious, but the acting is good, "presenting" the text, and so the actors never turn their backs on the audience* or use "atmospheric pauses" and similar modern innovations.*

MAYOR: I have invited you here, gentlemen, to inform you of a most unpleasant piece of news: we're to be visited by an Inspector.

LYAPKIN-TYAPKIN: What do you mean, an Inspector?

ZEMLYANIKA: What do you mean, an Inspector?

MAYOR: An Inspector from Petersburg, incognito. And with secret orders to boot.

LYAPKIN-TYAPKIN: How do you like that!

ZEMLYANIKA: We don't have troubles enough, so they send us some!

KHLOPOV: Heavens to Betsy! and with secret orders to boot!

MAYOR: I had a sort of premonition: all last night I was dreaming about a couple of extraordinary rats. Honest, I'd never seen anything like

---

* A comment on standard practice at the Moscow Art Theater, of acting with one's back to the audience.

them: black and of incredible size! They came, sniffed around a bit—and went away. Now I'll read you a letter I received from Andrey Ivanovich Chmykhov—you know who I mean, Artemy Filippovich. This is what he writes: "Dear friend, godfather and benefactor," [*mutters under his breath, skimming it rapidly*] . . . "and to inform you." Ah! here it is: "I make haste to inform you, among other things, that an official is coming with orders to inspect the entire province and in particular our district. [*Raises his index finger significantly.*]

I learned this from the most trustworthy people, although he is passing himself off as a private individual. Since I know that you, like everyone else, have your peccadillos, because you're no fool and don't like to let slip anything that swims into your grasp . . ."

[*Stops.*] Well, we're among friends . . . "I advise you to take precautions; for he might arrive at any moment, if he hasn't arrived already and is living somewhere incognito . . . Yesterday I . . ." Well, now he goes into family matters: "My cousin Anna Krillovna paid a visit with her husband; Ivan Kirillovich has got mighty fat and is always playing the fiddle . . ." and so forth and so on. That's the situation we're in now!

LYAPKIN-TYAPKIN: Yes, a most untoward situation, absolutely untoward. There's something behind this.

KHLOPOV: But what's it for, Anton Antonovich, why is this? Why are we getting an Inspector?

MAYOR: Why indeed! It's obvious—it's fate! [*Sighing deeply*] So far, thank God, they've only shown up in other towns; now our turn has come.

LYAPKIN-TYAPKIN: No, listen to me, you're all wrong . . . you don't . . . The government has subtle schemes: never mind the fact it's so far away, it has its finger in every pie.

MAYOR: Fingers or toes, gentlemen, you've all been forewarned . . .

[*Momentary blackout.* ANNA ANDREEVNA *and* MARYA ANTONOVNA *run onstage.*]

ANNA ANDREEVNA: Where are they, where oh where are they? Ah, for heaven's sake! . . . [*Opening the door*] Husband! Tony! Anton! [*Talks rapidly*] It's all your fault. It always is. You and your dawdling: "Just one teeny pin, just one teeny kerchief!" [*Runs to the window and shouts*] Anton, where are you off to, where? What, who's come? An Inspector? With a mustache? What kind of mustache?

MAYOR'S VOICE: Later, my love, later!

ANNA ANDREEVNA: Later? News won't keep till later! I won't wait till later . . . Just tell me one thing: Is he a colonel? Huh? [*Contemptuously*] He's gone! I won't forget this! You and your "Mama dear, Mama dear, wait a bit, just let me pin up this teeny kerchief; I'll only be a second." You and your second! We've found out nothing on account of you! It's all that damn primping; she heard the postmaster was here, so she had to go simper in front of the mirror; how does it look from this side and how does it look from that. She fancies he's stuck on her. Well, he's simply making fun of you behind your back.

MARYA ANTONOVNA: What am I supposed to do, Mama dear? It doesn't matter, we'll know everything two hours from now.

ANNA ANDREEVNA: Two hours! Thank you kindly. Most obliged for the information! Why didn't you think to say we'd know a lot more in a month! [*Hanging out of the window*] Hey, Avdotya! Huh? Listen, Avdotya, did you hear who it is that's come? . . . You didn't? What a ninny! He waved you away? Let 'im wave, you could have asked anyway. You couldn't find out! You've got a one-track mind, always thinking about boyfriends. Huh? They went off in a hurry! You should have run after the carriage. Go on, go do it now! You hear me? Hurry, hurry, hurry, hurry! . . .

[*Shouts until the curtain is down and we no longer see the two of them, standing at the window,* leaning out very "conventionally," so as not to rumple the backcloth, which makes no pretensions to solidity.*]

OFFICIAL ON SPECIAL ASSIGNMENT TO THE MANAGEMENT OF THE CROOKED MIRROR [*appearing before the curtain*]: The next interpretation of the very same excerpts comes from a director of the Stanislavsky school . . . But first, some biographical data about this guest director.

---

* The first part of the stage direction is a direct quotation from act 1 of Gogol's *Inspector General*.

He is a native of the Yaroslav district. He graduated from Agricultural School and became a specialist in reforestation, including grafting rare species of apple trees, for instance, the golden pippin. But then one day, seated on the banks of the Volga, where he used to think little thoughts, he heard the wondrous song of the nightingale. It was as if something had jolted him into restlessness, and from that time on the young man lost all peace of mind. Renouncing all his involvement in agrarian husbandry, renting out his pitch factory and distillery, our director-to-be headed for Moscow and became a diligent student of the great master. From the first he kept his eyes open, then learned, thereupon created and continually revered. For a year and a half he studied mood, two years theater as life; at night he worked on pauses. His dissertation, dedicated to Stanislavsky, bears the title "The Semi-pause and Full Pause of Mood."* Its thesis is "the square root of mood is in inverse proportion to the distance of theater from life."

Handpicked the next year to be a director by the Moscow High Art Theater, our young scholar responded with great alacrity to our proposal.

As everyone knows, the highly artistic productions of the Moscow Art Theater are distinguished first by the fact that they proceed as life proceeds, and second by the fact that everything happens not as in life, but in a "mood." Our director, first of all, ascertained the naturalistic locale of *The Inspector General*'s action. "You can ride away from our town for three years, and never reach any other country," says the Mayor. However, from a familiarity with Gogol's biography and his *Evenings on a Farm near Dikanka*, one may with great probability say that the action takes place in the town of Mirgorod. At the present time Mirgorod has ten thousand inhabitants, two tallow boileries, one tannery, and one shag tobacco mill. After traveling to Mirgorod and learning the town's history from its archives, our director actually established which house the Mayor had lived in at that specific time. The tobacco mill, which existed back then, was to the left of the Mayor's house, and to the right was the booth where Humpback Yakim sold bagels. Simultaneously he established the nature of the local Russian community, which elucidated Gogol's characters, who,

---

* The term "mood," *nastroenie*, is characteristic of the theatrical theories of Nemirovich-Danchenko and Stanislavsky.

although Great Russian in origin, are, for the most part, now naturalized to the Ukraine.

As to the "mood" which ought to permeate life in the Mayor's home, such a director will take his cue from Zemlyanika's line "We don't have troubles enough, so they send us some . . ." In view of this, the action first depicts the untroubled life of a sleepy little town, quiet and almost devoid of industry, apart from the aforementioned tobacco mill. But gradually the "mood" of a stifled spiritual state, anticipating the outcome of this unforeseen investigation, intrudes.

The greatest care went into the staging.* It is impossible to enumerate all the characteristic details. You will see them for yourself. I shall point out a few as examples: for instance, Anna Andreevna, who was educated, according to a stage direction of the author, "out of albums," appears with an old album in hand. Zemlyanika, who is said to be "a perfect swine in a skullcap," actually appears wearing a skullcap. Lyapkin-Tyapkin, who takes puppies as bribes and is prepared to give the Mayor "the very sister to that hound you know," really shows up with dogs, etc.

The director did not succeed in ascertaining exactly the kind of weather there was on the day the Mayor met Khlestakov. However, if you recall from *The Inspector General* that "the garrison was sauntering around the streets in uniform" but "with nothing on underneath," one may presume it to be a warm, cloudless day. Toward the end a slight drizzle occurs, as the ultimate artistic stroke, to create an inconsolably doleful mood, thus reconciling the highly artistic traditions of the play with the general mood. [*He exits. The curtain goes up.*]

2. Realistic Staging in the Spirit of Stanislavsky

As the curtain rises, there is almost total darkness onstage. Somewhere some old chimes are ringing hoarsely and rapidly. As the day begins to dawn, our eyes encounter a very lived-in room, with two windows in the back wall, through

---

* Another slap at the Moscow Art Theater's first principles. "The staging must create the necessary atmosphere . . . mood." Nikolay Éfros, *Moskovsky Khudozhestvenny Teatr* (Moscow: GIKhL, 1924), 128.

which we can see the yard, the fence, and a church in the distance. In the middle of the room is a large table with a wooden jug of kvass, surrounded by chairs; in front of it, downstage, back to the audience, is a settee. On the right wall is a large cupboard; at right in the corner are a small writing desk with inkwell and so forth. In the windows are pots of flowers and a caged canary; on the walls, portraits, a mirror, a clock, and two long tobacco pipes; on the narrow wall between the two windows, small knickknack tables and bookcases. The whole room presents almost entirely obstructed space. Door at right and door at left. We hear the crowing of a cock, then the mooing of cows and the neighing of horses. Someone, apparently in bare feet, is running hurriedly through the yard, pursued by the noisy barking of the aroused watchdog. The clock strikes again. A barefoot servant wench, in a sarafan *made of ticking and tucked up high, cautiously carries across the room a chamber pot, half covered by her apron. The rays of the rising sun spill over the room. Somewhere in the distance the merry sound of shepherd's pipes rings out. We hear a whole herd of cows pass by, lowing.*

The MAYOR, *sleepily, in an undershirt of Ukrainian cut, staggers in at right and opens a window, so that the sounds of the awakening town become clearer. A two-wheeled carriage with harness bells drives by. The* MAYOR *raises the jug of kvass to his lips and, after drinking greedily, groans, snorts, swats with his slipper a fly that has been pestering him, stretches, clears his throat, spits into the street, and exits right, after which the aforementioned serf wench runs by with a pitcher of water, and in the yard a lad from the local garrison begins to sweep up, raising an incredible cloud of dust. The* MAYOR *reenters, now washed, his hair combed, wearing a dressing gown and holding* CHMYKHOV's *letter. He rereads it, shakes his head, and eventually sits at the writing desk in the corner to pen a reply. We hear the scratching of a goose quill and the* MAY-OR's *slight wheezing. The clock strikes again. Enter* DR. HUEBNER *with a bottle of some kind of medicine; he utters the sound "Eh" and sits off to one side. A second or two later, enter* LYAPKIN-TYAPKIN *with two barking, pedigreed puppies on a leash, and a riding crop, which from time to time he swishes in the air. He greets the* MAYOR *just at the moment when the latter claps his hands to call the maid. The wench runs in and stops next to the* MAYOR; *he shows her the sealing wax, after which she runs out. Enter together* ZEMLYANIKA *in a skullcap and* KHLOPOV *carrying two books under his arm. All the characters must be dressed so that the audience senses at once the studious hand of an archaeologist–costume designer backstage. Fat* ZEMLYANIKA *pants after having some kvass.*

MAYOR [*seated, exchanges greetings with* ZEMLYANIKA *and* KHLOPOV; *he speaks with a Ukrainian accent, neither loudly nor softly, but just as in life*]: I have invited you, gentlemen, to inform you of a most unpleasant piece of news. [*Nodding her head affably to the guests,* ANNA ANDREEVNA *passes through the room with a large ring of jangling keys. After a pause.*] We're to be visited by an Inspector. [*He finishes his letter.*]

LYAPKIN-TYAPKIN: What do you mean, an Inspector? [*Hists to the pups to lie down and swishes his crop.*]

ZEMLYANIKA [*panting from the kvass, belches*]: What do you mean an Inspector? [*Belches again.*]

MAYOR [*shoving the letter into an envelope and writing the address*]: An Inspector from Petersburg . . . incognito. And with secret orders to boot.

[*The wench enters with a lit candle. The* MAYOR *melts the wax and seals his letter.*]

LYAPKIN-TYAPKIN: How do you like that! . . .

ZEMLYANIKA: We don't have troubles enough . . . so they send us some . . .

KHLOPOV: Heavens to B-B-Betsy . . . And with secret orders to boot. [*Hists to the pups to lie down.*]

MAYOR [*still sealing the letter*]: I had a kind of premonition . . . [UKHOVER-TOV *enters and exchanges greetings with everyone.*] All last night I was dreaming about a couple of extraordinary rats. Honest, I'd never seen anything like them before: black, and of incredible size . . . [*Hands the sealed envelope to the wench and points to his pipe. The wench exits.*] Now I'll read you the letter I received from Andrey Ivanovich Chmykhov. [ANNA ANDREEVNA *returns to her room, jangling the keys even more loudly.*] "Dear friend and benefactor . . . and to inform you." Ah . . . here it is. [*Reads the letter with no regard for coherence, as if to underline his relative illiteracy.*] "I make haste to inform you that an official is coming with orders to inspect the whole province and in particular our district. I learned this . . ." [*Church bells begin to peal, utterly drowning out the* MAYOR'*s reading. Everyone gives a start and squeezes in close to the* MAYOR. *The wench brings him a smoking pipeful of Zhukov tobacco and exits. When the bells subside, the* MAYOR *raises his index finger and says insinuatingly:*] That's the situation we're in now! [*Drums his fingers on the table. Everyone is silent.* ZEMLYANIKA *belches. Blackout.*]

[*The stage is empty. The wench runs across the yard, desperately flopping her bare feet. At left we hear the* MAYOR'*s voice, drowned out by the racket of the departing, jolting carriage and its bells: "Let's go, let's go, Pyotr Ivanovich . . . And don't let a soldier on the street without his full kit: that scum of a garrison only put a uniform over their shirt and nothing on underneath." At the same time, at right we hear the squabbling of the* MAYOR'*s wife and daughter. "Ah, for heaven's sake, for heaven's sake . . . It's all your fault, it always is. You and your dawdling: 'Just one teeny pin, just one teeny kerchief.'" The racket of the carriage driving away with the* MAYOR *drowns out the voices.*]

ANNA ANDREEVNA [*running across the stage in some kind of eye-catching "fully researched" shawl. Offstage left:*] Anton, where are you off to? What, has an inspector come? With a mustache! What kind of mustache?

[*The carriage drives away.*]

MAYOR [*offstage, over the rumbling of the wheels*]: Later, my love, later.

[*We hear the driver's smutty song and cries of "Gee up, m'hearties!" and so on.*]

ANNA ANDREEVNA [*offstage*]: Later? News won't keep till later . . . [*Howls*] I won't wait till later . . . just tell me one thing: Is he a colonel? Huh? [*Enter right* MARYA ANTONOVNA, *apparently comparing herself with a fashion plate.* ANNA ANDREEVNA *enters to confront her.*] He's gone . . . I won't forget you for this . . . You and your "Mama dear, Mama dear, wait a bit, just let me pin up this teeny kerchief; I'll be a second!" You and your second . . . [MARYA ANTONOVNA *looks out the window.* ANNA ANDREEVNA *speaks in "Chekhovian" tones.*] We've found out nothing on account of you . . . It's all that damn primping . . . [*The maid enters with a watering can and sprinkles the flowers on the windowsill.*] She heard the postmaster was here, so she had to simper in front of the mirror: how does it look from this side and how does it look from that. She fancies he's stuck on her. [*Weeps in vexation, then blows her nose into a handkerchief embroidered with some eye-catching pattern.*] Well, he's simply making fun of you behind your back.

[*The clock strikes nine. The sky clouds over.*]

MARYA ANTONOVNA [*not turning around, apathetically, looking out the window*]: What am I supposed to do, Mama dear? It doesn't matter, we'll know everything in two hours.

ANNA ANDREEVNA: Two hours! . . . [*Laughs a long while gloomily and sarcastically.*] Thank you kindly. [*The wench exits left.*] Much obliged for the information! . . . Why didn't you think to say we'd know a lot more in a month! [*Gets up from behind the table with the same laugh.*] Hey, Avdotya! . . . [*Turns around astonished that the wench is no longer in the room.*] Huh? [*Hangs out the other window from MARYA ANTO-NOVNA's and shouts.*] Avdotya, did you hear who it is that's come? You didn't? What a ninny . . . He waved you away? Let 'im wave, you could have asked anyway. [*Loud barking from the watchdog, whom ANNA ANDREEVNA tries to shout over.*] Go on, go do it now . . . Listen, run, ask questions where they went . . . what he's come for, what he's like—understand? Look through a chink and find out everything and what kind of eyes he's got, black or otherwise, and come back that very minute, understand? [*In unison with MARYA ANTONOVNA, in a voice of overwhelming grief.*] Hurry, hurry, hurry, hurry!

[*Rain begins to patter down on the yard. The curtain falls very, very slowly.*]

OFFICIAL ON SPECIAL ASSIGNMENT [*entering*]: The next version is in the spirit of Max Reinhardt. Some biographical data about the guest director!

The son of parents of reduced means, he was born in a small hamlet near Königsberg. Scanty rations, principally potatoes, conduced to his developing rickets. However, despite one leg being shorter than the other, he became successfully involved in teaching rhythmic gymnastics, following the Dalcroze system,* at a school. Needless to say, he

---

* A system of artistic gymnastics and eurhythmic training, created by the Swiss choreographer Émile Jaques-Dalcroze (1875–1950).

has brought his own Germanic seriousness to bear on the staging of *The Inspector General.*

Gogol's text first underwent a literary revision by Hugo von Hofmannsthal, as is customary with Reinhardt. Hugo von Hofmannsthal,* of course, took to his task very assiduously; having adapted Gogol into verse, he nevertheless preserved many of his expressions, totally integrally.

The music was composed by Humperdinck.† By introducing music, the director took as his rationale that letter of Belinsky‡ that begins, "Music, music, to hell with you!," etc.

All the favorite devices of the great innovator of German directing have been applied in this staging. A circus ring with a staircase, whose grandiosity demands a theater of five thousand, the entrance of the characters from the auditorium, changing the scene in the open air, and so forth. The foundation for the entire production was the following statement from Gogol's *A Theater Lets Out:*§

"It is a pity that no one noticed the one honorable character in my play. Yes, there was a single honorable, noble character, who acted throughout its entirety. This honorable, noble character was laughter. It was noble because it decided to appear despite the vile character it is given in 'society.'"

The director decided to appease the ghost of the great writer by introducing on the stage at long last this longed-for character in the shape of a ravishing young girl, in company with her steadfast friends—*satire* and *humor.* All are barefoot, again based on the words of Gogol himself: "Much may distress a man when reduced to his nakedness, but the bright power of laughter brings peace to his soul." [*He exits. The curtain goes up.*]

---

* Hugo von Hofmannsthal (1874–1929), Richard Strauss's favorite librettist, cofounded the Salzburg Festival with Reinhardt and wrote versions of *Elektra, Everyman,* and *The Great World Theatre* for him.
† Engelbert Humperdinck (1854–1921), composer of *Hänsel und Gretel,* wrote the score for Reinhardt's medieval spectacle *The Miracle.*
‡ The progressive essayist Vissarion Belinsky (1811–48) was both an admirer and a severe critic of Gogol.
§ "A Theatre Lets Out after the Performance of a New Comedy" (1836) was a playlet in which Gogol attempted to explain his theory of comedy.

3. Grotesque Staging in the Style of Max Reinhardt

Literary Adaptation by Hugo von Hofmannsthal

Music by Humperdinck

The stage represents the front of a house in the new Russian style, as it is under-stood by the Munich Secessionists.* A central porch, led up to by a few steps, ornamented with "Little Russian" plaquettes. Before the curtain rises, a trap ladder is put up through the orchestra, which, until the performance begins, plays a specially composed overture on a Russian theme.

As the curtain rises, LAUGHTER, SATIRE, *and* HUMOR *are onstage, per-forming a symbolic dance in the Russian spirit, as Humperdinck understands it. Thereafter, the* MAYOR *appears on the porch.* LAUGHTER *sits at his feet, while* SATIRE *and* HUMOR *stand by the footlights, against a background of side portals, right and left.*

MAYOR:

> Let them call me a gray gelding,
> Let me dream of rats all night,
> My firm conscience needs no welding.
> No inspector makes me fright.
> Me, whose cunning, dev'lish wily,
> Pulled the mask from each assayer!
> Skvoznik-Dmukhanovsky I be!
> Not for nothing am I mayor!
> To my house today I summon
> Each official by decree.
> We will figure out in common
> A way out. The light we'll see!
> I can hear their footsteps patter.
> Help me, friends, answer my call!
> Though my heart pounds at this matter,—
> The gelding gray will save you all.

---

* The Munich Secession, a union of German artists founded in 1892 by Franz von Schtuk, was active throughout the 1910s in Austria and Germany. It opposed official academic art and sup-ported impressionism. Its designs included pretentiously sophisticated structures and intricate, multicolored textural images. The theatrical branch included Ernst von Wolzogen, propagandist for the *Überbrettl.*

[*The sound of a defiant march is heard. Through the auditorium the officials in tricorn hats and fantastical uniforms march in step, presenting military salutes. As soon as they are drawn up onstage before the* MAYOR, *he addresses them with this speech.*]

> Gentlemen, I've called you here
> To learn news that will dismay.
> An Inspector's drawing near,
> Changing horses by relay.

ZEMLYANIKA:

> An Inspector?

MAYOR:

> Incognito.
> And with secret orders to boot.

LYAPKIN-TYAPKIN:

> War with Turkey?

MAYOR:

> Not a bitto.

KHLOPOV:

> Then with England?

ZEMLYANIKA:

> Spain's my vote.

LYAPKIN-TYAPKIN:

> Bribes of puppies and of harriers
> Hardly count as sins, and so
> Won't you take a little terrier
> Whelped by that hound you know?

MAYOR:

> I myself will go a-chasing
> Like a bloodhound, sniffing spoor,

Through the town. I will be tracing
This Inspector till I'm sure.

KHLOPOV:

Our hist'ry teacher's rage increases
When he hears Great Alec's name;
He breaks all our chairs to pieces,
And the State pays for the same.

ANNA ANDREEVNA [*enters with her daughter, both dressed as in a Ukrainian-style operetta*]:

An Inspector from Saint Peter?
Is he blond, brunet, mustached?
Answer me!

MARYA ANTONOVNA:

I'm all a-flutter!

MAYOR:

We don't know yet where he's cached.
Later, later, don't be prying!

ANNA ANDREEVNA:

Later? This *is* news, I mark!
Answer me! Don't be so trying!

MARYA ANTONOVNA:

I am blazing with love's spark.

ANNA ANDREEVNA:

Take it easy, darling daughter,
Don't fall in an am'rous trance!

MARYA ANTONOVNA:

I do only what I oughta,
Mama. What a circumstance!

ANNA ANDREEVNA:

On a throne you'll see me seated,
Soft strings strumming from the south,
Crown with ribbons red completed . . .
Only, Tony, watch your mouth!

MARYA ANTONOVNA:

A thousand messengers and over!
Wed a field marshal I may!
I can pick and choose a lover,
Once Dad has the court's entrée.

ANNA ANDREEVNA:

Soup across the seas by steamer
France will send us. We just heat.
Dressed in clothes fit for a queen, ah!
I will costly melons eat!

MAYOR:

Hold your horses, chatterboxes,
You don't know what all this meant.
'Cause of you, my pretty doxies,
To Siberia I'll be sent.

LAUGHTER:

Ha, ha, Mayor, circumspection!
Ha, ha, ha, my brother, hold!
Clouds won't hide you from detection
If corruption taints your soul!

[LAUGHTER, SATIRE, *and* HUMOR *dance around the bewildered* MAYOR. *Curtain.*]

OFFICIAL ON SPECIAL ASSIGNMENT [*entering*]: The next interpretation comes from a student of Gordon Craig, renowned among us for his mystical and cubist production of *Hamlet.** In the first "restructuring"

---

* Gordon Craig staged *Hamlet* at the Moscow Art Theater in 1911–12 with Vasily Kachalov in the lead and his own designs, featuring large screens.

this evening you have been shown, in part, Mirgorod in the clutches of fear. But what is Mirgorod? Please recollect the following words from "The Denouement to *The Inspector General*":* "Well now, what if this were the town of our soul and located within every one of us? . . . Awesome is the inspector who awaits us at the threshold of the grave. Know you not who this Inspector is? Why pretend? This Inspector is our awakening conscience which compels us of a sudden and all at once to subject ourselves to a thorough examination." In this town, according to Gogol, "our passions misbehave like corrupt officials and the mayor is the unclean soul itself." A mystical staging of *The Inspector General* can be realized, of course, only by an ardent follower of Gordon Craig. A young lord, former student at Oxford, and a well-known football player, has worked for some time under the tutelage of the illustrious Craig and has now come to Russia specially to exhibit the products of his creativity. You shall see them presently!—Suffice it to say that the action is played out in some point in infinite interplanetary space. The actual method of staging *The Inspector General*, however, we have decided to keep secret, so that the novelty of the spectacle will impress the audience. I will only allow myself to say with some assurance: the immortal comedy *The Inspector General* is, in this version, capable of reducing you to real tears. [*Exits, deeply affected.*]

4. Mystical Staging in the Style of Gordon Craig

The stage represents infinite space, hemmed in by cloth. Farthest upstage, extending into the upper reaches, are a symbolic watchtower and two enormous trumpets, drenched in a dead glare. Downstage, by the portals, the constables SVISTUNOV *and* DERZHIMORDA, *in the guise of winged angels, sound the trumpets at the audience, then in the opposite direction, then into the wings, and finally at one another. In the distance the mournful sound of an organ pours forth, to which music slowly enters left the* MAYOR, *or, as Gogol describes him, "more accurately, the unclean soul itself," followed by* LYAPKIN-TYAPKIN, ZEMLYANIKA, *and the others, in the guise of "misbehaving passions." Some are masked, others completely muffled up in black cloaks. The* MAYOR *stops center stage, the rest on a diagonal. Pause. A bell tolls.*

* The "Denouement" was another attempt by Gogol to explain his play by casting it as a moral allegory.

MAYOR [*mystically, in a singsong tone*]: I have invited you, gentlemen . . . to inform you of a most unpleasant piece of news . . . [*The bells tolls.*] We are to be visited by an Inspector . . .

[*Everyone reels about in a panic, uttering ponderous sighs.*]

LYAPKIN-TYAPKIN [*trembling*]: What do you mean, an Inspector?

ZEMLYANIKA [*ditto*]: What do you mean, an Inspector?

MAYOR: An Inspector from Petersburg incognito. [*The bell tolls.*] And with secret orders to boot.

[SVISTUNOV *and* DERZHIMORDA *blow the trumpets again.*]

LYAPKIN-TYAPKIN [*dismally*]: How do you like that . . .

ZEMLYANIKA [*in a quavering, staccato voice*]: We didn't have enough troubles, so they send us some . . .

KHLOPOV [*sobbing*]: Heavens to Betsy . . . And with secret orders to boot.

MAYOR: All last night I was dreaming about a couple of extraordinary rats . . . black and of incredible size . . . They came, sniffed about a bit, and went away. [*Offstage a mighty choir intones a passage from the "Requiem."*] Now I'll read you the letter I received from Andrey Ivanovich Chmykhov. [*He unrolls a long scroll.*] "An official has arrived with orders to inspect the whole province, and in particular our district . . . [*In a panic, everyone moves behind everyone else, cowering at right.*] Ivan Kirillovich has got mighty fat and always plays the fiddle." [*The plangent melody of a violin resounds behind the* SOUL. *He himself, contemplatively.*] That's the situation we're in now!

[*Clutching his head, he exits right, followed by the others. The violin plays on and on. Enter left* ANNA ANDREEVNA *and* MARYA ANTONOVNA, *in white winding-sheets: both are weeping, extending their arms in despair in the direction of the* MAYOR'S *exit.*]

ANNA ANDREEVNA: Where oh where are they? Ah, for heaven's sake, husband! . . . Tony! . . . Anton! . . . Where are you off to? . . . Where? . . . They've gone . . .

[*They sink into a posture of inconsolable grief. The tender notes of the violin are drowned out by the trumpets of* SVISTUNOV *and* DERZHIMORDA, *after which, to the cadenced tolling of the bell and the triumphant strains of the organ, the funereal chorus chimes in. Curtain.*]

OFFICIAL ON SPECIAL ASSIGNMENT [*entering*]: In accordance with the wish expressed by a Cinema Conference that's meeting in Moscow this summer, that the best works of classical literature should be adapted for the screen—the final version of *The Inspector General* will be staged in a purely cinematic style, the style of the well-known "Pathé" Company.*

Under the main title *The Inspector General* comes the original, intriguing credit "Dumbellov in the role of the Mayor." The director, one of the most able students of the famous Max Linder,† has drawn on all the gags available in the texts of *The Inspector General:* the tricornered hatbox taken for a hat, the rewarding scene with the letter, the Mayor's Wife's chase after the Mayor, in short, everything that, in this director's opinion, is funny about *The Inspector General* he exploits with all the expertise of movie technique.

The result being a "mighty comic comedy," *The Inspector General* is 650 meters long, made on the very best stock and accompanied by refined music from the modern repertoire.

5. Cinematic Staging

The music—a grand piano and a violin—plays "Gitanetta."‡ The characters are sitting, scrunched together around the Mayor, who leaps up quickly, pulls an envelope out of his pocket, and waves it in the air. Everyone rises in a fright, sits down again, changes places, and gesticulates forcefully. The Mayor, as if hit by lightning, removes the letter from the envelope and makes a show of reading it. At that very second,

---

* One of the earliest and biggest film companies, founded by the French Pathé Brothers.
† Max Linder (1883–1925), Pathé's leading silent-film comedian, was at the height of his popularity between 1912 and 1914.
‡ "The Little Gypsy" (1911) was a dance tune popular in music halls.

Chymkhov's letter with the complete signature appears on the screen. When the letter vanishes, all the characters bustle to say goodbye to the Mayor and run out left. But the Mayor, after putting his hatbox on his head, his left glove on his right hand, and vice versa, kneels down, mutters a quick prayer, gets up, and is about to run off left, when, at right, in a ridiculous state of undress, the Mayor's Wife appears, followed by her daughter, a flirtatious lady's maid, and Derzhimorda, who gives a salute. The Mayor's Wife yanks her husband by the coattails, but he tears himself away and runs off, with the Mayor's Wife after him, their daughter after the Mayor's Wife, the lady's maid after the daughter, Derzhimorda after the lady's maid, as he continues to make extremely comic salutes sometimes with his right hand, sometimes with his left. *The chase scene!* . . . When the characters have run across the stage a second time, the Mayor's Wife stumbles, her daughter falls on top of her, the lady's maid falls on top of the daughter, and Derzhimorda falls on top of the lady's maid.

THE FOURTH WALL
(Chetvyortaya stena)

A buffoonery in two parts

by Nikolay Evreinov

1915

Part 1

A corner of FAUST's *study in an ultranaturalistic staging. Not one single detail is missing! And everything is real. At right, a window; in front of it,* FAUST's *worktable. At left, a medieval bed in which there sleeps, beneath a medieval coverlet, in a medieval nightcap, the actor who plays the role of* FAUST. *Near the bed is a medieval washbasin. Under the bed is a medieval "convenience."*

As the curtain rises, the stage is dark. In the orchestra pit the musicians are gathering and lazily tuning their instruments.

ASSISTANT DIRECTOR [*a grouchy old theater rat, runs onstage flustered, looks at his watch, and shouts to the lighting booth*]: Let there be light! . . . Hey, where the hell are you, damn it? . . . Eleven o'clock and not hide nor hair of him! [*To* FAUST] Ivan Potapych! [*Rouses* FAUST.] Ivan Potapych! . . . It's eleven! . . . I'm here already! I've taken off my fur coat! The orchestra's already in place! . . . The prompter's already in his box!

FAUST: Haaw? . . . What? . . . What time is? [*He stretches. At the window a spotlight blazes into "daylight," and the footlights follow suit.*]

ASSISTANT DIRECTOR: It's been eleven o'clock now for the last fifteen minutes! [*To the electrician*] That spotlight of yours is flickering again! How many times do I have to call it to your attention?! Where did you ever see sunlight flicker like that?! Tell me! . . .

WATCHMAN [*bringing* FAUST *a glass of tea and a bun and the* Petersburg Gazette. *To the* ASSISTANT DIRECTOR]: Pal Palych is asking for you.

ASSISTANT DIRECTOR [*to* FAUST]: Ivan Potapych! Explain this! Explain what you're doing, having them bring you breakfast! The whole orchestra is in place! [*Mauling* FAUST *about.*] Will you wake up, for Chrissake! Do I have to drag you out by the feet? What am I to do with you? . . . Bloody hell! What a dog's life! [*He runs off right.*]

WATCHMAN [*to* FAUST]: Tea's gettin' cold.

[*From the orchestra comes a bang on the kettledrum and a burst of laughter.*]

FAUST [*shuddering and slipping his legs over the side of the bed*]: Bastard! . . . [*Puts on a medieval dressing gown and slippers, bites off a hunk of bun, and almost drinks off the tea in one gulp.*] I need a wash!

WATCHMAN: Right away, sir! [*Lays the newspaper on the bed and brings over a pitcher of water.*]

FAUST: Honest to God, I'll go back to the provinces ... This isn't a job, it's penal servitude, daily penance, being skinned alive! . . . [*He washes, assisted by the* WATCHMAN.] I'm not as young as I used to be . . . I can't

cope . . . It's all very well, their naturalism and all this "truth!". . .
What with the rats around this place you can't get to sleep before
three . . . [*Gargles and tests his voice.*] No consideration, it's incredible . . . To think they used to treat me with kid gloves back in the
provinces! . . . [*He wipes himself off with a medieval towel! . . . Backstage
we can hear the* DIRECTOR *clapping his hands and calling, "Places, chorus!
Look sharp! . . . Take your places! . . ." We hear the rumbling of a hundred
voices—an effect achieved by means of the lower notes of the organ—and
the stamping of feet. The* CONDUCTOR *appears behind his music stand.*
FAUST *puts on a beard attached with tapes, adjusts his nightcap before the
mirror, and avidly peruses the newspaper. The* WATCHMAN *carries away
the slop bucket and the tea glass.*]

DIRECTOR [*clean-shaven, with eyeglasses and a leonine head of hair, he
looks like a proper young academic; he carries the score of* Faust *and is jotting notes in a notebook, enters left with the words:*] Let's begin, ladies
and gentlemen, let us begin! [*Notices* FAUST's *newspaper.*] Ivan Potapych! . . . What's going on here! [*Takes the paper away from him.*] This
is really childish! . . .

FAUST [*embarrassed*]: Good morning!

DIRECTOR [*nodding to him*]: Aren't you ashamed! . . . Do we have to keep
a governess to look after you at all times?

FAUST: I just wanted to see if that review had . . . [*Bites off a hunk of bun.*]

DIRECTOR: Faust! And all of a sudden he's got a twentieth-century
newspaper in his hands. How does that fit in! . . .

FAUST: Well, I just . . .

DIRECTOR: You should be ashamed of yourself, my friend! The management reserves the stage for you after performances only so that you
can live yourself into the role, live it through!

FAUST [*munching on the bun*]: You're not fair—I do live it through. I live
Faust all night through and all morning too.

DIRECTOR: With the *Petersburg Gazette* in his hands! . . . Maybe it helps
you to chew a hunk of bun, but *Faust*, excuse me, is no Danish pas-

try!—it's sixteenth century, my lad! If you don't meld with the role of Faust, don't live your way into it as your own personal, innate role, I tell you straight out—don't expect it to be a success and don't come crying to me if someone else is cast in your part! Excuse me, but we're not here to slap together some farce! . . . Our work is far too serious! This is no puppet show!

FAUST: What did I do that was so wrong?

DIRECTOR: How can you even ask? Hasn't it sunk in yet why we put up this whole intricate setting of Faust's study every night, why we have you sleep on this set, wear Faust's costume all the time, his makeup, why, in short, we're giving you the possibility of breathing, as easily as you please, the atmosphere of a medieval scholar! . . . How can you fail to understand that the whole purpose of our production is to present a true-to-life, do you follow me, truuue-tooo-liiife Faust, to the nth degree!

FAUST: I'm giving my all.

DIRECTOR [unscrolling an old-fashioned manuscript on the table]: Is that so!—you haven't even unrolled this alchemical treatise on homunculi!

FAUST: I overslept a bit today . . . I got to sleep late . . . There are so many rats running around here . . .

DIRECTOR [sarcastically]: Ah, now it's the rats' fault! . . .

FAUST: The long and the short of it is, Karl Antonych, alchemy, chemistry, cosmography, they just aren't my kind of thing! . . . It's no secret, I flunked out of high school and then I went on the stage . . . And now I'm too old to begin!

[The PROPS MAN, who is even older than FAUST, brings in a chalice and puts it on the table.]

DIRECTOR [to the PROPS MAN]: Is the poison real?

PROPS MAN: Strychnine mixed with prussic acid.

DIRECTOR: Good. [PROPS MAN exits. To FAUST.] You see how far we go with details to give the actor the proper mood!—[Sniffs the contents *of the chalice.*] Real poison!—one sip and you'll be down among the dead men.

FAUST [*taking the poisoned chalice with trembling hand and singing*]: "Ah, thou, oh chalice of my forefathers! Thou wert wont to be full! Wherefore, wherefore dost thou tremble! Wherefore dost thy hand tremble so?". . . [*Fearfully he shoves away the chalice.*] I *am* beginning to tremble, damn it! . . . Is this really real poison?

DIRECTOR [*proudly*]: We have no truck with fakes.

MANAGER [*who is also the* ARTISTIC DIRECTOR, *a young man with a full beard, tall and imposing, although he makes an effort to seem unpretentious, enters accompanied by the* ASSISTANT DIRECTOR *and greets the* CONDUCTOR]: Good morning, Maestro! [*To the musicians, who stand up when he appears.*] Good morning, gentlemen . . . [*The* WATCHMAN, *who has come in behind the* MANAGER, *places two chairs on the right side of the stage, close to the footlights, and exits. The* MANAGER *sniffs around eagerly, then smiles.*] Smells like someone's been living here . . . Good . . . Feels real . . . Not a stage setting, but a lived-in dwelling! . . . That's how it should be . . . Although it's a shame there's not a greater stench of chemicals! . . . After all, it is an alchemist's laboratory!

DIRECTOR [*to the* ASSISTANT DIRECTOR]: More chemical smells!

ASSISTANT DIRECTOR: Right away, sir. [*Jots a note in the notebook.*] Add chemical pollution . . .

MANAGER [*to* FAUST]: How's it coming? Living into it? . . . [*Adjusts* FAUST*'s beard.*] Is it easy for you to live your way into Faust here?

FAUST: I do my best . . . [*Slips what's left of the bun onto the table.*]

MANAGER: Today I'll come up with something new . . . Along the lines of realism . . . Yesterday things were still a little murky . . . Lying in wait for today . . . Well now, let's begin! . . . [*He claps his hands—the* DIRECTOR *runs up.*] Take it from the allegretto chorus, A major, page 9! . . . [*To the* CONDUCTOR] Entrance tempo, maestro!

[*The orchestra plays the required music.*]

CHORUS [*offstage*]:

> Ah! . . .
> Why asleep, fair maiden?
> Welcome to the day!
> Soon the sun will gladden
> Heaven with its ray.
> Hark, the cocks are crowing
> Loudly to the morn,
> Heaven's vault is glowing
> As the light is born.
> Posies now are breaking
> Into buds of May,
> All the world is waking
> To love and joy today . . .

FAUST [*who has accompanied the words of the chorus with dramatic action, worked out in great detail, runs over the window with improbable tragicality*]:

> Joyous impulse, thou art so insensate!
> Be still!
> Begone from me, oh life! oh life!

MANAGER [*seated at right with the* DIRECTOR]: Sing with your back! . . . Your back! . . . Forget about the audience!

FAUST [*taking the chalice and turning his back full upon the audience*]:

> Ah thou, oh chalice of my forefathers!
> Thou wert wont to be full!
> Wherefore, oh wherefore dost thou tremble? . . .
> Wherefore does thy hand tremble so? . . .

MANAGER [*to* DIRECTOR]: Now that's what I call realism!

DIRECTOR [*flattered*]: Half strychnine, half prussic acid!

MANAGER [*shaking his head in approval*]: You can tell.

CHORUS [*offstage*]:

> The meadows with their beauty beckon,
> Over them are widely strewn

> Lovely patterns you can reckon,
> Made of fragrant, wondrous blooms.
> Everything is filled with magic,
> All things tempt us, charm our eyes,
> Everything is full of . . .

MANAGER [*clapping his hands*]: Sorry! . . . Sshh . . . [*They all fall silent. He walks to the window.*] Ladies and gentlemen of the chorus! . . . For heaven's sake, forget that this is an opera! . . . Sing the way you sing in real life! . . . After all, this is a chorus of German burghers, farmers, peasants! . . . Cut all this Italian stuff!—It's out of place here! Give me more vulgarity, simplicity, naturalness! . . . Have you ever heard barge haulers singing along the Volga? . . . That's what I'm after! . . . These people are just the same as barge haulers, only—German. [*Claps his hands and returns to his seat.*] From the top!

[*The chorus repeats.*]

MANAGER [*stopping chorus and orchestra*]: An appreciable improvement. But still far, far from ideal. [*To the* DIRECTOR] Call some extra rehearsals! Explain to the chorus again what truth in art is all about!

DIRECTOR: Right you are. [*Makes a note of it.*]

MANAGER [*to* CONDUCTOR *and* FAUST]: Allegro agitato, please! "What is God to me!". . .

[*The orchestra supplies the required introduction.*]

FAUST [*singing, lying wearily on the bed*]:

> What is God to me!
> He rewards neither faith nor love! . . .
> He will not give me back my youth.

[*He puts his feet on the floor and sings, sitting on the bed, straining with all the reality of a bilious, irritated little old man, while the* MANAGER, CONDUCTOR, *and* DIRECTOR *by gestures, stamping, and all other means possible try to extract from* FAUST *the maximum naturalistic annoyance.*]

> I curse you, earthly joys,
> And I curse the fetters of my earthbound prison!

I curse my fleshly, ailing, and imperfect form.
I curse all dreams of love!
What are life and fame to me?
What to me are hope and bliss?
I curse them too!
My patience is at an end . . .
Oh Satan! . . . Come to me!

[*From a trapdoor* MEPHISTOPHELES *appears, costumed according to our latest historical research.*]

MEPHISTOPHELES [*singing*]:

Here I am!
Wherefore do you wonder? . . .
I heard thine appeal at once
So I appear, sword at my side! . . .
A feather in my cap! . . .
A broad mantle on my back! . . .
And money in my purse.
Have I not all that's needful! . . .

MANAGER [*clapping his hands*]: Sorry! . . . [*They all stop.*] Good morning, Semyon Andreevich! [*Exchanges greetings with* MEPHISTOPHELES.] I didn't see you before. Don't get angry, dear boy, but I've got to eliminate this aria of yours.

MEPHISTOPHELES: What for? How come?

MANAGER: Don't get excited, dear old thing! It has absolutely nothing to do with your performance, but the fact is . . .

MEPHISTOPHELES: Is what? . . . What am I doing wrong?

MANAGER: It has nothing at all to do with you. It's far more serious. Mephistopheles, as I was reading in Eckermann* yesterday, is just one aspect of Faust himself. Understand?

MEPHISTOPHELES: So what?

---

* This is an ironic comment on F. F. Komissarzhevsky's "scholarship": in his chapter on Faust, Komissarzhevsky constantly refers to Johann Peter Eckermann's *Conversations with Goethe.*

MANAGER: So, for Goethe Mephistopheles is the same person as Faust,* but a Faust who's negative, compromised, earthbound in the meanest sense of the word. Mephistopheles is to Faust's tragedy what the devil is to Ivan Karamazov's!

MEPHISTOPHELES [*reeling*]: You can't mean . . .

MANAGER: My dear fellow! Truth above all! . . . If the Moscow Art Theater had no compunction in rejecting the devil as a separate character, then we, the producers of a realistic opera, should have done so long ago.

MEPHISTOPHELES: You must be joking!

MANAGER: Certainly not. In *The Brothers Karamazov*, Kachalov combined both the devil and Ivan in his own person,† and in our *Faust* Ivan Potapych [*points to* FAUST] will combine in his own person both Mephistopheles and Faust!

FAUST: Pa . . . pa . . . pa . . . pa?

MANAGER: What do you mean, pa-pa, pa-pa?

FAUST: Part's too low! . . . Mephistopheles is a bass, but . . . but . . . I'm a tenor.

MANAGER: Don't be silly!—sing it an octave higher and be done with it. I've thought of everything!

DIRECTOR: This had occurred to me as well. After all, what have we got here! . . . A work of realism, living characters, true-to-life images and all of a sudden an element of fantasy! . . . A bogeyman from a fairy tale! . . . The devil! . . . A goblin to scare children with! . . .

---

* Komissarzhevsky wrote: "In Goethe's tragedy Mephistopheles for me is Faust's alter ego; he is the devil but a special, namely Faustian devil . . . I would even have wanted this face and figure onstage to remind us of Faust." F. F. Komissarzhevsky, *Teatral'nye prelyudy* (Moscow: A. P. Korkin, A. V. Beydemon & Ko., 1916), 47.
† Vasily Kachalov as Ivan Karamazov in the Moscow Art Theater production of *The Brothers Karamazov* (1910) turned the dialogue of Ivan and the Devil into a soliloquy: "Ivan speaks his own words and those the devil speaks in the novel. Technically this was immensely difficult." Nikolay Éfros, *Moskovsky Khudozhestvenny Teatr 1898–1923* (Moscow: Gosizdat, 1924), 385.

MEPHISTOPHELES [*nonplussed*]: I ... I ... I can't find the words ... I ... have to speak frankly ...

MANAGER [*ever so sweetly and reasonably*]: For heaven's sake, Semyon Andreevich, if there's anything making you unhappy, put off your remarks to some other time! I'll be entirely at your disposal after the rehearsal! But right now, dear fellow, we're rehearsing! Show a little tact! You're an artist and should recognize how precious every hour of our creative work is. [MEPHISTOPHELES *staggers into the wings with an agonized look on his face. To* FAUST *and the* CONDUCTOR] Gentlemen, take it from Mephistopheles's entrance.

MEPHISTOPHELES [*turning around*]: What? ...

MANAGER: No, no! ... We'll manage without you! [MEPHISTOPHELES *exits.*] Ivan Potapych! If you please!

FAUST: I, you see ... I haven't learned Mephistopheles's part!

MANAGER: Can it be that after the 138th consecutive rehearsal* you don't hear the part ringing in your ears? ...

FAUST: But what sort of acting should I do in the meantime?

MANAGER: The same as before. Pretend that you are listening to somebody else! Imagine that Mephistopheles is your inner voice! ... a voice from within!

FAUST: And sing to myself in that voice?

MANAGER: Why, of course! ... but from within! [*Claps his hands. To the* CONDUCTOR.] Moderato! Entrance of Mephistopheles!

FAUST [*singing as* MEPHISTOPHELES, *acting as himself*]:

> Here I am!
> Wherefore do you wonder?
> I heard thine appeal at once!
> So I appear, sword at my side! ...

---

* A jab at the Art Theater's traditional rehearsal practice. Éfros: "Work was always feverish, but its tempo was deliberately slow." This led to "an unheard-of number of rehearsals": *Tsar Fyodor* took 74; *Antigone*, 36; and *The Brothers Karamazov*, 190. Éfros, *Moskovsky Khudozhesvenny Teatr*, 435.

MANAGER [*explaining to those around him*]: That's a symbol!

FAUST: A feather in my cap.

MANAGER [*as before*]: Another symbol.

FAUST:

> A broad mantle on my back! . . .
> And money in my purse.
> Have I not all that's needful!

MANAGER: Splendid! . . . From now on the problem of interpreting Mephistopheles on the stage is to be considered solved! . . . Without all those antinaturalistic entrances from trapdoors, colored flares, and the rest of the mumbo-jumbo, which is unworthy of a serious theater, of the true motto "Everything as it is in real life."* [*Shakes* FAUST's *hand.*] You must agree that this way is better, cleverer, nobler?

FAUST [*melted by the praise*]: Yes, of course, it's more original this way, much more original . . . although I really . . .

MANAGER: Nonsense, nonsense! Don't be modest! Naturally you're still a little shaky in your lines, but that's not what makes it so powerful! [*To the* CONDUCTOR] Have them transpose Mephistopheles's part for Faust! . . . [*To the* DIRECTOR] Call extra rehearsals for this scene! [*To the* CONDUCTOR] Now shall we go straight to the vision of Marguerite?

[*The orchestra plays the required music. At left, the form of* MARGUERITE *at the spinning wheel begins to glow through the wall.*]

FAUST [*as* MEPHISTOPHELES *in a spooky, coarse-grained voice*]: "How now? How dost thou like her?" [*As himself, tenorishly saccharine.*] "I am thine!"

MANAGER [*clapping his hands*]: Bravo! . . . [*The orchestra stops playing.*] You can feel at once that a duet is being sung. [*To those around him*] Am I right? . . . the illusion is complete! and totally plausible as well. Why

---

* Another swipe at Stanislavsky. His theory: "to be as close as possible to reality and its truth and overcome stage illusion." Éfros, *Moskovsky Khudozhestvenny Teatr*, 147.

this didn't occur to me sooner, I can't figure out. But this is what we're after!—And right after such plausibility comes the totally fabulous, by which I mean non-naturalistic, vision of Marguerite! True, science does acknowledge states of hallucination, but we can hardly attribute them to Doctor Faust, that sober intellect, tempered in the furnace of positivism, and it's not nighttime either, it's early in the morning! . . . What's your opinion, gentlemen? . . . Looking at it this way, I think that if we have to have "A Vision of Marguerite". . . the most suitable place for her would be somewhere out the window.

MARGUERITE: What do you mean, "out the window"?

MANAGER: Just that. Faust sees Marguerite out the window.

MARGUERITE: But this scene is called "the scene with the spinning wheel."

MANAGER: So what if it is! Let Marguerite pass by the window with a spinning wheel!—as if she's just bought it at the market, is taking it home and stops awhile to admire her new acquisition in front of the house where Faust lives.

DIRECTOR: Absolutely true to life. Maybe even Martha can go with her to lend a housewifely air to the whole scene.

MANAGER: Martha certainly can. Even more realistic!

DIRECTOR: I'll call her! [*He runs off right.*]

MANAGER [*to* MARGUERITE]: Please come over here, Alisa Petrovna! Just for a second! [MARGUERITE *leaves her place. To* FAUST *and the* ASSISTANT DIRECTOR.] I've just this minute noticed the whole inappropriateness of her costume! . . . A regular fancy-dress ball gown! [*To* MARGUERITE, *who has come downstage in her lovely traditional costume.*] Such dissonance, Alisa Petrovna!

MARGUERITE: What do you mean, dissonance?

MANAGER: Your costume. Clashes with the whole production.

MARGUERITE: It's made from the designer's sketch . . . You approved it yourself . . .

MANAGER: I know. [*Looks her over.*] It won't do at all . . . We need something else . . . And besides, you're too refined in general!—Unconvincing! Marguerite is lower middle class. More than that, she's a village lass! A foot soldier's sister. Lives with a bawd! . . . And in the rough-and-ready age of the Landsknechts at that. The makeup and the rest ought to be totally different. We have to make the audience feel that this kind of Gretchen wolfs down herrings, tail and all, her hands are covered with calluses from spinning, she's practically a beggar, earns her crust of bread by hard labor, runs to the market in the mornings in bare feet. Otherwise who would believe in your Marguerite!

MARTHA [*leaning out the window*]: You want me?

MANAGER: Yes, yes. [*To* MARGUERITE] Under the window, please! [MARGUERITE *goes to the other side of the stage and stands under the window with* MARTHA. *The* MANAGER *groups both of them in a pose, examining the spinning wheel, and returns to his seat. To the* CONDUCTOR.] Take it from where we left off! [*The orchestra proceeds.*]

FAUST [*as* MEPHISTOPHELES, *offering himself, from left hand to right, the chalice of poison*]:

> Take thou this chalice!
> Now no death, no poison is in't,
> But joy of life—just drink of it!
> No death lurks there! No poison's there!
> Youth lies therein and love!

[*Speaks.*] How can I drink it, if it's real poison?

MANAGER: Pretend to drink it!

FAUST [*as himself, timorously*]:

> I drink! . . .
> I drink!

[*With great caution he "pretends" to drink. The* DIRECTOR *runs offstage and gestures to* MARGUERITE *and* MARTHA *to come on. They cross slowly, arms around one another's waists, to the left.*]

I drink!
I drink for thy sake, divine image.

[MEPHISTOPHELES's *voice*] 'Tis well!

[*His own voice*] Shall I behold her!

[MEPHISTOPHELES's *voice*] Thou shalt!

[*His own voice*] Soon will't be?

[MEPHISTOPHELES's *voice*] This very day!

[*His own voice*] Oh rapture!

[MEPHISTOPHELES's *voice*] Let us be gone.

[*His own voice*] Let us be gone.

[*Speaking*] Now what?

MANAGER: What do you mean?

FAUST: Now I have a duet with Mephistopheles.

MANAGER: Sing it as Faust! [*To the* CONDUCTOR] Have the cellos come in as Mephistopheles's voice! Reorchestrate it!

[*The* CONDUCTOR *bows in compliance and, without stopping the orchestra, proceeds.*]

FAUST:

I crave the love, I crave the blisses
That must be found in stroking and in kisses,
I crave, with ardent love of bygone days,
To sup my fill of every young embrace.
O thou, bring back my youth, such is my plea!
Return to me my erstwhile ecstasy!

MANAGER [*during the singing urging him on, together with the* DIRECTOR]: Give us your back! More back! Forget about the audience! . . . More naturally! . . . More naturally still! . . . [*After the words "My erstwhile ecstasy," the* MANAGER *claps his hands, stopping the orchestra and the singer. To the* DIRECTOR.] It's all in verse.

DIRECTOR: What?

MANAGER: It's in verse, I said.

DIRECTOR: We adapted it as much as we could.

MANAGER: But even so you can sense the verse, the rhyme, the meter—in short, verse! Have you ever heard of a thing called verse?

DIRECTOR: Good grief, stop treating me like a child—as if I didn't know it myself.

MANAGER: Then we have to try and turn it into prose. After all, this isn't *Vampuka*, it's a realistic opera! What's verse doing in it, I ask you! If we can't manage to make it sound as trivial as everyday conversation, who would believe that this is life and not a stage production!

DIRECTOR [*making a note*]: Fine, I'll adapt it all over again.

MANAGER [*to the* CONDUCTOR]: Go on!

FAUST: Pardon me. I wanted to ask how you're going to handle my transformation from Faust into a young man? You promised to explain it to me several days ago, but in the meantime . . .

MANAGER [*interrupting*]: Transformation? . . . What transformation?

FAUST: The one into a young man! In the play, after Faust drinks the potion, he becomes young!

MANAGER [*roaring with laughter*]: Ha, ha, ha! . . . Good lord, Ivan Potapych, when are you going to scrap that childish notion of Faust! . . . It's a wonder you're not sickened by these penny-ante operatic miracles! . . . Do be serious! . . . For the last time, look at Faust not as a mountebank but as a psychologist! For the last time, understand that Faust is rejuvenated *spiritually*! Can't you understand? Spiritually, not physically. Why, where would we be if, in our realistic production of *Faust*, a sober interpretation, we went in for such infantile stunts as the instant transformation of a gray-haired old man into a raven-haired young man! . . . Is that the way you think of Faust's rejuvenation? Can't you live without the charade of sky-blue tights, a hat with an ostrich plume, and the rest of the folderol?

FAUST: Then what, am I to remain in my nightcap like this?

MANAGER: I assert that a nightcap is more worthy of Doctor Faust than a dunce cap!

DIRECTOR [*to* FAUST, *amicably taking him by the skirt of his dressing gown*]: You're an odd duck, Ivan Potapych! It's no secret that when we asked you to play Faust, we had in mind not so much your voice as your age.

FAUST: My age?

DIRECTOR: Why, of course! . . . Faust is an elderly man and, therefore, the best person to portray him onstage would be an elderly man like himself.

FAUST: But I . . . I'm not all that old!

DIRECTOR: You're just the right age. And you have the proper voice—a croaking, cracking, creaking voice . . .

FAUST: I've got a little cold today.

DIRECTOR: For heaven's sake, don't get well, otherwise you'll spoil our whole production. You should be exactly as you are now throughout the whole opera! . . . What's more, I would personally prefer it if, in the interests of realism, you rasped, croaked, hacked and coughed, blew your nose a good deal more—in short, it would make Faust's old age seem all the more naturalistic.

MANAGER [*to* FAUST, *from a position of superiority, upholding the* DIRECTOR's *opinion*]: Certainly, if an old man won't act onstage as an old man with all the infirmities appertaining to an old man, where is the realism in the acting, I ask you!

DIRECTOR: I even considered, in the interests of realism, releasing a sort of smell of old age into the audience! . . . Yes, yes! to fumigate the auditorium with some sort of mixture that would give off an odor of mustiness, snuff, mothballs, and a lot more! . . . So that the audience will actually sense the nearness of Faust! . . . Old codgers always give off a smell! . . .

ASSISTANT DIRECTOR [*offended on behalf of his venerable age group*]: What do you mean, they give off a smell?

DIRECTOR: For heaven's sake, I didn't mean you!

ASSISTANT DIRECTOR: Then be so good as to explain what you *did* mean!

MANAGER: Drop it, gentlemen, we'll straighten this out later! There's no time now for squabbling. [*To the* CONDUCTOR *and* FAUST] Let's go over the Faust-Mephistopheles duet again! "I crave love." [*To* FAUST] If you please! In the new interpretation!

FAUST: You mean, with a frog in my throat?

MANAGER: That's right!

FAUST: But it'll ruin my voice.

MANAGER: Be so kind as to obey the Director's directions!

FAUST: The Director won't get me a new voice!

MANAGER: You refuse? . . . All right. In that case don't complain if you're docked a month's pay! . . .

FAUST: What for?

MANAGER: For refusing to carry out the Director's directions! Clause 171 in your contract.

FAUST: But I was hired to sing, not croak!

MANAGER: You were hired to act. Would you rather *act* the role of Faust or pay two thousand rubles for breach of contract?—clause 183!

FAUST: But if I can't manage it, what then?

MANAGER: Why, then we shall rehearse until such time as you can!

FAUST [*after thinking it over*]: No, I better give it a try right now! . . . My voice is dear to me.

MANAGER: About time too! [*He claps to the* CONDUCTOR. *The orchestra plays the introduction.*]

FAUST [*singing in a very decrepit voice*]:

> I crave the love, I crave the blisses
> That must be found in stroking and in kisses, etc.

[*During his rendition the* MANAGER *and the* DIRECTOR *gesture to him with the inspired phrases* "Cough," "Blow your nose," "Clear your throat," "Hack a bit," "Good," "Expectorate," "That's it! That's it!," *and so on. The aria stops short because* FAUST *begins to cough in actual fact, spraying saliva about.*]

FAUST: Oof! . . . Give me some water! . . . [*The* ASSISTANT DIRECTOR *rushes to give him the chalice of poison.* FAUST, *enraged, shoos it away with the back of his hand.*] You can go to hell!

DIRECTOR [*calming him*]: You're just not used to it! It'll pass presently . . . Has it passed? . . . There, you see! Nothing to it! . . .

FAUST [*gasping for breath*]: I was choking there for a minute.

MANAGER: But the realism was total! The "old man" you gave us was a sight for sore eyes!

DIRECTOR: But don't make this gesture! [*Shows him.*] That's pure *Vampuka*. For heaven's sake don't vampukicize—and then the illusion will be complete.

ASSISTANT DIRECTOR [*walking over, in fear and trembling, to the* MANAGER *and the* DIRECTOR]: Beg pardon, gentlemen, might I offer a piece of advice concerning the realism?

MANAGER [*pompously*]: Any sensible advice will be received with thanks.

DIRECTOR [*equally pompously*]: Speak out! We're listening!

MANAGER: Don't be shy!

ASSISTANT DIRECTOR [*hesitantly*]: Of course I'm just an ordinary sort of man, I don't know anything about the more advanced directorial skills, and yet it occurred to me . . .

MANAGER: Yes?

ASSISTANT DIRECTOR: Please don't get angry now! . . . I mean this to be helpful . . . Well, after a good deal of cogitation, so to speak . . .

MANAGER: Get to the point!

ASSISTANT DIRECTOR: It occurred to me that if the opera is to achieve total realism, half measures aren't enough, so . . .

DIRECTOR: Say what you have to say.

ASSISTANT DIRECTOR: When did you ever hear a man in real life not talk—forgive me!—but sing instead?

DIRECTOR [*taken aback; after a pause*]: Yes, but this is an opera!

MANAGER [*to the* DIRECTOR]: Not an opera, but a music drama, if you want to be precise! In the first place. And in the second place . . . hmm . . . do you know, this very same thing just occurred to me!

DIRECTOR: Yes, but what can we do about it?

ASSISTANT DIRECTOR: Make it talking to music!

DIRECTOR: What do you mean "talking"?

ASSISTANT DIRECTOR: The same as we do in real life. Then the audience will both understand it and find it natural!

MANAGER [*mulling it over a bit*]: I see, I see what you mean . . .

ASSISTANT DIRECTOR: Simply have everything spoken . . .

MANAGER: Everything and everyone! . . . That's quite a head on your shoulders!

ASSISTANT DIRECTOR [*this shaft is aimed at the* DIRECTOR]: I don't know what sort of head it is, but at least it doesn't give off a smell! . . .

MANAGER: That'll do! . . . If you insist on taking it personally! What more do you have to add?

ASSISTANT DIRECTOR: Well, if they're going to talk instead of sing, they ought to talk in German, not our language.

MANAGER: Why so?

ASSISTANT DIRECTOR: Well, after all, it's taking place in Germany, and Faust is a German!

MANAGER [*after a pause of gleeful meditation*]: Goddamn it! You're a Columbus, a regular Columbus! . . . Why didn't I think of it sooner! [*To the* DIRECTOR] What do you think?

DIRECTOR: Obviously, you can't deny that Faust is a German, but . . . but in this case, if we're going to be consistent, I mean, if we're going all out for historical authenticity—our Faust ought to speak a Middle High German dialect.

MANAGER: Absolutely! We'll translate *Faust* into Middle High German . . . Naturalism means naturalism.

FAUST [*timidly*]: I ought to inform the management that not only don't I know Middle High German, but I can't get my tongue around any kind of German.

MANAGER [*profoundly, earnestly, thoughtfully*]: Yes, that is a fundamental difficulty . . . We might postpone the production for another two years, while you learn German like a native, live in Germany . . .

ASSISTANT DIRECTOR: Gentlemen, allow me to extricate you from your difficulty! . . .

MANAGER: Please do!

ASSISTANT DIRECTOR: There's no reason for Ivan Potapych to go to Germany, because from the naturalistic standpoint, from one end of the opera to the other, he doesn't have to sing—sorry—say more than a few words.

MANAGER
DIRECTOR } What do you mean?
FAUST

ASSISTANT DIRECTOR: Just this. In the part of Faust the lion's share of the monologues and dialogues are with Mephistopheles. Well, who holds long conversations with himself?—Only a lunatic. Marguerite does at the end of the opera, but that proves my point! The girl's gone out of her mind, so she can talk to herself to her heart's content! But Faust—where does the author say that he's out of his wits! . . .

MANAGER: Goddammit! . . . that's the barefaced truth! [*To the* DIREC-TOR] What do you think?

DIRECTOR [*embarrassed*]: In real life only madmen talk to themselves and Faust *isn't* a madman—I knew all this long ago.

MANAGER [*to the* DIRECTOR]: Then why didn't you say something all this time! . . . 138 rehearsals go by and not a peep out of you!

FAUST: Excuse me, I'm beginning to lose track of all this . . . I've got a terrific headache . . . Do you mean, I don't quite follow, in act 1, for instance, I'm not supposed to sing *or* talk?

MANAGER: Didn't you just hear our latest decision?

FAUST [*his hand to his brow*]: Do you mean you don't need me now? . . .

MANAGER: What do you mean, don't need you? . . . What about the inner feeling! the gestures! the acting! Faust is onstage the entire act! Who's going to perform in your place?

FAUST: Then it's a pantomime? Standing there tongue-tied like a dummy? . . .

MANAGER [*sternly*]: Ivan Potapych, remember clause 14 of your contract! . . .

FAUST [*terrified*]: What did I say that was so bad? . . . I just don't understand what I'm supposed to do onstage!

MANAGER [*dogmatically*]: Live through the role to music. [*To the* CON-DUCTOR] Take act 1 from the top! We'll re-rehearse it without wasting any more time!

[*The orchestra plays.*]

ASSISTANT DIRECTOR [*to the* MANAGER]: Sorry! One more thing!

MANAGER [*to the* CONDUCTOR]: Just a second! . . . Ssshh . . .

ASSISTANT DIRECTOR: The way I see it, if you want to achieve total lifelikeness in an opera, I mean—naturalism, you'd better set limits to the music!

MANAGER [*dumbfounded*]: What do you mean? You must be joking!

ASSISTANT DIRECTOR: Certainly not. Good grief, sir! A man wants to take poison, he's tired of living—do you want music playing during this? What's consistent about that? Where's your naturalism then?

DIRECTOR: Yes, but this is an opera!

MANAGER [*correcting him*]: A music *drama*.

DIRECTOR: Exactly so, a *music* drama! But you want to do away with the music altogether.

ASSISTANT DIRECTOR [*condescendingly*]: Altogether? . . . No, what for? Somewhere offstage—the play does say it's carnival time!! There's a little band playing and a choir singing, why not, sir! There's nothing against it! Maybe you can take some of the themes from *Faust* itself. But if it's to be as natural as in real life, sir, you can't have a full orchestra coming in and playing a symphony in front of the stage! Why, there's a man up there bidding his last farewell to life!

MANAGER [*nervously pacing*]: That's perfectly true . . . Perfectly true . . . It's really daring! . . . awfully daring! I'm even a bit worried we'd be somewhat . . . ridiculed in the papers for it, there'd be carica-tures—"an opera minus music," they'd call it, the cabarets would make us a laughingstock and so on, but . . . the principle of truth in art is above it all! As the saying goes, "If you fear wolves, keep out of the woods." [*Stops in front of the* CONDUCTOR. *Nervously.*] Maestro! . . . You are free for the time being . . . And so is the orchestra! . . . We have to work something out on this . . . I'm afraid it will take some time . . . and . . . in short, goodbye for the present. Don't be angry! . . . I'll give you all your instructions tomorrow.

[*The* CONDUCTOR *and the orchestra leave their places.*]

PROPS MAN [*has appeared onstage. To the* MANAGER]: Will you be need-ing me anymore? Things look fine and dandy on the props side, so . . . Time for dinner.

MANAGER: Hold on, my dear fellow. [*The* PROPS MAN *remains onstage until the end of the act.*] Ivan Potapych, let's try and re-rehearse your duet with Mephistopheles in the new staging!

FAUST [*crumbling to bits*]: You mean, the duet with myself? . . . without an orchestra? or singing? or words? Just plain mime?

MANAGER: Exactly.

FAUST [*his hand on his brow*]: I don't know if I can anymore! . . . my head's spinning round something awful . . .

MANAGER: Come now, none of your whims! . . . Pull yourself together!

[FAUST *takes a pose.*]

PROMPTER [*a tiny little old man with a tiny little bald head, bespectacled, leaning out of his box*]: Maybe you can let me go get something to eat while you're . . . Since you're doing it without words now, I . . .

MANAGER [*interrupting*]: Prompt the action! . . . Remind him what comes next in the mime! . . . [*The* PROMPTER, *groaning, flops back into his box.*] Only, for the love of God, not so much face to the audience! . . . Don't forget that right here [*he draws a line parallel to the footlights*] we're assuming a fourth wall.

ASSISTANT DIRECTOR [*definitely mocking*]: Excuse me, but why not give us the fourth wall itself, for the sake of verisimilitude?

MANAGER: How do you mean?

ASSISTANT DIRECTOR: Like so—put up a real fourth wall, and be done with it.

DIRECTOR: But that way we'll close off both the singer and the set!

ASSISTANT DIRECTOR: It's up to you. My job is only to point out that there are no such rooms in real life, rooms that dispense with a fourth wall! . . . If it's Faust's study, then it ought to follow the rules! Otherwise it makes no sense! A man is withdrawing from society, he wants to take poison in private, and there's an audience standing by, looking on, criticizing—basically *extraneous*. And why is it extraneous? Because no fourth wall has been put up—there's no way to hide things from prying eyes—you end up "slapping together a farce" as far as most decent people are concerned. It turns into a Punch-and-Judy show.

MANAGER [*nervously pacing the stage*]: Good grief, this gets trickier every minute!

ASSISTANT DIRECTOR: Forgive me for pointing out the naked truth!

MANAGER: Who the hell knows! Why I didn't think of this earlier I can't imagine! . . .

DIRECTOR: Well, I had an inkling of it before! . . .

MANAGER: Then why didn't you say something all this time!

DIRECTOR [*practically in hysterics*]: Because you kept clamping the lid on me! You kept my hands tied! You practically accuse me of wanting to be original, of wanting to contradict you! You want to hog all the fame for yourself! . . . That's why I've been as a dumb as a fish! . . .

MANAGER [*waving him away, flaring his nostrils, and turning to the* ASSISTANT DIRECTOR *with an imperiously commanding gesture*]: Put up a fourth wall! [*To the* PROPS MAN] Put up a fourth wall! [*To the* DIRECTOR] Put up a fourth wall!

FAUST: Is this what I get for living here, living-through here, spending my nights here onstage with rats? . . . As a final reward, I'm to be shut off from the audience?

DIRECTOR [*pompously*]: No wall, my dear fellow, can conceal truthful inner feeling from an audience. You just try and live it through and let us take care of the rest.

ASSISTANT DIRECTOR [*consoling* FAUST]: In the first place, if I may say so, your frantic nose-blowing, coughing and so forth, sir, will be distinctly heard from a window, because [*turning to the* MANAGER] you might build a window in Faust's study so the audience can see him through it . . .

MANAGER [*overjoyed*]: That goes without saying . . . There will be a window here. [*He points to the imaginary wall downstage.*] Right at this point . . .

FAUST [*interrupting*]: Ah, so there'll be a window? . . .

ASSISTANT DIRECTOR: But of course!

FAUST: And I can appear in it?

ASSISTANT DIRECTOR: As much as you like!

FAUST [*laboriously imagining it*]: Aha . . . now I get it . . . The window is here . . . I am here . . . the audience is over there . . . [*Puts his hand on his brow.*] Ugh, my head's spinning round . . . [*To the* MANAGER] Let me go, for heaven's sake . . . I can't understand anything anymore . . .

MANAGER: Go on, go on . . . [*Saying goodbye to* FAUST] I am more pleased with today than with anything that's come before. From now on we can consider the most important problems of the theater solved! [FAUST *exits.*] A fourth wall! . . . This is a veritable Columbus's egg! . . . Simple, clever, and natural all at once. [*Dreamily*] A fourth wall! . . . It marks the dawn of a new theater!—A theater free of lies, compromises, and the cheap hocus-pocus that's unworthy of pure art! . . . [*To the* DIRECTOR] Let's go! . . . We have to draw up a ground plan immediately, one that involves a fourth wall! . . . I'm coming up with such ideas . . . such ideas that . . . I won't leave one stone standing from the original staging!—That was pure *Vampuka*, no matter what you say. [*Shakes the* ASSISTANT DIRECTOR's *hand and kisses him on both cheeks.*] Thank you! . . . I am eternally obliged to you.

ASSISTANT DIRECTOR [*modestly*]: A tiny little bonus to my salary, if you'd do me the favor . . . Five measly rubles or so . . . comes in handy, a hat for the wife, laundry, the trolley . . .

MANAGER: Absolutely. I consider it an obligation.

[*Clasps his hand tightly and exits with the* DIRECTOR. *The* ASSISTANT DIRECTOR, *after accompanying the big shots out as far as the wings with obsequious bowing and scraping, turns back to the puzzled* PROPS MAN *and explodes into silent laughter. The* PROMPTER *pops out of his box; he systematically shoves his eyeglasses up on to his forehead, pulls from his pocket a sausage, a roll, some hard-boiled eggs, and a twist of paper containing salt, and settles in to have a bite at* FAUST's *worktable.*]

PROPS MAN [*to the* ASSISTANT DIRECTOR]: What are you so cheery about?

PROMPTER [*sniggering in approval*]: Well, you got them to take the plunge!

ASSISTANT DIRECTOR [*still laughing*]: And those idiots took it all for solid gold!

PROMPTER: Yes, that's some prank you played on them! No doubt about it! . . . I was almost scared stiff on the spot—they'll see through him, I was thinking.

ASSISTANT DIRECTOR [*still laughing*]: Not them! . . . They never had a clue! Their ideas were getting ahead of their brains! "You're a Columbus," they say! Ha, ha, ha . . . A Columbus! . . . [*Plants himself next to the* PROMPTER, *with his own lunch.*]

PROMPTER [*eating heartily*]: Yes . . . there's plenty of dimwits on God's green earth, but *naturalismists* like them, you won't find in a month of Sundays . . .

PROPS MAN: And I jest come in . . . hadn't a clue . . . What's up, thinks I, our Kuzma Ivanych is gone bonkers! . . .

PROMPTER [*correcting him*]: Columbus Ivanych, you mean! . . . [*He laughs, slapping the* ASSISTANT DIRECTOR *on the back.*]

PROPS MAN: So I figger, somethin's up! . . . From where I'm standin', you'd think it was the Boss layin' down the law. [*Plants himself down and decorously pulls a sandwich out of his pocket.*]

ASSISTANT DIRECTOR: Why not? Don't you think in a case like this I can be every bit as smart as the Boss? Nothing to it! Easy as pie! . . . If this were only *real* art, where there's imagination and beauty and what-have-you, genuine creativity—but that, if you please, isn't good enough for us. Now, making everything the way it is in life, an ersatz imitation, authentic naturalism—well, let's have a helping! . . . Any fool can do that! . . . What kind of art is that? . . .

PROMPTER [*chewing*]: But what if it's a subject from history?

ASSISTANT DIRECTOR: And what are picture books for? . . . Nowadays they take photographs for every archaeological artifact and publish it in a book! . . . That shouldn't stop you! . . . Better learn how to read.

PROPS MAN: You put in for a bonus, you scallywag! . . .

ASSISTANT DIRECTOR: And why not!—You think I'm going to teach them for nothing! . . .

PROMPTER: Columbus Ivanych, that's who you are! . . .

ASSISTANT DIRECTOR [*to the* PROPS MAN, *seriously, taking up the neglected "poisoned chalice"*]: You didn't really and truly put strychnine and prussic acid in this, did you? . . . What if somebody made a mistake and . . . Keep that in mind, my boy!

PROPS MAN: You think I'm dead drunk or somethin'! . . . I ain't riskin' my neck.—This here's a stomach tonic! . . . Doctor prescribed it for my wife—it tones her up.

ASSISTANT DIRECTOR [*pulling a bottle out of the* PROPS MAN'*s pocket*]: Is this the tonic?

PROPS MAN: Careful with that!—it's strychnine!

ASSISTANT DIRECTOR [*uncorking the bottle and sniffing the contents*]: It's very potent strychnine, you've got to admit! . . . You keep this for atmosphere too? [*They all guffaw.*] Well, let's drink our troubles away! [*They clink glasses.*] Maybe our little day really *is* done! . . . They're reducing us to "nontheater!". . . It's downhill all the way. [*They drink.*]

PROMPTER [*singing*]: "It happened in the Golden Age . . ."

[*The* PROPS MAN *joins in, the* ASSISTANT DIRECTOR *weeps quietly.*]

A STAGEHAND [*coming in after a pause*]: Should I let down the curtain?

ASSISTANT DIRECTOR: Hey, did you just wake up? . . . We've been done for a long time! . . . Do you think we're putting on a show here or what? You can see the rehearsal's over, so let down the curtain! [*The* STAGEHAND *exits.*] How many times do I have to tell him? . . .

PROPS MAN [*taking charge of the bottle and slapping it*]: Maybe they're gonna re-rehearse again! . . .

PROMPTER [*bursting into a sardonic laugh along with the* ASSISTANT DIRECTOR]: Maybe so! . . . That's another story! . . . [*The* PROPS MAN *pours, his hand wobbling with laughter.*] To the health of our Columbus! . . . [*They all eat and drink.*]

Part 2

The musicians of the orchestra, all in white tie and tails, ceremoniously take their places before an auditorium lit up for a gala. For a brief span, the carefully tuned instruments make music; then the CONDUCTOR *appears, bows to the audience and the orchestra, pompously sits in his seat, and imposes silence. The* DIRECTOR *appears before the curtain. He is in evening dress and white gloves, impeccably shaven and coiffed, and beaming with complacency.*

DIRECTOR [*bowing to the audience in several directions*]: Kind ladies and gentlemen! Before the overture to the immortal opera *Faust* commences, the management considers it fitting, nay, more—indispensable—to draw the audience's attention to the historic date of tonight's premiere. Today marks the 2,000th anniversary of the founding of the ancient Greek theater, the 715th anniversary of the founding of the Western European theater, and the 159th anniversary of the founding of our Russian national theater. Add up these figures and you will see that over the course of 3,473 years, the greatest minds in the theatrical world have been vainly striving to discover the "elixir of life"—if I may be fanciful—for verisimilitude onstage. But such is the fate of all outstanding discoveries!—they compel us fatefully to wait for them, century after century! . . . One need merely recall how much time preceded the discovery of America to realize that the discovery of the absolute in theatrical verisimilitude would need somewhat more time. Be that as it may, the one important thing is: there is now an end to the search, and this very day, this truly remarkable day, all who have hitherto sought for truth in the theater will at last receive the long-awaited solution. Today's premiere—and I am here on behalf of the management to inform you of it, proud that the allotted mission has fallen to me—today's premiere, ladies and gentlemen, is the total liquidation of old-fashioned, conventional art, steeped through and through with falsity! Today's premiere is a triumphal victory for unadorned truth in the theater. Today's premiere is the greatest event in the universal history of dramatic art—an event, the scope of whose originality can be measured only by the very performance that comprises this event. Regard it with the esteem it in all fairness deserves. But, whatever your opinions, the management is content in its mere awareness of having done its duty!—the duty of preferring, all in all, the truth of sober reality onstage, to tricks of theatrical deception.

[*He exits. The orchestra plays the overture to* Faust, *during which time a first curtain rises, revealing a second, on which Truth is depicted, tearing apart a wig in front of a mirror and trampling a heap of masks beneath her feet. Truth is represented as an unattractive, elderly woman, devoid of any kind of adornment. On either side of her are sewn laurel wreaths, with the inscriptions "Amicus Cato, sed magis amica Veritas"* on one and "Eat salt and bread, But Truth be said" on the other. At the conclusion of the overture an unendurable silence ensues, during which the* CONDUCTOR *leaves his place and the second curtain rises.*

Onstage, almost at the footlights, towers the notorious fourth wall. It is constructed with all the realism of the stonemason's art and observes all the archaeological findings relating to German architecture of the late Middle Ages. The half-light of early morning. The stage is empty. In one of the second-story windows we can see the flickering light of an oil lamp; judging by the two or three retorts, a globe and skull visible on the windowsill, it is the window of DOCTOR FAUSTUS's *study. As a matter of fact, his disheveled shadow flashes by! Then, at last, his characteristic old man's cough is heard! . . . As if in response, somewhere far, far away, the bell of the town hall rings out, tolling five o'clock in the morning. The light gradually grows brighter. At the right we can hear the drunken singing of the guild craftsmen to themes from the first chorus in* Faust:]

"Die Schaefer putze sich zum Tanz
Mit bunter Jacke, Band, und Kranz,
Schmuck war er aufgezogen.
Schon um die Linde war es voll
And alles tantzte schon wie toll."†

[*From right to left crosses a band of youths who have been up all night carousing, while one of them plays a Dutch chorus on a fiddle:*]

---

* "Cato is my friend, but Truth is a greater friend." The original quotation reads "Plato" and has been attributed to both Aristotle (*Nicomachean Ethics*) and Roger Bacon (part 1 of *Opus Majus*).
† Middle High German: "The shepherds dress up for the dance / With colorful jacket, ribbon and garland. / The finery's laid on. / Crowds had circled the linden tree / And everyone was already dancing like crazy."

"Es drueckte haftig sich daran
Da stiesz er an eine Maedchen an
Mit friche Dirne kehrt' sich um
Und sagte: Nun, da find ich dumm."*

[*The roisterers stagger off left.* FAUST *pops his head out of the window, wags it after the departing youths, and, shedding a tear for the memories of youth that well up in his mind, loudly blows his nose. From the right comes the sound of street sweeping.* FAUST, *having turned his head to the right, hides. In the open window on the third story appears an unattractive female figure, howling at the top of her lungs and scratching herself. A scruffy ragamuffin runs in at left and stops before the wall with an unequivocal intention. At that moment, the woman, noticing him from above and coming to a decision, disappears. A sweeper who shows up at right with the cry "Aber Donnerwetter, willst du Ruten kriegen" (Blast it, do you want a hiding?) runs at the urchin, waving his broom at him. The urchin, uttering an "Ow," rushes to escape the blow, which lands on the wall, while the sweeper trips and falls. The woman above pours on him the slops she had meant for the scruffy ragamuffin. The sweeper, shaking himself off like a poodle, lifts his head and roars, "Verfluchte Sau! So musz den doch die Hexen dran!" . . . (Damned sow! They must be witches in there), while the urchin with a shriek of laughter escapes left. The sweeper, crying, "Halt, dummer Jung" (Stop, stupid kid), runs out after the urchin. A few typical German villagers from the provinces cross the stage. The auditorium is filled with the stench of salt fish, onions, and pork.*]

CHORUS OF DRUNKARDS [*offstage left, to the tune "The meadows with their beauty beckon"*]:

"Ach wie und wo ich mich vergnuege,
Ach mag es immerhin geschehn,
Ach laszt mich liegen, wo ich liege,
Ach denn ich mag nicht laenger stehn."†

[MARGUERITE *and* MARTHA *appear right, both in dresses made of ticking.* MARGUERITE, *barefoot, holds a spinning wheel. They stop in front of the*

---

* "He was caught in the crush, / Then he bumped into a girl / Twirled around with a bold wench / And said, I think that's silly."
† "Oh, how and where I have my fun, / Oh, it may happen anyhow / Oh, leave me where I lie, / Oh, because I can't stand up anymore."

study window of FAUST, *who, having heard* MARGUERITE's *lewdly vulgar laugh, reappears in the window, but this time holding the poisoned chalice.*]

MARGUERITE [*admiring the spinning wheel*]: Ach, Gott! mag das meine Mutter sehn! [Oh, God, wait till my mother sees this!]

MARTHA: O, du glueckliche Kreatur! . . . [Oh, happy creature!]

MARGUERITE: Ach, seh Sie nur! Ach, schau Sie nur! . . . [Ah, look at you! Oh, just look!]

MARTHA: Geht! Ist schon Zeit! . . . [Go! It's about time!]

MARGUERITE [*slowly exiting left with* MARTHA, *singing, playing the spinning wheel*]:

> "Es war ein Koenig in Thule,*
> Gar true bis an das Grab,
> Dem Sterbend seine Buhle
> Einen goldenen Becher gab . . .
> Es ging ihm nicht darueber" etc.†

[*The music from a carnival is heard.*]

FAUST [*addressing the audience*]: I can't take any more of this! . . . Ladies and gentlemen, you are my witnesses! . . . [*He drains the chalice of poison dry and, staggering, disappears.*]

[*A tumult onstage. Voices can be heard: "What's happening?," "What's going on?," "Did you hear that?," "Let down the curtain," "Hold on," "Where's the director?," "Doctor," "What's come over him?," and so on. The curtain is rapidly let down. The* ASSISTANT DIRECTOR, *just the slightest bit tipsy, appears in front of the curtain.*]

ASSISTANT DIRECTOR [*bowing to the audience and clearing his throat*]: Ladies and gentlemen, owing to the stark raving madness of the per-

---

* The beginning of Goethe's ballad "Der König von Thule" (1774). Komissarzhevsky had recorded, "Marguerite's first soliloquy in her room is divided by the first two verses of the ballad of 'The King of Thule,'" and he had her sing the remaining verses after Faust's exit. Komissarzhevsky, *Teatral'nye prelyudi*, 58.
† "There was a king in Thule / True even unto the grave, / To him his dying paramour / A golden chalice gave . . . / Nought did he hold more precious," etc.

former who plays Faust, the rest of the opera cannot proceed . . . [*Steals a glance at the notes concealed in his hand.*] Which fact I bring to the attention of the most esteemed audience.

[*He bows and exits.*]

NIKOLAY URVANTSOV

INTRODUCTION

Nikolay Nikolaevich Urvantsov (1876–1941), youngest brother of the playwright Lev Urvantsov, graduated from the law school in Kazan and moved to Petersburg as a government civil servant. He gave up that position within a year and became an actor, performing in the troupe of an old classmate, N. A. Popov. From 1902 until the outbreak of the Great War, he was regularly employed, working for entrepreneurs and stars as diverse as Vera Kommissarzhevskaya and Lidiya Yavorskaya in Petersburg, the Adelheim brothers on tour, and Nikolay Sinel'nikov in Khar'kov. His usual line of business was comic simpletons and character roles. His experience as an actor may explain his careful attention to the costuming and interpretation of *Man's Fate*.

Urvantsov also performed for Evreinov in the Merry Theater for Grownup Children. He had already had a short comedy produced in 1906, exploiting the familiar theme of a scheming widow. Three years later, while simultaneously acting in professional companies, he joined the Crooked Mirror with his parody of melodrama *Jacques Noir and Henri Zaverny or The Missing Document*, with music by Érenberg. The 1909 season saw three of his novelties. *The Veterinarian* was viewed by the critics as a caustic parody of Ibsen and Maeterlinck but was in fact an adaptation of an homonymous playlet by Hans von Gumpenberg, first performed at the Munich cabaret the Eleven Executioners. The title of Urvantsov's next offering reveals it to be an updating of his melodrama sketch, now with "crook plays" at its target: *The Missing Millions, or The Genius of Detection. Nick Carter, Nat Pinkerton, Sherlock Holmes and the King of Thieves Arsène Lupin*. The genre of sensational crime dominated pulp fiction, commercial theater, and silent cinema, so it was ripe for mockery. Urvantsov was far from the first to exploit it, however. Even the creator of the "king of thieves," Maurice Leblanc, had published two novellas titled *Arsène Lupin vs Sherlock Holmes* in a French magazine in 1906; he then issued them as a book, which was turned into a play and then a film. Urvantsov's originality lay in reducing to absurdity the detectives' vaunted logic and powers of deduction, which ultimately lead nowhere.

His third effort, *The Raptures of Love* (*Vostorgi lyubvi*), adapted the *Vampuka* model to operetta, also set to music by Érenberg. The Viennese school of Johann Strauss II and Franz Lehár was mercilessly ridiculed for its clichés and kitsch; the operetta was so successful it stayed in the Crooked Mirror repertory for several years. Between 1911 and 1913 Urvantsov also served as second stage director, specifically invited to produce Evreinov's *Backstage at the Soul* (Evreinov typically claimed he'd been asking for someone to fill that function for three years). Evreinov admitted that he enjoyed attending his colleague's rehearsals, particular in contrast to those of Kugel'. The methods of the two chief directors were distinct: Urvantsov as an actor often turned to tried-and-true methods of the past, whereas Evreinov preferred to experiment. Kugel' referred to Urvantsov and Evreinov as "my two miracle-working Nikolays" (an allusion to the Orthodox saint). When Evreinov left the Crooked Mirror in 1914, Urvantsov stepped into the post of director-in-chief. As Khol'mskaya wrote, "Urvantsov as director and playwright, possessed of bright humor and comic fantasy, was, of course, more talented and more succulent than Evreinov."[1]

Simultaneously, Urvantsov mounted children's plays at Aleksey Suvorin's Society for Art and Literature Theater. He had long dreamed of a theater for children and in 1915 wrote a three-act play, *The Rubber Boy* (*Guttaperchevy mal'chik*), made into a film without his receiving a credit.

The war years proved to be Urvantsov's most productive at the Crooked Mirror, with new plays in almost every program. September 23, 1915, saw the premiere of *Moving Pictures* (*Kinematograf*), following Geyer's two earlier satires of silent film. Geyer had expressed the art world's distrust of the new medium, but by 1915 the attitude toward what Andreev had called "this aesthetic gangster and thug"[2] had gradually changed, especially in terms of its future potential. Urvantsov's sketch was organized along the lines of the average movie-house program of the day, a combination of short subjects and narrative films. It covers the standard genres, along with the primitive nature of the technology, including a lecturer, intertitles, and the overuse of letters to keep the plot moving. The clown Idiotkin was a direct caricature of the French comic André Deed (André de Chapais), star of Pathé's silent comedies, and known in the Russian releases as Glupyshkin (Dopey), soon the generic name for cinematic clowns in Russia. Urvantsov also had fun with the sound effects that usually accompanied film showings, created by a "universal sound machine," which in the smaller theaters was replaced by a metal washbasin, cap pistol, and police whistle.

As a playwright, Urvantsov had his ear to the ground, alert to what might intrigue the public and work in performance. As a follower of cinema, he noted that the theme of the woman of the future had become popular. The Zhanzonkov firm had issued a series of films in April 1914, including "A Woman of Tomorrow," with a scenario about a woman with a masculine temperament. A second series about heroines of the future and their struggle for independence was issued by the same firm in November 1915, this time with a variant, "The Man of Tomorrow."

Consequently, the fall program of the Crooked Mirror opened on October 6, 1915, with Urvantsov's *Man's Fate* (*A Psychological Drama of the Future*), a sarcastic prediction of the results of female suffrage and emancipation. Masculine and feminine psychologies, conceived in cartoon terms, have been switched. The conceit is played out within the framework of a drawing-room drama of adultery, with considerable allusion to the last act of Ibsen's *Doll's House*. The critics were enthusiastic: "The first premiere of the present season seemed highly successful . . . The caricature . . . proceeded to the accompaniment of uninterrupted laughter . . . wittily parodying the banal themes of domestic dramas with the help of a very simple device: men adopted female psychology, and vice versa. The author presents 'a picture of the future' when men will seem the frailer sex . . . Written with talent and staged by Urvantsov."[3] Khol'mskaya considered this the funniest play the Crooked Mirror produced during the war years, and even Evreinov admitted he could not keep from (mentally) applauding it. (He later noted that it was far superior to a "plagiarism" he saw in New York. He possibly meant George S. Kaufman's revue sketch "If Men Played Cards as Women Do.") *Man's Fate* held the boards until the theater's 1918 closure but was revived in the Soviet period, with a new opening and some substantial changes to the dialogue.

Urvantsov, in that same season, directed A. Deych's version of Gogol's *The Nose*, which sharply divided the critics. Following that he produced *The Sufferings of Sura and Yankel the Musician*, a parody of the dramas of Jacob Gordin, Semyon Yushkevich, and Osip Dymov. This reflected a fad for plays of Jewish life that stressed the hardships, travails, and alienation of the Russian Empire's most oppressed minority. In 1906 Kol'mskaya had played the lead in Sholom Ash's play *On the Road to Zion*, which was quite successful. Andreev had made a poor Jew the hero of his Faustian drama *Anathema*, and Yushkevich's tragedy of a suicide epidemic among ghetto youth, *Miserere*, was produced at the Moscow Art Theater. The popularity of such plays, often with Messianic themes, led to the development of stereotypes: accents, gestures, makeup, and costuming, along with sentimental plots and line delivery. While parodying these excesses, Urvantsov still managed to insert into his one-act the truth of the Russian Jewish tragedy—injustice, isolation, fear of persecution, and exile.[4]

The butts of Urvantsov's ridicule remained eclectic. *The Fame of Consul Duilius* (*Slava konsula Duiliya*, November 1916), drawn from ancient history, concerned the retinue of musicians who were to accompany the conqueror of Carthage wherever he went and announce him with fanfares. This tribute to his glory turns out to be a nuisance and forces the hero to abjure honors.

Urvantsov seemed eager to linger in remote periods, for his next offering in February 1917 was *Egyptian Darkness* (*T'ma egipetskaya*, an idiom implying a benighted state of mind), "an uncensored play on Egyptian life," which he directed in a highly stylized, cartoonlike format. The subtitle seems to refer to Evreinov's production of Oscar Wilde's *Salome* at Kommissarzhevskaya's Theater, which had been banned by the Holy Synod. The hieratic poses of the actors caricatured Meyerhold's conventionalized staging of Maeterlinck's *Sister Beatrice* at the same theater a few years earlier.

After the Revolution, when the Crooked Mirror was revived, Urvantsov continued to direct and write for it. The outstanding play of this period was *The Sundown and Sunrise of Europe* (*Zakat i voskhod Evropy*), whose title alludes to Oswald Spengler's *Decline of the West*. A monologue in the form of a lecture delivered by Jean Tryapichkin (the name, roughly Rag N. Tatters, is that of the offstage character in Gogol's *Inspector General* to whom Khlestakov sends his defamatory letter). A lying braggart like that comic hero, Tryapichkin concocts a lecture that is the equivalent of the stump speech in a blackface minstrel show; it is packed with bad French and German, mangled quotations, the dropping of culturally impressive names, puffed-up claims to celebrity: in short, a hyperbolic exercise in the grotesque. It soon becomes clear that the lecturer is a down-market dress designer, more interested in the minutiae of lady's fashions than in European politics. His tourist's view of Paris reflects the commercial vulgarity that derived from Lenin's New Economic Policy.

In all, Urvantsov contributed almost twenty pieces to the Crooked Mirror, most of them parodies. When it closed in March 1918, he found employment at the State Aleksandrinsky Theater in Petersburg, and with the Mirror's definitive end in 1922, he returned there as an actor and director until 1938, staging the farces of Molière and Chekhov. Throughout the 1930s, he performed in films, chiefly in character parts. His last years were difficult and lonely. He died in 1941 in his birthplace, Kazan, his plays uncollected and unpublished.

NOTES

1. Khol'mskaya, quoted in Nora Buks and Igor' Loshchilov, eds., *Kabaretnye p'esy serebryanogo veka* (Moscow: OGI, 2018), 447.
2. Leonid Andreev, "Pis'ma o teatre (Pis'mo pervoe)," *Maski* 3 (1913): 3–14.
3. N. N. Okulov [N. Tamarin], "Krivoe Zerkalo," *Teatr i iskusstvo* 41 (October 11, 1915): 749.
4. See Laurence Senelick, "Jews in Fashion at the Moscow Art Theatre," in *Jews and Theatre in an Intercultural Context*, ed. Edna Nahshon (Leiden: Brill, 2012), 221–42.

MOVING PICTURES
(*Kinematograf*)

A play in eight pictures

by Kolya Urvantsov

1914

Picture 1. Offended Honor, or The Bloody Revenge of Jealousy

Picture 2. Idiotkin Goes A-Courting

Picture 3. The Innocent Victim of a Criminal Passion

Picture 4. A Medical Operation

Picture 5. Newsreel, a Worldwide Survey—"I See All, I Know All"

Picture 6. Peter the Troubadour

*Picture 7. Wonderful Pictorial Tableaux of Interesting Scientific Expeditions
and the Beauties of Nature*

*Picture 8. A Ramble through Egypt—the Land of Pyramids and
Ancient Pharaoh Sphinxes*

*The stage is covered by a white screen, against which the actors perform as
silhouetted outlines. With this in mind, the poses must be shown either in a
clear-cut profile or full face. Individual figures must not overlap: they must
always be separated one from the other, lightly touching only the edges of the
outline when shaking hands, kissing, etc.*

*A practical note: so that a silhouette may look as if turned to face the specta-
tor, the performer must stand back to the screen or face to the light source, located
far upstage behind the screen. On the other hand, when wishing to present a fig-*

ure from behind, the performer must stand back to the light and face the screen so that the light, falling on his back, throws its outline on the screen.

In front of the screen in one of the downstage wings stands a small table holding objects for sound effects. At the table sits the DEMONSTRATOR, *who explains the pictures; he is also the sound man. Titles come from the light source, to which the actors turn their faces.*

Picture 1. Offended honor, or The Bloody Revenge of Jealousy

CHARACTERS

Gaston Poupée

Henriette Poupée, his wife

Comte de Fairelacour, in love with Henriette*

Messenger

Mob

A sophisticated drama from the life of foreign aristocrats. Music plays the waltz "The Hills of Manchuria."† The action takes place in time with the melody.

Demonstrator's Commentary	*Stage Directions*
1. The happiness of Gaston Poupée and his wife, the gorgeous Henriette Poupée, is unconfined:	Enter right from a hillock Gaston Poupée and Henriette with a lapdog on a leash.
2. They enjoy conjugal bliss amid the natural wonders of the south.	They sit on a bench, and, leaning in, exchange kisses, in profile. [*Sound of kissing*]
3. Gaston leaves on business, never suspecting that woe and disgrace are close at hand:	Gaston rises and exits left into the wings and waves his hat, Henriette, seated, waves her handkerchief.

---

* These are joke names from the French: *poupée* means "doll," *fairelacour* "to woo."
† *Na sopkakh Man'chzhurii* (1906) was an immensely popular waltz by Il'ya Shatrov commemorating a lost battle in the Russo-Japanese War.

4. A messenger brings a letter to Henriette from Count Fairelacour. The letter: "Dear Henriette, I love you and I intend to meet you on the bench: Respectfully, Count Fairelacour."

Enter right a messenger, gives a letter to Henriette, receives a tip, bows, goes out again. Henriette tears open the envelope [*crackle of torn paper*] and reads the letter.

5. Seduced Henriette, having plucked a flower, predicts the fate of her new crush:

Having plucked a flower, Henriette picks off its petals.

6. Count Fairelacour appears, the dart of love pierces them at first glance. They drown in the bliss of a criminal love.

The Count on the hillock right takes off his top hat, bows to Henriette. They both grab their hearts. They hold out their hands to one another. The Count runs up to Henriette and, taking her in his arms, sits beside her on the bench. Kiss.

7. The deceived husband catches them at the scene of the crime.

From the hillock right enters Gaston. When he sees the lovers, he grasps his head and wrings his hands.

8. The heart of Gaston Poupée is forever broken:

Gaston, sobbing, bends low. [*Sound of broken crockery*]

9. The fatal meeting of the rivals. Henriette's tears are in vain. The opponents exchange cards, and the jealous Gaston kills the Count in a duel.

The Count has jumped up on seeing Gaston. Henriette is on her knees. The opponents exchange simultaneous bows, simultaneously take out calling cards and exchange them, pull out pistols, and change places. The Count is on the hillock, Gaston by the bench. A shot. [*Sound of a stick hitting the table*] The Count falls on the hillock.

10. The murderer runs off, an enraged mob, summoned to Henriette's aid, pursues him:

Gaston, triumphant, runs off left. Henriette, turning to the right, waves her arms in appeal and runs after Gaston. Behind her from the hillock in single file run two gendarmes, a fat one and a thin one; an old man in a smock and wide-brimmed hat; a nursemaid with a baby carriage; an abbé under a sunshade; a little boy; a chimney sweep with a broom; a bicyclist; a young lady in an enormous hat; etc. They run from right to left twice. The Demonstrator whistles, rings, toots a horn, stamps his feet, etc.

11. The murderer escapes from his pursuers: Gaston sits down, but he still hears the groans of the murdered Count.

Gaston is alone. A powerful drama. He listens in horror, groans, automobile horns.

12. Wherever he goes, Fairelacour stands before him:

He goes right. From behind the hill emerges the figure of Fairelacour in a top hat, his arms down along his trouser seams. Gaston, terrified, falls to his knees, goes left, and there is the motionless Count who managed to run around the stage.

13. In desperation Gaston Poupée cuts his throat with a dagger.

Gaston pulls out an enormous dagger and plunges it into his chest. A gunshot. Gaston dies on the bench.

Picture 2. Idiotkin Goes A-Courting

Onstage the same setup as in picture 1. A comical sensation of a topical humorist, the music plays an "Oy-ra!"* The performers move to the rhythm of a polka.

---

* A partner's dance in three–four time and a rather quick tempo, often used as accompaniment to silent film. Possibly named after the Polish dancer Jan Oyra (born 1888).

CHARACTERS

*Monsieur Jacques Bouledegomme**

Marie Bouledegomme, his wife

Monsieur Idiotkin

A Messenger

1. The happiness of Jacques Bouledegomme and his wife, the splendid Marie Bouledegomme, is unconfined. They enjoy conjugal bliss amid the natural wonders of the South: Jacques leaves on business, while the scheming admirer spreads his toils for the splendid Marie. A messenger brings her a letter from Mr. Idiotkin, who is in love with her: The letter: "Dear Marie, I love you and intend to meet you on the bench: Respectfully, Idiotkin." Marie's mischief, plucking a flower, not averse to playing a trick.

1. Everything is the same as in the first picture, but in an exaggerated comic style.

2. Her laughter rings out like the sound of a tinkling bell: Idiotkin appears, with the expectation of imminent bliss.

Marie rejoices. [*Sound of a sleigh bell*]

3. Sly Marie seats him on the bench, which falls: No sooner has Idiotkin stood up than he falls again.

When Idiotkin falls, there is the sound of logs being dropped.

---

* Another joke name: *bouledegomme* is French for "cough drop."

4. Jacques Bouledegomme catches Idiotkin at the scene of the crime and, having punished him and no fooling, chases after him along with a mob.

Jacques has appeared on the hillock. When he sees Idiotkin, he does gymnastics with his arms and then slaps him on the cheek. [*Slap is a tambourine.*] Idiotkin runs away. Jacques, Marie, and the mob go after him. A low fence is rolled out on a diagonal, over which everyone jumps, and some fall down.

5. Idiotkin is caught, beaten to a pulp, and, one hopes, has lost the urge to play around with other people's wives.

Jacques, having caught Idiotkin, clutches him with one arm and, lifting him in the air, spanks him with the other. [*A drumbeat*] Total free-for-all.

Picture 3. The Innocent Victim of a Criminal Passion

A Gripping Melodrama from the serial
"Miseries and Mysteries of the Modern Maelstrom"
in Three Full-Length Episodes

CHARACTERS

Aneta, daughter of elderly Professor Spiridon Grigorievich
Spiridon Grigorievich, Aneta's elderly father
Mister Ivanov, Aneta's fiancé
Mister Petrov

EPISODE 1. Happiness Destroyed

Onstage, two stools, left and center.

Demonstrator's Commentary

Stage Directions

1. Aneta and her father, the elderly Spiridon Grigorievich, live in peace and contentment, on the pension

The father, with an enormous beard, in a skullcap and dressing gown, with a long pipe in hand, sits he receives. Aneta is industrious and occupies herself with needle-work, and their modest happiness defies description:

center [*full face*]. Aneta [*profile*] at right is sewing with a needle, by hand. Rattle of a sewing machine.

2. Mr. Ivanov, in love with her, arrives, and Spiridon Grigorievich, having blest their legal wedlock, goes into his room.

Ivanov enters left. He and Aneta, expressing love by gestures, get on their knees [*in profile*] on either side of Spiridon Grigorievich. Standing up and extending his arms over them, he blesses them and exits right.

3. The lovers' happiness defies description.

Aneta and Ivanov rise, cast glances to heaven and hold hands.

4. But here comes Mr. Petrov, and Aneta, pushing away Mr. Ivanov, rushes into Petrov's embrace and leaves with him.

Petrov enters right and, twirling his mustache, stares at Aneta. Aneta goes to him, they exit in an embrace, holding hands.

5. The grief of Mr. Ivanov defies description.

Mr. Ivanov acts out his grief.

EPISODE 2. In the Clutches of Debauchery

Onstage at the right a bench.

Demonstrator's Commentary	*Stage Directions*
1. Aneta's depraved life with Mr. Petrov.	In the middle of the bench sits Aneta, on the left Petrov. Petrov embraces Aneta with one arm, and holds a Champagne glass in the other.
2. In vain does the elderly Spiridon Grigorievich appeal to her to get on the road of virtue; Aneta laughs at the old man. The unhappy father's grief defies description:	Entering right, Spiridon Grigorievich waves his arms as if appealing to Aneta. Then he wrings his hands in grief and exits right.

3. Aneta carries on her criminal life with Mr. Petrov, and soon she appears to have a miraculous baby boy, Vanya, of extramarital origin.

Aneta sits with Petrov, as at the start of the picture, waves a handkerchief. Then she rises, goes backstage right, and returns carrying an undressed rag doll with jointed arms and legs:

4. Then a discomfited Mr. Petrov leaves in displeasure and sends a messenger with a letter. The letter: "Dear Aneta. I am abandoning you and our baby boy Vanya of extramarital origin. Respectfully, Mr. Petrov." The grief of the abandoned Aneta defies description:

Petrov has exited left. The messenger has come from there, bowed, given over the letter, and gone back again. Aneta unseals the letter. Aneta expresses grief.

EPISODE 3. Twenty Years Later

Demonstrator's Commentary

Stage Directions

1. Aneta wanders the world with her unhappy baby boy Vanya of extramarital origin, vainly seeking shelter and food. The wretched woman's desperation defies description:

Entering right, Aneta walks around the stage, as if exhausted.

2. She has met with her father, but Spiridon Grigorievich spurns her indignantly. The daughter's grief defies description:

Spiridon Grigorievich has entered right, indignantly brushed Aneta aside, and exited the same way.

3. She has met the father of her baby boy Vanya of extramarital origin, but Mr. Petrov turns away from her, laughing at her suffering. His cruelty defies description:

Heading left, Aneta bumps into Mr. Petrov coming in, and, falling to her knees, holds the baby out to him. Petrov roars with laughter, twirls his mustache, and exits the way he came. Aneta sobs.

4. But now Mr. Ivanov, having learned of Aneta's wretched plight, has sent a message with a letter: "Dear Aneta, I am very kind-hearted and love you, as I did twenty years ago. Respectfully, Mr. Ivanov."

The messenger enters left and acts as he did on his first appearance.

5. After this the lovers meet again, they are reconciled, and elderly Spiridon Grigorievich blesses her lawful marriage.

Ivanov from the left. Hugs. Spiridon Grigorievich stands between the kneeling couple.

6. The happiness of all three, along with that of the baby boy Vanya of extramarital origin, defies description.

Picture 4. A Medical Operation

On a table, covered by a tablecloth, lies a man with an enormous belly. The operator makes an incision with his knife, laying a hand on the table as if in the belly, and pulls various objects out of it, such as a lobster, a galosh, a bottle, etc. By placing behind the table an artificial leg inside the real leg, one may show the amputation of the leg and similar things, such as cutting off the head.

Picture 5. Newsreel, a Worldwide Survey: "I See All, I Know All"

Flight of the famous aviator parachutist.

Demonstrator's Commentary

Stage Directions

1. The undaunted flyer greets the public before the flight:

A gentleman enters and bows in all directions, waving his visored cap.

2. A hot-air balloon rises 1,524 meters above the ground:

On a string a cardboard cutout of a balloon with a parachute shape and a small human figure hanging beneath it is drawn up.

3. The descent of the insanely reck- When the balloon goes up, the
less aviator by parachute: shape of an opened parachute comes
down with the little human figure.

4. The undaunted flyer greets the Same as 1.
public after his flight:

Picture 6. Peter the Troubadour

*Very interesting historical scenes from the medieval era of world history, depict-
ing its contemporary manners, everyday life, and very interesting ferocious
feudal tortures. This picture, from the wonderful serial "An Artist's Golden
Album," besides its technical qualities and gripping subject matter, makes use of
a gramophone or so-called singing photograph. Very interesting.*

*In view of its historical, ethnographical, and artistic content, this picture
is specially recommended to students and coeds, members of parents' organiza-
tions, and in general all pedagogical personnel of both sexes. The picture has only
just been received from abroad. Very interesting.*

CHARACTERS

Count Conrad, huge mustache, pointed beard,
long broadsword almost as tall as a man

Berta, his wife, slender, tall, a kind of pointed sugar-loaf headdress,
with a long veil trailing behind it

Doctor, in a short robe with wide sleeves

Peter the Troubadour, curly hair, hat with a feather, tights, exaggerated
puffed trunk hose and sleeves. Short cape, guitar, long rapier.

Two soldiers.

*The two soldiers stand at either side of the stage in berets, holding halberds;
their figures are half outlined by the edges of the footlights.* BERTA *stands at the
left. At the right the* COUNT *sits on a stool holding a big goblet. Center stage
is a stake.*

Demonstrator's Commentary	*Stage Directions*
1. Count Conrad and his wife the Countess are in their castle. Oh, how joyless is the life of the gorgeous Berta with her sadistic husband:	The Count drinks wine and threatens with his fist. Berta weeps, wringing her hands.
2. A handsome youth arrives. Peter the Troubadour with his divine song enchants the heart of the Countess.	Peter enters left. [*Bows.*] Taking up his guitar, he sings, mouthing a gramophone: "Dearest, hearken to me, I am beneath thy window with my guitar" [*three times*].
3. Count Conrad goes off to war. But Berta, unable to withstand her ardent love, rushes into the arms of the troubadour.	The Count rises and, brandishing his broadsword, exits right. The soldiers are immobile at their posts. Berta and Peter rush into one another's embrace.
4. On returning from the war, the Count comes upon the lovers and wants to kill the troubadour with his broadsword, but doughty Peter, pulling out his rapier, proves a desperate opponent and, in the heat of battle, having run Conrad through, escapes with Countess Berta to his own land:	The Count enters right. The fight begins. The opponents jab at one another with their weapons. While in silhouette it seems they have run one another through, the Count drops his broadsword, presses Peter's rapier to his side with his elbow, and stands in profile, as if run through. Peter and Berta run off left.
5. The doctor-academician enters and in miraculous fashion cures Count Conrad, almost slain in the duel.	Doctor enters left. After perusing a book, he plants his foot on the Count's stomach and, having pulled out the rapier, respectfully hands it to him.
6. The enraged Count sends his forces in pursuit of the fugitives.	The Count waves the rapier, both soldiers march to center, turn around, and run out left.

7. The fugitives are captured, and wretched Peter is brought to confront the sadistic Conrad. In a rage the Count condemns his enemy to be impaled on the stake.

The soldiers enter left, holding a cutout cardboard effigy of Peter with legs spread to one side and arms held up, holding his guitar over his head. On the Count's order the effigy is impaled on the stake. Berta enters left.

8. But such a bloody torture is not enough for feudal vindictiveness: With his own hands the Count tears off a leg, an arm, and then the head of the unfortunate singer, weakened by his sufferings:

The Count walks over and tears off (a) a leg, (b) an arm, and then the head, tossing them at Berta's feet.

9. Grieving, Berta weeps bitter tears over her lover's lifeless remains.

Kneeling down, Berta sobs, clutching to her bosom Peter's torn-off leg.

Note: The cardboard cutout effigy of Peter is life-size in the pose of a jumping-jack jerked by a rod. On the effigy's back is a little pouch by which the effigy is mounted on the stake. The arm without the guitar is turned toward the COUNT, *the leg and head have been cut through beforehand so that when the time comes they may be easily detached. The whole effigy is full face.*

Picture 7. Wonderful Pictorial Tableaux of Interesting Scientific Expeditions and the Beauties of Nature

Our firm's cameraman's strolls across the seas in the high-speed yacht Molly Mamsha, *which is owned by an American millionaire. [The music plays "Down Mother Volga."]**

Demonstrator's Commentary

1. Here is the high-speed yacht *Molly Mamsha* sailing along the blue ocean waves, as our immortal poet puts it.

Stage Directions

At the bottom of the screen, running its full length, is a strip of cardboard, its edge in the form of waves. The strip is moved back and forth.

---

* "Vniz po matushke po Volge" was a Russian folk song set by Aleksandr Varlamov and a fixture in the concerts of the bass Fyodor Chaliapin.

2. In contemplation of the magnif-icent picture, the bold seafarers do not notice that a wonderful night has fallen over the sea: | The same as before, but the light is shone through a blue glass.

3. Day has come, and our voyagers have reached the Red Sea. | Red glass.

4. From there they head for the shores of the Black Sea. | Total blackout.

5. The further fate of the yacht *Molly Mamsha* and its owner, the American millionaire, as well as our firm's cameraman is unknown:

Picture 8. A Ramble through Egypt—the Land of Pyramids and Ancient Pharaoh Sphinxes

Demonstrator's Commentary	*Stage Directions*
1. Here amid the desert appear the flowering oasis and the royal pyramids of ancient Egyptians.	Two cardboard cutout triangles, a palm tree between them. Size about twenty-eight inches. The cardboard is held close to the screen.
2. The pyramids grow, because the traveler, sitting on a camel crossing the desert, rides closer and closer to the pyramids:	The cardboard is moved away from the screen toward the light, so that the light on the screen increases.
3. Admiring the pyramids in their natural dimensions, the traveler climbs to their top:	The cardboard is gradually moved downward, so that all that remains in silhouette are tops of the pyramids and the palm tree.
4. View of the desert from the pyramids.	Empty screen.

End

MAN'S FATE
(*Sud'ba muzhchiny*)

A psychological drama of the future in one act

by Nikolay Urvantsov

(1915 and 1920)

To the Performers

I entreat the kind performers to act this play not as a farce, but as an ordinary psychological study.

The more sincerely and intensely the inner experiences of the characters are presented, the easier it will be for my set task to be accomplished. As to the nature of the performance, of course, the women's movements and voices should be masculine and firm, and the men's soft and feminine, but this must not go beyond certain limits and hence not turn into an imitation of women by the men and vice versa. It is all a matter of intonation. Because this caricature is written in the form of a stage play, I would suggest to the performers that they clearly emphasize the line of business of the role played: Varvara Petrovna by her position in the play ought to be a dramatic *raisonneur*; Paul an ingénue, at first flirtatious, then dramatic; Hélène a romantic lead, a ladies' man; Semyon Ivanovich a middle-aged heroine; Kolya a parlor maid with a touch of everyday realism.

And, of course, the women in the play should be acted by women, and the men by men.

The costumes should be extremely illustrative. For the men I should suggest trousers made out of ladies' material with layers of frills and slit below to reveal the leg in a light-blue stocking, dainty shoes with high heels. The waistcoat adorned with ribbons. Short little jackets with a tapered waist and short sleeves. Lace trim, lace collar. Ornaments. Hair style halfway between masculine and feminine. For instance, Kolya, somewhat long hair with waved bangs; Semyon Ivanovovich, definitely a bald spot, with his hair hanging in bandeaux, like Cléo de Mérode.* Mustaches, beards, sideburns.

The ladies in plain skirts with a slit in front. Beneath them ordinary trousers. Plain dark waistcoats. Stiff collars.

Frock coats and tailcoats a bit longer and more tight-waisted than ordinary. Plain and simple haircuts, perhaps crew cuts.

The furniture is the usual sort, but the pictures are of amorous subjects depicting a half-naked man and a lady with a bouquet, peeping from behind a drapery. A lover with a bunch of grapes or a dove in his hand. A lady with a bottle of wine, etc.

CHARACTERS

Varvara Petrovna Gortseva, a construction engineer of underground railways. Age forty.

Paul, her husband. A young man, age twenty. Refined and delicate, dressed tastefully and flirtatiously.

Elena Petrovna Raiskaya (known as Hélène), a young defense attorney.

Semyon Ivanovich, her husband, a middle-aged man of fifty, with traces of former good looks on his faded face.

Kolya, parlor-lad of the Gortsevs

Nurse-Lad to the Gortsevs' children (in the 1920 version, *the Tutor*)

Feofilakt Feomentovich Propagandov, a coed and bluestocking

Scene 1

PAUL's *boudoir. An elegant writing desk. A nook with soft furnishings. A cheval glass, a cottage piano, flowers, knickknacks. The cozy little nest of a flirtatious man. Evening. A standard lamp and a hanging colored lamp are lit.* PAUL, *indolently sprawled on a daybed, is reading a novel. Enter from her study* VARVARA PETROVNA *with a briefcase, looking over papers. Walking over to the desk, she puts the papers in the briefcase.*

---

* The French dancer Cléo de Mérode (1875–1966) parted her hair in the middle, and it hung down either side of her face in symmetrical bandeaux.

PAUL: You're going out again?

VARVARA PETROVNA: Yes, Paul dear, I'm going out . . .

PAUL: Where to?

VARVARA PETROVNA: You've know I've got a meeting today.

PAUL: Those nasty meetings again . . . Couldn't you stay at home with your husband at least one night?

VARVARA PETROVNA: I can't, Paul, it's a very important meeting.

PAUL: An important meeting. An important meeting . . . Always leaving a young husband alone—that's not important. The fact that your husband is bored every night all on his own—for you that's not important. [*Weeps.*]

VARVARA PETROVNA: Tears again . . . Aren't you ashamed, Paul. Don't be a baby, stop pouting, my little boy.

PAUL [*capriciously*]: Leave me . . .

VARVARA PETROVNA: Don't be angry, you little ninny, I'll try to be back soon.

PAUL: Please don't hurry on my account.

VARVARA PETROVNA: All right, my little boy. If my leaving distresses you so much, I'll stay home.

PAUL [*hurriedly*]: Oh no, no. You've got business—go.

VARVARA PETROVNA: But weren't you just asking me to stay?

PAUL: No, no. Go, my dear. I'm ashamed of my whims. Forgive your silly little hubby.

VARVARA PETROVNA: A child, a mere child. How can one not love you?! All right, I'm going, but you be a clever boy and wait up for me. Because I'm bringing you a surprise.

PAUL: A surprise? What kind of surprise?

VARVARA PETROVNA: Remember, you liked that fashionable waistcoat Semyon Ivanovich had? Well, my little boy is going to have that very waistcoat . . . And in addition, today I'll bring up your favorite candy . . . I love you!

PAUL [*kissing* VARVARA PETROVNA]: Varvara Petrovna, you're so sweet, the way you spoil me!

VARVARA PETROVNA: Don't be silly, my little boy. What are such trifles compared with the happiness you bring me with your love? Well, give me a kiss . . . Kolya, lock the door behind me and try to keep the mistress from being bored while I'm away. You hear me? Goodbye again. [*Exits.*]

Scene 2

PAUL [*coming to life once* VARVARA PETROVNA *is gone, glances at the door*]: Kolya, has the mistress gone out?

KOLYA: Yes, sir.

PAUL: Fine. Now I'm going to give you a letter. Take it quick as you can to Elena Pavlovna and be sure to do it so that Semyon Ivanovich doesn't see it. Understand? [*Sits down to write the letter.*]

KOLYA: Don't worry, master. Semyon Ivanovich never leaves the nursery, and Elena Pavlovna always receives the letters herself.

PAUL: Is that so? Well, that's fine. [*Reads over what he has written.*] "Hélène, my dream boat. My wife, as always, has gone to a meeting. Come. I'm waiting. I'm waiting for you impatiently. I send you all my hugs and kisses. Your crazed Paul." Yes, crazed . . . Make sure she gets it, Kolya, and come back here quickly.

KOLYA: Wait for an answer?

PAUL: No, no answer needed.

[KOLYA *exits.*]

Scene 3

PAUL: Oh, Hélène, Hélène. My heart is full of you. One word from you and I will give myself to you entirely. My honor, my life, my name—I will sacrifice it all to you, my goddess, my lord and mistress. [*Doorbell.*] The doorbell? Who can that be? Kolya's gone, I'll open it. [*Exits into the hallway. Offstage voices, his and* SEMYON IVANOVICH's.]

Scene 4

PAUL: Goodness me, do my eyes deceive me?! Semyon Ivanovich. What a pleasant surprise. [*Exchange of kisses.*] So glad to see you, darling. Have a seat, have a seat here, it's comfier over here.

SEMYON IVANOVICH: Thank you. Dear Paul . . . Forgive me for calling you that, but my age and my sympathy give me the right to this friendly familiarity.

PAUL: Please, please, darling. Is that a new outfit? Very nice. Very tasteful.

SEMYON IVANOVICH: Is it? Vanechka does all my sewing. You know, my regular modiste.

PAUL: Wonderful. And the trousers—with little flowers. Very sweet.

SEMYON IVANOVICH: The latest style.

PAUL: I absolutely must order myself one like it. Polka dots will soon be old hat. Little flowers are much cuter. And this fabric suits you so well.

SEMYON IVANOVICH: Ah, darling, does it matter? What do I care? [*Powders his nose.*]

PAUL: Darling, what's wrong? You're out of sorts? Your eyes have been crying?

SEMYON IVANOVICH: Yes, Paul dear, my grief is unbearable. I can't settle down, while you, you are so young, so life-loving, so happy, I felt like resting my heart in your presence. But alas! The sight of your untroubled happiness only increases my suffering and torment. [*Weeps.*]

PAUL: Semyon Ivanovich, what's wrong? You're crying? Calm down.

SEMYON IVANOVICH: Ah, Paul, you will never understand my sorrow. You are young, you are loved. Your life is paradise, and you cannot understand my torment.

PAUL: You? Are you really unhappy?

SEMYON IVANOVICH: If you are not afraid, my child, that my tale of woe will overshadow your cloudless happiness, I shall tell you the story of my wretched life. After the death of my first wife, a respectable businesswoman who worshipped me, I was free, with a large fortune and a heart no longer young, but still ignorant of the happiness of love. A crowd of suitoresses flocked around me, to win my hand. Some were attracted by my wealth, others were sincerely attracted by my beauty, vestiges of which you can still discern on my face even now. [*Powders his nose.*] But all their courtship remained pointless. My heart slumbered serenely, unacquainted with the flame of passion. But alas. It was silent until my path was crossed by Hélène. Ah, Paul, how much mad happiness, but how much mad torment, tears, and despair that encounter brought me. Hélène at that time had only just passed the bar exam and taken up the legal profession. A young assistant defense attorney, she immediately attracted attention and was clearly distinguished among her colleagues. All they talked about in society was her brilliant pleading and talented, winning speeches. But, you probably know yourself how witty, eloquent, and enchanting my Hélène is.

PAUL: Oh, yes, yes . . . I do know . . .

SEMYON IVANOVICH: The first time I met her was at a ball. She invited me to a quadrille, and that evening decided my fate. I fell in love, but was afraid to admit to myself the outburst of feeling. Hélène began to woo me. Meetings, dates, her ardent self-confidence won me over. Mad passion overwhelmed me. And once when Hélène in my boudoir, kneeling at my feet, asked for my hand, I forgot everything, forgot the difference in our ages and social position, and fell into her embrace . . .

PAUL [*enviously*]: Hélène loved you?

SEMYON IVANOVICH: Oh, our love overflowed with unclouded happiness. I boldly broke with all the prejudices of our circle and, openly associating with Hélène, cast a daring challenge to society. Gossip, tattle began, many families stopped receiving me. But I laughed at it and swam in bliss, until we had our first child. Then a new problem arose before me. I could scorn the opinion of the world and be reconciled with my unsanctioned situation, but how was that the fault of the unhappy infant? Why should he, because of his father's frailty, have to bear the covert glances, the remarks and, perhaps, hear the insulting label "illegitimate." [*Weeps.*]

PAUL: Calm yourself, Semyon Ivanovich, have a sip of water.

SEMYON IVANOVICH: Never mind, it'll pass. So, I decided to have it out with Hélène and demanded that she seal our bond with lawful matrimony and give our baby a name. Hélène agreed, but the thought of losing her freedom obviously terrifies her. Three years have gone by. Now we have four children, but the question of marriage for various plausible reasons she keeps putting off and putting off.

PAUL: Wait a bit, Semyon Ivanovich, since Elena Pavlovna promised, she'll probably keep her word.

SEMYON IVANOVICH: Oh no, Paul, don't try to comfort me. I have noticed with horror that Hélène has grown cold to me. She is no longer the same. My caresses chill her. In vain I devote myself to her with the same love and passion as before, she pays more and more attention to young, fresher beauties who, like a swarm of bees, buzz round her with their brilliance and gaiety. How can I compete with them, I, the fading husband of a certain age?

PAUL: What are you saying, Semyon Ivanovich? You are still a very interesting man. If I were a woman, I would be ready to woo you. You have such a beautiful beard.

SEMYON IVANOVICH: Ah, Paul, when a man begins to grow old and become uninteresting, people reassure him with "You have a beautiful beard." Dismal reassurance! Oh, the nights of jealous tears, anxiety, and suspicions. Who knows them the way I have learned to know them? Hélène began to feel oppressed by family life. Irritable and sullen at home, she came to life whenever she went into society, where easy victories among the lush flowerbed of men awaited her. Our domestic life became a living hell. Hélène left no one I knew in peace, none of my acquaintances, and my best friends became my enemies, as they fell into his captivating net. Young chamber-lads in my house, even they benefited more from Hélène's full attention and affection than I did, a neglected and hated husband. I forgave her everything, and shut myself up in my suffering and devoted my life to my dear little ones. The rare evenings when Hélène stayed at home were for me radiant holidays . . . But alas, this was the last flicker of happiness . . . Now I am losing my last hope.

PAUL: What has happened, Semyon Ivanovich dear?

SEMYON IVANOVICH: Dear Paul, Hélène has a new attachment . . .

PAUL [*embarrassed*]: A new attachment?

SEMYON IVANOVICH: And this time, it would appear, a serious and irresistible one.

PAUL [*controlling himself*]: Elena Pavlovna is in love? With whom?

SEMYON IVANOVICH: Alas. I don't know. Jealous suspicions torment me. I try to discover the man responsible for my suffering, but in vain. I see only that Hélène is moving away from me every day, every hour.

PAUL: Semyon Ivanovich, darling, calm down. I feel sorry for you.

SEMYON IVANOVICH: Dear Paul, my sweet boy. You treat me with such sympathy, but I . . . I confess I don't trust even you. I was ready to suspect even you. My jealousy was directed at you. I lost my reason because of my insane suspicions. [*Sobs.*]

PAUL: Calm down, Semyon Ivanovich, have a sip of water.

SEMYON IVANOVICH: Thank you, Paul dear. You're so young, with such a trustful, open gaze, you are incapable of injecting, snakelike, a new poison into the lacerated heart of a ridiculed, abandoned husband. [*Embraces* PAUL.]

PAUL: Calm down, Semyon Ivanovich, please don't cry.

SEMYON IVANOVICH [*suddenly alarmed*]: Paul, what's this! What is this, Paul?

PAUL: What's wrong, Semyon Ivanovich?

SEMYON IVANOVICH: What is that perfume? For heaven's sake. Where did you get that perfume?

PAUL: Semyon Ivanovich, dovie, it's my perfume, I always wear it . . .

SEMYON IVANOVICH: When Hélène returns home at night, she always smells of that perfume.

PAUL: What's surprising about that? The perfume "Scent of a Male" is the favorite fragrance this season . . . It's more than likely that Elena Pavlovna uses it.

SEMYON IVANOVICH: Paul dear, how naive you are?! Not Hélène, but the one she's betraying me with . . . It's his perfume. Hélène carries it away with her after their meeting and embraces. Forgive me, I seem to be upsetting you.

PAUL: Oh no, don't be silly. As you know, Varvara Petrovna and I are anticipating the imminent arrival of a blessed event, and actually my nerves are frayed. I was just expecting the doctoress.

SEMYON IVANOVICH: Oh, then I won't get in your way. I've stayed far too long. Forgive me if my tears upset you. But you can see for yourself—a man's tender heart always looks for sympathy and affection, and only tears can relieve his sufferings . . .

PAUL: Oh no, Semyon Ivanovich, I'm always glad to see you. Do drop by, pretty please.

SEMYON IVANOVICH: Thank you, thank you. Ah, I left my handbag here. I have to powder my nose . . . Can you tell from my eyes I've been crying?

PAUL: Oh no, not at all . . .

SEMYON IVANOVICH: I need to freshen up my perfume.

PAUL: Perhaps you'd like some of mine?

SEMYON IVANOVICH: No, no . . . I use only my own perfume. Anyone with a faithful heart never changes perfume. Remember that, Paul. From the day I met Hélène I have used only "The Scent of Spain." This scent reminds me of the dawn of my happiness . . . But I'm getting carried away again. Goodbye, Paul. Thank you for the sympathy, thank you.

PAUL: Kolya, are you back?

KOLYA: Yes, mistress, what are your orders?

PAUL: Lock the door. Goodbye, Semyon Ivanovich, do drop by.

Scene 5

PAUL: An unhappy man. I almost feel sorry for him. But is it my fault that Hélène has grown cold to him and loves me. "Anyone who can't protect his happiness deserves to lose it." That's what Hélène said in one of her brilliant speeches for the defense, and these words have become my motto. I'm young, beautiful, and don't want to fade away in the joyless embraces of a spouse . . . I love and will take from love all its happiness, because love, love alone means life for a frail man. [*Sits at the piano, plays a waltz. Doorbell.* KOLYA *enters.*]

Scene 6

KOLYA: There's someone at the door, sir. Shall I let them in?

PAUL: If it's Elena Pavlovna, do so. I'm stepping out for a moment. Tell anyone else I'm not at home.

KOLYA: Yes, sir. [*Exits to the vestibule.*]

PAUL: She is here. I'll go and fix my hair in my dressing room.

Scene 7

KOLYA [*showing in* HÉLÈNE]: If you please, madam. The master will be here soon; the gentleman is in his boudoir.

HÉLÈNE: And where is the mistress? At a meeting?

KOLYA: Yes, ma'am, our mistress is always out on business, but the master is alone, bored. The gent is a pitiful sight.

HÉLÈNE [*walking over to* KOLYA]: How about you, Kolya, are you bored? Eh?

KOLYA [*embarrassed*]: Why should I be bored? I've always got work to do, no time for boredom.

HÉLÈNE: We know all about your men's work. The cooks and the wet nurses probably give you no peace, you little rascal . . . Your eyes blaze so . . . . A cute little black mustache, my beauty.

KOLYA: What're you on about, madam? What's so beautiful about me?! You're only teasing me. There's our master, actually, now he's worth looking at.

HÉLÈNE: Never mind the master. Kolya, you don't know your own worth. If you were dressed up and your hair done the right way, with a bit of polish, you could give any master a run for his money.

KOLYA: Ah, what are you saying, madam?

HÉLÈNE: Believe me, believe me, I'm right. Then you'd be living in the lap of luxury, riches. Would you like me to take an interest in you? [*Tries to embrace* KOLYA. KOLYA *pulls away, indignantly.*]

KOLYA: Stop it, madam. Stop your pinching . . . Honest to goodness, I'll tell the master . . . Aren't you ashamed? Pestering me like I was "the likes of them," a man of the streets. For you to toy with for a while and then throw away, so I'd spend my life with no reputation and drowned in tears. It's shameful, madam. God be with your grace, and so rich. I'm respectable—I can get on without your grace. I'm engaged. And I gave her my word and I keep myself to myself.

HÉLÈNE: A fiancée? So that's how it is. Who's this fiancée of yours?

KOLYA: A young janitress. She used to work next door . . . A girl who doesn't drink, works hard, thinks deep thoughts.

HÉLÈNE: That's fine. When is the wedding to be?

KOLYA: Any minute. My Tanya is off doing military service, but when she gets back, we'll have the wedding.

HÉLÈNE: Congratulations, congratulations. That means, Kolya, I'll have to give you a present . . . Little babies and little sucklings . . . in the future. There will be kids, won't there? Why are you blushing, you little rascal?

KOLYA: The things you say, madam. They get me all embarrassed.

HÉLÈNE: No need to be embarrassed—they're the facts of life. Come here, give me a kiss and you'll get . . . Only the kiss first . . . Well, hop to it.

KOLYA: How can you, madam? When folks are around, you gotta keep from acting indecent . . .

HÉLÈNE: What rot, who's around? [*Embraces* KOLYA.]

KOLYA [*with false modesty*]: Let go, honestly. Isn't it a sin . . .

HÉLÈNE: You little coward, I'll show you something to be scared of. [*Kisses* KOLYA.] Well, here's a dowry for you.

KOLYA: No need, madam . . . Thank you kindly.

HÉLÈNE: However, I think the master is coming. Get out. March.

KOLYA: Enjoy your visit. A humble *merci* to you, madam. [*Exits.*]

Scene 8

PAUL [*entering*]: Hélène, my love. Here you are at last.

HÉLÈNE: Paul, my lucky star, my dickey bird, my dear, dear little boy . . .

PAUL: Ah, don't call me your little boy, for pity's sake.

HÉLÈNE: Why not, Paul?

PAUL: That's what my wife calls me. Don't remind me of her . . . Don't remind me about my criminal betrayal.

HÉLÈNE: What a child you are, Paul. Happiness is so rare and so beautiful: it is criminal to pass it by. And just as we love one another in the bright light of day, just as we gaze upon the beautiful flowers, which entrance us with their sweet, thrilling fragrance, so we should revel in resplendent happiness and pluck the infinitely beautiful moments of pleasure . . .

PAUL: Oh, the way you talk, Hélène. You intoxicate me with your words.

HÉLÈNE: You're committing a crime against your spouse? Am I not betraying *my* husband, my children? And I do not speak of them. I forget everything when I am with you, Paul.

PAUL: No, no, Hélène. By all that's holy, for the sake of our love, do not speak to me about your husband.

HÉLÈNE: What's come over you? You're trembling all over. What has happened?

PAUL: Your husband, the unhappy Semyon Ivanovich, has just been here.

HÉLÈNE: Here? My husband?

PAUL: If you had arrived only a few minutes earlier, you would have bumped into him here.

HÉLÈNE: What did he want? What new quirks of a capricious and quarrelsome man?

PAUL: He is jealous of you. He suspects . . .

HÉLÈNE: I'll break him of that stupid jealousy.

PAUL: Don't be so cruel, Hélène. He is unhappy. He loves you very much. How he wept and grieved at your treachery. I am afraid of you, Hélène. You seduced me the same way and you will deceive me the same way you are now deceiving your own husband.

HÉLÈNE: I? Deceive you, Paul? When I first met Semyon Ivanovich, he was already a man of advanced years, while I was a high-spirited, madcap girl, who had only just set foot on the road of life. As an experienced coquette, he knew how to entice me into the sweet toils of his voluptuousness, but he could not, could not take possession of my heart. And when the first year of passion has passed, I grew cold to him, I realized my mistake and in despair flung myself into the maelstrom of fleeting attractions. But when I saw you, my young, my pure Paul, my soul was resurrected for the world and for virtue. Your youth, your purity won my heart. I was in agony that you belonged to another, in agony until I could see you, my own Paul, love me, give yourself to me, belong to me. Now, when happiness has opened up before me, you want to bestow your beauty and youth on the cold embraces of your prosaic spouse, while I, in the name of duty, return to the cheerless caresses of a husband. Paul! We are young! We are in love! Paul, I worship you, and you want on account of prejudices to destroy our life, our love, our happiness . . .

PAUL: Destroy our love? Lose you? No, no, Hélène. I cannot live without you. Take me, do with me what you will. Disgrace, dishonor—I will accept it all for your sake. [*He collapses into* HÉLÈNE's *arms.*]

Scene 9

VARVARA PETROVNA *enters through the door center with a box of candy. On seeing her husband in* HÉLÈNE's *arms, she stops and involuntarily drops the box on the floor. At this sound,* PAUL *tears himself out of* HÉLÈNE's *embrace.*

PAUL: Varvara Petrovna . . . you're home?

VARVARA PETROVNA: Yes, I . . . I'm home . . . [*Staggering and leaning her back against the door, she sobs gutturally, hiding her face in her hands.*]

PAUL: What's the matter? Calm down, Varvara Petrovna.

VARVARA PETROVNA: Never mind . . . never mind . . . a moment's weakness . . . I came back early . . . I wanted to hurry and cheer you up and brought you your favorite candy . . . [*Tramples it underfoot.*] Damn it!

HÉLÈNE: I see that I am in the way here. I am very sorry for what just happened, Varvara Petrovna, you may demand satisfaction, I am always at your service.

VARVARA PETROVNA: No, I shall get satisfaction for my offended honor in a different way. [*Pulls out a pistol.*]

PAUL [*with a cry of horror*]: Varvara Petrovna, stop . . . For the love of God, stop . . .

VARVARA PETROVNA: Don't be afraid, my despicable one. I will not soil my hands by killing a *man*. *Your* life is in no danger. But you will leave my house at once, the house you have disgraced with your vile betrayal. Elena Pavlovna will remain. From you, a woman, I demand an answer: What do you intend to do? How will you act now?

HÉLÈNE: I have already said that I am at your service and at any hour ready to give you satisfaction.

VARVARA PETROVNA: Oh no! You are unworthy of the honor of fighting a duel with me. Besides, what would be the point? If you shoot me or run me through with your sword, will that settle the matter? No. Before I kill you like a dog, if you don't immediately answer me what you intend to do for the man whom you seduced and who now, on your account, is bereft of house and home.

HÉLÈNE: You are referring to your husband?

VARVARA PETROVNA: I no longer have a husband . . . I speak of your lover. He has no place here, beside my domestic hearth. The concern for the future fate of the man you seduced is a matter for your conscience and your honor.

HÉLÈNE: Forgive me, Varvara Petrovna, but you seem to forget that I have a family of my own.

VARVARA PETROVNA: A family of your own? Why didn't you think about your family when you seduced this wretched creature? And you speak of it now when the hour of reckoning has come.

HÉLÈNE: I was infatuated. Paul's beauty blinded me. I forgot everything in the world. But I cannot for the sake of an infatuation betray my duty and leave to the mercy of fate the children and husband who worship me and to whom, alas, I am so obliged.

VARVARA PETROVNA: You speak of duty, you disreputable seducer. I am sure that your husband, that cultured, saintly man, will spurn you in indignation. Therefore, I demand an answer: How will you provide for the fate of your victim?

PAUL: Wait, wait . . . Hélène, you speak of your duty. But where are your dreams of our happiness? Where are the insensate words of love, with which you seduced me? This means that it is all a deception, a joke. Oh God, God . . . To joke so mercilessly, so pitilessly with a man's heart.

Scene 10

[SEMYON IVANOVICH *enters.*]

SEMYON IVANOVICH: What has happened? For heaven's sake, what is this? Your chamber-lad Kolya ran to me in tears and urged me to come here. What's the matter?

VARVARA PETROVNA: The matter is, most esteemed Semyon Ivanovich, that your wife seduced my husband, taking advantage of his youth and frivolous nature. My life is in pieces. There is no place in my family for a wanton, deceitful man. He is unworthy to be the father of my children and must leave my house. If your wife is a decent woman, she has no right to abandon a well-provided-for man and must peacefully return to the bosom of her own family. A choice lies before her: you or Paul. Talk it over. I shall not stand in your way and I shall return when you have evaluated your situation and have come to a final decision. [*She exits into her study.*]

Scene 11

SEMYON IVANOVICH: There it is, Hélène. You have to make a choice: me or Paul. A husband who has given you his love, his loyalty, his fortune, or that beautiful, frivolous boy, who attracted you with his carefree youth. The whirlwind of infatuation or duty, the sacred duty to your husband, father of your children. And still you waver? You have doubts about where you belong?

HÉLÈNE: Senya, forgive me. I am grievously at fault to you, but there are moments when the voice of passion deafens the demands of reason and imposes a new duty on a woman.

SEMYON IVANOVICH: Hélène, what are you saying?! For an infatuation over a boy you are ready to abandon me. Pity, pity . . . On my knees I implore you, come back, do not desert me. You are my happiness, you are my last joy. I know, loving a middle-aged man is ridiculous, but why is fate so unequal, why can a middle-aged woman boldly and freely take to husband a young man, while the ardent and insane love of a man is ridiculous and contemptible if he bestows it on a woman younger than himself . . . You are silent, Hélène . . . You do not love me . . . You laugh at my suffering. Your heart is closed to my tears . . . What am I to do, what am I to do? . . . Paul, I turn my prayers to you. You have destroyed my heart with your flirtation, but I forgive you everything, only do not destroy the happiness of my children. Do not take away my family's support, its breadwinner. Do not take from an unhappy man in his declining years his last joy. Give me back, give me back my Hélène!

PAUL: Get up, Semyon Ivanovich, don't degrade yourself before me. I ought to be on my knees asking your forgiveness. I am guilty toward you and your little ones. Be calm, I will not claim any rights to Elena Aleksandrovna. Let her return with a clear conscience to her domestic hearth. I do not want to be the reason for your little ones' grief. Elena Aleksandrovna, all is over between us, you are free.

SEMYON IVANOVICH: Hélène. Again you are mine. Noble Paul, how can I thank you? If you are ever in difficulties, if you meet with need, when my friendship, my fortune . . .

PAUL: That's enough. Be still. I tender you my love as a sacrifice, and we cannot be friends. The offer of money merely insults me.

SEMYON IVANOVICH: I didn't mean to . . . Believe me. What I . . .

PAUL: Be still. Be still . . . I need nothing from you, only leave this place . . . Go away with her . . . quickly, quickly.

[SEMYON IVANOVICH *and* HÉLÈNE *exit.*]

Scene 12

PAUL [*standing in place, turning in circles. Unable to contain himself, running to the door*]: Hélène, Hélène . . . Come back . . . She doesn't hear . . . She's gone . . . The villainess . . . God. What ruination, what despair reigns in my house . . . [*Falls onto the settee and sobs.*]

VARVARA PETROVNA [*entering from the study*]: Ah, you're alone? And where are Semyon Ivanovich and Hélène? Gone? Splendid. That means, the problem is solved. The noble heroine has returned to the bosom of her family hearth. Virtue triumphs, vice is punished. A beautiful ending to a poetical romance.

PAUL: Varvara Petrovna, why this ridicule and scoffing? Can't you see how much pain I'm in now?

VARVARA PETROVNA [*with deep sorrow*]: And I'm not? Wasn't it hard for me to behold your treachery? Didn't I love you? Didn't I give you everything a wife who passionately loves her husband can give him? And this is your thanks . . . I shall be interested to see what you do now: run after your mistress or crawl to the threshold of my home which you have disgraced?

PAUL: Oh no, no . . . Don't worry. I know I am in the wrong and I shall not ask for mercy. I shall go and never more return.

VARVARA PETROVNA: You're going? Where to? What will you do, so pampered, unfit for a man's life?

PAUL: I can make myself a small, modest living teaching French or music . . . I acted in amateur theatricals, perhaps happiness will smile on me on the stage.

VARVARA PETROVNA: The stage? In that swamp, that quagmire where hundreds of men perish, transformed from priests of high art into low, fallen creatures . . . Where will you get the means for the brilliant outfits and the flamboyant, free life of an actor? Do you know how to fight off the hundreds of temptations that will ensnare you like a glistening spiderweb? Will you find the strength to preserve unsullied my name, which you, unfortunately, now bear?

PAUL: Oh, don't worry, your name will remain unspotted. I will take my bachelor name or a stage name that befits my bitter fate, and if ever you hear of the actor Woebegone or Hartbroke,* you will know that it is I—the once happy and carefree Paul . . .

VARVARA PETROVNA: But you may perish, Paul . . .

PAUL: So what of it? One fallen man more or less, it doesn't matter . . .

VARVARA PETROVNA: Stay, Paul. Perhaps I can find the strength to forget it all and forgive you . . .

PAUL: Oh no. I don't want your forgiveness. I shall go. But before that I want to tell you all that I have been pondering and feeling while you and Hélène, you proud women, mistresses of life, were deciding my fate here. You set some conditions and talked about me, while I—a docile man—silently awaited your verdict. Please understand, once and for all, that a man is a human being, the same as you women. We too have our own will, our own desires and feelings. Who gave women the right to be mistresses of the fates of men? Who gave you the right to belittle me, to make me the plaything of your egoism and vanity? Enough! I have done you wrong, Varvara Petrovna, but I do not crave forgiveness, because for all the mistakes we make it is your fault, you women's and no one but yours . . .

VARVARA PETROVNA: How is that? I am hearing such words for the first time . . .

PAUL: Of course, you find it strange that I—a man—dare to raise my voice and tell you women the bitter truth to your face. You women from the day of your birth are preserved by nature from falling and

---

* In Russian, Gorev and Neshchastlivtsev. Gorev ("Woeful") was in fact the name of two actors, father and son, on the Moscow stage; Neshchastlivtsev ("Unhappy") is the name of a tragedian in Ostrovsky's comedy *The Forest*.

temptation. Before you fall, you have to cross a secret line. On you lies the responsibility for future posterity, while we men are defenseless from all the attractions and snares which you women lay in our paths. Meanwhile, for each of our mistakes, for each of our wrong moves you throw stones at us and stick us with the disgraceful label of fallen man. But what do you do, stern judges, to keep us on the path of virtue? Have you ever thought how you have educated us men? From childhood you train us to care for our looks, polish our manners, train us for luxury and adornment; do you ever say a word about high ideals, obligations to society and social welfare? Tinkling on the piano, prattling in French, scraps of superficial learning stand in for our education and conceal our spiritual emptiness and impoverishment . . . You fashion us into playthings for your feminine whims, slaves in your harems, submissive husbands in your family—more like a dark prison than a joyous union of love and happiness . . . And what a pitiful role we play, we men, in such a family . . . You women are busy with your activities in society, while on us lies the sacred obligation to educate our children; you have arrogated to yourselves the role of lawgivers in creativity and art, while we men are deprived of the sacred right to work. We cheerlessly choke on the fumes of the domestic cookstove, we waste our manliness on pointless dilettantism, on trivia such as china painting or embroidering sofa cushions for your study. Turkish odalisques once knew how to recover their freedom and rights, but we men drag out our fate. They throw us, innocent youths, ignorant of life, not even understanding the obligations of a spouse, into the arms of women who have long enjoyed the pleasures of love and dissipated their strength and purity in the embraces of wanton men . . . And you call such a union holy matrimony . . . When in the desecrated, cheerless heart of a man the thirst for life, for love erupts, the thirst for real living happiness, and when he, responding to this sacred thirst, attempts to throw off the shackles of female power—that's when you get upset, when you load him with disgrace and scorn for some little error, for every false step. Like sportsmen in pursuit of their quarry, you women hunt down men, you snare us in your nets, you seduce us with your sweet speeches and promises, and when a man falls into the trap, you are the first to smear us with your scorn. Where is the justice in that? You said that I disgrace your home. But this is not the home of a true marriage, but a doll's house, in which your Nora once was smothered. I too am Nora. Now my eyes are open, and, like Nora, I shall leave your doll's house for a new free life.*

VARVARA PETROVNA: Stop, Paul. Think it over. Nora is no model for you. What a woman can accomplish, the weak powers of a man cannot manage. I cannot, cannot let you go . . . Remember our children, Paul. Do not deny them the tender affection of a father.

PAUL: Children, my children.

[*The* NURSE-LAD *enters, in a white apron, a frilled cap with white ribbons.*]

NURSE-LAD: Master, the children are awake and calling for their papa to come and kiss them.

[*Offstage children's voices are heard: "Papa, Papa."*]

PAUL: My children, my poor little ones. God, what am I to do? [*The* NURSE-LAD *exits.*] No, no, I do not have the right to go to my innocent, pure babes. When I have learned life, when I have turned from a doll into a human being, only then will I have the right to educate my children.

VARVARA PETROVNA: You're leaving?

PAUL: Yes. Here is your ring. Give me back mine. We both ought to be entirely free. I left the household keys on the sideboard. It's all over now.

VARVARA PETROVNA: Where will you go? It's night.

PAUL: I shall find shelter with my friends. I cannot spend the night under a roof with a woman who is a stranger to me.

VARVARA PETROVNA: Will you never remember me, Paul? Will I always remain a stranger to you?

PAUL: Ah, Varvara Petrovna, for that the miracles of miracles will have to transpire.

---

* The reference is to the last act of Ibsen's *Doll's House*, frequently performed in Russia. Vera Kommissarzhevskaya had made the role one of her triumphs.

VARVARA PETROVNA: What is that?

PAUL: For that you and I must change so that our cohabitation may become a marriage. [*Exits.* VARVARA PETROVNA *sobs, her head on the table.*]

Postrevolutionary Variant*

PAUL's *boudoir. An elegant writing desk. Upstage, a door to* GORTSEVA's *study; down right, a door to the nursery. Center the entrance door. A nook with soft furnishings. In the corner an upright piano, flowers, knickknacks. The cozy little nest of a flirtatious young man. Evening. A standard lamp and a colored hanging lantern are lit.* PAUL *is sprawled indolently on a daybed.* FEOFILANT, *waving around cigarette smoke, is walking around the room.*

FEOFILANT: No, Paul, it can't go on like this.

PAUL: I don't understand, Feofilant, what you want of me?

FEOFILANT: Living the way you live cannot go on. I don't recognize you. How can two years of marriage have changed you so much? Where is your fervor, where is your inquiring mind, your inquisitive spirit? You left the university, you've stopped reading, stopped taking an interest in anything outside the narrow limits of your personal life. You do nothing . . .

PAUL: What am I supposed to do?

FEOFILANT: What? Struggle, protest, and join the fight for our male equality.

PAUL: That's old hat, Feofilant, old and stale. I don't understand how you aren't sick and tired of repeating the same thing over and over. Have some candy.

FEOFILANT: You make me angry, Paul . . . I am always, always ready to assert one and the same thing: Fight. Fight to the death, fight to the

---

last drop of blood . . . Enough! We must throw off the hated yoke of women. Down with women and three cheers for male equality. Remember what our poet said. The poet is a martyr, the poet is a suffering man:

> The shame and slavery of years shall pass,
> A blessed beginning will be made, ·
> I scent the breeze of freedom
> And the equality of man.

PAUL: Hush, hush, Varvara Petrovna might hear you. And you know how little she cares for your harangues.

FEOFILANT: Of course, of course. "Varvara Petrovna might hear." Again the power of women, again the fear of women . . . Oh, if marriage always offers such a future, then I would rather stay single forever than put my fate into a woman's hands.

PAUL: Words, Feofilant, mere words. All it would take is for some interesting, well-to-do girl to propose to you and you'll quietly go up the aisle.

FEOFILANT: Never. To willingly make oneself dependent on a woman, to take your wife's name, to live amid fumes of cooking, scads of children and dirty diapers . . . No, I'd rather refrain from love, from the joys of life, than burst into tears over this illusory joy at such an awful cost . . .

PAUL: Refrain from love, refrain from the happiness of having a child, that's crazy! Yesterday I was walking with my toddler. I led him by his little hand, and he prattled all the way, peppering me with questions: "Papa, our mama lives to work for us, but you, papa, you live to love us." Yes, we men were made for love! Let women work, toil, struggle—that's their affair, while we men must bring to life beauty, poetry, joy, the light of love and pleasure.

FEOFILANT: I'm ashamed to listen to you, Paul. You're wallowing in philistine satiety; male bourgeois comforts have extinguished all idealism, all aspiration.

PAUL: Of course, of course, you run down male "bourgeois comforts," but ask yourself what your independent life provides you: a rented room, vile food, a half-naked existence, the eternal window ledge for books, the notorious courses set aside for men, screechy friendly meetings of coed "Bluestockings". . . I reject such independence.

FEOFILANT: Oh, yes, my life is devoid of creature comforts, but it is rich in cultured pleasures. Art, theater. When one of us succeeds in getting a ticket to the opera or the play—how much spiritual joy we feel.

PAUL: In the "gods," the stifling gallery.

FEOFILANT: Yes, in the gallery. But there we experience the highest pleasure, which never reaches you, sitting in an expensive box, surrounded by flirtatious ladies . . . And courtroom trials, clamorous lawsuits we always attend! The speeches of the prosecutors and defense attorneys! A while back I was at a public showing of a friend of yours.

PAUL: Elena Pavlovna?

FEOFILANT: Yes, Elena Pavlovna Raiskaya. I once caught a glimpse of her here; she impressed me as a foppish, self-satisfied woman, but then, in court, I didn't recognize her. She was defending some cashier who had lost at the racetrack and squandered other people's money.

PAUL: The same old story.

FEOFILANT: Yes, but Raiskaya, making her speech, was transfigured: her eyes blazed, her voice shed tears, and we all wept. The defendant was acquitted, of course. Paul, darling, if you could have seen it! We made such an ovation that Her Honor the Presiding Judge ordered them to clear the court. We waited for Raiskaya on the stairs. When she came out, she dropped her handkerchief and . . . I picked it up as a souvenir . . . Paul, I would very much like to meet Elena Pavlovna. Call me when she comes here!

PAUL: Feofilant, you are such a contradictory person. I think you're in love!

FEOFILANT: Don't talk nonsense, Paul. In love . . . No, I bow to genius, to the magnetism of a social activist. I hate women, but a woman such as Raiskaya, I would devote myself to totally.

PAUL: Very nice. And what would your Dasha say to this?

FEOFILANT: Dasha is my comrade, my friend. We are bound by the communality of cultural work and leading convictions. We are close, that's true—but it's no vulgar romance of woman and man, but a free bond of different and equal individuals. Paul, you're wallowing so far in bourgeois comforts that you can't understand what I'm saying.

PAUL: Of course, how could I understand! But, forgive me, Feofilant: by denouncing me, at the bottom of your heart you're simply envious of me, jealous of my life, my material security . . . If only because Raiskaya visits here . . . She'll never visit you, whereas I can spend whole evenings with her.

FEOFILANT: I'm envious? Never! Just because you have changed your principles, don't think that everyone's capable of being such turncoats.

PAUL: For heaven's sake, what big words! I ought to be offended, if it weren't simply so funny.

FEOFILANT: There's no point in thinking that way. There's nothing funny about it. The struggle of men and woman is an eternal, centuries-long struggle . . . But the hour is near when all men will understand how shameful it is to be faint-hearted and, bonding together, will throw off the shameful yoke of womankind.

> I scent the breeze of freedom
> And the equality of men . . .

[*Enter* KOLYA.]

KOLYA: Master, the mistress wishes me to inquire where you put the mistress's stiff collars and handkerchiefs? The lady is about to go out, is in a hurry, and can't find anything on her own.

PAUL: Ah, Kolya, you should know this. Collars are in the chiffonier and hankies in the cupboard, on the right . . . in mine, the one with the mirror. I'll get them myself right now.

KOLYA: Please don't trouble yourself, I'll get them.

[*He exits.*]

FEOFILANT: Such is man's fate . . . Go on, Paul, prepare your wife's collars, hand her her handkerchiefs, be a subservient slave, but I can't watch it, I'm going. Here are some of those wonderful pamphlets. Read them.

PAUL: What are they? "Men's Right to Holy Labor," "From Darkness to Light," "The Road to a Free Man."

FEOFILANT: Hush, be more careful.

PAUL: Are they banned books?

FEOFILANT: Of course, printed abroad in Geneva. Would a female censor allow such daring ideas?

PAUL: That's very interesting. I'm very fond of banned books.

FEOFILANT: Read them. I'm going. I don't want to run into your wife. We share a mutual antipathy. Right now I have a meeting, our meeting of the leaders of the men's movement; I hope it won't be a failure. Goodbye. [*He exits.*]

[*Enter* VARVARA PETROVNA.]

VARVARA PETROVNA: That Feofilant was here again?

PAUL: Yes.

VARVARA PETROVNA: Where is he?

PAUL: He left.

VARVARA PETROVNA: Good riddance. He knows perfectly well that I don't care for his visits and sermons. Of course, he got all excited again, enlightened you, and recited inept poetry by suffragists . . . I don't understand, I do not understand why he hangs around here so much.

PAUL: We went to school together. We've been friends from childhood.

VARVARA PETROVNA: All the more reason it's time you broke up. What a boring and awkward subject. To sit still like a little schoolboy and vent your anger at all the world. He badmouths women, but dreams of figuring out how to get the first slut he comes across to hang round his neck. Not that anybody would be tempted by a face like that. He's not a man, damned if I know what he is . . . Hold on, hold on, what are you reading? Hand it over . . . "The Road to Men's Equality?" More of this illegal stuff . . . More of that crew-cut idiot wanting to bestow his moronic pamphlets on you?

[*Doorbell.* KOLYA *enters.*]

PAUL: Varvara Petrovna, what am I supposed to do?

VARVARA PETROVNA [*to Kolya*]: Kolya, take these booklets to the kitchen and throw them in the stove. You may go. [*He exits.*] [*To* PAUL] Tell your Feofilant that his library is serving as kindling for the hearth he so clearly wants to destroy. Paul, I categorically forbid you to receive such gentlemen. I do not want such subjects to cross my threshold. [*Pause.*] Are you displeased, Paul?

PAUL: Oh no, for pity's sake. You're the mistress in your own home and can do whatever you please.

VARVARA PETROVNA: Be aware, my dear, that the visits of that Feofilant always upset you. On his account we always have some sort of quarrel and disagreement, and your peace and happiness are dearer to me than all the Feofilants in the world. [*Stuffs papers into his briefcase.*]

[*The play proceeds as in the original until just before* VARVARA PETROVNA'S *first exit.*]

. . . Kolya, lock the door after me and try to keep the mistress from being bored in my absence, and if Feofilant comes back, she's not at home. Goodbye again, my child. [*Exits.*]

[KOLYA *exits behind him.*]

PAUL [*alone*]: He's gone, another whole evening on my own. [*Enter the* TUTOR.] Ah, it's you, nanny. Are the children asleep?

TUTOR: They're having their milk. I'll put them bed now. Look in on them, sir, they're waiting for you.

[PAUL *exits.* KOLYA *brings in a basket of flowers.*]

TUTOR: What's all that?

KOLYA: Flowers for our master. Can't you see?

TUTOR: More flowers? Somebody throwing away money on nothing. Who sent it?

KOLYA: The one who had to, that's who sent it.

TUTOR: Don't be rude.

KOLYA: Your place is the nursery. You've got no call poking your nose into the master's business.

TUTOR: Is that so, is the master a stranger to me? Mind you, I nursed him, fed him, and now I don't dare say a word. Well, to business. They're not sending these flowers to our master for anything good, oh no they're not. [*Enters the nursery as* PAUL *comes out of it.*]

PAUL: Ah, flowers! Who from?

KOLYA: How should I know, a messenger brought them. There's a note. [*He exits.*]

PAUL [*taking the note*]: Of course, Hélène . . . Dear Hélène . . . [*Reads.*] "Paul, I have to see you this very day. When your wife goes out, call me on the 'phone. I'll wait for your ring. I send you flowers. May they, these beautiful, fragrant flowers, silently tell you of my love. I kiss your dainty hands. Hélène." [*She picks up the telephone.*] Operator, young man? . . . 528–25. . . *Merci*. Hélène, is that you? . . . I got them . . . thank you . . . Well, of course . . . No, Hélène, no . . . You mustn't, please . . . What? . . . Yes, she's just gone out . . . No, don't come here . . . Why? . . . It's better that way . . . I don't believe you . . . What? . . . You're going out? . . . No, no, I beg of you . . . For heaven's sake, you mustn't . . . No, no . . . Well, all right . . . Drive over . . . Yes, drive over, I'll be waiting . . . [*Hangs up the receiver.*] Good heavens, what am I doing? . . . Heavens above, give me strength! . . . [*Doorbell.*] The doorbell? . . . That's odd! . . . Who can it be?

[*The play then proceeds much as in the original, but with heavily cut dialogue and an "impassioned kiss" before the reentrance of* VARVARA PETROVNA. *Later, when* SEMYON IVANOVICH *"runs in":*]

SEMYON IVANOVICH: What's the matter? For heaven's sake, what is it? What's happened?

VARVARA PETROVNA: The matter is, most respected Semyon Ivanovich, that Elena Pavlovna has seduced my husband, taking advantage of his youth and frivolousness. [SEMYON IVANOVICH *faints*.] Semyon Ivanovich, what's wrong?

HÉLÈNE: Senya, get up, Senya!

VARVARA PETROVNA: Unbutton your husband's waistcoat! Kolya, bring some water, smelling salts!

SEMYON IVANOVICH: Where am I? What came over me?

HÉLÈNE: Calm down, Senya . . . Let's go home . . . Paul, I realize the error of my ways, forgive me, all is over between us. Let's go.

[*They exit.*]

[*The final scene begins as in the original, but after a cut version of the speech about the stage:*]

VARVARA PETROVNA: I've been considering. Of course, to go on with life as before is unthinkable, but I don't want to deprive our children of a father's tender care. Outwardly our relationship will remain as of old: you will run the household as before; everyone will assume you are my husband, but we will live in different wings. Later, perhaps . . . I shall forgive you.

PAUL: Oh no, I don't want your forgiveness . . . because for all the mistakes we make, we men, you women are responsible and no one but you . . .

VARVARA PETROVNA: We?

PAUL: Yes indeed! Have you ever thought about how you raise us men? From childhood on you train us to concern ourselves with our looks, train us for luxury and adornment . . . You make us into dolls for your feminine whims, slaves in your harems, humble husbands in your family! . . . And what a paltry role we men play in such a family! We joylessly suffocate in the fumes of the domestic cookstove, we squander our talents on trifles, such as china painting or embroidering sofa pillows for your study . . . We, innocent youths, who know nothing of life, not even understanding the obligations of a spouse, are thrown into the embrace of women who have long tasted the joys of loves and have dissipated their vital forces in the society of bought-and-sold men! . . . And you call such a union holy! . . . [*Quickly.*] You said that I disgrace our home. But this is not the home of a true marriage, but a doll's house, in which your Nora has suffocated. I am Nora too! . . . Now I see clearly and, like Nora, I am leaving for a new, free life!

VARVARA PETROVNA: Stop, Paul! Nora is no model for you! What a woman could achieve, a man's feeble strength cannot endure . . . Finally, remember your children, Paul! Don't deprive them of a father's tender care!

PAUL: Children, my children! . . . [*Goes to the door and turns back.*] No, it's too late, I have no place at the domestic hearth! [*Takes a shawl and goes to the door.*]

VARVARA PETROVNA: You're leaving?

PAUL: I am.

VARVARA PETROVNA: Will you never come back to me, Paul?

PAUL: I reply with Nora's words: "For that to happen the miracle must take place."

VARVARA PETROVNA: What miracle, what is it?

PAUL: For that to happen the difference between men and women must disappear! [*Exits.*]

VARVARA PETROVNA: Oh hell!

AFTERWORD

When Evreinov resurrected the ludicrous figure of Koz'ma Prutkov to be patron saint of the Crooked Mirror, he was hoping to show that the parodic strain in Russian literature was of long standing. Foreign readers in particular had, by the beginning of the twentieth century, based their notions of Russian culture on the lyricism of Turgenev, the hysteria of Dostoevsky, the moralizing of Tolstoy, the wistfulness of Chekhov, and the grimness of Gorky. If they knew a Russian comic author, it was probably Gogol, and he was regarded as a local colorist; one early English translation of his picaresque epic *Dead Souls* was subtitled "Home Life in Old Russia."[1]

Obscured by spiritual, reformative, or socially engaged movements, humor was not what first sprang to mind in defining the Russian character. In Saki's Edwardian novel of bad manners, *The Unbearable Bassington*, there is a passage illustrative of outsiders' view of the Russian intelligentsia:

> "Does this sort of thing appeal to you?" she asked the young Russian, nodding towards the gay scrimmage of masqueraders and rather prepared to hear an amused negative.
>
> "But yes, of course," he answered; "costume balls, fancy fairs, café chantant, casino, anything that is not real life appeals to us Russians. Real life with us is the sort of thing Maxim Gorki deals in. It interests us immensely, but we like to get away from it sometimes."[2]

Although Russian comic authors rarely achieved star status, they did exist in abundance. The severity of tsarist censorship waxed and waned according to the regime in power, but satirical publications flourished, so long as the targets could not be construed as political. Chekhov, after all, began his career writing captions for his brother's cartoons in the Moscow equivalents of *Punch*. The proliferation of such journals and of the artistic

409

cabarets before the Great War did benefit from a relaxation of state oversight, but their authors could draw on a tradition of mocking manners, fashions, and ideas that went back to the reign of Catherine the Great.[3]

In the diaspora that succeeded the October Revolution, could an indigenous Russian satire be transplanted abroad? Those Russian cabarettists who fled westward attempted to preserve past successes in aspic. In Berlin the Teatr Kikimora (Bogeyman Theater), Van'ka-Vstanka (the Wibbly-Wobbly), and Chyornaya Roza (Black Rose) of the chansonnier Vertinsky had limited success, died natural deaths, or were shut down by the Nazis. In Paris, Fyodor Komissarzhevsky and N. N. Aslanov created a short-lived Theater of Miniatures in 1926. Evreinov himself was responsible for the Brodyanskie Komedianty (Strolling Players), "halfway between the Crooked Mirror and the [avant-garde] Stray Dog," which revived some of the Mirror's sketches. A revival of *The Guest Star* in 1934 boasted a dream cast that included Lapitsky, the former director of the Petrograd Theater of Musical Drama; Moscow's best Carmen, M. S. Davydova; and the great basso Fyodor Chaliapin.[4] Such phenomena were, however, more the intermittent products of nostalgia than a vital source of creativity.

Within Russia, the Bolshevik takeover, the ensuing Civil War, famine, international blockade, and social instability eliminated the audience for the kind of comedy offered by the Crooked Mirror. The urbane, well-informed public for parody was largely dispersed by emigration, expulsion, or extermination. Once a form of social stability returned under Lenin's New Economic Policy in the early 1920s, satire seemed to enjoy a resurgence—Mikhail Zoshchenko, Il'f and Petrov, Nikolay Érdman, Vladimir Mayakovsky, Mikhail Bulgakov, and Evgeny Zamyatin are usually cited as standard-bearers of a new "Soviet comedy." Much of what they mocked was the discontents of everyday life under the new order often camouflaged as fantastic dystopias. By the late 1920s they and their works were under attack as a key question was raised: What sort of satire, if any, was appropriate to promote socialism and communism for a proletarian public?

Far from banning comedy outright, the leading ideologues of the Soviet Union devoted a good deal of thought and debate to this question, the powerful and influential Commissar of Enlightenment Anatoly Lunacharsky among them. Lunacharsky had been one of the contributors to the prerevolutionary *Theater: A Book about the New Theater*, presenting a Bolshevik commentary on the discussion of the theater's viability in the modern world. In 1920, his essay "Let Us Laugh" made the bold statement "Laughter is a sign of strength . . . it is strength itself," but "it should be channeled in the right direction."[5] Citing Bergson as his authority, he characterized laughter as a "*refined* weapon." The problem came in identifying targets at which to aim the weapon.[6]

The usual suspects—the monarchist opposition, the White army, capitalist plutocrats, the clergy, the petty bourgeoisie, "ex-people," the émigré Fifth Column, hostile nations—stood outside the norms of inchoate Soviet society. At first, revolutionary satire continued the attack on bureaucracy that had been a regular feature of tsarist comedy, but even there, boundaries of the permissible were unclear. The traditional peasant belief had been that abuses and injustices were the result of lower-level officials and if only the tsar knew of them, he would sweep them away. This kind of magical thinking could not be maintained under socialism. Attacks on individuals might reflect badly on the system as a whole.

Cabarets and miniature theaters were particularly problematic. As the formalist critic Osip Brik pointed out, they, along with other forms of light entertainment such as farce and operetta, had been created "to sate bourgeois lust"; they might conceivably be "repurposed" as instructional agitprop (agitational propaganda), turning "a well-staffed brothel into a workers' hostel."[7] The poet Vladimir Mayakovsky, who cofounded a Satire Studio in 1920 and projected a Revolutionary Theater of Satire, praised music halls and any form of entertainment that did not produce a yawn. However, the experiments in "eccentricity" and the hybrid form known as agit-hall (*agit-kholl*), as practiced by such young directors as Eisenstein and Foregger, were condemned by establishment critics as inappropriate to Marxism. It may also be that the great popularity in Western Europe and America of such émigré cabarets as the Chauve Souris (formerly Moscow's Bat) and the Blaue Vogel prompted a negative reaction to similar enterprises.[8]

Sketch comedy had to be made functional and didactic. Teresvat (the Theater of Revolutionary Satire) was created in 1919 in the predominantly Jewish town Vitebsk, where Marc Chagall became commissar of art and El Lissitzky and Kazimir Malevich organized street festivals. *Teresvat* became the generic term for agitprop troupes, and its center was moved to Moscow. It was supplanted by the more proletarian Blue Blouse movement, founded in 1923, which served as a living newspaper to inform an illiterate public of the events of the day. By the end of the decade, it constituted five thousand teams of nearly one hundred thousand members. Its proponents recommended "liveliness and varied action and humor" for success,[9] but since its raison d'être was propaganda and its intended audience the unenlightened, the level of comedy remained rudimentary.

Remnants of the prerevolutionary theaters of miniatures managed to survive in the early days of Bolshevik rule. An improvisational studio in a Moscow apartment became the Semperante in 1919, moving to the big auditorium and bare stage of the Polytechnic Museum. It was a two-person operation made up of Anatoly Bykov, an "unsmiling clown" like Buster Keaton, and Anastasiya Lyovshina, considered the brains of the operation. They played everything from Yankees to Chinese coolies, characterized by "a clownish superciliousness punctuated by little notes of malice."[10]

The Bat's former premises were occupied by the Crooked Jimmy cabaret in 1924, where from 1926 to 1929 David Gutman, a veteran of Teresvat, directed current-event sketches and revues with startling titles—*You're Not a Hooligan, Are You, Citizen?* and *Quiet, I'm Stealing*. To keep abreast of the times, it moved to full-length comedies, such as Valentin Kataev's hit *Squaring the Circle* (1927), a farce about wife-swapping caused by the housing shortage. It was one of the few plays to be retained when the cabaret was reorganized in 1929 as the Moscow Theater of Satire; despite its name, it featured innocuous situation comedies. A similar fate was in store for the Leningrad Theater of Satire and Comedy, opened by Gutman in 1929. After numerous alterations, it was renamed the Leningrad State Comedy Theater in 1935. Under the leadership of Nikolay Akimov, it featured the satirical fairy tales of Evgeny Shvarts, but his most mordant comedy, *The Dragon*, was banned, and Akimov himself was dismissed in 1949 when Stalinist officials walked out halfway through a performance.

Just as these theaters were being founded and the Crooked Mirror was uttering its last gasp, a major debate took place concerning the future of Soviet satire. Tsarist satirists had adopted an oppositional stance vis-à-vis the establishment, but Communists had to view their government as benign and well intentioned. The theater critic Vladimir Blyum spent his career insisting that all "archaic" forms of satire (allegoric fables, metaphoric innuendo, anecdotes) be rejected; indeed, satire *tout pur* was at best superfluous in a society where redress to abuses was accessible and at worst a weapon in the hands of the class enemy. Artists were now citizens with a stake in supporting the state. As "ideologists of the proletariat," their satire must have a point of view; otherwise it was to be condemned as bourgeois.[11]

Blyum, who made a career of fulminating against satire, was at first in the minority. Other writers cited satire as a significant tool for forming a new Communist culture. Lunacharsky retrenched his earlier position, insisting on the importance of laughter as "a class weapon of enormous power," "of the social self-discipline of the collective." His definition of laughter as a medium of self-criticism became instrumental to the idea of forging *Homo sovieticus*, the new Soviet human being. The very first issue of *Literaturnaya gazeta* (April 22, 1929) reiterated the need for corrective satire. The Soviet Academy of Sciences created a Commission on Researching Satirical Genres, although its historical survey of past practices failed to inaugurate new forms.

The need to consolidate every effort to realize the Five-Year Plan stifled the diversity of opinion. With the imposition of a government policy stating that socialist realism was the only acceptable form of art, Blyum's censorious dismissal of satire became all but unanimous. Entertainment as individual escapism or leisure was sidelined. Comedy had to serve the state's aims by breeding positive heroes, so "proletarian literature will not create any classics of satire or humor."[12] Despite the periodic calls for Soviet Gogols and Saltykov-Shchedrins (Sergey Gusev in 1927, Georgy Malenkov in 1952), any sanctioned satire had to demonstrate how negative characters behave in the positive environment nurtured by socialist doctrine. In the circus the clown Karandash could make fun of Hitler, and on the variety stage the comedian Arkady Raykin could joke about long queues and middle management, but sophisticated parody was out of the question.

Raykin was a star of the Soviet Union's most popular form of light entertainment, *éstrada*. A loanword from the French *estrade*, it means literally "platform" or figuratively "the boards" and became the standard term for "variety" or "vaudeville."[13] (Nowadays it also describes a genre of pop music.) Cabaret was rapidly eclipsed by *éstrada*. Everything from "gypsy" choirs to crooners to circus acts came under this rubric; an equivalent might be the kind of variety shows seen on early American television. The comic styles preferred in *éstrada* were stand-up performed by a *conférencier*, simple sketches, and clown routines. As a state-supported and -funded institution, it was in no position to develop an oppositional stance or elitist attitude. The level of reference was pitched to the average Soviet citizen, although the average Soviet citizen had become alert to "wink-wink nudge-nudge" allusions, the so-called Æsopic code that Russian satire had always exploited.

With the dissolution of the Soviet Union, music edged out the spoken word on the variety stage. Revivals of Ostrovsky's comedies about corrupt merchants were often meant as glancing blows at a new class of plutocrats. The 1920s absurdist group the OBERIU and its chief exponents, Vvedensky and Kharms, sidelined in their own time, were rediscovered and served as models, much as Evreinov had resuscitated Koz'ma Prutkov. Political satire was widely broadcast by the television show *Kukly* (*Puppets*), a current-events revue based on the British original *Spitting Image*. New cabarets with old names opened, but aimed at a wider, fun-seeking audience. The Bat, for instance, became a showplace for tap dancing.

Under Putin, satire and parody have once more become endangered species. Already in his first term as president (2000–2004) he ordered *Kukly* off the air. More recently, various stand-up comedians and sketch troupes throughout the country have been banned, investigated, or forced to take refuge abroad. Public performance has been replaced by social media and Twitter accounts, which can, until blocked, disseminate a joke or a caricature more widely and safely. The explosive and foul-mouthed protest of Pussy Riot may be a far cry from the Crooked Mirror's polished experiments, but it is probably an appropriate response to its society's descent into barbarism.

NOTES

1. In 1914 Ethel Voynich published a collection of translations, *The Humour of Russia* (London: Walter Scott, 1914); aside from Gogol, Ostrovsky, and Saltykov-Shchedrin, the authors included were minor recorders of anecdotal tales of peasant and provincial life.
2. Saki [H. H. Munro], *The Unbearable Bassington* (London: John Lane, 1913), chap. 15.
3. See Arthur P. Coleman, *Humour in the Russian Comedy from Catherine to Gogol* (New York: Columbia University Press, 1925).
4. Nikolay Evreinov, *Pamyatnik mimoletnomu (iz istorii émigrantskogo teatra v Parizhe)* (Paris, 1953).

5. A. Lunacharsky, "Budem smeyat'sya," in *Sobranie sochinenii*, 8 vols. (Moscow: Khudozhe-stvennaya literatura, 1964), 3:76–79. See also Daniel Gerould, "Lunacharsky on Revolution-ary Laughter," *Slavic and East European Performance* 26, no. 1 (Winter 2006): 519–62.

6. An excellent account of these debates is Serguei Alex. Oushakine, "'Red Laughter': On Re-fined Weapons of Jesters," *Social Research* 79, no. 1 (Spring 2012): 189–216.

7. Osip Brik, "O neprilichnom" (1922), in *Éstrada bez parada*, ed. T. P. Bazhenova et al. (Mos-cow: Iskusstvo, 1991), 29–30.

8. Laurence Senelick, "Émigré Cabaret and the Re-invention of Russia," *New Theatre Quarterly* 35, no. 1 (January 2019): 44–59.

9. Editorial, *Zhivaya gazeta* (1925): 3.

10. Boris Golubovsky, *Bol'shie malenkie teatry* (Moscow: Izd. Im. Sabanikovykh, 1998), 338.

11. See Robert Russell, "Satire and Socialism: The Russian Debates, 1925–1934," *Forum for Modern Language Studies* 30, no. 4 (1994): 341–52. The remark about "point of view" may have been aimed at Nikolay Érdman's Teresvat revue *Moscow from the Point of View of . . .*

12. I. Nusimov, "Voprosy zhanra v proletarskoy literature," *Literatura i iskusstvo* 2–3 (1931): 43. Zoshchenko regarded the notion of "positive satire" as "wishy-washy" (*rykhlaya*).

13. There is an extensive literature on *éstrada*. Basic texts are E. D. Uvarova, *Éstradny teatr: Min-iatyury, obozreniya, myuzik-kholly (1917–1945)* (Moscow: Iskusstvo, 1983); E. D. Uvarova, ed., *Russkaya sovetskaya éstrada, 1917–1929: Ocherk istorii* (Moscow: Iskusstvo, 1976), *1930–1945* (1977), and *1946–1977* (1981); and D. I. Zolotnitsky, ed., *Mastera éstrady* (Moscow: Iskusstvo, 1964).

BIBLIOGRAPHY

Archive of Crooked Mirror scripts, documents, newspaper articles, repertory lists, programs, etc., owned by Laurence Senelick. Includes typed and printed variants of *A Little Night Music*, *Man's Fate, Memories,* and *Backstage at the Soul.*

Alyansky, Yury. *Uveselitel'nye zavedeniya starogo Petersburga.* Saint Petersburg: Avrora/Stroyizdat SPb, 2013.

Bazhenova, T. P., et al. *Éstrada bez parada.* Moscow: Iskusstvo, 1991.

Buks, Nora, and Igor' Loshchilov, eds. *Kabaretnye p'esy serebryannogo veka.* Moscow: OGI, 2018.

Dmitriev, Yury. "Teatry miniatyur." In *Khudozhestvennaya kul'tura kontsa XIX–nachala XX veka (1908–1917): Kniga trety'ya. Zrelishchnie iskusstva muzyka*, 191–207. Moscow: Nauka, 1977.

Énukidze, Natéla. "Russkie *Vampuki* do i posle 'Vampuki.'" *Uchenie zapiski russkoy akademiy muzyki imeni Gnesenikh* (2012): 37–58.

———. "Vladimir Georgevich Érenberg: Sud'ba peresmeshnika." *Materialy Mezhdunarodnoy nauchnoy onlain-konferenii 24–27 noyabrya 2002 goda*, 181–90. Moscow: Nauchnye shkoly v muzykovedenii XXI veka, 2020.

Evreinov, Nikolay. *Dramaticheskie sochineniya III–I tom. (P'esy iz repertuara "Krivogo Zerkale").* Petrograd: Academia, 1923.

———. *Histoire du théâtre russe.* Paris: Éditions du Chêne, 1947.

———. *Pamyatnik mimoletnomu (iz istorii émigrantskogo teatra v Parizhe).* Paris: n.p., 1953.

———. *V shkole ostroumiya.* Edited by Aleksandra Deich and Anna Kashina-Evreinova. Moscow: Iskusstvo, 1998.

Geldern, James von, and Louise McReynolds, eds. *Entertaining Tsarist Russia, 1771–1917.* Bloomington: Indiana University Press, 1998.

Golub, Spencer. *Evreinov: The Theatre of Paradox and Transformation.* Ann Arbor, MI: UMI Press, 1984.

Kotova, T. V., ed. *Izvestnaya i neizvestnaya éstrada kontsa XIX–nachala XX veka 1846–1917. Katalog fonda tsenzury . . .* Saint Petersburg: Baltiiskie sezony, 2010.

Kugel', Aleksandr. *List'ya s dereva.* Leningrad: Vremya, 1926.

———. *Teatral'nye portréty.* Moscow and Petrograd: "Petrograd," 1923.

McReynolds, Louise. *Russia at Play: Leisure Activities at the End of the Tsarist Era.* Ithaca, NY: Cornell University Press, 2003.

Polyakova, M. Ya., ed. *Russkaya teatral'naya parodiya XIX nachala XX veka.* Moscow: Iskusstvo, 1976.

Rudin, Rudolf Grigor'evich. *Teatr malykh form.* Moscow: Znanie, 1980.

Senelick, Laurence. "Boris Geyer and Cabaretic Playwriting." In *Russian Theatre in the Age of Modernism*, edited by Robert Russell, 36–63. London: Macmillan, 1990.

———, ed. and trans. *Cabaret Performance: Europe, 1890–1920*. New York: PAJ Press, 1989.

———, ed. and trans. *Russian Dramatic Theory from Pushkin to the Symbolists*. Austin: University of Texas Press, 1981.

Teatr i iskusstvo: Ezhenedel'ny illyustrirovanny zhurnal. Edited by A. R. Kugel'. Saint Petersburg, 1897–1918.

Tikhvinskaya, Lyudmila. *Kabaré i teatry miniatyur 1908–1917*. Moscow: RIK "Kul'tura," 1995. Reprinted as *Posednevnaya zhizn' teatral'noy bogemy serebryanogo veka*. Moscow: Molodaya gvardiya, 2005.

Uvarova, E. D., ed. *Éstrada Rossii XX vek. Éntsiklopediya*. Moscow: Olma-Press, 2004.

———, ed. *Russkaya sovetskaya éstrada 1917–1929: Ocherk istorii*. Moscow: Iskusstvo, 1976.

Znosko-Borovsky, Evgeny A. *Russky teatr nachala XX veka*. Prague: Plamja, 1925.

Zolotinitsky, David. *Fars . . . i chto tam eshchyo? Teatr farsa v Rossii (1893–1917)*. Saint Petersburg: Nestor-Istorik, 2006.